P9-ANY-030

DISCARDED

Inside World Politics

Inside World Politics

DIANE P. ROGERS
formerly of Oakwood Collegiate Institute
Toronto

and

ROBERT J. CLARK
formerly of Pauline Johnson Collegiate-Vocational School
Brantford

Macmillan of Canada / Toronto

For permission to use copyrighted materials, grateful acknowledgement is made to the copyright holders listed on pages 351-3, which are hereby made a part of this copyright page.

Cover Photos: Miller Services, Toronto, The Canadian Press, and Wide World Photo

Printed and bound in Canada by
T. H. Best Printing Company Limited

To
Thora Denton Tracy McIlroy
for her inspiration

Preface

Politics on our "village planet" – this is the subject under consideration in this resource book. And it is politics in its widest context, namely, a phenomenon which "arises whenever there are people living together in associations – whenever they are involved in conflicts – and whenever they are subject to some kind of power, rulership or authority."

Each theme contains relevant selections of varying difficulty that represent a number of disciplines, such as English, Sociology, Philosophy, and Political Science. Much of the material has been student tested. This testing indicates that, if used thoughtfully, the resources should increase respect for the various sources of learning, and assist students to consider possible solutions to human problems and political issues.

Certainly it is hoped that the book will serve as a partial answer to teachers and students who are searching for interesting, imaginatively treated material that provokes individual thought and meaningful discussion.

How to Use the Book

This resource book has been organized to permit maximum flexibility in the teaching of the material. Its themes may be studied either consecutively or at random, so that it may be used either as a text or as a "resource centre". And because the excerpts related to each theme may also be considered either in sequence or out of sequence, teaching arrangements such as large and small discussion groups are possible. It is hoped, moreover, that students will be frequently encouraged to examine the material independently. Each excerpt can be allowed to speak for itself and the student allowed to react by himself. And he can be permitted to find the selection that "speaks" most easily to him, with the understanding that he will proceed to an appreciation of the other sources later. An introduction precedes only those excerpts where it was felt some background description was necessary to understand the reading fully. Otherwise, the student is invited to "plunge right in".

The Discussion Guidelines have been carefully designed to help each student discover valuable concepts, to engage the students in value judgments, and to encourage clear thinking. Students are asked to base their judgments on first-hand personal experience, on the particular excerpts that promoted discussion, on the suggested cross references, and on supplemental material. After studying a theme, a student might be encouraged to react personally to it by briefly developing his own thesis on the topic, either orally or in written form. Such an exercise would, with practice, promote honesty of thought.

Some excerpts are grouped, and in such cases questions follow each grouping rather than each selection. This arrangement is intended to encourage students to read and digest more than one viewpoint without interruption, and to consider the grouping as a whole in their assessment. Discussion Guidelines are not given for illustrations, cartoons, and most poems, in order to permit maximum freedom for imaginative interpretation of the material. It is important to realize that the cartoons, quotations, and illustrations are included to add new perspectives or to reinforce a given opinion.

As he becomes familiar with the book, the student should understand that a balanced evaluation of any subject requires the weighing of a number of viewpoints from a variety of sources. Thus, before discussing the merits of a particular point of view, he should know the author's credentials and should consult the biographic notes at the back of the book. He will, in addition, need to consider his own biases, his particular experiences in life, and his training, before reaching conclusions. And, because many of the problems of mankind are not peculiar to one generation, he should realize that a balanced view also requires the use of resources drawn from both the past and the present.

To determine the value of sources such as maps, advertisements, case studies, statistics, or news reports, it will be necessary to assess the peculiar quality and accuracy of the data, the bias of the author, the completeness and representative quality of the material, and the calendar date it represents.

Few excerpts, be they documents, poems, or essays, are intended as sources for laborious analysis. On occasion, careful examination of wording and sentence structure will enhance the study of the material; however, the readings are included primarily for their idea content and should be considered in that light.

If used selectively, this resource book can be an exciting experience for students of world politics. It can create a new appreciation of the role of individuals, ideologies, institutions, and nations in international affairs. It can, as well, make students aware of their own potential role as citizens of the world.

Authors' Note

A special debt is owed to Miss Gladys E. Neale, Manager of the School Book Department of the Macmillan Company of Canada, to Miss Margaret L. Ford, former Head of the English Department, Forest Hill Collegiate, Toronto, and to Professor J. M. S. Careless, former Chairman of the Department of History, University of Toronto, whose enthusiasm for the concept of the book, perceptive comments on the manuscript, and unflagging support were essential to its initiation and completion.

We are indebted also to Professor H. Simmons, of the Department of Political Science, York University, who kindly read the manuscript and offered suggestions valuable to its political orientation and structure.

The very nature of the book made it a particular challenge to its editor, Mr. Terry Leeder, who played a vital role in its production. His originality, constructive observations, and assistance in the selection of photographs and material were considerable and much appreciated.

The visual impact of the book was, we believed, especially important to the realization of its purposes. Mr. Peter Maher's artistic contribution, in this regard, speaks for itself.

Thanks are due, also, to Miss Christine Chamberlain and others who provided a student assessment of the resources.

And, finally, to Jean Clark, to families and friends, our appreciation for their patience and encouragement while "the book" commanded allegiance.

Contents

PART ONE: MEN AND THEIR GOVERNMENT

The Challenge of Underdeveloped Nations

The Meaning of War

Our planet is a very, very small place, what I have called "A Village World", because that which you can go around in 90 minutes is a village. That in which you can communicate instantly, as we can now, is a village. That which depends upon the interdependencies of work, of exchange, of trade, of commerce – that too is a village.

What we lack is that we have very little else that belongs to a village. We do not in fact have the village policeman, we do not have the village welfare system, we do not in fact know that we are living in a village. All these fundamental changes are still to be made. We have been handed the brute fact, the raw material of a world society, but we haven't yet shaped it into something which is truly human, truly civilized and which can in fact survive.

The Village Planet
Barbara Ward

PART ONE

MEN AND THEIR GOVERNMENT

Organizing a Society

from *The Wonderful World of J. Wesley Smith*, by Burr Shafer, by permission of Vanguard Press Inc.

"You're right – I picked out the wrong hunting ground, I'm too inexperienced to lead – we need a new chief – I resign."

If you had the opportunity to organize a society, how would you do it? What sort of state would you create? There are many courses you could follow. Would you seek the ideal – a Utopia? Would you pattern a system of government on a familiar one? Would you reorganize the existing framework? Indeed, how democratic would your government be? Many answers have been proposed. How would a novelist, a prisoner of war, a biblical writer, a black power advocate, or two opposing philosophers answer these questions?

FIVE VIEWS

Government without Adults

from *Lord of the Flies*
by William Golding

[Because of an atomic war, some schoolboys are being flown from England when their plane is forced to crash-land on a coral island. The novel *Lord of the Flies* is an imaginary account of their attempts to adjust to each other and to their strange surroundings.

This excerpt is from the first part of the novel. Ralph, one of the boys, has discovered a conch (sea shell) and, directed by his companion, Piggy, proceeds to summon other survivors by blowing it. The boys make their way to the platform on which Ralph stands.]

At last Ralph ceased to blow and sat there, the conch trailing from one hand, his head bowed on his knees. As the echoes died away so did the laughter, and there was silence.

Within the diamond haze of the beach something dark was fumbling along. Ralph saw it first, and watched till the intentness of his gaze drew all eyes that way. Then the creature stepped from mirage on to clear sand, and they saw that the darkness was not all shadow but mostly clothing. The creature was a party of boys, marching approximately in step in two parallel lines and dressed in strangely eccentric clothing. Shorts, shirts, and different garments they carried in their hands: but each boy wore a square black cap with a silver badge in it. Their bodies, from throat to ankle, were hidden by black cloaks which bore a long silver cross on the left breast and each neck was finished off with a hambone frill. The heat of the tropics, the descent, the search for food, and now this sweaty march along the blazing beach had given them the complexions of newly washed plums. The boy who controlled them was dressed in the same way though his cap badge was golden. When his party was about ten yards from the platform he shouted an order and they halted, gasping, and sweating, swaying in the fierce light. The boy himself came forward, vaulted on to the platform with his cloak flying, and peered into what to him was almost complete darkness.

"Where's the man with the trumpet?"

Ralph, sensing his sun-blindness, answered him.

"There's no man with a trumpet. Only me."

The boy came close and peered down at Ralph, screwing up his face as he did so. What he saw of the fair-haired boy with the creamy shell on his knees did not seem to satisfy him. He turned quickly, his black cloak circling.

"Isn't there a ship, then?"

Inside the floating cloak he was tall, thin, and bony: and his hair was red beneath the black cap. His face was crumpled and freckled, and ugly without silliness. Out of his face stared two light blue eyes, frustrated now, and turning, or ready to turn, to anger.

"Isn't there a man here?"

Ralph spoke to his back.

"No. We're having a meeting. Come and join in."

The group of cloaked boys began to scatter from close line. The tall boy shouted at them.

"Choir! Stand still!"

Wearily obedient, the choir huddled into line and stood there swaying in the sun. None the less, some began to protest faintly.

"But, Merridew. Please, Merridew . . . can't we?"

Then one of the boys flopped on his face in the sand and the line broke up. They heaved the fallen boy to the platform and let him lie. Merridew, his eyes staring, made the best of a bad job.

"All right then. Sit down. Let him alone."

"But, Merridew."

"He's always throwing a faint," said Merridew. "He did in Gib; and Addis; and at matins over the precentor."

This last piece of shop brought sniggers from the choir, who perched like black birds on the criss-cross trunks and examined Ralph with interest. Piggy asked no names. He was intimidated by this uniformed superiority and the offhand authority in Merridew's voice. He shrank to the other side of Ralph and busied himself with his glasses.

Merridew turned to Ralph.

"Aren't there any grown-ups?"

"No."

Merridew sat down on a trunk and looked round the circle.

"Then we'll have to look after ourselves."

Secure on the other side of Ralph, Piggy spoke timidly.

"That's why Ralph's made a meeting. So as we can decide what to do. We've heard names. That's Johnny. Those two – they're twins, Sam 'n Eric. Which is Eric –? You? No – you're Sam."

"I'm Sam."

"– 'n I'm Eric."

"We'd better all have names," said Ralph, "so I'm Ralph."

"We got most names," said Piggy. "Got 'em just now."

"Kids' names," said Merridew. "Why should I be Jack? I'm Merridew."

Ralph turned to him quickly. This was the voice of one who knew his own mind.

"Then," went on Piggy, "that boy – I forget –"

"You're talking too much," said Jack Merridew. "Shut up, Fatty."

Laughter arose.

"He's not Fatty," cried Ralph, "his real name's Piggy!"

"Piggy!"

"Piggy!"

"Oh, Piggy!"

A storm of laughter arose and even the tiniest child joined in. For the moment the boys were a closed circuit of sympathy with Piggy outside: he went very pink, bowed his head, and cleaned his glasses again.

Finally the laughter died away and the naming continued. There was Maurice, next in size among the choir boys to Jack, but broad and grinning all the time. There was a slight, furtive boy whom no one knew, who kept to himself with an inner intensity of avoidance and secrecy. He muttered that his name was Roger and was silent again. Bill, Robert, Harold, Henry; the choir boy who had fainted sat up against a palm trunk, smiled pallidly at Ralph and said that his name was Simon.

Jack spoke.

"We've got to decide about being rescued."

There was a buzz. One of the small boys, Henry, said that he wanted to go home.

"Shut up," said Ralph absently. He lifted the conch. "Seems to me we ought to have a chief to decide things." "A chief! A chief!"

"I ought to be chief," said Jack with simple arrogance, "because I'm chapter chorister and head boy. I can sing C sharp."

Another buzz.

"Well, then," said Jack, "I –"

He hesitated. The dark boy, Roger, stirred at last and spoke up.

"Let's have a vote."

"Yes!"

"Vote for chief!"

"Let's vote –"

This toy of voting was almost as pleasing as the conch. Jack started to protest but the clamour changed from the general wish for a chief to an election by acclaim of Ralph himself. None of the boys could have found good reason for this; what intelligence had been shown was traceable to Piggy while the most obvious leader was Jack. But there was a stillness about Ralph as he sat that marked him out: there was his size, and attractive appearance; and most obscurely, yet most powerfully, there was the conch. The being that had blown that, had sat waiting for them on the platform with the delicate thing balanced on his knees, was set apart.

"Him with the shell."

"Ralph! Ralph!"

"Let him be chief with the trumpet thing."

Ralph raised a hand for silence.

"All right. Who wants Jack for chief?"

With dreary obedience the choir raised their hands.

"Who wants me?"

Every hand outside the choir except Piggy's was raised immediately. Then Piggy, too, raised his hand grudgingly into the air.

Ralph counted.

"I'm chief then."

The circle of boys broke into applause. Even the choir applauded; and the freckles on Jack's face disappeared under a blush of mortification. He started up, then changed his mind and sat down again while the air rang. Ralph looked at him, eager to offer something.

"The choir belongs to you, of course."

"They could be the army –"

"Or hunters –"

"They could be –"

The suffusion drained away from Jack's face. Ralph waved again for silence.

"Jack's in charge of the choir. They can be – what do you want them to be?"

"Hunters."

Jack and Ralph smiled at each other with shy liking. The rest began to talk eagerly.

Jack stood up.

"All right, choir. Take off your togs."

As if released from class, the choir boys stood up, chattered, piled their black cloaks on the grass. Jack laid his on the trunk by Ralph. His grey shorts were sticking to him with sweat. Ralph glanced at them admiringly, and when Jack saw his glance he explained.

"I tried to get over that hill to see if there was

Miller Services, Toronto

Choirs, such as the one described in the story, form an élite group in many English schools. The choristers shown here sing at King's College Chapel, Cambridge University.

water all round. But your shell called us."

Ralph smiled and held up the conch for silence.

"Listen, everybody. I've got to have time to think things out. I can't decide what to do straight off. If this isn't an island we might be rescued straight away. So we've got to decide if this is an island. Everybody must stay round here and wait and not go away. Three of us – if we take more we'd get all mixed, and lose each other – three of us will go on an expedition and find out. I'll go, and Jack, and, and . . ."

He looked round the circle of eager faces. There was no lack of boys to choose from.

"And Simon."

The boys round Simon giggled, and he stood up, laughing a little. Now that the pallor of his faint was over, he was a skinny, vivid little boy, with a glance coming up from under a hut of straight hair that hung down, black and coarse.

He nodded at Ralph.

"I'll come."

"And I –"

Jack snatched from behind him a sizeable sheath-knife and clouted it into a trunk. The buzz rose and died away.

Piggy stirred.

"I'll come."

Ralph turned to him.

"You're no good on a job like this."

"All the same –"

"We don't want you," said Jack, flatly. "Three's enough."

Piggy's glasses flashed.

"I was with him when he found the conch. I was with him before anyone else was."

Jack and the others paid no attention. There was a general dispersal. Ralph, Jack, and Simon jumped off the platform and walked along the sand past the bathing-pool. Piggy hung bumbling behind them.

"If Simon walks in the middle of us," said Ralph, "then we could talk over his head."

The three of them fell into step. This meant that every now and then Simon had to do a double shuffle to catch up with the others. Presently Ralph stopped and turned back to Piggy.

"Look."

Jack and Simon pretended to notice nothing. They walked on.

"You can't come."

Piggy's glasses were misted again – this time with humiliation.

"You told 'em. After what I said."

His face flushed, his mouth trembled.

"After I said I didn't want –"

"What on earth are you talking about?"

"About being called Piggy. I said I didn't care as long as they didn't call me Piggy; an' I said not to tell and then you went an' said straight out –"

Stillness descended on them. Ralph, looking with more understanding at Piggy, saw that he was hurt and crushed. He hovered between the two courses of apology or further insult.

"Better Piggy than Fatty," he said at last, with the directness of genuine leadership, "and anyway, I'm sorry if you feel like that. Now go back, Piggy, and take names. That's your job. So long."

He turned and raced after the other two. Piggy stood and the rose of indignation faded slowly from his cheeks. He went back to the platform. . . .

[Having explored the island, Jack, Ralph, and Simon return to make their report.]

By the time Ralph finished blowing the conch the platform was crowded. There were differences between this meeting and the one held in the morning. The afternoon sun slanted in from the other side of the platform and most of the children, feeling too late the smart of sunburn, had put their clothes on. The choir, noticeably less of a group, had discarded their cloaks.

Ralph sat on a fallen trunk, his left side to the sun. On his right were most of the choir; on his left the larger boys who had not known each other before the evacuation; before him small children squatted in the grass.

Silence now. Ralph lifted the cream and pink shell to his knees and a sudden breeze scattered light over the platform. He was uncertain whether to stand up or remain sitting. He looked sideways to his left, towards the bathing-pool. Piggy was sitting near but giving no help.

Ralph cleared his throat.

"Well then."

All at once he found he could talk fluently and explain what he had to say. He passed a hand through his fair hair and spoke.

"We're on an island. We've been on the mountain-top and seen water all around. We saw no houses, no smoke, no footprints, no boats, no people. We're on an uninhabited island with no other people on it."

Jack broke in.

"All the same you need an army – for hunting. Hunting pigs –"

"Yes. There are pigs on the island."

All three of them tried to convey the sense of the pink, live thing struggling in the creepers.

"We saw –"

"Squealing –"

"It broke away –"

"Before I could kill it – but – next time!"

Jack slammed his knife into a trunk and looked round challengingly.

The meeting settled down again.

"So you see," said Ralph, "we need hunters to get us meat. And another thing."

He lifted the shell on his knees and looked round the sun-slashed faces.

"There aren't any grown-ups. We shall have to look after ourselves."

The meeting hummed and was silent.

"And another thing. We can't have everybody talking at once. We'll have to have 'Hands up' like at school."

He held the conch before his face and glanced round the mouth.

"Then I'll give him the conch."

"Conch?"

"That's what this shell's called. I'll give the conch to the next person to speak. He can hold it when he's speaking."

"But –"

"Look –"

"And he won't be interrupted. Except by me."

Jack was on his feet.

"We'll have rules!" he cried excitedly. "Lots of rules! Then when anyone breaks 'em –"

"Whee-oh!"

"Wacco!"

"Bong!"

"Doink!"

Ralph felt the conch lifted from his lap. Then Piggy was standing cradling the great cream shell and the shouting died down. Jack, left on his feet, looked uncertainly at Ralph who smiled and patted the log. Jack sat down. Piggy took off his glasses and blinked at the assembly while he wiped them on his shirt.

"You're hindering Ralph. You're not letting him get to the most important thing."

He paused effectively.

"Who knows we're here? Eh?"

"They knew at the airport."

"The man with the trumpet-thing –"

"My dad."

Piggy put on his glasses.

"Nobody knows where we are," said Piggy. He was paler than before and breathless. "Perhaps they knew where we was going to; and perhaps not. But they don't know where we are 'cos we never got there." He gaped at them for a moment, then swayed and sat down. Ralph took the conch from his hands.

"That's what I was going to say," he went on, "when you all, all . . ." He gazed at their intent faces. "The plane was shot down in flames. Nobody knows where we are. We may be here a long time."

The silence was so complete that they could hear the fetch and miss of Piggy's breathing. The sun slanted in and lay golden over half the platform. The breezes that on the lagoon had chased their tails like kittens were finding their way across the platform and into the forest. Ralph pushed back the tangle of fair hair that hung on his forehead.

"So we may be here a long time."

Nobody said anything. He grinned suddenly.

"But this is a good island. We – Jack, Simon, and me – we climbed the mountain. It's wizard. There's food and drink, and –"

"Rocks –"

"Blue flowers –"

Piggy, partly recovered, pointed to the conch in Ralph's hands, and Jack and Simon fell silent. Ralph went on.

"While we're waiting we can have a good time on this island."

He gesticulated widely.

"It's like in a book."

At once there was a clamour.

"Treasure Island –"

"Swallows and Amazons –"

"Coral Island –"

Ralph waved the conch.

"This is our island. It's a good island. Until the grown-ups come to fetch us we'll have fun."

Jack held out his hand for the conch.

"There's pigs," he said. "There's food; and bathing-water in that little stream along there – and everything. Didn't anyone find anything else?"

He handed the conch back to Ralph and sat down. Apparently no one had found anything.

The older boys first noticed the child when he resisted. There was a group of little boys urging him forward and he did not want to go. He was a shrimp of a boy, about six years old, and one side of his face was blotted out by a mulberry-coloured birthmark. He stood now, warped out of the perpendicular by the fierce light of publicity, and he bored into the coarse grass with one toe. He was muttering, and about to cry.

The other little boys, whispering but serious, pushed him towards Ralph.

"All right," said Ralph, "come on then."

The small boy looked round in panic.

"Speak up!"

The small boy held out his hands for the conch and the assembly shouted with laughter; at once he snatched back his hands and started to cry.

"Let him have the conch!" shouted Piggy. "Let him have it!"

At last Ralph induced him to hold the shell but by then the blow of laughter had taken away the child's voice. Piggy knelt by him, one hand on the great shell, listening and interpreting to the assembly.

"He wants to know what you're going to do about the snake-thing "

Ralph laughed, and the other boys laughed with him. The small boy twisted further into himself.

"Tell us about the snake-thing."

"Now he says it was a beastie."

"Beastie?"

"A snake-thing. Ever so big. He saw it."

"Where?"

"In the woods."

Either the wandering breezes or perhaps the decline of the sun allowed a little coolness to lie under the trees. The boys felt it and stirred restlessly.

"You couldn't have a beastie, a snake-thing, on an island this size," Ralph explained kindly. "You only get them in big countries, like Africa, or India."

Murmur; and the grave nodding of heads.

"He says the beastie came in the dark."

"Then he couldn't see it!"

Laughter and cheers.

"Did you hear that? Says he saw the thing in the dark –"

"He still says he saw the beastie. It came and went away again an' came back and wanted to eat him –"

"He was dreaming."

Laughing, Ralph looked for confirmation round the ring of faces. The older boys agreed; but here and there among the little ones was the dubiety that required more than rational assurance.

Discussion guidelines

1. The author states that the boys had no "good reason" for selecting Ralph. Their choice seemed to be determined by "stillness", "size", "attractive appearance", and his possession of the conch. In choosing leaders of a government, to what extent are modern voters motivated by the same kinds of influences?
2. "Every society has its 'beastie' rumours, which threaten stable government." Discuss with reference to some specific current events.
3. Comment on the value and limitations of a fictional account such as *Lord of the Flies* for a student of politics.

Cross references

Leaders and Followers, page 136
The Culture Concept, page 146

[Throughout history, man has often identified God as the source of law, and as the authority behind government. Are man's claims for God justified? What are the effects of such claims? And why has man just as frequently denied these roles to God?]

a

God and Society
from Deuteronomy 5: 1-22

[At first glance, some of the jet-age generation might be tempted to dismiss the Ten Commandments as being out of their "orbit". However, the covenant which Jews believe was made with them after they escaped from bondage in Egypt, and began looking for a promised land, reveals man's search for divine guidance in structuring a society.]

And Moses called all Israel, and said unto them, Hear, O Israel, the statutes and judgments which I speak in your ears this day, that ye may learn them, and keep, and do them.

The Lord our God made a covenant with us.

The Lord made not this covenant with our fathers, but with us, even us, who are all of us here alive this day.

The Lord talked with you face to face in the mount out of the midst of the fire,

(I stood between the Lord and you at that time, to shew you the word of the Lord: for ye were afraid by reason of the fire, and went not up into the mount;) saying,

I am the Lord thy God, which brought thee out of the land of Egypt, from the house of bondage.

Thou shalt have none other gods before me.

Thou shalt not make thee any graven image, or any likeness of any thing that is in heaven above, or that is in the earth beneath, or that is in the waters beneath the earth:

Thou shalt not bow down thyself unto them, nor serve them: for I the Lord thy God am a jealous God, visiting the iniquity of the fathers upon the children unto the third and fourth generation of them that hate me.

And shewing mercy unto thousands of them that love me and keep my commandments.

Thou shalt not take the name of the Lord thy God in vain: for the Lord will not hold him guiltless that taketh his name in vain.

Keep the sabbath day to sanctify it, as the Lord thy God hath commanded thee.

Six days thou shalt labour, and do all thy work:

But the seventh day is the sabbath of the Lord thy God: in it thou shalt not do any work, thou, nor thy son, nor thy daughter, nor thy manservant, nor thy maidservant, nor thine ox, nor thine ass, nor any of thy cattle, nor thy stranger that is within thy gates; that thy manservant and thy maidservant may rest as well as thou.

And remember that thou wast a servant in the land of Egypt, and that the Lord thy God brought thee out thence through a mighty hand and by a stretched out arm: therefore the Lord thy God commanded thee to keep the sabbath day.

Honour thy father and thy mother as the Lord thy God hath commanded thee: that thy days may be prolonged, and that it may go well with thee, in the land which the Lord thy God giveth thee.

Thou shalt not kill.

Neither shalt thou commit adultery.

Neither shalt thou steal.

Neither shalt thou bear false witness against thy neighbour.

Neither shalt thou desire thy neighbour's wife, neither shalt thou covet thy neighbour's house, his field, or his manservant, or his maidservant, his ox, or his ass, or any thing that is thy neighbour's.

These words the Lord spake unto all your assembly in the mount out of the midst of the fire, of the cloud, and of the thick darkness, with a great voice: and he added no more. And he wrote them in two tables of stone, and delivered them unto me.

b

A Twentieth-Century Prophet?

from *A Black Muslim Code*
by Elijah Muhammad

[In the current American scene, the Black Muslims represent one black power group that claims to know how oppressed Negroes can create a new society. The reading contains some of the guidelines given by Elijah Muhammad to male Muslims for gaining their "promised land".]

I am here to tell you that I myself have been sent directly from the face of God. He has given to me that which is written by the prophets that will give you life, bring light to you, your understanding will return.

'In the name of Allah, the Beneficent, the Merciful': Violations of these laws are subjected to 30 days to indefinite suspension from the Temple:

Sleeping in the Temple.

Keeping late hours.

Using narcotics (dope, heroin, marijuana).

Married and taking up time with sisters.

Abusing your wife.
Socializing with Christians.
Drinking alcoholic juices.
Unclean homes.
Personal hygiene.
Lying and stealing from one another.
Gambling (shooting pool, dice, cards, etc.).
Eating pork.
Gossiping on one another.
Adultery.
Disobeying your officers.
Disrespecting Ministers and the Supreme Captain.
Talking about your Leader and Teacher.
Misrepresenting the teachings of Islam.
Disrespecting the Messenger of Allah.

ELIJAH MUHAMMAD

Discussion guidelines

1. Suggest some reasons why man has claimed divine approval for the organizing of societies.
2. "God and/or Caesar!"
   (a) Explain the meaning of this predicament.
   (b) ". . . let us go forth to lead the land we love, asking His blessing and His help, but knowing that here on earth God's work must truly be our own." (John F. Kennedy, Inaugural Address)
   To what extent does this statement reflect society's continuing belief in the necessity of divine approval?

Cross reference

The Use of Symbols, page 44

Miller Services, Toronto

by permission of Johnny Hart and Field Enterprises Incorporated

Men Need Rulers

from *Leviathan*

by Thomas Hobbes – a modern paraphrase

[What are the laws of nature? What determines man's actions? If nature and man are in opposition, how can a stable government be formed? The philosopher Thomas Hobbes (1588-1679) used his observations of the society of ants and bees to answer these political questions.]

Certain living creatures, such as bees and ants, live sociably with one another and yet have no other direction than their personal judgments and appetites. Some people may want to know, perhaps, why mankind cannot do the same. The answer is this:

Firstly, men are continually in competition with one another for honour and dignity, whereas bees and ants are not. Consequently there arises among men envy and hatred, and finally war.

Secondly, among bees and ants, the common good of all is the same as the private good of each bee or ant. But man, whose joy consists in comparing himself with other men, can enjoy nothing but that which brings personal status.

Thirdly, creatures like bees and ants, since they cannot reason, do not see any fault in the administration of their common business. On the other hand, among men, there are very many who think themselves wiser, and better able to govern the public, than others. Such men strive to reform government, one this way, one that way. By the collision of such reformers, civil war is created.

Fourthly, although such creatures can make known to each other their desires and other affections, yet they lack that skill at words by which some men can make good seem evil, and evil seem good. By so doing, men spread discontent among their fellows, and trouble the peace.

Lastly, the agreements among such creatures are natural. Agreements among men are by covenant only, which is artificial. Therefore it is no wonder that there is something else required to make agreements among men lasting. That something is a common power. The only way to create a common power that can defend men from the invasion of foreigners, and the injuries of one another, is to give all men's power and strength to one man, or to one assembly of men.

The man who has this power conferred on him is called sovereign, and has sovereign power. Everyone else is his subject.

Discussion guidelines

1. Ashley Montagu, the noted biologist, has stated: "The impulses towards co-operative behaviour are already present in [man] at birth and all they require is cultivation." Suggest reasons why you agree with either Hobbes or Montagu.
2. "Given man's nature, the only practical form of government is a dictatorship." Discuss.

Cross references

Student Rebellion, page 97
Leaders Are More Important, page 106
The Ideal State, page 107

In Defence of Equality

from *Second Treatise on Civil Government*
by John Locke – a modern paraphrase

[John Locke (1632-1704) disputed Hobbes's defence of absolute monarchy, and in so doing wrote his own defence of individual rights and limited government. An understanding of his views is basic to an understanding of Western liberal-democracy.]

Of the State of Nature

To understand political power correctly, we must consider the state that all men are naturally in – that is, a state in which they have perfect freedom to dispose of their possessions and persons as they think fit, within the bounds of the law of nature.

This state is also a condition of equality, so that no one has more power than any other. This is true of all men, unless God should set some one person above another, and give to him, by clear appointment, the right to rule.

But though this state is a state of liberty, yet it is not a state of license. Man does not have the liberty to destroy either himself, or any creature in his possession. The state of nature, which I spoke of, has a law of nature (that is, reason) to govern it, and this law obliges everyone, since all are equal and independent, to do no harm to any other person's life, health, liberty, or possessions.

Of the Ends of Political Society and Government

If man in the state of nature is as free as I have said, and if he is equal to the greatest and subject to no body – why will he part with his freedom? The obvious answer is that his enjoyment of his freedom is very uncertain, and constantly exposed to the invasion of others. Since every man is his equal, and the greater proportion of his fellow men are not fair and just, the enjoyment of the property man has is very insecure. This condition makes man willing to give up his freedom and to join in the society of others who are already united, or have a mind to unite, for the mutual preservation of their lives, liberties, and property.

Of the Dissolution of Government

The reason men enter into society is to preserve their property. Therefore, the purpose they have in choosing and authorizing a legislative assembly is the making of laws to guard the properties of all the members of the society. Whenever the legislators try to take away and destroy the property of the people, or to reduce them to slavery, these legislators put themselves into a state of war with the

The Globe and Mail, Toronto

Aftermath of the Chicago riots, 1968. How might Locke have reacted to the destruction of property evident in this picture?

people. In this situation, the people are freed from any further duty to obey their legislators. They have, moreover, a right to resume their original liberty, and, by the establishment of a new assembly, to provide for their own safety and security. What I have said concerning the assembly holds true for the supreme executive power, which has a double trust, both to take part in the assembly and to carry out the law. If the executive acts against both of these trusts by making his own arbitrary will the law of society, he frees the people from the duty of obeying him.

Discussion guidelines

1. (a) To what extent would you agree that human beings are born with certain absolute rights – life, liberty, and property?
   (b) Evaluate Locke's view of the political significance of property.
2. In your opinion, are all men created "equal and independent"? Comment.
3. Which of Locke's arguments regarding revolution could be used to justify the political aims of black nationalism and Quebec separatism?

Cross references

Canadian Sins Against Minorities, page 115
A Dialogue on Protest, page 177
The Watts Riot: An Incident, page 180
Civil Disobedience: National and International, page 181

Government in Captivity
from *Stoerpenberg Camp*
by Gerald Haines

There were a hundred and sixty of them. They had been counted by the Germans and the count had been checked. They moved about the building peering out the windows at the drab winter landscape, or sat around the tables, now and then dropping down on a bunk, hands under head, to lie staring at the ceiling. One hundred and sixty American prisoners of war, who had been captured in the Battle of the Bulge two months ago, were now organized as a prisoner-of-war labor unit at Stoerpenberg, somewhere in western Germany.

During the first two days they had nothing to do but lie on their beds and wait to be fed. As men drifted from one bunk to another, they began to talk about their situation. They discovered that they were all privates who had been in combat units of one kind or another. They represented a fair cross section of the United States, with men from every region of the nation included. Some of the men who had been able to talk to the guards had discovered that the camp was at the edge of a large town. The prisoners were to be used as laborers in nearby fields or for general utility work about the town.

The prisoners were housed in a gymnasium that had been part of a group of factory buildings. It evidently had been used as a workers' recreation center. At one end of the building a few tumbling mats and gymnastic bars were all that remained of the building's former equipment. An aisle formed by two rows of tables ran down the center of the building. Behind the tables, on each side were rows of double-decked bunks, while at the far end of the gymnasium three rooms were partitioned off from the central part. The center room was fitted with washing troughs; to the north was a storage room, and to the south a lavatory. At the south end of the building on the outside lay a long narrow plot of ground used as an exercise yard for the prisoners. Within the building and the exercise yard the American prisoners formed a little society of their own.

By the second day the men had picked out bunks and taken regular places at the tables. There were ten tables, so sixteen men were grouped at each. Men who had known each other before they were captured tended to cluster together. None of the men could have known anyone else in the group for more than two months, but under the circumstances, any familiar face was a welcome sight. A few men who had not yet made friends tended to drift to the table closest to their bunk.

On the third day the German officer in charge told the prisoners to choose a group leader. This leader would pass on to the group the regulations and orders of the German officers and would be responsible for carrying out rules for health and sanitation made by the prisoners.

After the interpreter told the prisoners this, they began to discuss the matter among themselves. They were seated around the tables where there was enough space for two or three of them to get together. They decided to hold an election. Very shortly men began to move from table to table campaigning for their favorite. Finally a few men were selected as candidates. Votes were taken by a show of hands.

If a proposed candidate seemed to have a fairly large number of people behind him he was considered in the running, and if not, his name was dropped. The choice soon narrowed down to a few men. Each man was presented to the group by his backers who made campaign speeches in his favor. After the speeches were finished, a final vote was taken by a show of hands. The choice was George Kent, a man of good physical appearance, who had demonstrated a commanding personality and superior social presence during the election of the leader. A college graduate, Kent had at one time been an acting sergeant, and had distinguished himself in battle.

Kent immediately brought up the vital matter of how food was to be distributed. In a prisoner-of-war camp with limited rations, food was of vital importance to everyone and was without doubt the subject most constantly on every prisoner's mind. Kent suggested that the entire ration of food should be divided into ten parts, one for each table, and then distributed at the tables to the men. In order to supervise this final distribution of food, he suggested that each table elect a table leader to take charge. The men quickly responded to this suggestion. Gathered around the tables, they talked informally, and finally each table chose its representative. The men who were finally chosen as leaders had a few characteristics in common. Several were college graduates and all the remainder had finished high school. A number of them had acted as noncommissioned officers at one time or another. Every one of them was a good talker who could communicate well with his fellows.

Shortly after the table leaders were chosen, several of them suggested to Kent that they set up a council to govern the unit. Kent agreed. In the following weeks the council met regularly. It consisted of Kent and the ten table leaders. At each meeting Kent passed on orders and information from the German administration of the camp so that the table leaders could inform the men in their group. The members of the council also discussed living arrangements, such as the choice of bunks, and made assignments to clean-up details.

If a man felt he had a legitimate "gripe" he complained to his table leader. If the table leader was unable to settle the matter on the spot, he would bring it before the council at the next meeting. Most matters brought up in this way were settled at the council, but when a new problem seemed to be particularly important, it was referred to the tables for discussion and a referendum. Through this procedure the men were able to make rules by which they could govern themselves.

In a few weeks the camp was functioning very effectively. The men were organized into compact units. The routine of their lives had been worked out with each man having certain duties to perform in a regular rotation for the benefit of all. Behind this formal organization was the code of the group. The code was not formal – no one had written it down or made speeches about it – yet everyone knew what it was and lived by it, or knew what to expect if he did not.

The first and most important rule of this informal code was that no prisoner would steal from another, particularly that he would not steal food or tobacco. Stealing from the Germans was quite all right as long as a prisoner did not get caught. If he were caught, the prisoner's duty was clear – to identify himself as the sole participant and to bear the brunt of German displeasure. There were a few other important parts of the code. Everyone was expected to keep as clean as possible, although keeping clean required a great deal of effort. As to the work being done for the Germans, it was quite all right to do as little as possible as long as a prisoner did not get caught.

Within two weeks after the 160 prisoners had been thrown together in the gymnasium at Stoerpenberg, they had developed a small but complete society. They had organized a government; they had made some laws; they had worked out an economic organization to distribute food; they had built up a social structure; and they had accepted an informal code which everyone obeyed.

In the third week of March, 1945, as the result of an incident among the members of Table Five, the leaders of the work unit suddenly found themselves with a difficult problem. One of the men at the table was accused of stealing food and the uproar over it threatened to break up the society. One of the members of Table Five was a man named Court. From the very first, Ainslee, the table leader of Number Five, had been aware that Court did not fit into any of the informal groups at the table, nor did he seem to have friends at any of the other tables. His manner was listless and apathetic. He seemed withdrawn from the life about him and his reactions seemed rather slow and confused when any situation arose that required him to participate in some activity. His personal habits were very lax to the point that he was filthy, even though a room for washing was available. Ainslee thought that Court was mentally ill or had suffered some intense experience during his capture.

Whatever the reasons, Court was one of the few men who did not actively participate in the life of the group. His sole interest was food. Soon he began to save bread from his daily rations. Each day he added another small portion to his store. He concealed the chunks of bread about his clothing and bunk. Court was very suspicious of his fellow-prisoners and spent much of his free time carefully checking his hoard. By the middle of March much of the bread he had managed to save was stale and unpalatable. He was not seen to eat any of it, but he seemed to get satisfaction from handling it and knowing that it was there when he wanted to look at it.

Bartrum, a tall, heavy man from Table Five, had been observing Court's behavior carefully. In casual conversations with others, he pointed out the futility of Court's actions. Many others agreed with him and, because food was so scarce, some felt that it was wrong for one man to waste what could be used so well by others.

Each evening the men of the work unit stood in the aisle to be counted by one of the German noncommissioned officers. Late in March Bartrum was late to formation. Immediately after the men were dismissed, he returned quietly to his bunk. A short time later the men around Table Five were startled by hoarse cries. Court was moving around and around his bunk, searching here and there, uttering moans and weeping. Ainslee and several others moved quickly over to Court to discover that much of his hoard of bread had been stolen. In a few minutes a large crowd had collected about Court's bunk. The news of his loss passed quickly among them. The low hum of many voices began to comment on the fact that Bartrum had been late to head count. The men began to suspect that he was the thief.

Ainslee had decided to go to Kent to organize a search among the members of the group when a few of the men walked over to Bartrum's bunk and began looking around. Bartrum protested when suddenly one of the men found a chunk of bread tucked away at one end of the bunk. He shouted aloud and turned upon Bartrum. A thick knot of men rapidly swirled about him, cursing, shouting, and striking at him. Bartrum attempted to fight clear, stammering incoherently, as more and more men joined the melee. The room was filled with uproar which spread rapidly until every man in the room was involved.

Kent, the group leader, quickly caught the significance of the cries of the outraged men around Bartrum and realized that if he did not act quickly, Bartrum might be killed. Throwing himself into the crowd, he fought his way to Bartrum. Seizing him by the collar, Kent managed to get on top of a table where he could be seen above the mob, still holding Bartrum firmly. At first he could not make himself heard, but as more and more of the men saw who it was that held Bartrum, they became more quiet. Taking a deep breath Kent tried again. "Okay," he said. "I hate the —— as much as you do, but this isn't the way to do it." Howls of protest greeted this statement but Kent kept on talking, arguing that Bartrum must be handled by regular procedure and not by a mob. Meanwhile several of the table leaders had fought their way to Kent and now began to ring about him. Slowly the protests began to lessen. Kent bore down on the fact that the group would have its chance to take action after the council had tried Bartrum. As the crowd became quieter, Kent felt that the immediate danger was over. Calling to the table leaders to come with him, he jumped down from the table and, holding tightly to Bartrum, pushed his way through the men. They let him pass. The leaders walked with Kent and Bartrum to the end of the room. Here on the old tumbling mats they sat down to consider what they should do.

Bartrum's trial was conducted with some formality. Kent presided and asked most of the questions. Bartrum began by denying the theft but soon admitted his guilt, justifying himself by saying that the bread was being wasted and should do someone some good. He surprised the council by saying that he was ready to accept any punishment that seemed fitting.

The council, after some deliberation, passed sentence on Bartrum. First they placed him in isolation for a month; no one was to speak to him or have anything to do with him at all. Second, during this same month he was assigned to two hours of additional work in the barracks each night after the work unit had returned from the fields. Finally, he was to replace from his own bread ration an amount equal to the bread he had stolen.

After passing the sentence, the table leaders returned to their tables and consulted their men. In general, most of the men seemed satisfied and only a few felt that the sentence was too light. After each table had voted to accept the decision, the leaders returned to Kent and informed him of the results. Kent then sent Bartrum back to his bunk with a stern reminder that if he did not carry out his sentence properly, the next action would be very severe.

During the following two weeks, Bartrum was cut off from his fellow prisoners. No one spoke to him. Each evening he put in his two hours of extra labor. Each day he turned over part of his bread ration to Court who either ate it or stored it away with the rest of his hoard. Ainslee supervised the return of the stolen rations and kept an accurate day-by-day record. He appointed a different man each day to make sure that Bartrum worked steadily during his extra hours in the evening. By refusing to have anything to do with Bartrum, every member of the group helped to enforce the rest of the sentence.

Two weeks after the sentence began, the gymnasium was hit by a bomb during an Allied air attack. The Germans then bundled the American prisoners into small groups to distribute them among a number of other work camps. The society which they had formed came to an end. Most of the prisoners never saw each other again.

Discussion guidelines

1. Assess the value of the Stoerpenberg case study in helping students to understand how a government is structured, and how workable decisions are made.
2. (a) Do you think a similar structure of government would have been established by (i) Russian prisoners of war and (ii) Canadian prisoners of war? Suggest some reasons to support your opinion.
   (b) To what degree do you think people form a government modelled on what they are used to?
3. "A democratically organized government is the most responsive to human needs." To what extent do you agree with this viewpoint?

Cross references

Democracy in the Modern World, page 125
The Culture Concept, page 146

Nazi Totalitarianism

Miller Services, Toronto

We live in a world in which forms of government, whether democratic or non-democratic, have already been established. Of the latter type, Nazism is perhaps the most spectacular modern example. Is it dead? To answer this question involves understanding the origins and development of Nazi theories and party apparatus in Germany. Did it owe its emergence to the charismatic appeal of Hitler? Was it rooted in authoritarian German traditions? Was it the product of economic despair? Futhermore, how did Nazi totalitarianism function and how effective was its operation? Indeed, to what extent is this form of non-democratic ideology and/or government still present in the world today?

THE PROGRAM

The Aims of the Nazis

from *The Program of the National Socialist German Workers' Party*

The National Socialist German Workers' Party at a great mass meeting on February 25, 1920, in the Hofbräuhaus-Festsaal in Munich announced their program to the world.

In Section 2 of the Constitution of our Party this Program is declared to be inalterable.

The Program of the German Workers' Party is limited as to period. The leaders have no intention, once the aims announced in it have been achieved, of setting up fresh ones, merely in order to increase the discontent of the masses artificially, and so ensure the continued existence of the Party.

1. We demand the union of Germans to form a Great Germany on the basis of the right of the self-determination enjoyed by nations.

2. We demand equality of rights for the German people in its dealings with other nations, and abolition of the Peace Treaties of Versailles and St. Germain.

3. We demand land and territory (colonies) for the nourishment of our people and for settling our superfluous population.

4. None but members of the nation may be citizens of the State. None but those of German blood, whatever their creed, may be members of the nation. No Jew, therefore, may be a member of the nation.

5. Anyone who is not a citizen of the State may live in Germany only as a guest and must be regarded as being subject to foreign laws.

6. The right of voting on the State's government and legislation is to be enjoyed by the citizen of the State alone. We demand therefore that all official appointments, of whatever kind, whether in the Reich, in the country, or in the smaller localities, shall be granted to citizens of the State alone.

We oppose the corrupting custom of Parliament of filling posts merely with a view to party considerations, and without reference to character or capability.

7. We demand that the State shall make it its first duty to promote the industry and livelihood of citizens of the State. If it is not possible to nourish the entire population of the State, foreign nationals (non-citizens of the State) must be excluded from the Reich.

8. All non-German immigration must be prevented. We demand that all non-Germans who entered Germany subsequent to August 2, 1914, shall be required forthwith to depart from the Reich.

9. All citizens of the State shall be equal as regards rights and duties.

10. It must be the first duty of each citizen of the State to work with his mind or with his body. The activities of the individual may not clash with the interests of the whole, but must proceed within the frame of the community and be for the general good.

We demand therefore:

11. Abolition of incomes unearned by work.

12. In view of the enormous sacrifice of life and property demanded of a nation by every war, personal enrichment due to a war must be regarded as a crime against the nation. We demand therefore ruthless confiscation of all war gains.

13. We demand nationalization of all businesses which have been up to the present formed into companies (trusts).

14. We demand that the profits from wholesale trade shall be shared out.

15. We demand extensive development of provision for old age.

16. We demand creation and maintenance of a healthy middle class, immediate communalization of wholesale business premises, and their lease at a

cheap rate to small traders, and that extreme consideration shall be shown to all small purveyors to the State, district authorities and smaller localities.

17. We demand land-reform suitable to our national requirements, passing of a law for confiscation without compensation of land for communal purposes, abolition of interest on land loans, and prevention of all speculation in land.

18. We demand ruthless prosecution of those whose activities are injurious to the common interest. Sordid criminals against the nation, usurers, profiteers, etc., must be punished with death, whatever their creed or race.

19. We demand that the Roman Law, which serves the materialistic world order, shall be replaced by a legal system for all Germany.

20. With the aim of opening to every capable and industrious German the possibility of higher education and of thus obtaining advancement, the State must consider a thorough re-construction of our national system of education. The curriculum of all educational establishments must be brought into line with the requirements of practical life. Comprehension of the State idea (State sociology) must be the school objective, beginning with the first dawn of intelligence in the pupil. We demand development of the gifted children of poor parents, whatever their class or occupation, at the expense of the State.

21. The State must see to raising the standard of health in the nation by protecting mothers and infants, prohibiting child labour, increasing bodily efficiency by obligatory gymnastics and sports laid down by law, and by extensive support of clubs engaged in the bodily development of the young.

22. We demand abolition of a paid army and formation of a national army.

23. We demand legal warfare against conscious political lying and its dissemination in the Press. In order to facilitate creation of a German national Press we demand:

(a) that all editors of newspapers and their assistants, employing the German language, must be members of the nation.

(b) that special permission from the State shall be necessary before non-German newspapers may appear. These are not necessarily printed in the German language.

(c) that non-Germans shall be prohibited by law from participating financially in or influencing German newspapers, and that the penalty for disobeying the law shall be suppression of any such newspaper, and immediate deportation of the non-German concerned in it.

It must be forbidden to publish papers which do not conduce to the national welfare. We demand legal prosecution of all tendencies in art and literature of a kind likely to disintegrate our life as a nation, and the suppression of institutions which oppose the requirements above-mentioned.

24. We demand liberty for religious denominations in the State, so far as they are not a danger to it and do not oppose the moral feelings of the German race.

The Party, as such, stands for positive Christianity, but does not bind itself in the matter of creed to any particular confession. It combats the Jewish-materialist spirit within us and without us, and is convinced that our nation can only achieve permanent health from within on the principle: THE COMMON INTEREST BEFORE SELF.

25. That all the foregoing may be realized, we demand the creation of a strong central power of the State. Unquestioned authority of the politically centralized Parliament over the entire Reich and its organizations; and formation of Chambers for classes and occupations for the purpose of carrying out the general laws issued by the Reich in the various States of the confederation.

The leaders of the Party swear to go straight forward – if necessary to sacrifice their lives – in securing fulfilment of the foregoing points.

Discussion guidelines

1. Give evidence that the Nazi political platform was totalitarian in nature.
2. "A successful party program should have something in it for everybody." Argue the validity of this statement with reference to (a) the program of the Nazi party and (b) a political program of which you have first-hand knowledge.
3. Why is racism frequently made an issue by would-be dictators?

Cross reference

The Aims of the Communists, page 65

Miller Services, Toronto

Young men demonstrating for the Nazi Party during an election campaign. Can you suggest why the Nazi movement had a strong appeal to youth?

GERMANY'S ACCEPTANCE OF HITLER

German Response to Versailles

from *Woodrow Wilson and the Lost Peace*
by Thomas A. Bailey

On April 14, 1919, when it seemed as though a settlement was in sight, the German delegates were summoned to Versailles to receive the Treaty. Upon arriving late in the month, they were assigned as virtual prisoners to a hotel, about which a fence was hurriedly erected to shield them from the stares of the curious and from the possible violence of the mob. This precaution was far from foolish, for several weeks later the delegates were assailed by a crowd of angry Frenchmen, and two of the Germans were injured by stones. Nothing could better illustrate the poisonous atmosphere surrounding the Conference.

The German delegates had arrived, but still there was no treaty. . . . The first printed copies were not available until the early morning of May 7, 1919 – the day of the presentation of the pact to the German delegates. It is an almost incredible fact that probably no single one of the Allied statesmen had read the Treaty as a whole until the day it was handed to the Germans.

Herbert Hoover remembers that a messenger brought a copy to him on the morning of May 7, and he was so disturbed by what he found that he went for a walk in the early morning air. He met General Smuts, who was similarly agitated, and who was also walking to cool off. The two men despondently compared notes and expressed fear for the future. . . .

As one examined the individual clauses of the Treaty by themselves the various provisions did not seem altogether unreasonable. But when they were all put together, and when it was observed that certain exactions made it difficult or impossible to carry out other exactions, the whole effect was stunning.

The Treaty of Versailles was formally presented to the German representatives on May 7, 1919, by coincidence the fourth anniversary of the sinking of the *Lusitania*.

The scene was the Trianon Palace at Versailles. The day was one of surpassing loveliness, and brilliant spring sunlight flooded the room. . . .

The crowd was small, for the room was small – merely the delegates of both sides, with their assistants, and a few carefully selected press representatives. The grim-visaged Clemenceau sat at the center of the main table: Wilson at his right, Lloyd George at his left.

The air was surcharged with electricity: German and Allied diplomats had not met face to face since the fateful summer of 1914. Would the Germans do something to offend the proprieties?

When all were seated, the doors swung open. At the cry, "*Messieurs les plénipotentiaires allemands!*" the whole assembly rose and stood in silence while the German delegates filed in before their conquerors and sat at a table facing Clemenceau.

The Tiger rose to his feet and, his voice vibrant with the venom of 1871, almost spat out his speech with staccato precision: "It is neither the time nor the place for superfluous words . . . The time has come when we must settle our accounts. You have asked for peace. We are ready to give you peace."

Already a secretary had quietly walked over to the table at which the Germans sat, and laid before them the thick, two-hundred-odd-page treaty – "the book".

With Clemenceau still standing, the pale, black-clad Count Brockdorff-Rantzau, head of the German delegation, began reading his reply – *seated.*

An almost imperceptible gasp swept the room, for the failure of the German to rise was taken as a studied discourtesy. Some felt that he was too nervous and shaken to stand. Others felt that he wanted to snub his "conquerors". The truth is that he planned to sit, not wishing to stand like a culprit before a judge to receive sentence.

Nothing could better reflect the spirit of the Germans. They felt that the war had been more or less a stalemate; they had laid down their arms expecting to negotiate with a chivalrous foe. As equals, why should they rise like criminals before the Allied bar?

If Brockdorff-Rantzau's posture was unfortunate, his words and the intonation of his words were doubly so.

The Germans had not yet read the Treaty, but they had every reason to believe that it would be severe. They had not been allowed to participate in its negotiation; they would not be allowed to discuss its provisions *orally* with their conquerors. Brockdorff-Rantzau decided to make the most of this, his only opportunity to meet his adversaries face to face and comment on the unread Treaty. Both his manner and his words were sullen, arrogant, unrepentant.

Speaking with great deliberation and without the usual courteous salutation to the presiding officer, he began by saying that the Germans were under "no illusions" as to the extent of their defeat and the degree of their "powerlessness". This was not true, for both he and his people were under great illusions.

Then he referred defiantly but inaccurately to the demand that the Germans acknowledge that "we alone are guilty of having caused the war. Such a confession in my mouth would be a lie." And the word "lie" fairly hissed from between his teeth.

Bitterly he mentioned the "hundreds of thousands" of German noncombatants who had perished since Armistice Day as a result of Allied insistence on continuing the blockade during the peace negotiations. This shaft struck home, especially to the heart of Lloyd George.

When the echo of Brockdorff-Rantzau's last tactless word had died away, Clemenceau spoke. His face had gone red during the harangue, but he had held himself in check with remarkable self-restraint. Harshly and peremptorily he steamrolled the proceedings to an end: "Has anybody any more observations to offer? Does no one wish to speak? If not, the meeting is closed."

The German delegates marched out, facing a battery of clicking moving picture cameras. Brockdorff-Rantzau lighted a cigarette with trembling fingers.

Lloyd George, who had snapped an ivory paper knife in his hands, remarked angrily: "It is hard to have won the war and to have to listen to that."

Thus, within a half-hour, was compressed one of the greatest dramas of all time.

Discussion guidelines

1. (a) "The time has come when we must settle our accounts. You have asked for peace. We are ready to give you peace." How accurate was this statement of the French premier?
   (b) "Every treaty which brings a war to an end is almost inevitably accepted by the loser under duress" (E. H. Carr, *The Twenty Years of Crisis 1919-1939).*
   In the light of subsequent historical developments, do you think too much duress was placed upon Germany at Versailles? Comment.
2. Compare the Allied treatment of the defeated Germans at Versailles (1919) with that of the German treatment of the defeated Russians at Brest-Litovsk (1918).
3. A peace treaty has not yet been signed between the victors of the Second World War and Germany. What is to be said for and against this situation?

Cross reference

Statecraft, page 243

2

a

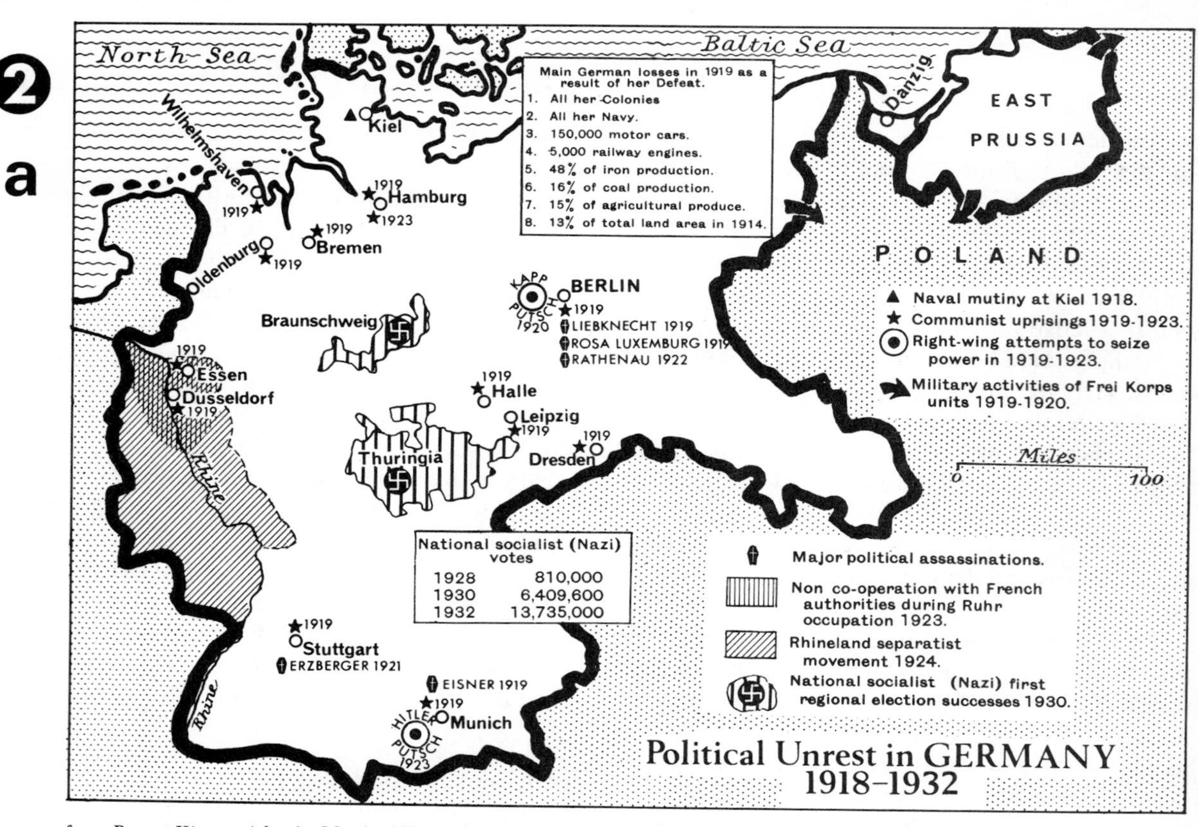
North Sea
Baltic Sea
Main German losses in 1919 as a result of her Defeat.
1. All her Colonies
2. All her Navy.
3. 150,000 motor cars.
4. 5,000 railway engines.
5. 48% of iron production.
6. 16% of coal production.
7. 15% of agricultural produce.
8. 13% of total land area in 1914.
Danzig
EAST PRUSSIA
POLAND
Kiel
Wilhelmshaven
Hamburg
Bremen
Oldenburg
BERLIN
KAPP PUTSCH 1920
LIEBKNECHT 1919
ROSA LUXEMBURG 1919
RATHENAU 1922
Braunschweig
Essen
Dusseldorf
Halle
Leipzig
Dresden
Thuringia
Rhine
Stuttgart
ERZBERGER 1921
EISNER 1919
Munich
HITLER PUTSCH 1923
Naval mutiny at Kiel 1918.
Communist uprisings 1919-1923.
Right-wing attempts to seize power in 1919-1923.
Military activities of Frei Korps units 1919-1920.
Miles
0
100
National socialist (Nazi) votes
1928 810,000
1930 6,409,600
1932 13,735,000
Major political assassinations.
Non co-operation with French authorities during Ruhr occupation 1923.
Rhineland separatist movement 1924.
National socialist (Nazi) first regional election successes 1930.
Political Unrest in GERMANY 1918–1932

from *Recent History Atlas*, by Martin Gilbert and John Flower, by permission of Weidenfeld and Nicolson

b

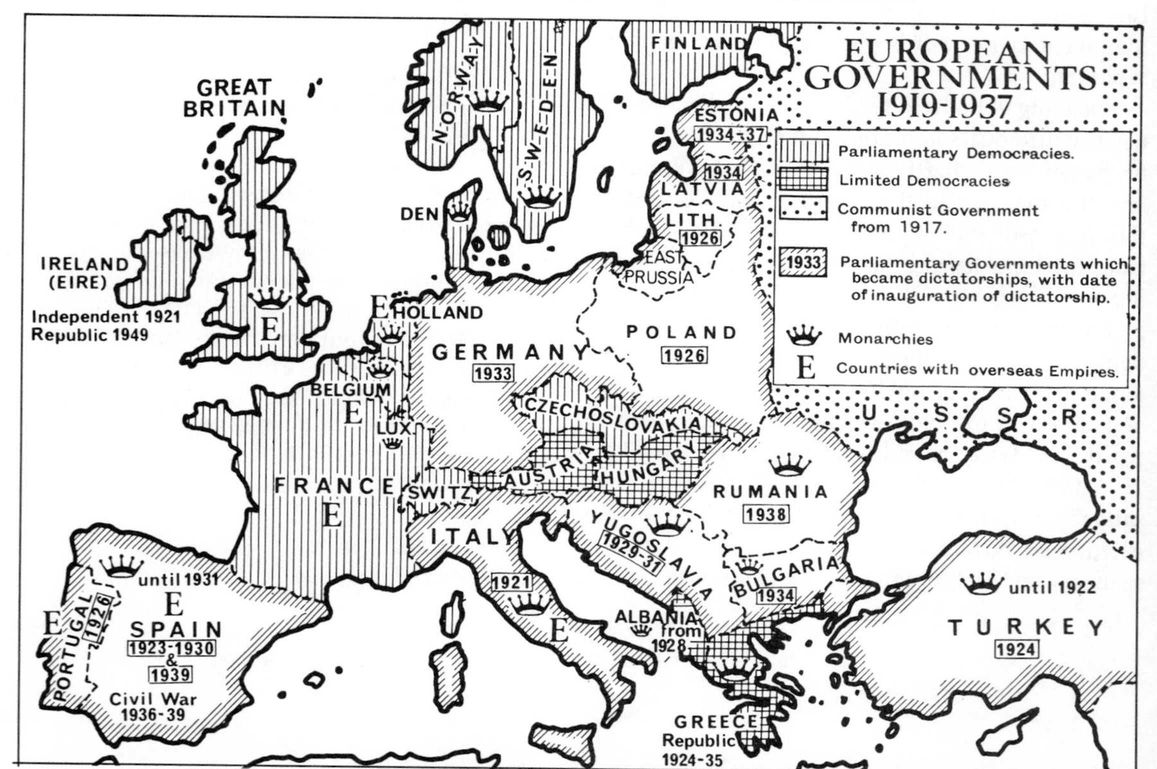
EUROPEAN GOVERNMENTS 1919-1937
Parliamentary Democracies.
Limited Democracies
Communist Government from 1917.
1933 Parliamentary Governments which became dictatorships, with date of inauguration of dictatorship.
Monarchies
E Countries with overseas Empires.
GREAT BRITAIN
IRELAND (EIRE)
Independent 1921
Republic 1949
NORWAY
SWEDEN
FINLAND
ESTONIA 1934-37
LATVIA 1934
LITH. 1926
EAST PRUSSIA
DEN
HOLLAND
GERMANY 1933
POLAND 1926
BELGIUM
LUX
CZECHOSLOVAKIA
AUSTRIA
HUNGARY
FRANCE
SWITZ
U S S R
RUMANIA 1938
ITALY 1921
YUGOSLAVIA 1929-31
BULGARIA 1934
ALBANIA from 1928
GREECE Republic 1924-35
TURKEY 1924
until 1922
PORTUGAL 1926
SPAIN 1923-1930 & 1939
until 1931
Civil War 1936-39

C

Political Divisions in German Parliamentary Elections, 1919–1933

[Figures indicate number of seats]

	Communists	*Independent Socialists*	*Social Democrats*	*Centre*	*Democrats*	*People's Party*	*Nationalists*	*National Socialists*	*Others*
Jan. 1919	—*	22	163	71	74	22	42		7
June 1919				Versailles					
June 1920	2	81	112	68	45	62	66		30
1923				Inflation; French Invasion of Ruhr					
May 1924	62	—†	100	65	28	44	96	38	45
Dec. 1924	45		131	69	32	51	103	20	48
May 1928	54		152	61	25	45	78	12	67
1929				Depression					
Sept. 1930	77		143	68	14	30	41	107	91
Apr. 1932				Presidential Election					
May 1932				Dismissal of Brüning					
July 1932	89		133	75	4	7	40	230	33
Nov. 1932	100		121	70	2	11	51	196	32
Jan. 1933				Hitler Chancellor					
Mar. 1933	81		125	74	5	2	52	288	25
Nov. 1933								661	

*The Communists boycotted the election.
†The Independent Socialists split between the Communists and the Social Democrats.

Discussion guideline

To what extent do the maps and the election chart contribute to an understanding of the Nazis' success?

A Stormtrooper's Reaction

from *The Mark of the Swastika*
by Louis Hagen

My father was a market gardener in Weissensee. Although my brother Karl carried on the family tradition when he left school, I [Fritz Muehlebach] felt that it did not lead anywhere. When I left school, I got a job as assistant to a chemist, but, owing to the bad times, that did not last long. After my father passed away, I would have liked to have stayed at home with my mother. But there was no work to be had, so I finally decided to try my luck at sea. I left home at the age of twenty – that was in 1927 – and went to Rotterdam. There was a lot of unemployment there too, but I was lucky enough to get a ship right away.

For the next five years I was a sailor and enjoyed myself very much. I went all over the world, saw foreign countries and foreign people, and brought back souvenirs and curios from all over the place: Chinese beads, snakes in bottles, painted coconuts, native weapons, and brass idols. My mother was very proud of them and used to show them off whenever one of the family came to an evening meal.

In 1931 we were in the North Sea when there was a bit of a rough-house between several lads and some of the older seamen. As the youngsters seemed to be getting the worst of it, I sided with them. I got a broken wrist and a torn ear, but we mastered them, and when the mate caught us, we had two of the older fellows locked up. I never did find out the reason for the row.

When we landed at Stettin, I was told by two of the youngsters that they were in the Hitler Youth. To show their gratitude, because I'd helped them in the fight, they asked me to come to one of their gatherings at what they called their *Sturmlokal* (a pub in which Party members regularly met). Here I was introduced to other Party members and men who were in the S.A.

Until then I had only heard vaguely about the National Socialist doctrine. Now, I began to realize that it was a very large party and its leaders really did know what they wanted, not like all the other parties.

One of the lads, called Erwin Eckhart, took me back to his flat. As we had been signed off and it looked as though I would have to stay ashore a bit, I rented a room from Erwin and used to share his kitchen. He told me a whole heap of things about politics that I never knew before. We hadn't talked about politics at home. I suppose my mother and father were only simple, old-fashioned people and they couldn't grasp the new, modern ideas about politics. Erwin knew it all and used to jaw away by the hour. And then he started taking me to the Party meetings and lectures. It's wonderful how it broadens your mind to think about important things like politics. I was bowled over by some of the lectures – I was beginning to get my eyes opened to a few things. The way all the other parties were just muddling through because they hadn't got one ideal and one leader. The way our German industry was being smothered by Jewish moneylenders. And the way the other countries were trying to pin the war guilt on the German people. We had to throw the Versailles lie back in their teeth, and throw over all the unjust burdens which the Treaty had laid on us. Socialism was the answer – finish the class struggle, and no one must earn more than a thousand marks a month. Put Germany in the hands of the Germans, and throw out the Jews and foreigners.

At these meetings there was often a good deal of heckling by Communists and other political groups. It annoyed me that people holding different political views should disturb these lectures. I, for one, wanted to know what the Nazis stood for, so that I could form an opinion. The shouting and heckling

Miller Services, Toronto

Stormtroopers saluting Hitler at a rally. Why might the S.A. have appealed to a person such as Fritz Muehlebach?

often made it impossible for the speaker to complete his speech. The S.A. men always tried to keep order, and I always used to give them a hand with the disturbing elements so that the lectures could continue undisturbed. Quite often it led to serious fights.

In the Sturmlokal near the place where I lived I met a lot of students and unemployed S.A. men. I went there a lot, and the talk was mostly on political problems. I enjoyed these discussions, which were interesting and always to the point. But the others were much better talkers than I was, for I had not had any political training. But I liked the general atmosphere of comradeship, and, in the end, I decided to send in my application forms for the S.A. It was time for me to belong to an organization and take an active part in shaping the future of my country. I felt that this party was on the right road and that I would learn a great deal about politics in its ranks. I wanted to know what was going on; I wanted to be able to answer questions and have the strength and confidence which all the other S.A. men seemed to have.

As soon as my wrist was better I went to sea again. Whenever we put into a German port, I found my way to the nearest Sturmlokal and spent what free time I had there. Wherever I went I found the same comradeship and sense of purpose. I was more and more proud and happy that I was part of this movement.

Back in Stettin I was very disappointed to learn that I had not been accepted by the S.A. in my absence. In April, 1932, the S.A. had been prohibited, and they now had to be very careful about new members. And they didn't know anything about my past and thought I might have been a spy for the Communists or for the police. I was very sorry, of course, but it did mean that the party was very alive to the dangers. Every member had to show his worth and reliability before being accepted. This really made me admire them more than ever.

I couldn't get a ship after this and was again out of work. Times were bad, and I was very depressed. When I realized that there were six million unemployed in the same position as myself, the responsibility of getting a job seemed completely hopeless. Depression and panic were in the air; some of the biggest banks had closed, and no one could see any end to it. Of course Moscow started making mischief in this atmosphere of unrest and discontent, and almost six million people went over to the Communists. The Reds were busy with strikes and the picketing of offices and factories and intimidating the workers. They were at the root of all the street brawls and shooting. The government was always changing and couldn't do anything, and the police didn't seem to care. They were all making it easy for the Communists to terrorize the whole German population.

In July, 1932, three of the local S.A. men were murdered by the Reds. This strengthened my resolve to try again to join the S.A. and avenge them. I was careful to get references from home, and Erwin vouched for me. This time it worked.

It was wonderful to know at last that I was taking an active part in the welfare of my fatherland. We S.A. men were the soldiers of the movement. It was our job to maintain order at all Party meetings. The speakers and leaders were protected by the S.S., which was a special corps of picked S.A. men limited to ten per cent of our strength. Members of the S.A. and S.S. were strictly forbidden to make speeches or take part in public discussions. All that was entrusted to the political leaders and those members of the Party who had received special political training. We were not trained to talk and argue, but it was up to us to make the best possible impression through our discipline and military bearing.

Life was still tough. Ninety per cent of our Sturm (roughly equivalent to a company of soldiers) were unemployed, but now we had something to fight and live for; and this made it so much easier for us all to bear the hardships. We were all in the same boat.

I got 8.40 marks a week unemployment benefit. Five marks went on rent, and the remaining 3.40 had to pay for all my living expenses. Thirty pfennigs were spent on tobacco. Ten pfennigs I paid toward the Party insurance fund in case I was disabled while fighting for the Party. When I drew my benefit, I just spent one mark on eleven small sausages from a stand outside the labor exchange. They cost ten pfennigs, but you could get eleven for the price of ten. The free sausage I ate immediately. The rest I kept for my breakfasts and suppers for the rest of the week. Another 1.20 marks I kept for buying bread and other things. For my main meal of the day I was able to go to the S.A. home, where for only ten pfennigs we got a really good midday meal. The well-to-do party members made regular contributions to the S.A. home. We often had real butter, and also venison and wild pork from their hunting estates, and in the season we often got jobs as beaters and loaders. Whenever a big shot came to the Sturmlokal, we got a free meal and free beer all round. Being members of the Party, they weren't a bit stuck-up and stand-offish, but talked to us man to man and made us see that we all had the same ideas and the same hopes for Germany. My membership fee was paid by what we used to call a "Godfather", who owned a shoe shop. Once I was really on the rocks and he lent me some money. When I wanted to pay it back in weekly instalments, he wouldn't have it, and let me off the whole amount. Many of us had Party godfathers – people we could always go to when we were in trouble, and who would invite us to Christmas and other festivals.

I was very badly off for clothes, because you never needed much on board ship and I never had bothered about them. Now, of course, I had no money, and I couldn't even afford a uniform. I felt rather ashamed of this. Most of the men in our Sturm wore at least part of a uniform, and all I could do was to wear a swastika armlet. In November my only pair of boots gave out and a heel came off in the snow. When I limped to the Sturmlokal, my *Sturmbandführer* took me straight to the S.A. offices and saw to it himself that I was given a complete uniform free of charge. I was very happy to get the uniform in time for the big November (1932) elections, because now I was able to undertake more important public duties, such as standing in front of the polling booth with a sandwich board. The results were very disappointing because we got even less votes than last time. But the leaders weren't at all downcast. They explained to us that this was really a victory for us. What it meant was that the lukewarm elements had now shown themselves in their true colors and left the Party. Now we knew where we stood. And those of us who were left would be true to their oath and their Führer.

The elections were the excuse for renewed outbreaks of violence on the part of our opponents. We had fights every day and several hospital cases each week. I got my nose broken with a knuckle duster during a scrap with the *Kampfring Junger Deutschnationaler*, the military youth organization of the German National Party.

Each party had its own fighting force: the Communists had the *Rotfrontkampferbund*, the Social Democrats had the *Reichsbanner,* and so on. And they all did everything they possibly could to provoke us. There was not one large-scale meeting that was not disturbed in some way or other, and not a single propaganda parade that took place without a disturbance. But now and again we got our own back.

I remember a large Communist rally where 150 of our people got in in ordinary clothes and took up the end seats on each side of the center gangway right down the hall. When all the speeches were well under way, one of our men slipped a stick of cordite into the stove. There was a fine explosion, the windows were shattered, and the whole hall was filled with thick sooty smoke. At the moment of the explosion we all stood up, put on our armlets and S.A. caps, and stood to attention giving the Hitler salute. The Reds were taken completely by surprise. They started shouting and dashing round the hall like a lot of scalded cats. Then, as the smoke cleared away and they saw the solid wedge of disciplined S.A. men standing shoulder to shoulder down the whole length of the hall, they squealed with terror and made a rush for the doors. Then we all seized chairs, smashed them as we had been taught, and, armed with the legs, waded into them. We always had to work fast and scientifically as the police were against us and were always liable to turn up. They were always pro-Red and beat us up whenever they could catch us. I remember once we broke up a *Deutsch-National* meeting at the Stettin Kaisergarten. The police got word of it and surrounded us. We had to come out through a long narrow corridor; the police had lined up all along the passage, and as we tried to get through, they thrashed us with rubber truncheons, and some of them weren't above using their feet. I was ill for a week after this meeting.

What made it worse was that we had strict orders not to resist the police, and we weren't allowed to carry guns. Anyone caught with a gun was expelled from the S.A. All we were allowed to do was to defend ourselves against insults with our fists. There was a lot of grumbling about the unfairness of this, but our leaders explained to us that we mustn't give the government the chance to get us banned. They were really terrified of us and would take the first opportunity. We just had to put up with it as best we could while our enemies tried their very best to incite us. Many of our comrades were murdered by the Reds, and we couldn't lift a hand to avenge them. But we were able to stick it out because we knew our time would come.

We were not allowed to wear our uniform or badges when we went to the labor exchange, where we had to get our cards stamped each day. Waiting in the queue, arguments would break out, and they often led to fighting. By the end of 1932 things got to such a pitch that a man couldn't go to the labor exchange without being beaten up if it was known that he was in the S.A. or a Party member. To avoid trouble and protect ourselves, the whole Sturm used to go together in a group. That usually kept the troublemakers quiet.

Everything we did now had to be organized in groups. Regularly, after midnight, parties armed with ladders, paint brushes, and pails went out until dawn, sticking up posters and slogans on walls and houses. Then, after we'd finished, we used to march through the town chanting in chorus, "All power to Adolf Hitler". Smaller groups of four to six men were busy all day pushing leaflets and party newspapers into mailboxes. We were always told to begin at the top of the house, as fights usually started if the people on the lower floors had time to give the alarm. Then members of the *Hauschutzstaffel* (military self-protection squads organized for the protection of houses and apartment houses against rival political parties) would sometimes lie in wait for us at the entrance and grab our leaflets and attack us with clubs and knuckle dusters. Another group was specially detailed to escort home S.A. members who lived in streets mainly inhabited by our opponents. Pommersdorf, for example, was a hot-bed of Communists, and if we hadn't escorted home the only two S.A. men who lived there, they would certainly have been attacked and probably murdered.

The struggle continued and our ideas spread, and by the end of 1932 we had the satisfaction of knowing that we were by far the strongest party. We all felt that final victory was just around the corner and the decision could no longer be delayed. General von Schleicher's government was all the time on the edge of a crisis, and it was obvious that nothing could save it. Then in January of the new year we heard that our Führer had been asked to join this government, obviously in a last desperate effort to keep it on its feet. This was a terrible moment for us. We were scared that he might be compromised and go with the reactionaries. But we needn't have worried, for this was followed by the news that the Führer was prepared to take all or nothing. He would not prop up anybody else's government but was perfectly willing to form his own. We hung on from day to day, with our excitement rising to fever pitch, and then, on January 30, standing around the wireless in the Sturmlokal, we heard the news we were waiting for. Reichspräsident-Feldmarschall von Hindenburg had charged the Führer with the formation of a government.

We had been waiting for it. We had always known it had to happen, and yet, when it came, it hit us like an explosion. We were beyond happiness. We sang the Horst Wessel song, we shouted "Heil!" until we were hoarse – and then we drank to the Führer till our throats were clear again. Then we dashed into the streets, where groups of other brown-shirts and Party members had already begun to gather. Swastika flags had appeared as if by magic. The day went by in a fever of activity, and a great torchlight procession was organized for the evening.

That night, as we marched singing through the streets, we had it all our own way. Now the police were on our side and guarded our procession. Our enemies were laying low, and there were no fights until we came to Pommersdorf. There, in spite of our strict order not to leave formation, a few of our more enthusiastic members could not resist the chance of getting their own back on the Reds. Some of them were afterwards expelled from the S.A. for lack of discipline.

During the months that followed there was a sudden stream of newly converted Party members. The German National Party had already come over to us, and after the March elections the so-called March casualties started pouring in. We had a pretty poor opinion of them, and I heard of cases in Berlin where the Sturms, particularly in the north, were now made up almost entirely of former Communists. My own Sturm in Stettin was certainly not what it had been; forty per cent of it had recently been Reds, ten per cent Social Democrats, and a lot were ex-Stahlhelm, Free Corps, and old Landsknechte. These people had turned their coats just in time to reap the rewards of the victory for which we had fought.

A Businessman's Answer
from *The Mark of the Swastika*
by Louis Hagen

I [Alfred Voss] was born [in 1895] in Lüneburg into the confining and depressing atmosphere of a small bourgeois home. My father was a minor official in the Lüneburg Town Council, assistant secretary of the Land Registry. We had no other sources of income, and it was only my mother's economy and good housekeeping that enabled him to keep up a style compatible with his rank as one of His Majesty the Kaiser's civil servants.

We never experienced outright need – that might have been bearable. But what seemed to me worse than that, we were forever scrimping and scraping. We had always to think twice before spending a penny; we had to go without most of the ordinary little pleasures and luxuries of life, and often we did not have quite enough to eat. I was the unwitting cause of much of this, since it was a point of honor in a civil servant that his son should go to the ancient and celebrated Lüneburg Gymnasium.

The sacrifices which sent me to the Gymnasium were, to my mind, completely wasted. Why should I be stuffed up with old dry Latin and Greek? What good would Sophocles and Virgil be in modern life? I would rather have gone to the modern school where I could have learned science and economics and things that could help me to get on in the world. For I meant to get on. I swore to myself that on no account would I become a civil servant and rot in genteel poverty in a county town. I wanted money – a lot of money. Not for itself, but for all the things money can buy. And all the things I had been denied up to then. I wanted to wear smart modern clothes, eat rich food, drink choice wines, know rich gay women, and go to theatres and night clubs and cabarets. All these I wanted. But how to get them I had no idea.

When my chance did come, it was at a time and in a way that I had never imagined. In 1911, quite suddenly, my father died. The State pension was wretchedly inadequate, and I had immediately to leave school and start to earn my living as quickly as possible.

At that time a Lüneburg metal firm was looking for a young man to learn the trade. Although I had no references, I applied for the job. The owner of the firm was a certain Samuel Marcus, a small, lively Polish Jew with a narrow and highly intelligent face. He interviewed every applicant personally.

He asked me why I wanted to start in his firm. I replied that I had no particular leanings toward the metal trade; I would just as gladly sell soap or wicker chairs. But I particularly wanted to work for a Jew, for in my opinion Jewish merchants were generally more liberal-minded and also more successful than others. This got me the job, and Samuel Marcus subsequently took a great deal of interest in me.

Very early I had found out the secret of success in business. From the very first day I concentrated all my interest on the metal trade as though nothing in the world existed beside it. I read innumerable books on metallurgy and attended evening classes in commercial subjects. In this way I very quickly surpassed my more easygoing colleagues. For their part, they scorned me as an upstart climber and a would-be boss's bright boy. They were right, of course, but I didn't worry. I knew I was on the right road.

I became very friendly with Marcus's only son, Mischa, who was heir to the business. He was a few years younger than I but seemed older than his age. We got on very well together.

We planned to go into a business partnership when we were older. This was our great secret, which no one, not even old Marcus, knew anything about.

In 1919 we started. The firm of Voss & Marcus, metal merchants, with offices in Berlin, was duly entered on the company register. Our first object was to obtain capital quickly.

Our big chance was the surrender of war materials ordered by the Treaty of Versailles. Trains carrying airplanes, guns, and tanks were continually rolling west to be turned into scrap metal. Like many others, we managed to secure a part of this valuable scrap. Through the agency of French buyers, whom we had met in a Cologne night club, we even contrived to have some of this material sent back to Germany as soon as it had arrived in France. At that time it was impossible to do business on any other basis. A "respectable" businessman might think this procedure corrupt; to us it merely demonstrated our "commercial elasticity".

The inflation which now led to the sudden depreciation of the currency worked to our advantage. By accident we hit on a very profitable routine which we made the model for a great number of other deals. For the sum of 5,000 marks we had bought a rather large item of scrap copper which was lying in Duisburg and which we forgot about for several months. To our great amazement, we noticed one day that its value had meanwhile risen to 20,000 marks. Our next step was simple; by selling a quarter of the copper we recovered our original outlay, which left us with 15,000 marks' worth of copper.

The fall of the mark continued unabated. In May, 1920, the dollar stood at sixty marks; in January, 1922, it was worth 200. No one could fail to see that capital funds were worth nothing while nonperishable goods could be worth anything. We decided to risk everything on a really big coup.

One of our former colleagues in the supply office, called Petersen, who was still engaged in winding up its operations, had told us confidentially that a cargo of copper was lying in the east port of Berlin. Its nominal value was five million, but through him it might be secured for three million, since this material was "listed" for delivery to the Allies. The only difficulty was how to raise this gigantic sum of three million, which was far beyond the capacity of our small business. To this problem, which I thought insoluble, Petersen provided the answer.

One of his friends was Dr. Rudolf von Struven, a director of the Darmstädter Bank. This bank advanced a credit of 2,400,000 marks to us on the security of the cargo of copper which was not yet ours. And then with great difficulty we succeeded in raising the remaining 600,000 marks ourselves.

From then onward we had a spell of good fortune. The credit of the Darmstädter Bank was at first repayable after three months; but Petersen knew how to get our payment postponed for another nine months. When, at length, we paid it in October, 1922, the dollar stood at 7,000 marks. And our copper had risen in value to 105 million; after the sale of about twenty per cent of it we were left with a clear profit of eighty million marks' worth of copper. It was like a fairy tale.

Then came 1923 and the occupation of the Ruhr. The mark reached dizzy heights. We no longer traded in metal alone; like everyone else, we bought whatever valuables there were: landed property, jewelry, works of art, and antiques. We even bought the all-powerful dollar on the black exchange; officially it was not quoted.

Our speculations were, of course, complete tightrope walking. But we stepped with such a hypnotic sureness and such constant good luck that even to think of it today makes me dizzy. This kind of life needed the vigor and iron nerves of youth. And it needed the callousness of youth too. For we were surrounded on all sides by hunger and dire need. Old people who depended on pensions or savings found that their monthly income would buy no more than a tram ticket. For a few crusts of bread they had to sell all that they possessed. And the younger men of the working and salaried classes were little better off. Their pay was generally worthless a few hours after they had received it, and they lived from hand to mouth. Businessmen who didn't ride the wave soon went under, and suicides were the order of the day.

We were living in the most luxurious style. I had furnished a complete floor in a house in Hubertusallee in the Grünewald district, which was in no way inferior to Mischa's Lützowufer flat. My servant and my driver wore cream-colored liveries, which today I consider a little showy, and I drove a six-seater Mercedes, which was the most expensive car one could get.

Despite our youthful lightheartedness, we saw that this kind of business could not go on flourishing indefinitely. Germany seemed to be heading for economic disaster. The idiotic Versailles Treaty and the impossible Allied reparation demands put Germany in a desperate situation. On the strength of the untrue charges of war guilt, the enemy nations were all out for the biggest pickings from our unhappy country. They should have known that Europe needed Germany and our economic collapse would damage their economies no less than ours. But such an obvious truth was beyond their vision.

Meanwhile, the rate of inflation still increased. Between September and November, 1923, the dollar rose from 320 million to 2,500 million marks. It was obvious that this state of affairs could not go on.

Our business intuition now told us to reverse our strategy. While everybody else went on buying, we got rid of everything as quickly as we could, retaining only our stocks of metal. The proceeds came to a sum of astronomical dimensions, whose true value could only be gauged by expressing it in terms of dollars. Everyone thought us mad to sell; but we had a plan.

Our most valuable possession was our stock of metal. We were prepared to part with that too, but only in return for foreign currency, preferably dollars or sterling. This would have been strictly illegal. But we knew quite well that deals of that kind were made every day, usually with members of Allied military and trade missions. Through Petersen we got to know some smart American businessmen who, in their turn, introduced us in the bar of the Adlon Hotel to Captain Gadsby, a young Englishman whose father owned large factories in the English Midlands.

Gadsby was fair, slender, with a bored and hard face. He was not at all upset about the tight currency restrictions; but his suspicions, the most prominent English characteristic, were at once aroused. Why should we want to sell at a time when everyone else was buying? We managed to convince him that we were in urgent need of capital in order to get a footing in a large concern. He believed us, and from that moment everything went smoothly.

At his request we had lowered the purchase price by fifteen per cent, but in return we demanded that a quarter of the price should be paid in sterling into a special account with the Bank of England. Gadsby was agreeable to that, and as this keen young businessman had the use of military telephone lines, we knew that our deal would be put through promptly.

We were not a week too soon; a few days after our contract had been signed the mark was stabilized. Through Gadsby's connections the permission to ship the metal to England was easily obtained, and soon after, we received payment of £300,000. This represented six million marks in the new currency; our remaining property was valued at four million.

The following period of deflation was marked by a considerable scarcity of ready money. Our ten million placed us in a powerful position. The time for speculation was now past, and I began looking around for some more solid investment.

At that time I made the acquaintance of Kommerzienrat von Eberstein, a leading personality in German industry, owner of steel mills and machine-tool and motor works. These had been in the possession of his family for three generations. He had been ruined by the inflation and was desperate for capital. He had to have at least three million on six months' credit.

I advanced this sum to him at the rate, not then thought excessive, of one per cent per day. Then I sat back and awaited developments. After six months, as I had expected, I was asked by von Eberstein to his country house near Brandenburg. I was received by von Eberstein's daughter Traute, a fair-haired capable-looking girl with considerable charm. She was nervous and anxious to please, and I thought perhaps she had been crying. After dinner von Eberstein confessed his inability to repay the loan which, with accumulated interest, was now eight million. I asked him what terms he could offer.

He suggested that I should join his group of companies as an active partner. Von Eberstein's son Heinz, who was an engineer, was to run the technical side. This offer was too good to miss. But it meant that I had to sever my business relations with Mischa, which I did on the best of terms.

The time had now come when the German economy was helped to its feet by British and American loans. I have always been nauseated by the hypocrisy with which these loans were offered under the guise of charity. They cared no more for us than we did for them. It was a pure business deal. They knew that if they wanted to exploit us and extract reparations from us they had first to make us financially solvent. Their credits were virtually paid into their own pockets. Whatever their motives, though, the good effects soon became noticed. The general position became easier, factories were running again. I could only welcome these developments; I was sick of the strenuous and nerve-wracking life I had been leading and wanted nothing more than rest. Moreover, I felt it was time my cultural development caught up with my business development. I had started reading avidly and wanted time to study and absorb, and a place of my own where I could build up a library.

At that time I heard of an old aristocratic estate in Babelsberg being offered for sale. I went there and found a beautiful old house with a park of about forty acres, both in a somewhat neglected condition. As the price was reasonable, I bought the house and gave orders for it to be restored and furnished.

I was now well off enough to afford this. Thanks to Heinz Eberstein's efficient technical direction, the Eberstein works had recovered very quickly, and there was no shortage of orders. Only one thing worried old Eberstein.

We had large factories at Landshut, in Bavaria, where tractors, trucks, and armored cars used to be made. But by the Treaty of Versailles the manufacture of armored cars had been forbidden, while the German market was glutted with tractors released from army stocks. Unable to sell his machinery, Eberstein was faced with the necessity of having to shut down these factories.

At that time it came to my knowledge that tremendous orders for tractors and trucks were being placed by a Soviet purchasing commission. In a Berlin bar I met a German businessman who was already in contact with the Russians, and I was taken by him to the mysterious Soviet headquarters in Lindenstrasse.

Everything there was reminiscent of the way Russians are depicted in comic papers; there was an atmosphere of complete suspicion. Behind every painting one suspected an automatic camera, in every lamp a hidden microphone. The Russians argued with a dogged persistence and with some lack of the social graces. However, after much hard bargaining we concluded the deal. Shortly after, we received orders for about twenty million marks' worth of goods.

I went down to Brandenburg to report my success to Eberstein. This time Traute seemed a different woman. When I had seen her before, she had been expecting ruin daily. Now she greeted me with a warm smile. She was acting as her father's private secretary, and I was very impressed with her grasp and knowledge of business details. Eberstein was delighted by the Russian orders and asked me to take over the direction and the expansion of the Landshut works.

Once the factories were running smoothly, I decided to travel abroad. Hitherto I had had no time for traveling and, apart from what my military service had shown me of France, I knew no foreign countries. It was not merely to be a holiday; I intended to revive some of my old connections and to establish new ones. I also wanted to study conditions in the tool and motor industry in other countries.

On my return I called on Eberstein at his castle in Thuringia. He showed a keen interest in doing business with Britain. But quite evidently he was no longer in the best of health, and it seemed to me that it was time for the old gentleman to take a rest. I asked Traute what she thought and found she had been anxious about her father for some time. He had been sleeping badly and had lost much of his keen grasp of business matters, and Traute had been doing more and more herself. She agreed with me completely that he ought to give up but said that he wouldn't because it would be like handing over the family business to a stranger. An obvious solution occurred to me – and looking at Traute I saw that it had occurred to her too. A few weeks later I asked old Eberstein for the hand of his daughter in marriage.

Like many others, we might have had to shut down our factories during the great depression of the thirties if our Russian orders had not kept forty per cent of our production capacity employed. It became increasingly clear that through the system of foreign loans German industry was so tied to other countries that it responded very sensitively to the ups and downs of their economies. This only screened the German economic plight. The number of unemployed rose steadily. The Darmstädter und Nationalbank and the Dresdner Bank, as well as most of the smaller banking firms, had to stop payments. This resulted in general panic, widespread bankruptcy, and a fresh wave of suicides. Everybody saw that this state of affairs could not go on. Everybody said, "This cannot go on," but nobody did anything.

Our government proved itself incompetent in the face of a situation for which, apart from the shortsightedness of other nations, our own lunatic swarm of more than thirty political parties was to blame. The whole fabric of the Weimar Republic was corrupt, and rotten. A people like the Germans could not be ruled in that way. We should have modeled our government to a much greater extent on the Soviet system. By this I do not mean to endorse the Communist doctrine, any more than the Russians themselves do. What I mean is that a group of leaders of superior intellect and endowed with dictatorial powers was best suited to lead a country out of an unbalanced economic situation.

I probably do not go far wrong in assuming that the Allies deliberately supported the Weimar Republic because they wanted to prevent a German economic revival. Through that policy they gave indirect support to the National Socialist movement and thus achieved the very thing that they had set out to avoid.

The attitude of a businessman or industrialist to the National Socialist movement and its program could only be one of bewilderment. No one among my friends could take the Nazis seriously. The economic foundations of the Nazi program were both vague and crude. They took no account of the complex nature of the international economic situation, and no one could trust these amateurs to repair the dislocated German economy. The vague and hardly comprehensible tone of their speeches, slogans, and propaganda might serve to stir up certain sections of the population or to inflame unstable youths, but a businessman had no time for this kind of Valhalla hysteria.

None of the leaders of that party were of recognized social standing. Apart from a few impoverished noblemen and superannuated soldiers, they consisted mainly of shipwrecked middle-class people and a few young desperadoes who had nothing

Miller Services, Toronto

Alfried Krupp, who controlled an industrial empire based on steel production and heavy industry, was the most important of the businessmen who supported Hitler. After World War II, he was imprisoned for war crimes. On his release, he revived his vast business interests and played a leading role in the reconstruction of West Germany.

to lose and everything to gain. To imagine this clique in power seemed even more farfetched than the possibility of a Communist Germany. All the same, I discerned certain danger signals in the situation and thought it advisable to interest myself in politics and also to sound my fellow industrialists on the matter. I began talking politics at my clubs: the Düsseldorf Association for Heavy Industry, whose influence on the country's economic life was enormous, and the Herrenklub in Jägerstrasse in Berlin.

The latter had a very diverse membership – landowners, artists, industrialists, lawyers, and politicians. The members were held together only by a common and pronounced leaning toward the right. But the most important club I belonged to was the Unionklub in Schadowstrasse. As I had kept racing stables at Karlsborst, I was eligible for this club, which was outwardly a meeting place for those who were interested in racing but which, in reality, I found was far more. Membership in the first place was confined to followers of Hugenberg's right-wing Deutschnational Party and extreme right-wing army officers. The committee included Herr von Papen, with whom I had two important discussions, together with Reichsbank president Schacht, concerning the participation of Germany in an international steel cartel. Papen, of whom I thought highly, convinced me that the policy of the ineffective cabinet of Herr Brüning had become intolerable; and as the Communists were gaining more and more ground, it was essential to give active and financial support to the parties of the right, of whatever shade they were.

I need hardly say that I was not at all keen on being harnessed to any one party vehicle; but, on the other hand, there was no denying that the present policy would lead us nowhere. I must confess quite frankly that I had confidence in a man like Papen, who represented the good old national school and who was so superior to the Nazi ruffians.

In the summer of 1931 I went to Brussels for the cartel talks. I now found a noticeable improvement in our relations with other countries. The same crisis gripped us all, the same anxieties worried us all; and so our smaller differences were readily sunk in our common problems. Sir Charles Gadsby was also in Brussels. He spoke openly and apprehensively about the state of his factories. Like everyone else, he had been obliged to dismiss great numbers of his workers, and his production had been switched over to small commodity goods. Though the talks were not completely successful, an international price control for steel was agreed upon.

On that occasion I made the significant discovery that the industrialists of all countries, and not Germany alone, had become increasingly afraid of Communists. As a natural consequence, their politics had become more conservative and nationalist than before. I found nothing strange in this; but I think it should be placed on record, since we Germans are now blamed for a development that was not confined to our own country.

Our continuing business with Russia shielded the Eberstein concern from the worst effects of the depression; we had even been able to acquire some more factories, in Nuremberg, Landshut, and near Brunswick. Owing to the crisis, these factories were idle, and we did not put them into production until later.

In the autumn of 1932 Traute and I went on a tour of the Mediterranean. After a few lovely months in Split on the Dalmatian coast, we went to Corfu. There we heard, in February, that Hitler's Cabinet had assumed power in Germany. I cannot say that I was upset by this news; nor were some British businessmen who were spending their holidays there. At the same time, I thought it better to return at once to Berlin.

I found that several of our old employees, some of them men of more than thirty years' service, were suddenly sporting the Nazi Party badge and were tending to throw their weight about.

Early in April, 1933, Schacht asked some twenty

or thirty industrialists to come to the Reichsbank for talks. Through Petersen I learned that those summoned to Berlin were all the important industrialists. I went keyed up with expectation. After we had waited for about ten minutes in the great hall of the Reichsbank building, Schacht came in accompanied by several others. "Gentlemen, I have the honor to present you to the Reichskanzler." It was Hitler. He was wearing a well-cut dark gray lounge suit and for a few moments seemed very shy and embarrassed. Then he began.

He pointed out that in his work of political reconstruction he depended very largely on our assistance. German economy was the crucial point for Germany's recovery. Although his Party had made a strong appeal to the masses, he thought that a reasonable capitalist system was the only possible one; we needed to have no fear of overly radical reforms. Then someone assured Herr Hitler that German industry, whose representatives were here assembled, knew very well who was its true enemy; and that they welcomed the strictly anti-Communist policy of the government. He then turned to us. He explained that during its hard struggle against reactionary and radical elements the N.S.D.A.P. had run into grave financial difficulties and had incurred heavy debts. He was sure the industrialists would think it their duty to make a small contribution to the struggle of this "truly national Party". He had, therefore, taken the liberty of dividing the Party's total debt into several small portions, each quite reasonable; and he would be glad if we could consider taking over these insignificant obligations.

The upshot of it all was that every one of us had to shoulder an obligation that was by no means trifling. Our own share was something over a hundred thousand marks. This cunning move gave us an idea of what to expect from the new régime.

In common with other industrialists, I thought it was only a question of time before the Nazis fell. Personally I gave them half a year, or at most a year, after which, I was convinced, our national economy would have broken down. Furthermore, I could hardly imagine that other countries would allow Germany to be governed by a gang of sword-waving, war-happy thugs.

Discussion guideline

How valuable do you think each of the case studies is for explaining Hitler's rise to power? Give supporting evidence for your opinion.

METHODS

 **a**

The Use of Symbols

from *Mein Kampf*
by Adolf Hitler

I myself after innumerable attempts, had laid down a final form; a flag with a red background, a white disk, and a black swastika in the middle. After long trials I also found a definite proportion between the size of the flag and the size of the white disk, as well as the shape and thickness of the swastika.

And this remained final.

And a symbol it really is! Not only that the unique colors, which all of us so passionately love and which once won so much honor for the German people, attest our veneration for the past; they were also the best embodiment of the movement's will. As National Socialists, we see our program in our flag. In *red* we see the social idea of the movement, in *white* the nationalistic idea, in the *swastika* the mission of the struggle for the victory of the Aryan man, and, by the same token, the victory of the idea of creative work.

Miller Services, Toronto

b

Nazi Rituals

from *Berlin Diary*
by William L. Shirer

[On September 5, 1934, and March 17, 1935, American correspondent William Shirer telegraphed his impressions of the Nazis' use of the flag and other symbols in the staging of political rallies. Note the relationship between Hitler's theories and Shirer's observations.]

Nuremberg, September 5
I'm beginning to comprehend, I think, some of the reasons for Hitler's astounding success. Borrowing a chapter from the Roman church, he is restoring pageantry and color and mysticism to the drab lives of twentieth-century Germans. This morning's opening meeting in the Luitpold Hall on the outskirts of Nuremberg was more than a gorgeous show; it also had something of the mysticism and religious fervor of an Easter or Christmas Mass in a great Gothic cathedral. The hall was a sea of brightly colored flags. Even Hitler's arrival was made dramatic. The band stopped playing. There was a hush over the thirty thousand people packed in the hall. Then the band struck up the *Badenweiler March*, a very catchy tune, and used only, I'm told, when Hitler makes his big entries. Hitler appeared in the back of the auditorium, and followed by his aides, Göring, Goebbels, Hess, Himmler, and the others, he strode slowly down the long center aisle while thirty thousand hands were raised in salute. It is a ritual, the old-timers say, which is always followed. Then an immense symphony orchestra played Beethoven's *Egmont* Overture. Great Klieg lights played on the stage, where Hitler sat surrounded by a hundred party officials and officers of the army and navy. Behind them the "blood flag", the one carried down the streets of Munich in the ill-fated putsch. Behind this, four or five hundred S.A. standards. When the music was over, Rudolf Hess, Hitler's closest confidant, rose and slowly read the names of the Nazi "martyrs" – brownshirts who had been killed in the struggle for power – a roll-call of the dead, and the thirty thousand seemed very moved.

Berlin, March 17
The first paragraph of my dispatch tonight sums up this extraordinary day: "This Heroes Memorial Day in memory of Germany's two million war dead was observed today amid scenes unequalled since 1914 as rebirth of Germany's military power brought forth professions of peace mixed with defiance." The Germans call the day *Heldengedenktag* and it corresponds to our Decoration Day. The main ceremony was at the Staatsoper at noon and it was conducted with all the color which the Nazis know how to utilize. The ground floor of the Opera House was a sea of military uniforms, with a surprising number of old army officers who overnight must have dusted off their fading gray uniforms and shined up their quaint pre-war spiked helmets, which were much in evidence. Strong stage lights played on a platoon of Reichswehr men standing like marble statues and holding flowing war flags. Above them on a vast curtain was hung an immense silver and black Iron Cross. The proper atmosphere was created at once when the orchestra played Beethoven's *Funeral March*, a moving piece, and one that seems to awaken the very soul of the German.

Howling House okays new flag by 163 to 78

By RICHARD SNELL
Star Staff Writer

OTTAWA – Canada's new red maple leaf flag was born at 2.13 a.m. today in a howling, angry Commons exchange brought to an end by closure.

Then, in an emotion-packed scene, the MPs and public galleries rose to their feet to sing "O Canada" and "God Save the Queen" as the vote – 163 for the new flag and 78 against – was announced.

It took 33 days of debate, four recorded votes yesterday, and millions of words to give Commons approval to a stylized red maple leaf on white background flanked by two red bars.

Dominion Wide

M.P.s after the debate

Toronto Daily Star, December 15, 1964

Discussion guidelines

1. "Hitler's rallies were almost religious services in celebration of German nationalism." Fully explain the meaning of this statement.
2. Comment on the significance of colour selection in the creation of symbols.
3. To what extent would the Canadian flag debate support or refute the idea that political symbols are important?
4. Assess the indoctrination possibilities of various symbols and rituals in (a) your school and (b) advertising.

Cross references

Propaganda and the Mass Meeting, page 133
A World Symbol? page 302

The Breakdown of Society

from *The Nazi Seizure of Power*
by William Sheridan Allen

[Thalburg, during the first years of Hitler's Third Reich, was a small German town located in the valley of the Grade River, in the former kingdom of Hannover. It was a predominantly middle class, Lutheran town, more closely connected with the countryside than with industry.]

> Behold how good and how
> pleasant it is for brethren to
> dwell together in unity.
> Psalms 83: 1

Very early in the Nazi era an event occurred in Thalburg which effectively fused propaganda and terror. This was the boycott of the Jews, April 1 to 4, 1933. In addition to being the beginning of that process which ended ten years later in the gas chambers of the S.S. extermination camps, this particular action was also a miniature example of what the Nazis intended to do to the entire German population. For the essential effect of the boycott of the Jews was to atomize them socially: to cut them off from the rest of German society so that normal human ties could not work to restrain the dictatorship.

Thalburg had a very small Jewish population. The census of 1932 showed 120 men, women, and children professing the Jewish faith out of a total population of ten thousand. There was no significant increase in their number; a generation before there had been 102. Most Jews in Thalburg were small businessmen: cattle brokers, grocery- or clothing-store owners, and artisans. One Jewish merchant celebrated, in 1932, the 230th anniversary of the founding of his haberdashery – during all of which time it had been located in Thalburg. There was no Jewish section in Thalburg: Jews were well assimilated into Thalburg society. The town had very little anti-Semitism before the advent of Nazism. Jews belonged to the shooting societies, patriotic clubs, and choral groups, and if they were differentiated it was by class, not religion. Some were elected to offices in their clubs, some were very highly respected, all were accepted as a normal part of the town's life.

The Nazis were determined to change this, since anti-Semitism formed one of the cornerstones of their ideology. This was not generally realized by Thalburgers, especially not by the Jews, who saw Nazi propaganda as an electioneering device or a manifestation of intellectual bankruptcy, but hardly as a concrete program.

There had been occasional anti-Jewish utterances in speeches by Kurt Aergeyz,[1] but the real campaign against the Jews opened on March 29, 1933, with an advertisement in the T.N.N.,[2] sponsored by Local Group Thalburg of the N.S.D.A.P.[3] It declared that "international Jewry" was spreading "gruesome propaganda" against Germany and "mishandling our German brothers in foreign lands". In response to this, declared the statement, the N.S.D.A.P. was calling a boycott against all Jewish businesses: "Germany will force Judah to his knees!" Three days later a second advertisement appeared which gave a specific list of individuals and businesses to be boycotted. The advertisement, marked "Clip and save", listed thirty-five firms representing forty individuals (in other words, almost all the adult male Jews in Thalburg).

The itemized appeal for a boycott was followed

[1]The Nazi Deputy Leader in Thalburg.
[2]*Thalburger Neueste Nachrichten*, the local newspaper.
[3]The National Socialist German Workers' Party (Nazi Party).

by action. Beginning on April 1, S.A.[4] men were posted before the doors of Jewish stores or offices. This "counteraction against the Jewish hate propaganda" was, according to the statement issued by the N.S.D.A.P., to continue "until the hate campaign and boycott against German goods ceases".

The boycott was also backed by the County Agricultural Society, which urged farmers to "crown your fight for nationalism by dealing a blow to the Jews". To provide farmers with an alternative to dealing with Jewish cattle brokers, a Cattle Brokerage Society was incorporated under the auspices of the County Agricultural Society, the only organization to support openly the Nazi boycott in Thalburg.

After three days the boycott was halted, ending with a parade featuring placards against the Jews.

The application of the boycott varied in its effectiveness. One of the firms listed in the advertisement was Braun's Banking House, a solid and well-respected establishment. There were no S.A. posts before its doors on April 1, 1933, and business went on as usual. In most other cases there were S.A. posts, but only for a few hours. No violence occurred. Some Thalburgers were actually unaware of the action. But all Thalburgers eventually came to know that Jews were now outcasts and that the

[4]Sturmabteilung – Hitler's Storm Troopers.

Ullstein Bilderdienst

Members of the S.A. enforcing a boycott of Jewish stores in Berlin, April 1933

Nazis were deadly serious about this aspect of their program.

The effect of the boycott upon the Jews of Thalburg was shattering. Gregor Rosenthal and his wife could not at first believe that it would take place. But when they saw the two S.A. men posted before their door the full significance of it broke upon them. They did not dare to leave their home at all that day and Rosenthal himself sat crumpled up in his chair for hours repeating, "Was it for this that I spent four years defending my Fatherland?"

The economic effect of the boycott extended beyond the formal period. While Banker Braun's business apparently did not suffer at all, Gregor Rosenthal's practice declined rapidly and his income fell from 9,000 marks in 1932 to 6,000 marks in 1933. This was probably true of most Jewish businesses; as people became more fearful, dealing with Jews became more of a luxury.

The Jews themselves aggravated the situation by withdrawing into themselves while the other Thalburgers, even if they might be opposed to the persecution of the Jews, abetted the system by their own efforts at self-protection. The day after the boycott began, a chain store with branches in Thalburg placed a large advertisement in the T.N.N. which announced that theirs was a "purely Christian family-enterprise" with no "outside capital" to mar their "Economic Independence – The Pride of Our Firm". Shortly after the boycott more stores blossomed forth with signs proclaiming "German Merchant". Once the principle was accepted it was a simple step to the poster, "Jews Not Admitted". Early in May the cigar factory in Thalburg announced that "a thorough examination by the N.S.D.A.P. has conclusively shown that the firm is a purely German enterprise".

As for the Jews themselves, they reacted in various ways. Banker Braun, a man who belonged to the uppermost circles of Thalburg society, ignored the whole matter as much as possible. On the occasion of celebrations he hung an Imperial flag before the bank. He was happy to do this anyway since he was a nationalist, a monarchist, and had served as an officer in World War I. Braun greeted friends on the street in a courtly manner by tipping his hat, thus avoiding the "German greeting" (i.e., *Heil Hitler* plus the Nazi salute). To the anxious advice that was given him to leave Thalburg, he replied, "Where should I go? Here I am the Banker Braun; elsewhere I would be the Jew Braun." Secure in his position as a member of Thalburg's upper class, he was convinced that the trouble would soon pass. To avoid unpleasantness he quietly resigned from his shooting society and singing club, giving "the press of business" as his reason.

Others were not so self-confident. Gregor Rosenthal withdrew from all social contact and crossed the street to avoid meeting erstwhile friends. His own sense of persecution intensified the growing feeling among Thalburgers that it might be unwise to be seen talking to a Jew. Soon Rosenthal received letters from the Veterans' Club and the shooting society dropping him from membership "for non-attendance at meetings". The chairman and the secretary of the Men's Singing Society of 1850 came to see him personally; Rosenthal was entertainment chairman of the club and therefore not to be dealt with by a simple letter. They urged him to attend meetings and help them keep the club going in these difficult times. Rosenthal had developed new sensitivity, and reading their faces carefully he told them that unfortunately his practice kept him so busy that not only would he have to resign his position as entertainment chairman, he could not even be a member any longer. They expressed profound regrets and left. Most of Thalburg's Jews probably reacted in this way.

Some townspeople went out of their way to talk to Jews or to buy in Jewish shops, especially the Socialists. But to counter-balance this there were S.A. men to mutter insults at them when they passed by street corners, and yet other S.A. men who bought heavily at Jewish stores, running up bills

Miller Services, Toronto

For many Jews, the isolation from society that began in places like Thalburg ended in ghettos or concentration camps – or in death. Here, Jews are lined up to be shot at the end of the Warsaw Ghetto uprising, May 1943. Would Jewish resistance in 1933 have prevented such an end? To what extent have such experiences influenced the history of modern Israel?

which they never paid, sometimes perhaps because the bills were never tendered.

Thus the position of the Jews in Thalburg was rapidly clarified, certainly by the end of the first half-year of Hitler's regime. Every speech given by a Nazi leader on the subject of the Jew as a Marxist-Capitalist international prisoner of the *Volk*, every newspaper item in the same vein, every new joke or rumor reinforced the situation. The new state of affairs became a fact of life; it was accepted.

Thalburg's Jews were simply excluded from the community at large. At the same time the Nazis undertook their most Herculean task: the atomization of the community at large. Though the methods differed, the result was the same, and by the summer of 1933 individual Thalburgers were as cut off from effective contacts with one another as the Jews had been from the rest of the townspeople. The total reorganization of society was the most important result of the Nazi revolution. Eventually no independent social groups were to exist. Wherever two or three were gathered, the *Fuehrer* would also be present. Ultimately all society, in terms of human relationships, would cease to exist, or rather would exist in a new framework whereby each individual related not to his fellow men but only to the state and to the Nazi leader who became the personal embodiment of the state.

The usefulness of a general shakeup of social organization for dictatorial control can well be imagined. In the first place it would mean that people could be more easily observed, since all clubs would be Nazi controlled. Secondly, with old social ties broken down there would be less opportunity for the spreading of discontent. Thirdly, by giving a Nazi cast to all organizations, the members would become involved in the general Nazi system.

Promoting dictatorial control was not the only reason for Nazi reorganization of social units. There was also a tendency to simplify social organization and thus provide more efficiency and less diversity. On the one hand, for example, it was thought that by lumping together the various sports clubs one could arrive at the best combination of athletes. On the other hand, an attempt was made to unite all clubs which had the same function but which were formed along class lines, since the new guidelines were to be German citizenship and good Nazism, not the old traditions or class distinctions.

In the case of mass organizations such as sports clubs, fusion did not take place in order to maintain control over the societies, since they were already well infiltrated. But in the case of small class-oriented groups, fusion might be needed to end their exclusive nature so that Nazis could bring the groups under control.

Most of this was accomplished in the first few months of the Nazi era. Clubs were dissolved; others were fused together; others lost their purpose and went into rapid decline. All societies came under Nazi control since they were required to have a majority of N.S.D.A.P. members in their executive committees. If an organization was ordered by the N.S.D.A.P. to dissolve its present executive committee and elect a new one with a Nazi majority, the assumption was that this would be necessary to comply with the law. They might have discovered differently had they challenged the legality of the order. But no one did this in the first few months of the Nazi rule, and after that it was too late. Thus the enormous social reshuffle took place without open resistance.

Discussion guidelines

1. Outline the methods used by the Nazis to guarantee a community's loyalty to their political system.
2. (a) Suggest reasons why the Jews were singled out for persecution and extermination.
   (b) If you had been a German citizen living in Thalburg in 1933, would you have spoken up in defence of the Jews, even if you were the only one to do so? Defend your position in the light of conditions in the town in 1933.

Cross references

What Would You Have Done? page 169
The Right to Resist – Did It Exist? page 174

NAZISM IN OPERATION

What Hitler Did for Germany

from *The Rise and Fall of Nazi Germany*
by T. L. Jarman

Party Membership

Membership of the Party was distinguished from membership of the many organizations and formations attached to it. Actual membership of the Party was under 1 million at the beginning of 1933; four months later it was claimed to be 3 million. Then a stop was put to further applications for membership. But exceptions were made, and in 1937 and again in 1939 the conditions of admission were altered and became easier. Boys and girls who had served in the Hitler Youth for four years were, after a careful process of selection, transferred to the Party. By 1943 it was claimed that there were 6½ million members. With a membership of that size, the Party had evidently become something larger than the political *élite* which, earlier on, it had claimed to be. But the idea was retained in that members could, for certain offences, be expelled from the Party. As membership of the Party was an essential qualification for most higher positions – in Government employment, for example – expulsion was a serious matter, not to mention the danger of arousing the interest of the political police. . . .

Controls

[The] Party also possessed a [frightening] . . . apparatus of control, coercion, and destruction – the S.A., the S.S., the Gestapo, and the concentration camps. Secret police, detention, imprisonment, and execution are typical of police-states, but in Germany they were organized with . . . thoroughness and efficiency. The cruelty was therefore all the worse: it was not the cruelty involved in being in the hands of uncouth and primitive guards and in lack of proper facilities, food, clothing, and housing, as often is the case with atrocities committed by backward peoples; it was a refined brutality without parallel in modern times. . . .

The S.S., which had originated in the specially picked men of Hitler's personal bodyguard and had been developed by Himmler, was the *élite* of the Nazi fanatics. But these fanatics were not wild men in the ordinary sense; they were selected men of strong physique and intelligence, carefully trained, and devoted to the carrying out of the *Führer*'s purposes. The men of the S.S. were trained men, but they were more than that: they made up a racial *élite*, and through them the policy of building a super-race was developed. When an S.S. man married, he and the woman he married had to meet special racial and [physical] standards; their children would be born in a special S.S. mothers' house and under the care of an S.S. doctor; the family might live in a special S.S. settlement; an S.S. boy would have open to him certain educational advantages and would do his military service with an S.S. unit. . . . The S.S. was respected and feared. The S.S. was the most active and merciless agent of coercion: in police duties, the concentration camps, and the expulsion and murder of Jews. . . .

The concentration camps were . . . a carefully planned instrument to crush opposition and deter all forms of criticism or discontent. . . . At the beginning of the war in 1939, according to a report by the S.S. general, Pohl, there were six camps, Dachau with 4,000 prisoners, Sachsenhausen with 6,500, Buchenwald with 5,300, Mauthausen with 1,500, Flossenburg with 1,600 and Ravensbrück with 2,500. . . .

Religion

Hitler himself, though he had been brought up a Catholic and appealed from time to time in his speeches to God and Providence, showed little but contempt for religion. But he was astute in his dealings with the Churches. He did not make a frontal attack on them; rather, he encouraged decay from the inside, and drew away the young by providing them, in the Nazi Party and its organizations, with a more exciting alternative to the Churches. . . . For Christianity, a religion of love and international brotherhood, Hitler had no use. It could be left, he thought, to decay in the new, Nazi Germany, where the sentiment of German nationalism would take its place. Hitler turned with hope to the German peasantry in the matter of a basic faith, as in that of racial expansion eastwards. "It is through the peasantry that we shall really be able to destroy Christianity because there is in them a true religion rooted in nature and blood."

. . . Nothing could be more false, indeed, than to imagine that under the Nazi régime the Germans were a people browbeaten and cowed by fear of the secret police, and driven to work against their will by the methods of terror employed by a ruthless dictator. This was [a] mistake – coupled with the equally false idea that the German workers were suffering unbearable economic hardships. . . . Those who thought in this way were also likely to regard Russia as a people's paradise. In fact, it was more correct to see the roles as reversed: in Russia the use of force was more evident than in Germany and poverty and squalor were prevalent everywhere in Russia, in keeping with an Asiatic rather than a European way of life. Once the Nazis were in power and all open opposition had been overcome, terrorism was kept in the background.

The New Germany

The most striking thing about Nazi Germany was the new spirit which animated the country: a new hope, a new self-confidence and pride, a new energy and determination filled a people who since 1918 had suffered the heavy blows of defeat, the collapse of the currency, and, finally, the economic depression of the world slump. *Deutschland erwache!* (Germany awake!) – that had long been a popular slogan with the Nazis. Now that they were in power it seemed, indeed, as if Germany had awakened. Germans found a new faith in the greatness and future of their country. As a German headmaster wrote in 1937 in reference to the plebiscites which produced mass votes in favour of Hitler's policies: "In fact 98% have voted for Hitler *of their free will*. And they would do it at any time. So would I."

. . . Germans, those who were not politically suspect in any way, could travel abroad; the currency they could take out was limited, but exchanges could be arranged with foreigners visiting Germany. The Nazi leaders did not fear that if Germans visited foreign countries they would come back with their own national allegiance weakened. The foreign visitor was welcome in Germany . . . [and what he saw] was generally overwhelmingly in Germany's favour. He found what was apparently the most orderly and well-directed country in the world; people were at work and appeared to be contented, all the [comforts] of life were there: opera, theatres, the cinema, cafés and restaurants, hotels, books, sports, hiking and sun-bathing in summer, skiing in winter. The young, or those who saw Germany for the first time, were liable to feel that all this . . . had been created by the Nazis. . . .

Economic Recovery

At the basis of Nazi success was Germany's economic recovery. . . . That the men could get jobs again, and were back at work – that in itself was a source of pride to the Germans when they were told of the faltering and fumbling methods of foreign countries to deal with the problem. The reduction of the German unemployment figures by 5 million was a remarkable achievement, and of the greatest propaganda value also. When Hitler had come to power, there were 6 million unemployed out of Germany's 20 million workers; by the end of 1936 only 1 million were listed as unemployed. That was what the *Führer* had brought about. He had asked for four years: he had kept his pledge. . . .

Public works were an essential part of the Nazi policy for dealing with unemployment. In itself, this was not new, and it was a policy adopted in other countries also. During the Weimar period loans had been used to finance public building, and in the United States Roosevelt's New Deal made extensive use of organized public undertakings to relieve unemployment. But Hitler had the apparatus of dictatorship in his hands. . . . Hitler could fix wages and use certain measures of compulsion. It was easier in Germany to organize those who were unemployed into work-gangs and move them from place to place wherever they were most wanted. Thus towns could be planned, housing estates created, and new factories built as a nucleus around which the residential quarters were arranged. Hitler, with his youthful interest in art and architecture, took a personal interest in the new building schemes, and attention was also given to layout and landscape gardening. . . .

Perhaps the most striking of all Hitler's public works, and best known, were the *Autobahnen*, or great motor roads. . . . These roads were wide and straight, with parallel tracks, providing one-way traffic in each direction separated by a broad stretch of grass and shrubs. There was no cross-traffic on these roads; bridges or viaducts were used when other roads or railways had to cross. Cars coming onto or leaving the *Autobahn* did not do so at right angles, but moved on or off gradually at special points. The building of these great roads certainly helped to relieve unemployment; it was a large-scale

Section of an *Autobahn* built during the Nazi Régime

Miller Services, Toronto

and long-term programme, which stimulated the motor industry and the iron and steel industry also, for the building of the numerous bridges created a demand for steel. The roads were also of propaganda value: they impressed foreigners, and they impressed the Germans themselves. In addition, they were of strategic value: important roads led to the Austrian, Czech, Polish, and Belgian frontiers, and such roads were well calculated to serve the needs of modern mechanized armies. . . .

At a rather later stage, rearmament became of great importance. . . . Military expansion could only be based on economic expansion, on the fullest development of the heavy industries which offered employment to the workers and provided the basic materials of war. Here, then, was a dilemma for the Nazis: a nationalist policy meant making Germany independent of foreign countries, yet economic expansion must necessarily mean the import from abroad of raw materials not found, or not found in sufficient quantities, in Germany. The policy of . . . economic self-sufficiency . . . was followed in every possible way. *Ersatz*, or substitute, goods produced by the skill of German chemists were used wherever possible in place of goods formerly imported. Such research had been going on long before the Nazis, and was now intensified; much use was made of *Buna* (synthetic rubber) and substitutes for wool and petrol. The materials to be imported from abroad were reduced as far as possible and a drive undertaken for the production of foodstuffs at home; only materials essential to the country's development plans were to be admitted, and elaborate quotas, licence arrangements, and exchange restrictions were worked out. Bilateral agreements were made with a number of individual countries for trading purposes. . . .

Labour

Even a dictator cannot afford to ignore altogether the wishes of the people, and the success of the Nazi régime depended to a large extent on the goodwill of the workers. The Nazis laid a firm foundation in the way they dealt with unemployment, and they strengthened their position by building up the *Arbeitsfront* (Labour Front). . . . Strikes and lockouts were made impossible – they were condemned as political sabotage – and the *Arbeitsfront*, which included the employers as well as workers, provided machinery for industrial conciliation and arbitration. That industrial disputes could be settled without strikes meant a considerable economy, and aided the Nazi drive for increased production. . . .

The Labour Front had also visibly attractive ways of appealing to the workers. Wages, if low, could be supplemented, with the German genius for careful and elaborate organizations, by providing special facilities – for holidays and travel, for entertainment, for sport. Inside the Labour Front there was the department known as *Kraft durch Freude* (Strength through Joy), and this was an excellent means of providing cheap holidays for the lower-paid workers, who might otherwise have had to stay at home. Workers who wished to take advantage of the scheme made weekly contributions. As the number who did so ran into millions, things could be organized in mass and the cost of the holidays to each person could be low. . . .

Arrangements were also made to bring within reach of workers the theatre and classical concerts. . . .

The German Race

Quite apart from the workers, for whom careful consideration was given, the Nazis waged a constant struggle for youth, for woman as the mother, and for the physical well-being of the whole German race. . . .

At every stage of development the Nazis sought to mould and influence the young with the object of creating a race of splendid Germans, a true *Herrenvolk*. Little boys and girls had their own Nazi organizations, and at fourteen the boys joined the *Hitlerjugend*. The Nazi youth movement undoubtedly

Miller Services, Toronto

German girls in a government-sponsored camp

captured the imagination of the children; it was a real punishment to remain, for any reason, outside. Children wanted to march and sing and salute, they wanted to go to the Nazi camps, they wanted to enjoy the wonderful, exciting life that was organized for them. And no other youth movement was allowed to compete for their loyalty. Children became, from an early age, the devoted followers of the *Führer*, like those who demonstrated at a great cinema meeting in Cologne and chanted in unison: "*So war es* (So things were). We were slaves; we were outsiders in our own country. So were we before Hitler united us. Now we would fight against Hell for our leader." Then for the young men there came six months of compulsory labour service in a camp before their two years' military service. The labour service had as its object to let manual labour break down the barriers of social class, mould the character still further to the Nazi pattern, and strengthen the physique of the potential soldier and worker. Outdoor manual labour and military drill (with spades instead of rifles) were the means. The physical training of the young began to make its mark on the whole nation; the Germans carried off many of the prizes at the Olympic Games held in 1936 in Berlin, and the foreign visitors were impressed both by German athletic prowess and by the splendid spectacle offered in the German capital. There was before their eyes a new Germany: of youth, of power, of faith – though its future was in the hands of one man whose megalomania would lead its people to disaster. But for the moment this was hidden: each September at Nuremberg the *Parteitag*, or rally, was held, with the most magnificent pageantry. The marching of thousands of disciplined, uniformed figures, the massed bands, the forest of flags, the simple glories of the vast stadium of the Zeppelin Field lit at night by hundreds of searchlights meeting in a dome overhead – all had their effect, intense and hypnotic, on German and foreigner alike.

Discussion guidelines

1. How was the Nazi Party organized to maintain control over the state, and sustain public morale?
2. "At the basis of Nazi success was Germany's economic recovery."
   (a) Estimate the validity of this statement.
   (b) If the statement is true, does it mean that man prizes material security more highly than political liberty? Explain the reasons for your decision.
3. "In actuality, Hitler's program impoverished and brutalized the German nation." Argue this point of view.

Cross references

Stalin: Creator or Monster? page 71
What Would You Have Done? page 169
Controlling the Mind, page 322

A DEAD ISSUE?

❶

The Awesome Authoritarian Power of a Pale Minority

By CHARLES TAYLOR

JOHANNESBURG – Within a facade of parliamentary democracy, South Africa's ruling Nationalists are putting the finishing touches to their awesome collection of authoritarian powers.

After 20 years in office, the Nationalists have established an unassailable majority in a House of Assembly that owes its mandate to one-fifth of the population – the white minority.

Sapped courts' power

They use that majority to pass a host of restrictive laws and have steadily eroded the power of the courts to modify or disallow these measures.

In Parliament itself, they receive only token opposition from a weak and dispirited United Party that is almost equally wedded to a doctrine of permanent white supremacy.

Their only true opponent is Helen Suzman, the sole representative of the tiny Progressive Party, which advocates multi-racial politics on a heavily qualified franchise. Elected from a wealthy Johannesburg suburb, the petite and attractive Mrs. Suzman is a lonely and courageous gadfly.

In the parliamentary session which ended in Cape Town last month, Mrs. Suzman delivered 17 major speeches, spoke on 14 votes and tabled 139 questions. But none of these deterred Prime Minister John Vorster from using his Nationalist steamroller to pass new laws that further entrench white political domination.

With one law, the nation's 1,860,000 Coloreds have lost their right to elect four white members to the Assembly – a last vestige from the days when they shared a common roll with white voters in Cape Province.

Then there is the Prohibition of Improper Interference Bill, an Orwellian title for an act that bans all multiracial political parties. While the Progressives are remaining in existence as an all-white grouping, the even smaller Liberal Party has decided to disband.

Under author Alan Paton, the national president, the Liberals advocated ultimate universal suffrage for all races, and felt that to become an all-white grouping would be a contradiction in terms. Long harassed by the Security Branch, they have now been legislated out of existence.

While dissent is stifled among the nation's 3½ million whites, it is totally prohibited among the 13 million blacks. Both their major political organizations, the African National Congress and the rival Pan-African Congress, are banned, and their leaders are either jailed or in exile.

"We assume there must be some underground activity, but we never hear about it anymore," a white liberal said. "The police are so effective that no African would dare to approach us."

The Government is confident that it has either banished or jailed most of its dangerous opponents. Anxious to maintain a semblance of legality, it relies on a fantastic body of restrictive laws and decrees. The most notorious of these is the Suppression of Communism Act, which effectively equates communism with any determined opposition to apartheid.

1,000 held prisoner

Nearly 1,000 political prisoners are confined on Robben Island, South Africa's Alcatraz. Mainly non-whites, they include Robert Sobukwe, the former P.A.C. leader who has been in jail since 1960, when he led anti-pass demonstrations that resulted in the Sharpeville massacre. Although he completed his sentence for incitement in 1963, Sobukwe is detained from year to year under a special clause of the General Laws Amendment Act, which Parliament solemnly confirms in its annual session.

Another 800 South Africans of all races are banned or restricted, which means that they live a harrowing existence in the shadows of their society. They include Helen Joseph, a 62-year-old veteran campaigner for African political rights, who has been under house arrest for six years.

Those who are banned become virtually non-persons. They can be confined to their homes, forced to resign from any organizations and forbidden to meet more than one person at a time outside their family circles. They are kept under constant surveillance by the police, and nothing they say or write can be reported.

No proof needed

With Mrs. Joseph and the others, the Government simply claims that their activities furthered the Communist cause. There is no need to prove these charges in court, and there is no chance of appeal.

"There's always something of an outcry when anyone is banned or detained," a Nationalist M.P. remarked. "But you can't expect the police to reveal all their sources. That would only play into the hands of our enemies.

"And I can assure you that in time, all their Communist connections will be established."

Mrs. Joseph and most of the others could have their freedom at any time – but at the cost of leaving South Africa on a one-way exit permit. Some have accepted such an exile, but most refuse to abandon their homeland.

The threat of banning hangs over any South African who opposes the Government's apartheid policies. Under the circumstances, many find it advisable to stifle the stirrings of their conscience.

Apart from Mrs. Suzman, the strongest dissent is found in the English-language newspapers, which maintain a barrage of strong and caustic criticism against the Government for its larger lunacies. (Although they vary in their approach, the Afrikaans dailies all support the Nationalists.)

Here, too, the limits of dissent are carefully circumscribed. After numerous delays – and with mounting legal costs – charges are still pending against Laurence Gandar, editor-in-chief of the Rand Daily Mail, over a series of articles in 1965 which contained allegations that prisoners are maltreated in South African jails.

It is one of the typical refinements of South African justice that the Prisons Act not only forbids the publication of "false" information about prisons or prisoners, but also thrusts upon the newspaper the onus of proving that reasonable steps were taken to establish that the reports were not false.

Other laws weigh equally heavily upon editors and reporters. They give the Government the power to prohibit the publication of any "documentary information" which it considers "calculated to engender feelings of hostility" between whites and non-whites. They also forbid publication of any material which "brings any section of the inhabitants of the Republic into ridicule or contempt."

Bold criticism

With such threats hanging over their heads, it is remarkable that the English-language newspapers persist in their bold criticisms. Yet it is more relevant that their attacks fail to evoke any significant response.

In most democracies, such serious allegations as those of the Rand Daily Mail would lead to a full public inquiry and might well topple the Government. In South Africa they are quickly brushed aside and their perpetrators are persecuted.

Most white South Africans are content to acquiesce in this steady erosion of their political rights. Most seem bemused by their growing prosperity and readily accept the Government's assurance that the dissenters are a handful of crackpots and Communists. Only a few recognize that the growing body of repressive legislation is undermining the prospects for peaceful political change.

"It's so easy to despair," one veteran liberal remarked. "I often think the only solution is a bloody revolution.

"Of course, that's impossible – at least for the foreseeable future. But the way things are moving, it could become inevitable."

The Globe and Mail, Toronto
July 19, 1968

Apartheid in Action
by Paul Hogarth

"Your pass, Kaffir!"

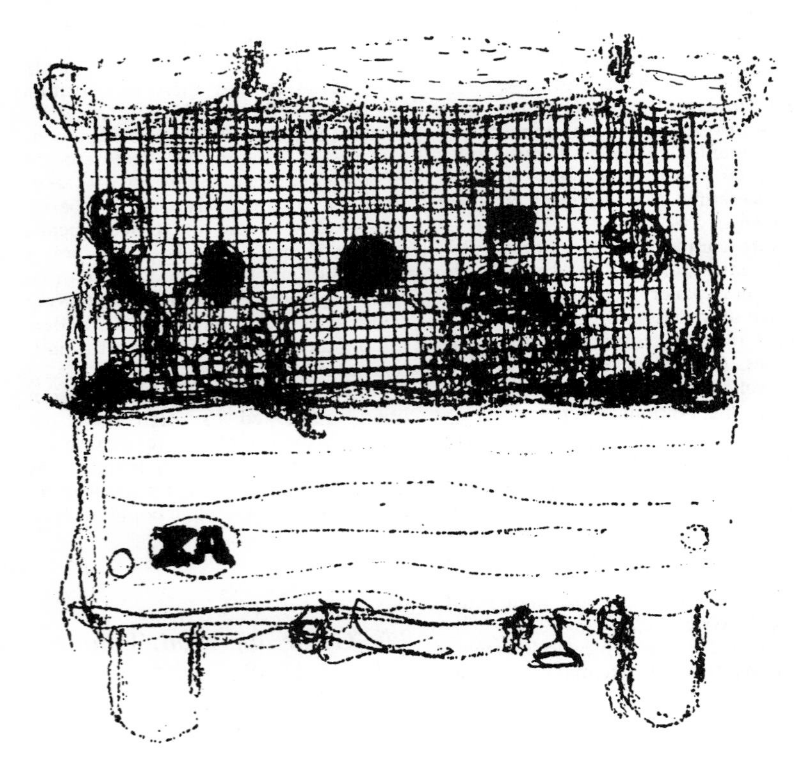

Africans without passes taken off to jail

A pass court

Sentenced to forced labour on isolated farms

Sons of Adam, originally published by Dennis Dobson in London and Thomas Nelson and Sons in the U.S.A.

Discussion guidelines

1. Is Charles Taylor's evidence sufficient for his claim that South Africa's Nationalists have an "awesome collection of authoritarian powers"? Defend your opinion.
2. To what extent does the South African government's policy compare with the program of the National Socialist German Workers' Party?
3. "There is no workable alternative to authoritarian government in present-day South Africa, if 'white civilization' is to survive." Cite evidence to defend or refute this claim.

Cross reference

My Dungeon Shook, page 165

The Many Faces of Communism

from *L'Express*, by Tim

Communism claims the allegiance of more than half the world's population. Why? And why have Marx, Lenin, Stalin, and Mao figured so prominently in its history? The more one looks at Communism, in fact, the more intriguing it appears. How can it claim to be democratic? Why did it triumph first in Russia, of all places? How close are Russian Communists to the ideas of Marx? What, finally, are the many faces of Communism in the world today, and why is an understanding of their similarities and differences of vital concern to western democracies?

THE PROGRAM

The Aims of the Communists
from *The Communist Manifesto*
by Karl Marx and Friedrich Engels –
an abridged text

[In 1848, caught up in the excitement of a series of revolutions sweeping Europe, Marx and Engels published the following statement of Communist ideas.]

The history of all previous society is the history of class struggles.

Middle Class Society
The modern bourgeois (middle class) society that has sprouted from the ruins of feudal society has not done away with class conflict. It has but established new classes, new conditions of oppression, new forms of struggle in place of the old ones.

Our age, the age of the bourgeoisie, possesses this distinctive feature: it has simplified class conflict. Society as a whole is more and more splitting up into two great classes directly facing each other: Bourgeoisie and Proletariat (working class).

The bourgeoisie, wherever it has got the upper hand, has pitilessly torn asunder the feudal ties that bound man to his "natural superiors", and has left remaining no other bond between man and man than naked self-interest.

The Working Class
But not only has the bourgeoisie forged the weapons that bring death to itself; it has also called into existence the men who are to wield those weapons – the modern working class – the proletarians.

In proportion as the bourgeoisie grows, in the same proportion the modern working class grows – they are a class of labourers who live only so long as they find work, and who find work only so long as their labour increases wealth. They are a class who must sell themselves piecemeal; they are thus a commodity, like every other article of commerce, and are consequently exposed to all the changes of competition, to all the fluctuations of the market.

Class Conflict
But with the development of industry, the proletariat not only increases in number, it becomes concentrated in greater masses, its strength grows, and it feels that strength more. The members of the working class become more equal as machinery removes all distinctions of labour, and nearly everywhere reduces wages to the same low level. The growing competition among the bourgeois makes the wages of the workers ever more unstable. The constant and rapid improvement of machinery makes their livelihood more and more uncertain; and thus the collisions between individual workmen and individual bourgeois take more and more the character of collisions between two classes. Thereupon the workers begin to form combinations (Trades' Unions) against the bourgeois; they club together in order to keep up wages; they establish permanent associations in order to prepare for these occasional revolts. Here and there the contest breaks into riots.

The Communists
(a) aims
In what relation do the Communists stand to the proletarians?

The Communists do not form a separate party opposed to other working-class parties.

They have no interests separate and apart from those of the proletariat as a whole.

They do not set up any principles of their own, by which to shape and mould the proletarian movement.

The immediate aim of the Communists is the same as that of all the other proletarian parties: formation of the proletariat into a class, overthrow of bourgeois rule, and conquest of political power by the proletariat.

In a sense, the theory of the Communists may be summed up in the single sentence: Abolition of private property.

The proletariat will use its political power to take, bit by bit, all capital from the bourgeoisie, to give the state control of all production, and to increase productive forces as rapidly as possible.

(b) programme

In the most advanced countries, the following changes will be pretty generally adopted:

1. Abolition of property in land and application of all rents of land to public purposes.
2. A heavy progressive or graduated income tax.
3. Abolition of all right of inheritance.

Miller Services, Toronto

According to Marx and Engels, the growth of modern industry would reduce the working class to poverty, since it would drive wages down "to the same low level". And yet, in Canada today, many members of the working class are able to own homes in suburban areas like that shown above. How do you account for this development?

4. Confiscation of the property of all emigrants and rebels.

5. Centralization of credit in the hands of the State, by means of a national bank with State capital and exclusive monopoly.

6. Centralization of the means of communication and transport in the hands of the State.

7. Extension of factories and instruments of production owned by the State; the bringing into cultivation of waste lands, and the improvement of the soil generally in accordance with a common plan.

8. Equal liability of all to labour. Establishment of industrial armies, especially for agriculture.

9. Combination of agriculture with manufacturing industries; gradual abolition of the distinction between town and country, by a more equable distribution of population over the country.

10. Free education for all children in public schools. Abolition of children's factory labour in its present form. Combination of education with industrial production, etc., etc.

In place of the old bourgeois society, with its classes and class conflict, we shall have an association, in which the free development of each person is the condition for the free development of all.

The Communists everywhere support every revolutionary movement against the existing social and political order of things.

In all these movements they bring to the fore, as the leading question in each, the property question.

Finally, they labour everywhere for the union and agreement of the democratic parties of all countries.

The Communists openly declare that their ends can be attained only by the forcible overthrow of all existing social conditions. Let the ruling classes tremble at a Communistic revolution. The proletarians have nothing to lose but their chains. They have a world to win.

Working men of all countries, unite!

Discussion guidelines

1. In what respects did Marx and Engels misjudge the future role of the middle class?
2. What elements in the Manifesto explain the fact that Communism is still a world-wide movement?
3. "All modern governments, including the Canadian, practise part of the 1848 Communist program." How do you account for this?

Cross references

The Aims of the Nazis, page 25
Our "Free Society", page 108

RUSSIAN COMMUNISM

Lenin: Portrait of a Revolutionary

from *Inside Russia Today*
by John Gunther

Vladimir Ilich Ulyanov organized and led the October Revolution, and was the founder of both the Communist party and the Soviet Union, enough revolutionary achievement for one lifetime. . . . What Marx put into words, Lenin, by reason of his extraordinary capacity for leadership, was able to put into deeds. By crude definition "Marxism" is a philosophy; "Leninism" is Marxism applied to government in Russia.

What Lenin did, in effect, was to cut through millions of words of Marx to reassert and achieve a series of simple propositions, based in part on the *Communist Manifesto*. First, the creation of a party; second, the overthrow of bourgeois supremacy; third, setting up of the dictatorship of the proletariat; fourth, the introduction of socialism; fifth, the conquest of political power. Lenin was pragmatic, direct, logical – such un-Russian characteristics!

His life story may be told briefly. He was born Vladimir Ilich Ulyanov in Simbirsk, now called Ulyanovsk, a small city on the Volga, in 1870. . . . Lenin took the name "N. Lenin" in his early revolutionary days. The "N" does not represent "Nikolai", as is commonly thought; it was simply part of his pseudonym, and, like the "S" in Harry S. Truman, stands for nothing. . . .

Lenin's father, Ilya Nikolaevich Ulyanov, was a member of the minor nobility, having reached a rank in the bureaucracy corresponding to that of major general in the army; he was inspector of schools in the Simbirsk district. . . . He was of sound middle-class Russian stock. . . . Lenin's mother, Maria Alexandrovna Berg, was the daughter of a doctor, and had German blood. She was a devout Lutheran. . . .

Lenin's family was upstanding, well-off, and intellectual. Young Lenin wore an Eton collar to school, and, of all things, read *Tom Sawyer*. By this time youths all over Russia were being swept headlong into the revolutionary movement. Lenin's elder brother, by name of Alexander, joined a terrorist society, and, in a juvenile . . . way, became involved in a plot to murder Czar Alexander III; although the plot failed and although he had only the most peripheral connection with it, he was executed. This broke his mother's life, and was, not without reason, a puissant influence on Lenin's subsequent development. Vengeance! On the other hand Lenin was too hard-headed to think much in terms of personal outrage, retaliation, or "romantic" violence. . . . He had, in the words of Hamilton Fish Armstrong, "grandiose visions of the betterment of mankind" plus "total contempt for human life".

Lenin was expelled from the University of Kazan for revolutionary activity, moved to St. Petersburg, and studied law. He became a barrister, and practiced law for a time at Samara. In about 1890 he discovered Marx. This was the controlling event of his life. Back in St. Petersburg, he went into revolutionary work in earnest. He was arrested in 1897, spent a year in prison, and was shipped off to Siberia. He wrote several books, and, in 1900, was allowed to leave Russia and become an *émigré* in Switzerland, where he helped to found and edit the important revolutionary paper *Iskra*, or *Spark*. He moved to London in 1902. When he returned to Petrograd in 1917 to lead the Revolution, he had not been in Russia for ten years.

Lenin was an extraordinarily intricate character, although Soviet idolaters today say that "he was as simple as the truth". He had several homely traits and characteristics, loved children and pets, and was wont to make mild little jokes, such as that no woman could understand chess, a railway timetable, or dialectical materialism. He lived in austere simplicity, did not smoke, refused to have easy chairs in his office, disliked cut flowers, and, a curious point, always kept his watch fifteen minutes slow. He had a passion for reading. . . . The main elements in his character were a piercing realism, pertinacity, and magnetism. He could meet a man once, and win him for life. Maxim Gorky records that he read a newspaper as if his eyes were "burning holes in it"; also that his mind had "the cold glitter of steel shavings". Marx was neither a fanatic, a demagogue, nor even an orator; Lenin was all three, and, besides, *loved facts*, a combination that can be terrifying.

The story of the [October] Revolution we shall interpolate later. Let us first round out the bare

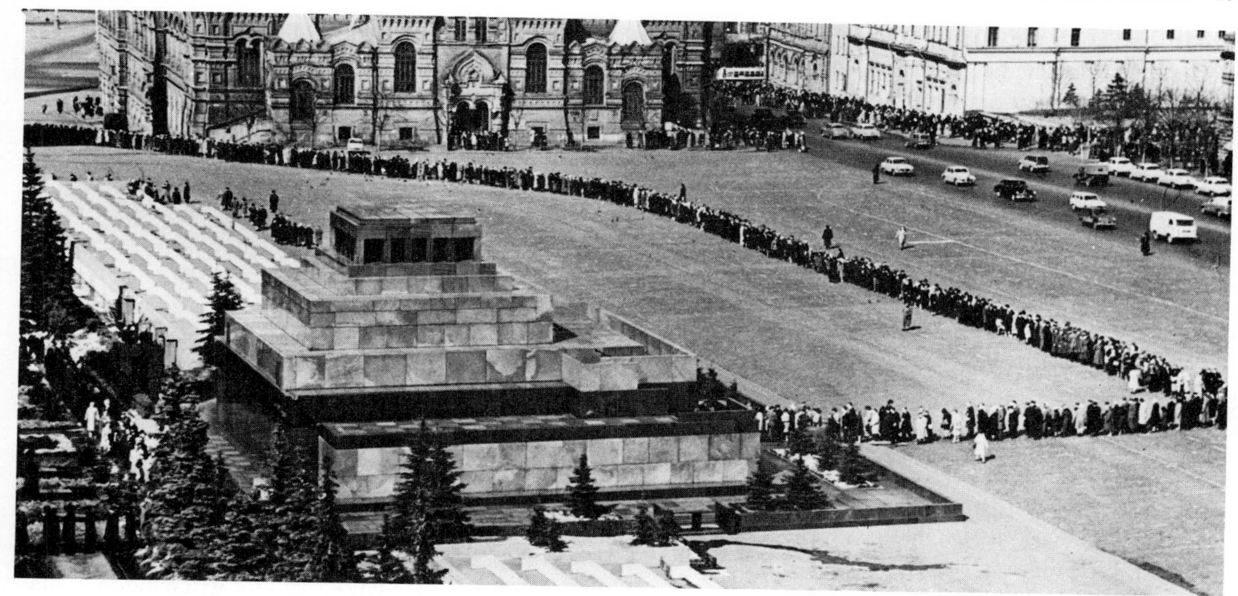

Miller Services, Toronto

Russians line up to pass through Lenin's tomb in Red Square, Moscow. What reasons might there be for such continuing devotion to Lenin?

details of Lenin's life. Before the October Revolution was a year old, on August 30, 1918, he was shot and seriously wounded by a young woman Social Revolutionary, by name Fanny Kaplan. He recovered his powers fully, but was shaken. He suffered a severe stroke in 1922, had several other strokes, and died on January 21, 1924. His funeral was one of the supreme events in Soviet history, and, among other things, proved that the Revolution had been won. Even the blindest of observers, suffocated by their hatred of Bolshevism amid the passions of that time, could not but be impressed at the demonstration of mass devotion that occurred. "Three quarters of a million people waited an average of five hours in the Arctic cold of 30 degrees below zero, night and day alike, before passing through the hall where Lenin's body lay in state."

Today, needless to say, Lenin is gospel in the Soviet Union, much more so than Marx. More than 7,300 editions of his works have been printed . . . He is seldom referred to by name alone, but is called "great Lenin", or something of the sort. He is not only used as a stick to beat opponents with, but is quoted affirmatively on every known variety of topic. . . . At the moment the Leninist line is used to support two main considerations: (a) socialist legality, and (b) the necessity for collective leadership.

In 1917 there were, as everybody knows, two . . . revolutions. The one known universally today as the "February" Revolution occurred on March 8. . . . Factors which played a role were disgust with the course of World War I, which was eating the life of the nation away; mass desertions in the army; a severe breakdown in domestic economy; moral, ethical, and social dissatisfactions; disintegration in the court, culminating in the murder of the Czarina's favorite, Rasputin. Riots broke out in St. Petersburg (since 1914 called Petrograd) which Czarist troops refused to put down; in fact they fraternized with the strikers. The Duma [Russian Parliament] declined to accept an imperial decree ordering its dissolution, and, on March 12, established a provisional government. There was practically no resistance, and very little bloodshed. Nicholas II abdicated on March 15, and, a few days later, the dynasty ended. The monarchy was not forcibly wrenched off the throne; it fell of its own torpid weight. In the following months the provisional government, under Alexander Kerensky and others, vainly sought to hold power.

The Bolsheviks had little, if anything, to do with the February Revolution, which was almost completely unorganized, or with the fall of Czardom....

But the October Revolution was quite a different story. With this the Bolsheviks had a great deal to do: they made it, although they were a minority among the revolutionaries. Lenin, on the outbreak of war in 1914, was living in Galicia; the Austrian authorities arrested him as an undesirable alien, and deported him to Switzerland. In 1917 the German general staff conceived the idea that . . . [he] might provoke a new revolution in Russia, which in turn might reverse the pro-Ally policy of the provisional government, or even seek a separate peace and take Russia out of the war, which would immensely serve German ends. Lenin and a handful of companions were shipped across Germany in a sealed train, and arrived in Petrograd on April 16, 1917. It is of the utmost interest that Lenin, although revolution in Russia was what he had hoped and worked for all his life, was not exclusively interested in Russia by any means. . . . The October Revolution was made . . . by a handful of outsiders. Moreover, let us repeat, they were a minority. Only five Bolshevik deputies had been in the Duma. They were also a distinct minority in the first All-Russian Congress of Soviets of Workers and Soldiers Deputies (June 16), and . . . were fanatically opposed by elements in the army, the trade unions, and even the Central Committee of the Party.

How, then, were Lenin and his men able to reach and hold power? The chief weapons were three. First, he converted the *party*, even if small, into an extremely effective and sharp instrument, the élite "vanguard" of the proletariat. Second, he was a masterful political manipulator, who did not hesitate to use force brutally. Third, and above all, he promised peace, and the people were mortally sick of war. Also consider the "technological" aspect of the Revolution, for which Trotsky was responsible. He invented the technique of the modern coup, in which extensive military effort is avoided, and effort concentrated on seizing key points of power, like the telegraph office and other means of communication.

In any case, the Bolsheviks duly seized power.... Slogans like "Peace! Land! Bread!" and "All Power to the Soviets!" reverberated through the country. Before long these became transmuted into other slogans, like "He who does not work, neither shall he eat", and, not quite so menacing, "From each according to his abilities, to each according to his needs". The means of production were seized by the state, and the land nationalized; banks were taken over, and the public debt repudiated. Not the least astounding thing about this revolution was that it was almost bloodless. Total casualties were probably not more than a few hundred. What sober historians have called "the greatest event in human history since the Reformation" duly occurred, and, except for a good deal of oratory and noisy scratching of pens, it was as if a button had dropped.

Discussion guidelines

1. "Lenin was an improbable Marxist revolutionary." Argue this viewpoint.
2. "Luck and a denial of the basic Marxist theory of revolution account for Lenin's success in October 1917." Discuss.

Cross reference

Leaders and Followers, page 136

2

Stalin: Creator or Monster?
from *Stalin: A Political Biography*
by Isaac Deutscher

[Although Lenin established Communism in Russia, it was his successor, Joseph Stalin, who worked out the details of the modern Communist state in the U.S.S.R.]

Miller Services, Toronto

This huge poster was displayed in Moscow University in 1954. Why would Stalin have wished it to be drawn this way?

The complexity of Stalin's character and of his role becomes most apparent when a comparison is attempted between him and Hitler. Their similarities are numerous and striking. Each of them suppressed opposition without mercy or scruple. Each built up the machine of a totalitarian state and subjected his people to its constant, relentless pressure. Each tried to remould the mind of his nation to a single pattern from which any "undesirable" impulse or influence was excluded. Each established himself as an unchallengeable master ruling his country in accordance with a rigid *Führerprinzip* [leader principle].

Here the similarities cease and the differences begin. Not in a single field has Hitler made the German nation advance beyond the point it had reached before he took power. In most fields he has thrown it back far behind, terribly far behind. The Germany he took over in 1933 was, despite economic depression and social strains and stresses, a wealthy and flourishing country. Its industry was the most efficient on the continent. Its social services were the most modern that any European nation had had. Its universities were great centres of learning, priding themselves on famous men of science. The better part of the German youth was serious, alert, and idealistic. The German theatre was the object of the highest admiration and of imitation. The best German newspapers were the most intelligent and the best informed of the continental press.

The Germany that Hitler left behind was impoverished and reduced to savagery. We are not speaking about the effects of Germany's defeat, but about the state of the nation, regardless of defeat. The material apparatus of production which the country possessed under Hitler was, apart from special armament plants, not essentially greater than that which it had possessed before. Its social services were half destroyed. Its universities became drilling grounds for a generation of horrible brutes. Its famous men of science were compelled either to emigrate or to accept the guidance of S.S. men and to learn racialist gibberish. Its medical men were turned into specialists on the racial purity of blood and into the assassins of those whose blood was deemed impure. Twelve years of "education" by a nazified press, radio, cinema, and theatre left the collective mind of Germany ruined. These terrible losses were not redeemed by a single new idea, unless one chooses to regard as new the idea that one nation or race is entitled to dominate or exterminate the others. Nor was the social structure of the nation essentially changed by national socialism. When the Nazi facade was blown away, the structure that revealed itself to the eyes of the world was the same as it had been before Hitler, with its big industrialists, its Krupps and Thyssens, its Junkers, its middle classes, its *Grossbauers* [large landowners], its farm labourers, and its industrial workers.

What a contrast, after all, Stalinist Russia presents. The nation over which Stalin took power might, apart from small groups of educated people and advanced workers, rightly be called a nation of savages. This is not meant to cast any reflection on the Russian national character – Russia's "backward, Asiatic" condition has been her tragedy, not her fault. Stalin undertook, to quote a famous saying, to drive barbarism out of Russia by barbarous means. Because of the nature of the means he employed, much of the barbarism thrown out of Russian life has crept back into it. The nation has, nevertheless, advanced far in most fields of its existence. Its material apparatus of production, which about 1930 was still inferior to that of any medium-sized European nation, has so greatly and so rapidly expanded that Russia is now the first industrial power in Europe and the second in the world. Within little more than one decade the number of her cities and towns doubled; and her urban population grew by thirty millions. The number of schools of all grades has very impressively multiplied. The whole nation has been sent to school. Its mind has been so awakened that it can hardly be put back to sleep again. Its greed for knowledge, for the sciences and the arts, has been stimulated by Stalin's government to the point where it cannot be satisfied. It should be remarked that, although Stalin has kept Russia isolated from the contemporary influences of the West, he has encouraged and fostered every interest in what he calls the "cultural heritage" of the West. Perhaps in no country have the young been inspired with so great a respect and love for the classical literature and art of other nations as in Russia. This is one of the important differences between the educational methods of Nazism and Stalinism. Another is that Stalin has not, like Hitler, forbidden the new generation to read and study the classics of their own literature whose ideological outlook does not accord with his. While tyrannizing the living poets, novelists, historians, painters, and even composers, he has displayed, on the whole, a strange devotion for the dead ones. The works of Pushkin, Gogol, Tolstoy, Chekhov, Belinsky, and many others, whose satire and criticism of past tyranny have only too often a bearing on the present, have been literally pressed into the hands of youth in millions of copies. Nor can the fact be ignored that the ideal basic to Stalinism, one to which Stalin has given a grossly distorted expression, is not domination of man by man, or nation by nation, or race by race, but their fundamental equality. Even the proletarian dictatorship is presented as a mere transition to a classless society; and it is the community of the free and the equal, and not the dictatorship, that has remained the inspiration. Thus, there have been many positive, valuable elements in the educational influence of Stalinism, elements that are in the long run likely to turn against its worse features.

Finally, the whole structure of Russian society has undergone a change so profound and so many-sided that it cannot really be reversed. It is possible to imagine a violent reaction of the Russian people itself against the state of siege in which it has been living so long. It is even possible to imagine something like a political restoration. But it is certain that even such a restoration would touch merely the surface of Russian society. For of Stalinist Russia it is even truer than of any other revolutionary nation that "twenty years have done the work of twenty generations".

For all these reasons Stalin cannot be classed with Hitler, among the tyrants whose record is one of absolute worthlessness and futility. Hitler was the leader of a sterile counter-revolution, while Stalin has been both the leader and the exploiter of a tragic but creative revolution.

Discussion guidelines

1. "Uninformed people say that all dictators are the same – totally evil." By referring to the régimes of Hitler and Stalin, defend or refute this statement.
2. In 1956, the Russian leader Khrushchev referred to Stalin, who died in 1953, as a "criminal murderer". To what extent do you think Deutscher and Khrushchev would be in agreement?

Cross reference

Men Need Rulers, page 14

Wide World Photo

German troops entering Stalingrad. Did Stalin's purges help the German invaders?

Does Dictatorship Create Order?

from *Fifty Years of Soviet Communism*
by Louis Fischer

[An observation frequently made is that order and efficiency are obvious benefits of a non-democratic government, whereas disorder and inefficiency must be accepted as part and parcel of democracy. But is this necessarily true?]

Even persons devoted to individual freedom and horrified by the high cost of dictatorship often assume that dictatorship brings order. The champions of dictatorship argue that the democratic system means political chaos and economic instability. Under a dictatorship, they hold, decisions are quickly made and carefully executed.

Soviet experience proves all these views wrong.

For seventeen years, from 1917 to 1934, the Soviet Union was torn apart by civil wars, peasant revolts, workers' strikes, and fierce, openly publicized struggles within the Soviet Communist party. Policies were adopted not after a careful scientific evaluation of their possible or probable results, but in the hope that they would undermine and defeat the opposition. At times, policies were adopted not because of their desirability, but to steal them from the opposition. This happens in democracies too. After 1934, when Stalin had established his personal supremacy, the true chaos commenced when tried, experienced, loyal Communists were murdered at his will, with ruinous effect on the national economy, the people's morale, and the ability to ward off invasion. This disarray continued under Stalin's dictatorship for nineteen years.

Stalin was succeeded by Malenkov, who was

ousted with the aid of the army by Khrushchev, who was ousted by Brezhnev and Kosygin. In the post-Stalin period the national economy was decentralized by Khrushchev for political purposes; dozens of federal ministries were abolished. Then the economy was recentralized and the ministries were re-established. Presently it occurred to Khrushchev to divide the party control over the economy in two; one set of party bureaucrats would manage industry, another set agriculture. The confusion was fantastic and it lasted until he lost his job. His successors restored the unified party management over the economy.

All of these gigantic manipulations involved millions of bureaucrats, thousands of extended, smoke-filled conferences, and millions of pounds of paper, not to speak of the money and materials wasted in each reorganization and the undermined morale of the great army of officials who never could know what would befall next.

Similar upheavals on a smaller scale have taken place in regions, districts, ministries, and party groups where the frequent turnover of top personnel brings in its train transfers, promotions, demotions, and dismissals of lesser figures.

Insecurity and nervous tension are the accepted way of life in the Soviet Union. In Stalin's time, life was a lottery. On a visit to Yugoslavia in the 1950s, I met in a bull session with a group of Belgrade's Communist authors. They told me that they had recently had a visit from Leonid Leonov, the Soviet novelist. He was asked why Boris Pilnyak, a Soviet novelist, had been executed. Leonov replied, "It is pure chance that Pilnyak is not sitting here and listening to your question why Leonov was executed." The murder lottery has ended, but it is still pure chance that Comrade X who managed Trust Y was here yesterday and is gone today. Lack of tenure is part of the system. It breeds fear, on which a dictatorship feeds, and envy and competition; it encourages intriguers and informers to do their worst.

Many misconceptions exist about planning. In the minds of some, planning equals order. It does not. I once asked Ivan Smilga, a former chairman of the Federal State Planning Commission (Gosplan), whether planning was possible when combined with overfulfillment of the plan. He said, "Of course not." The moment the Kremlin adopts the national economic plan, propaganda begins for overfulfilling the plan. Factories are hailed in the Soviet press for carrying out their plan not on December thirty-first but on November seventh, the anniversary of the revolution, and rewards are granted to the zealots who inspired the achievement.

But a plan assumes order. To make one hundred units of a given machine will require a hundred men, a hundred units of material, a hundred units of energy. All requirements should be available in time. If, however, the hundred units of the machine are to be manufactured in ten months or less, as the party usually urges, the factory may have to recruit more workers, find more metal for them than it has stored, and call for more energy. The Soviet press frequently complains that factories raid one another for their requirements. If planning were real this would not be possible.

Time without number *Pravda* complains about "storming" the plan. The plan normally reaches a plant in January or later. The management begins to study and prepare. By the second half of the year, the director and engineers grow apprehensive they may not fulfill the plan. So they "storm" the plan. The speed-up begins, the search for more of everything. Chaos reigns. Fortunately for the Soviet dictatorship, the management and workers submit to this system and produce results. But the losses are surely considerable.

It is not a guess that Soviet planning operates under enormous disadvantages. The Soviet leadership admits it. For decades, the plan prescribed only quantities. A certain industry was to produce so much and each of its units so much. Since failure to meet these assignments was hazardous even in the post-Stalin era, trusts and their branch factories did their utmost to fulfill the plan, to produce the required number of shoes or tractors. Very frequently this was accomplished at the expense of quality. The Soviet newspapers constantly stressed the importance of quality. But the plan demanded quantity and that was the first concern of all involved in production.

The Soviet shoe industry might manufacture a hundred million pairs of shoes which should take a year of wear. But if they wore out in six months the industry, in effect, had produced only fifty million pairs of shoes.

Nevertheless, the procedure of quantity-planning worked, at great cost to the national economy to be sure, as long as everything was in short supply. The desert easily absorbed all available water, no matter how polluted.

In recent years, the Kremlin made a discovery: goods worth billions of rubles filled the warehouses because nobody wanted to buy them; they were inferior. And this applied not only to shoes but to tractors that broke down after a few months and dynamos that lacked the necessary wiring. But the factory that produced these shunned items remained aloof; its responsibility ended when the item was shipped from its gates.

After decades of such planning, a Soviet economist in Kharkov named Professor Yevsey Liberman suggested a radical change: factories should not only produce, they should also sell and what they earned would be used for investment and improvement of the lot of the working staff.

This wisdom, timidly launched, was attacked as capitalism. Authoritative spokesmen denied the slander. Discussion swirled around Liberman's idea for more than two years. Finally, two factories were cautiously designated to undertake the experiment. Success. More factories joined the parade. Today, Libermanism seems to have been accepted by the Kremlin.

There is no social bookkeeping for the losses through chaos of the pre-Liberman era. Libermanism does not replace Leninism, but it breaches the walls of that tight centralization which Lenin regarded as the essence of communism. Factories will now be ordered to work independently though, of course, within the national plan. How long this new system will continue nobody knows. Independence opens doors wide to corruption which has always been the curse of the Soviet economy.

To cope with corruption and with the suspicion of corruption the Soviets have constructed a mechanism of checks and balances. Any Soviet store reveals its method. In a butcher shop, the housewife joins a queue to the butcher's table. She inquires about the cost of a cut of pork. He tells her. She then joins another queue at the cashier's window to buy a receipt equal to the amount. She then joins a queue to the butcher. The butcher wields his chopper, weighs the meat, and finds he has chopped off more than the pound the woman wanted; this will cost a few kopeks more. She then returns to the cashier's queue, and again to the butcher's queue. But the butcher has no right to hand her the pork. There might be collusion between him and the customer. He passes the meat to a packer. The housewife joins that queue. The packer checks the meat against the woman's receipt and finally relinquishes the purchase to her.

Eating a meal in a Soviet restaurant takes an extraordinarily long time. I have often inquired why. The waiters and the head waiters give the same explanation: no waiter can himself take food in the kitchen. He must write out an order for the glass of tea and hand the order to a person who will fill the glass for him. Then he stands in line for a pat of butter, and for fruit preserves which go into the tea. A bookkeeper behind the scenes watches over the entire process.

Mistrust creates jobs, wastes time, and pyramids disorder.

Soviet history and Soviet life have been the conclusive proof that the dictatorship is not order but its opposite. (It is only necessary to mention the prolonged convulsions in Red China during dictator Mao Tse-tung's so-called Cultural Revolution, and the war and its horrors brought upon Germany by Hitler's dictatorship.) How dictatorship came to be identified with order is one of the baffling riddles of modern times.

Discussion guidelines

1. "Dictatorship is more efficient than democracy." Support your viewpoint.
2. "The best government is always the most efficient government." From your contact with government at school or in the community, discuss this claim.

Cross references

Leaders Are More Important, page 106
The Ideal State, page 107

Russian Government in Action

from *Main Street U.S.S.R.*
by Irving R. Levine

Lenin is supposed to have remarked that there could be any number of political parties in the Soviet Union but only on one condition. The Communist Party must be in power and all the other parties must be in jail.

The Communists justify their political monopoly by explaining that there is no need for an opposition party. Opposition parties are necessary only when they represent *opposing* class interests. In the Soviet Union, runs the Communist argument, there are no *opposing* classes. The only classes, the workers and peasants, have similar rather than contradictory interests. The Communist Party defends their interests. The workers and peasants would not tolerate any attempt to undermine their interests by an opposition party.

The Communist Party consists of only seven million members out of a population of more than two hundred million people [1960]. Less than four per cent of the Soviet people are members of the Party. And, in fact, it is only a small portion of this four per cent that runs the country. It is the élite class, the privileged few in a country of under-privileged people. It is small wonder that *Pravda* could not restrain itself and ignore the book, *The New Class*, written by disillusioned Yugoslav Communist leader Djilas. Djilas's first-hand appraisal of the Communist Party as a new exploiting class burned deep into Communist conscience. Without mentioning the actual content of the book, *Pravda* denounced it for "insinuations and hostile attacks on the Communist Party". Djilas himself was described as a renegade belonging to the "miserable set of a demoralized, cowardly movement", a traitor to the people and the revolution. *Pravda*'s real rage lay in the fact that Djilas was a traitor to the Communist class in a society which claims to be classless.

At the time of the 1917 Revolution the Party claimed to have numbered only 240,000 members; in 1938 its membership had grown to 2,300,000 and at the end of World War II, in 1945, there were about six million. The growth since then has been much slower; the leadership apparently preferring exclusivity to broad membership. A small, selected group can be more effectively controlled than a mass representative party.

It is no easy matter to join the Communist Party

in Russia. It is considered an honor to belong. No one knows how many millions of Russians, if given the chance, would refuse to join because they oppose Communist principles, but it is certain that the Party could be at least several times larger than it is today if the Kremlin leadership were to decide to expand. No one can estimate, either, how many Party members pay only lip service to the Party's principles. Certainly there are many who belong because it is one of the few ways of achieving a privileged position in the Soviet Union. Money does not obtain a roomier apartment in Russia. Party membership will. Neither money nor, in fact, a responsible position as a plant manager, a scientist, or a writer in itself wields real influence in Russia. Party membership does. Prestige and influence, if not always respect, go with Party membership in Russia. One of the first adjustments a correspondent has to make in reporting from Russia is to rid himself of a feeling of self-consciousness in asking people if they are members of the Communist Party. In interviewing a person in the United States, such a question is usually regarded as an insult. In Russia, of course, an affirmative answer is given with pride.

To join the Party a Russian must be nominated by three Party members (each of whom has been in the Party at least three years) in the office or factory or institution where he works. Sponsorship is not lightly given, because sponsors are held responsible for their candidates. The would-be member is interviewed and investigated by members of the Party unit to which he has applied first. To be admitted as a candidate member, he must receive a majority vote. His period as a candidate member or, in effect, as a Party apprentice, may run for months or years before he is again voted on for full membership. Usually the period of probation runs one year. A person is eligible for Party membership at the age of eighteen.

Party units of varying size in every factory, collective farm, every city district, every town and village, in schools, in offices, in military units, and aboard navy ships form the base of the Communist Party. There are more than 400,000 units, ranging in membership from tens to hundreds.

Delegates from these units meet irregularly in Party congress. There is one delegate elected for every 5,000 members. A congress, according to Party rules, should be convened at least every four years.

Between congresses the Central Committee is summoned periodically – at least twice a year, according to Party rules – either to resolve disputes within the Presidium [a small group of Communists who are the real rulers of the Party], during periods when that degree of democracy is in effect, or simply to give formal approval to decisions of the Presidium. At all times, Party members are kept abreast of the thinking and decisions of the leadership by Party publications and by personal conferences and communications. The Presidium is presided over by the first secretary of the Central Committee, commonly referred to abroad as chairman of the Communist Party.

As chairman of the Party, a man is able – as did Stalin and, to an extent, Khrushchev – to arrange for men of loyalty to him to be members (and candidate members, a group almost equal in size to the Central Committee and a rung lower in importance) to ensure support of his programs. Control of the Party means, in effect, potential control of every phase of Soviet life. Members of the Party hold all key positions in the government, in industry, in science, in the arts. Stalin used the secret police as an instrument to ensure his control of the Party by keeping an eye and ear on the thoughts and plans of other Party members and eliminating any he suspected.

The Communist Party has been described as a tightly disciplined civilian army, a dedicated priesthood. Membership entails many privileges and opens horizons of limitless opportunity. But the demands and responsibilities are tremendous too.

Miller Services, Toronto

Diamond-drilling by open-pit methods near the Arctic Circle in Siberia. To what extent do you think state control as opposed to private enterprise accounts for the development of such regions?

A Party member may be called on to uproot his home and move to a Siberian farm to spur production. He may find himself at a remote army post to observe a unit's proper political indoctrination. He and other members of his unit will be held responsible for an outbreak of juvenile delinquency in their area. A drop in a factory's production will require explanations by the plant's Party members.

A Party member's personal conduct is also under close scrutiny. Ekaterina Orestova, textile factory foreman and a Party member for twenty-five years in good standing, was summoned by her Party superiors. She had accepted a gift from workers on her birthday. Some disgruntled workers had complained that they were forced to contribute. The magazine, *Party Life*, discussed the case. *Party Life* investigators had determined that Miss Orestova had not suggested that money be raised. Her best friend at the factory had initiated the collection, and some workers felt obliged to contribute because of Comrade Orestova's position. The magazine granted that allowances must be made for Comrade Orestova's excitement and confusion at the surprise presentation, and also that some workers would have been offended by her refusal to accept the gift. However, in similar cases, Party members should be guided by Orestova's error. They should refuse the gift and suggest instead that the workers hold a meeting and present a certificate of honor as a birthday present. As this case demonstrates, the Party is characterized by often oppressive, self-righteous earnestness with a total absence of any lightness of spirit or humor.

The composition of the 7,215,505 Party members (including 419,609 candidates) at the time of the twentieth congress was reflected in statistics issued on delegates to the congress. Among the 1,436 delegates about half, or 758, had higher education. There were 193 women. Twenty per cent of the delegates were under 40 years of age. Fifty-five per cent were between 40 and 50. Twenty-five per cent were over 50. Only twenty-two of the delegates had entered the Party before the 1917 Revolution. These statistics reflect the gradually changing complexion of the Party. The core of revolutionary fanatics who plotted in cellars and fought in the streets against Czarist soldiers is fast dying. The new Communist is a man of vested interests. Stability rather than revolution benefits him. He has acquired position and property.

The Communist Party starts its training of the nation's young at a tender age, starting with "Little Octobrists", in pre-school, nursery age, "Pioneers" in grade school, and the "Young Communist League" (or Komsomol) after the age of 14.

In 1938 Komsomol had 4,800,000 members. By 1949 it had grown to 8,000,000. In 1958 there were 18,000,000 members in an age group that comprised probably 25,000,000. The potentialities of the Komsomol as an instrument for indoctrination and direction of the youth are evident in these figures. It's also significant in this regard that by 1959 more than 80 per cent of the Soviet populace had been born and educated under the Communists.

The principle of separation of church and state has its counterpart in the religion of Communism. The Kremlin maintains there is a distinct division between the Communist Party and the Soviet Government. On paper there is. The organization of the Communist Party, from the Presidium at the top and down to the Party units, is separate from the government structure administering the affairs of the nation. But the line between Party and state is usually meaningless because the main jobs in government are held by members of the Party, and where this is not the case, the government official receives his guidance from the Party. The Party [influence is felt everywhere]. Every military commander, for example, has a Party political worker of equal rank in theory, and greater influence in fact, by his side. Party members fall into two classes: those whose full-time activities are devoted to Party organization and administration, and those who hold other jobs – as factory managers, university rectors, government officials – and whose influence and importance are enormously enhanced by Party membership.

The government structure is, theoretically, rooted in the people. Elections (with only one candidate for each office) are held for deputies to the Supreme Soviet – the U.S.S.R.'s two-chamber congress or parliament. The Supreme Soviet elects a Presidium. This is the Presidium of the Supreme Soviet, not of the Communist Party, but many of its members are the same. The Presidium elects a chairman, who is president of the country. There is also a Council of Ministers, consisting of the heads of various ministries. The chairman of the Council of Ministers is the Premier of the nation. He is, of course, chosen from among the members of the Communist Party's Presidium.

The Supreme Soviet, by an invariably unanimous show of hands, converts the ukases – the decrees – issued by the Presidium of the Supreme Soviet (which acts for the whole body between sessions) into law.

Discussion guidelines

1. (a) "The difference among the major political parties in Canada is like the difference between Tweedledum and Tweedledee." Give the reasons for your agreement or disagreement with this statement.
   (b) To what extent do you think it would be wise for Canadians to follow the Russian example and officially adopt a one-party system?
2. Compare the structure of the Russian Communist party with that of a major Canadian and/or American political party.
3. In the *Communist Manifesto,* Marx had insisted that Communists wanted power to get rid of "the old bourgeois society, with its classes and class antagonisms", and in its place set up "an association in which the free development of each is the condition for the free development of all". To what extent can Communists in the U.S.S.R. claim to have followed these particular ideas of Marx?

EASTERN EUROPEAN COMMUNISM

[Since the end of World War II, Communist governments have dominated Eastern Europe. What light does the 1968 invasion of Czechoslovakia throw on the nature of Eastern European Communism, and on its relationship to Russian Communism? The following news articles, printed at the time, present some ideas on the subject, and provide an opportunity to evaluate news coverage of the event. It should be noted that the first of the articles was written prior to the invasion.]

1

Soviet-Czech Relations—See-Saw Between Pressure and Reconciliation

By ROBERT M. SMITH

The recent dispute between the Soviet Union and Czechoslovakia has been a teeter-totter of pressure and reconciliation.

On July 19, Moscow summoned the entire Presidium of the Czechoslovak party to go to the Soviet Union to explain its liberalization. Normally, such invitations are not made public until their acceptance. Prague felt that Moscow had issued it as a means of pressure.

The Czechoslovak leaders, nervous but steadfast, refused. Three days later the Russians took what seemed the first step in their retreat. They agreed to come to Czechoslovakia.

For three days the Russians tried to bring the Czechoslovaks into line. They began with bluster, then became more reasonable. On the fourth day, with the Czechoslovakia still unyielding, the Russians relented.

On August 3, the Czechoslovak victory was ratified in Bratislava. An empty document proclaiming unity of purpose was signed. Even a token Soviet effort to save face by including in the declaration some of its earlier position was defeated by Czechoslovak editing.

The feather was added to the Czechoslovak cap August 9 with the arrival in Czechoslovakia of President Tito of Yugoslavia, the most famous Communist dissident, who had broken from Moscow in 1948.

Ignoring a summer downpour, thousands of Czechoslovaks poured out on to the runway at Prague airport waving Yugoslav flags and shouting: "Long live Tito."

One Czechoslovak interpretation of the apparent Soviet backdown was that the Russians knew the problems of the Czechoslovak economy. They theorized that the Soviets, Poles, and East Germans hoped that the economic condition of the country would get worse and that the Czechoslovaks would demand a new government to replace the liberals.

Another important factor seemed the reliance of Czechoslovak heavy industry on the Soviet Union for new materials and crude oil.

The question of how the ideologically conservative Russians, East Germans, and Poles would react had been uppermost in the minds of the Czechoslovaks since January, when the New Communist Party leadership under Alexander Dubcek, the first secretary, began its "democratization progress".

At one point last winter the Old-Guard ideologist in the Soviet leadership, Mikhail Suslov, demanded a military intervention to "save socialism" – meaning dogmatic party rule – in Czechoslovakia. But Mr. Suslov was overruled by more cautious men around the party chief, Leonid Brezhnev.

According to Zdenek Mlynar, a member of the new Czechoslovak party Secretariat, the only Soviet action was the temporary cut-off of wheat deliveries.

He attributed the stoppage to "nervousness" in Moscow over the developments in Czechoslovakia.

But apparently the Soviet Union had second thoughts, because on April 1 it resumed wheat shipments.

In addition, the Soviets discreetly offered the Czechoslovaks a $400-million loan in hard currency to be paid back with goods which Moscow normally buys in the West. The Prague Government desperately needs hard currency to bolster its economy.

The economy suffered under 20 years of central direction, by the dogmatic system of former President Antonin Novotny.

It was in September, 1967, that Mr. Novotny called for a hardening of Communist discipline and warned liberal elements that the Communist Party would not tolerate political compromise.

In June, 1967, Czechoslovakia followed the Soviet Union's example and severed diplomatic relations with Israel.

In February, 1967, at the end of an unpublicized visit by Mr. Brezhnev to Czechoslovakia, an official statement said that the talks he had held with Czechoslovak leaders showed "complete identity of views" of the two sides on "problems of the international situation . . . and on the necessity to strengthen the cohesion of the socialist community and the unity of the international Communist movement."

In September, 1966, the Soviet Union and Czechoslovakia signed an agreement in Moscow by which the Czechoslovaks agreed to provide more than $550-million in credits for the development of the Soviet oil industry in Western Siberia. In exchange, the Soviet Union agreed to deliver oil above the quantity called for in the existing long-term trade agreement.

At the beginning of June, 1966, during the 13th congress of the Czechoslovak Communist Party, in Prague, Mr. Novotny called for unity within the Warsaw Pact and said the Soviet armed forces remained "the core of the defense of the entire socialist camp".

But by January of this year [1968] the younger generation had gained enough power to oust Mr. Novotny, who in combining the presidency with the first secretaryship of the Communist Party had since 1953 wielded supreme power.

In his place as secretary, the Party appointed 46-year old Alexander Dubcek, a Slovak who had spent his formative years in the Soviet Union.

His accession was the result of a long power struggle in which he charged that Mr. Novotny had imperilled the country's economy.

By mid-summer a program of drastic reform was under way. Secret police powers were cut back, censorship was for a while abandoned. A new 11-man Presidium of the Communist Party was announced, packed with Dubcek supporters known for liberal views.

The Soviet Union began to get restive. The first open sign was a spate of attacks in the Soviet press on Czechoslovak personalities and programs.

The Russians called a series of East bloc meetings all clearly designed to pressure the Czechoslovaks back into line. They announced massive Warsaw Pact maneuvers and used them to put Soviet troops into Czechoslovakia for the first time since the Second World War.

Once the maneuvers ended, the Soviets delayed pulling out their troops and the war of nerves built up.

But in two historic meetings on Czechoslovak soil, one at Cierna between the Soviet and Czechoslovak Presidiums, another at Bratislava bringing the rest of the dwindling East bloc face to face with the Czechoslovaks, it seemed that Mr. Dubcek would be given license to try his reforms.

Mr. Dubcek had used these talks to insist that Czechoslovakia remained true to the Warsaw Pact, and that its reforms were essential to making a success of communism within its borders.

But in the past week the Soviet press became critical again.

The Soviet Government newspaper Izvestia complained yesterday night that Sudeten Germans were staging a "revengist bacchanalia" over Czechoslovak territory that Germany lost after the Second World War.

The Sudentenland is a Czechoslovak frontier territory which had a population of about 3 million Germans and 800,000 Czechoslovaks before the war.

The Munich agreement of Sept. 29, 1938, opened the door for Adolf Hitler's occupation of the Sudentenland as peace started to crumble in Europe. The Germans were expelled after the Allies won the war.

The New York Times,
August 21, 1968

2

The Fears That Spurred the Russians into Action

By JOHN GELLNER

If ever there was an anxious balancing of the pros and cons of a major political-military move, it must have taken place these past two weeks in the Kremlin when the Russian leaders were struggling toward a decision on whether to invade Czechoslovakia.

Perhaps we will know one day precisely what tilted the scales on the side of aggression. Right now, it seems inconceivable that hard-headed political leaders like the Russians, even if they are accustomed to ruling by coercion, should think the reasons for violent action outweigh the very cogent reasons that militated against it.

Thought it a threat

Clearly, the Russian leaders put a much higher evaluation than did the West on the significance, and thus on the probable long-range effects, of the reform movement in Czechoslovakia. Surprising as it may seem, they at least seem to have considered it a threat to their own power position, at home and abroad.

They may have found that there were strong historical reasons for such a conclusion. History plays, and always has played, a considerable role in the formulation of Soviet policy. This can be seen again and again, for instance, in the pathological fear of encirclement, rooted in civil war experience; in the exaggerated sensitivity whenever the Soviet Union believes it can see an incipient move toward the erection of a "cordon sanitaire" such as existed in the Nineteen Twenties and Thirties; in the fear of German revival which is difficult to comprehend considering the disparity of power.

The Czechs and Slovaks have, on several occasions in the past, exhibited a capacity for ideological leadership quite out of proportion to their material strength. To go back a long way, the Reformation started in Bohemia and it was there that the first Reformed Church was founded. More recently, the first republic of Thomas Masaryk and his disciples built a model for a democratic middle-power, exercising a pacifying influence upon the world – and this a generation before the middle-power concept was recognized as desirable.

There were always too few Czechs and Slovaks – situated in just about the most awkward geographical position in Europe – to make a lasting impact, but something of their political idealism always influenced European developments.

The Marxist reform movement of these past seven months was not a Czechoslovak invention, of course. What has been called humanized Marxism has been propounded since Stalin's death made a modicum of theoretical discussion possible within many Communist parties. But in Czechoslovakia for the first time humanized Marxism from being a suppressed or, at best, a tolerated intellectual deviation, became the official, practical policy of a ruling Communist Party.

Ideologically, this meant an advance beyond Leninism, the admission that its body of dogmas, the "revealed religion" as it were, was neither complete nor unchangeable. Practically, it meant the end of dictatorship.

According to the new policy, the Communist Party would still remain the leading political force in the land and Marxism the state religion, and this would still restrict the area within which any opposition would be able to maneuver. But there would be persuasion in place of coercion. Minority opinion would be heard.

Tried selling Marxism

In brief, Marxism would be sold, not imposed. The Czechoslovak reformers believed that this was possible if it was done in a way acceptable to intelligent people. They were equally sure that Marxism, which in Czechoslovakia has almost 100 years of tradition, would die unless it was propounded this way.

The Soviet leaders obviously came to the conclusion that they could not permit the Czechs and the Slovaks to make theoretical changes in Marxism and Leninism, or to live under any other than dictatorial government. The risks involved clearly seemed too great.

The Soviet leaders could have been under no illusion as far as the attractiveness of the Czechoslovak experiment was concerned. It appeared to offer the kind of organization of society which the majority of the peoples of East-central Europe wished for, and which has been more and more insistently demanded in the Soviet Union itself.

The wave of repression which has swept through the Soviet Union in these past two years shows how concerned the Soviet leaders are about the stirrings within their own society. This is also why Wladyslaw Gomulka in Poland, who started 12 years ago as a reformer of sorts (admittedly, in a limited way) has tightened the screws more and more in recent times, and why Walter Ulbricht persists in running the mustiest kind of Stalinist satrapy in East Germany.

Freedom is catching

Freedom is always contagious. Propagated, if only cautiously and strictly for home consumption, by a government such as in Czechoslovakia in these past months, it could conceivably become the one great motivating force to inspire all the long-oppressed peoples in the area.

There is yet another possible explanation for the Soviet action, and it is a frightening one. What if the Soviet leaders have come to the conclusion that the next few months offer the best opportunity for gaining the upper hand (or at least a significant temporary advantage) in their global power struggle with the United States? To them, it would seem like the proper moment.

Deeply affected at home and abroad by the political consequences of the Vietnam war, the United States seems less able and willing than at any other time in recent years to assert itself in the world. Moscow may be right to count on a feebler U.S. response to, say, violent Soviet action in the Middle East than it encountered six years ago in its Cuban venture.

If the Soviet leaders, having decided to take advantage of assumed U.S. weaknesses in means and moral fibre, plan to launch a major, militarily backed political offensive in some part of the world, they would naturally want to batten down elsewhere. Consequently, they would make sure that they were firmly in command in their own area, that there was no weak spot along the periphery, and that there was discipline at home.

It is conceivable that by their seizure of Czechoslovakia the Russians wanted to close what they judged to be a gap in their defenses before they hit out elsewhere. It is a chilling thought, but one not to be dismissed out of hand.

At any rate, the Iron Curtain has come down again with a loud rattle and it is the Russians who have lowered it. This comes as no surprise to those in the West who never believed that there really was a detente, certainly not after early 1965. It will shock – hopefully, into some good sense – the starry-eyed optimists who have already been seeing the dawn of peace and fraternity on the international horizon and who thought that it was the West (and especially the United States) which was lagging in the march toward that dawn.

It will probably put a stop to talk about dismantling NATO. Born as a consequence of the Communist coup in Czechoslovakia in February, 1948, the alliance will be revitalized by Russia's aggression against Czechoslovakia of August, 1968.

That this must be one of the immediate effects of the Soviet action is nothing to rejoice over, but no doubt it is the inevitable result. The Soviet leaders must have taken this into account when they made up their minds about Czechoslovakia.

For the Czechs and Slovaks, the future looks bleak. They have suffered a stunning setback, the harder to take because it comes after a period of national euphoria. On the other hand, a store of self-confidence has been accumulated in the nation which will probably make the disaster of 1968 easier to overcome psychologically than those of 1938 and 1948. The past seven months cannot be wiped off the slate.

The Globe and Mail, Toronto
August 23, 1968

Miller Services, Toronto

Czechoslovakian youths argue with Russian soldiers in Prague on the day after the invasion. Why might they have felt they could get away with this? Does this appear to be a typical invasion?

3

Russians Descended Like Vultures, Czechoslovaks Say

By ZENA CHERRY

I spent all Saturday afternoon in the white sunken living room of Mr. and Mrs. John C. Lockwood on Forest Hill Road to meet Czechoslovak refugees Mr. and Mrs. Juri Klobouk. They arrived in Toronto last week with their son Michael, 9, and Yolande, whose fourth birthday was yesterday.

An estimated 8,000 Czechoslovak refugees are coming to Canada because of the August invasion of their country by Soviet-led troops. Eva and Juri Klobouk are the first ones I've met. The Lockwoods did not know them before but were at Malton to welcome them. They became involved through their son-in-law, Lubomir Chmelar of Albany, N.Y. – he is Juri's cousin.

It was a happy afternoon. Eva speaks English, her husband does not, so we had two languages going, and much laughter.

Juri is a playwright and when your life is wrapped around words it's frustrating, to put it mildly, when you can't communicate. However, he can say quite a bit with his face and hands and has already picked up a few key words. For instance, "secretary, please", to his wife when he wants her to translate. I'd guess she's never held the floor from him before and we all sensed this amusing switch.

Eva and Juri are each 35 years old. They have healthy round fresh faces.

She has auburn hair and was so well groomed. She wore a charcoal grey suit which could go from winter to summer, breakfast to dinner, with a change of accessories. I thought, if I had to emigrate I don't own one thing as perfect. She has her degree in mining engineering from the University of Prague. From teaching oil geology she turned to popular science journalism and broadcasting.

Juri is a TV photographer, "to make my bread and butter". He is as well, the author of one novel and 10 plays including The Rocking Chair which won first prize in the 1965 Prague Festival.

"When did you decide to leave Czechoslovakia?" I asked Mrs. Klobouk.

"On Aug. 22, the day after the invasion. Like everyone we were in a terrible daze but we finally realized hopelessness. The history of our country is one of pogroms, wars, reprisals, and purges. We had had six months of political freedom under Alexander Dubcek – then the Russians descended like vultures. Communism is no longer a political idea, but a front for the brute power of Russian imperialism. Remember, we are completely indoctrinated Communists, yet we decided we could not live with it anymore – it's a terrible condemnation.

"The radio and TV stations were demolished; newspapers taken over. And grisly events such as the student on her way to the university to get her degree. She had put a little Czechoslovak flag in her lapel with a black band under it. A Russian murdered her right on the street car with his machine gun.

"The first wave of Russians were desperadoes and they had been deliberately kept hungry, on five potatoes a day. They brought no rations and so had to loot. We lived in an apartment and in the shopping section a butcher refused to give up his last piece of meat, so they killed him. The official figure of those killed on Wenceslas Square the first day were 80, and 2,000 in Forestry Park – but there were many more.

"They even shot their own. One soldier had his leg run over and he was shot on the pavement. They brought no medical corps with them. A doctor friend of ours was called to the Russian barracks and taken to a sick man. 'Is this contagious?' he was asked. 'Yes, it's hepatitis.' They shot the patient in bed."

Was it hard to get permission to leave Czechoslovakia?

"We were officially allowed out to work for one year. The Canadian embassy in Prague told us once we were in another country we could get a visa. We got out on Oct. 25, went to Bern and applied for our visas at the Canadian consulate. The Canadian Government lent us $726 for our air fares. Now the Canadian Government is giving us $120 per month for rent, plus $120 for food and other expenses."

Did they expect this help?

"No. Even in the United States there is nothing like this. Immigrants are helped only by private persons."

What did they bring to Canada?

"We brought a few clothes and our two typewriters. We had a car and a weekend chalet. We sold them. But the exchange rate is so ludicrously low that we left the money to care for our parents."

Eva's mother is a widow on a state pension. Juri's father is a retired chartered accountant.

I wondered if they thought student revolts on this continent are Communist-inspired.

"Definitely not. Students today have known no depression, no war – there are not these outlets for their tremendous energies. All over the world student uprisings are the mode, nothing to do with Communism."

For the present the Klobouks have furnished rooms in the home of a man who came from Yugoslavia to Toronto two years ago. "He now owns two houses, a Buick, and a $1,500 color TV set. Imagine!"

And finally, how do they feel now that the move is completed?

"We have a terrific sense of relief. We see ahead lots of tasks, and these are confusing, but not overly worrisome. We want to stay in Canada for the rest of our lives. We hope you realize how lucky you are to live here – you have freedom. Now we have freedom too," said Mrs. Klobouk.

The Globe and Mail, Toronto
November 25, 1968

Discussion guidelines

1. Compare the value of the three news accounts by considering the following criteria:
   (a) the nature of the news article (e.g., syndicated column, news agency, or free-lance journalist)
   (b) the dateline
   (c) the author's credentials
   (d) the validity of the headline in relation to the article
   (e) the reliability of the evidence
   (f) the validity of the opinions expressed
2. From the point of view of the Czechs, was the 1968 crisis a national revolution, or an ideological reformation?
3. "A common fear of Germany is the strongest tie that holds Russia and her satellites together."

   or

   "The standing of the satellites inside the soviet empire at any one time, and the measure of independence that they can gain and hold, depend on the strength of the U.S.S.R. domestically, in its orbit of power, and in the world." (John Gellner, *Political and Social Trends in Eastern Europe*)

   In your judgment, which of the above statements comes closest to explaining the relationship between Russia and her Eastern European satellites?

Cross references

Spheres of influence and Soviet aggression, page 276
Rigidity "the Most Dangerous Aspect of Two-Bloc System", page 278

CHINESE COMMUNISM

Adapting Communism to China

from *Mao – and the Chinese Revolution*
by Jerome Ch'en

Mao is a Marxist-Leninist seeking to strengthen his country by the application of Marxist-Leninist doctrines to Chinese conditions. In his view, China could not become powerful and wealthy until she was freed from imperialist and feudal bondage. He believed that the only force strong enough to bring about her emancipation was a Marxist party supported, in theory, by urban workers and rural peasants, but, in practice, mainly by peasants, especially armed peasants . . .

Because he is a Marxist, Mao differs from other Chinese revolutionaries in another sense. His revolution, essentially a military one, also has far-reaching cultural implications. The reforms prior to the 1911 Revolution started with firearms, spread to industries and railways, and finally raised the demand for a constitution. The revolutions of 1911 and 1926-8, aiming at democratic republicanism, were accomplished much too quickly. They absorbed so many opportunistic elements into the ranks of the revolutionaries that both the revolutions lost their social meaning. From another point of view, one may see how in the process of reform and revolution China borrowed from the West. The borrowing began with weapons, then extended to machinery and means of transport, and finally to political and legal institutions. Even the pattern of revolution was borrowed from France and Russia. Both the reformers and the revolutionaries felt the need for talented and trained people but, apart from sending students to study abroad, they seemed to be unaware of the importance of an adequate policy of training cadres [training small groups of people who can then control and train others]. Without well-trained and incorruptible cadres to form the middle and lower ranks of the civil service, all the high-minded objectives of a revolution would be lost. Here Mao borrowed from Stalin and the Russian party the policy of training cadres. Moreover, because of his reliance on politically backward peasants, Mao had to find ways to arouse them, such as the reduction of rent and interest rates and the redistribution of land. So he attacked the vested interests of the land-owning class and has in fact dismantled the traditional structure of Chinese society.

Mao's social revolution does not stop here. He is a feminist, treating women as the equals of men and expecting them to live up to such treatment. He is fully aware of the value of science, though without much understanding of it himself. Literature and the arts he believes should serve the people, the labouring people, and the Chinese should in learning from other nations be selective, discarding the "undesirable", bourgeois elements. He advocates borrowing from abroad, but is opposed to "wholesale Westernization". What is borrowed must be "integrated with the characteristics of the nation and given a definite national form before it can be useful". He himself has given the Marxist revolution in China a national form and expects others to do the same to sciences, literature, and the arts.

The national form of the Marxist revolution in China cannot fail to have international implications. What Mao has in mind may be the application of the Chinese, and his own, form of revolution to other backward countries. The basis of this form or pattern, according to Mao, is the uneven development of a large and populous country, which is caused by an under-development of industries and communications. Therefore at places where there are transport difficulties and the Government's control is weak the Communists can set up base areas from which to wage a protracted war. The Mao pattern is consequently an extension of the Leninist theory of the weakest link. Lenin justified the outbreak of a revolution in Russia, rather than in an industrially advanced country, by saying that it was in Russia that the bourgeois control was weakest. Mao likewise justified his reliance on the poor peasants when waging a protracted war from revolutionary bases by saying that it is at places where the control of the Government is the weakest that the sparks of revolution can be lit.

The weakest link alone is not enough; there must also be a large group of pauperized and discontented peasants. The millions of poor peasants in China in recent years were, in all probability, the result of the extortions and civil wars of the warlords and the dislocations and upheavals caused by the Resistance War and the hyper-inflation. That Chinese society underwent drastic changes between 1911 and 1949 is beyond question. Mao himself studied these changes and drew his conclusions, and his success may justify his views.

Miller Services, Toronto

2

Working with the Masses: A Case Study
from *Report from a Chinese Village*
by Jan Myrdal

In 1953 I [Ching Chi] joined the League of Youth, and, in 1956, I became a member of China's Communist Party. My work is that of secretary in Intourist in Sian. I earn seventy-four yuan a month, am married and have two sons, one of eight and one of five. I did thirteen months' lao dung, from the spring of 1959 to the spring of 1960, that is voluntary physical work. I did this in Liu Ling.

I come from a background that is not proletarian. We have always been well off. My father is a doctor, and when I was small he was in charge of a clinic. My mother went to college. My father was a Christian. He despised traditional medicine, which he called quackery. What he thinks about it now, I don't know. I expect he was reformed after the liberation, along with the rest. At the moment he is in Moscow studying neuro-surgery. I don't know whether or not he is still a Christian. I was sent to a school run by Canadian nuns. They taught me to play the piano. We used to sing psalms.

Life was never difficult for us, nor were we ever short of food. My father loved cleanliness above all else. I was forbidden to go out to the kitchen; if I did so despite this, then I was beaten. He would give me ten strokes. This was because in our district food is cooked over wood fires, and I could have made myself grimy. I looked down on our servants. They were dirty. I grew up thus and became lazy. I could not use a broom or even wash myself. Those were not things that I needed to do. After 1949, I became a bit better, perhaps. At school I was on my own and had to wash and dress myself; but my sentiments were far from being those of the workers. I knew nothing of the seriousness of life either. I did not know where the food that was set on my table came from. Nor did I bother about it. After the liberation, I learned a lot about how the proletariat felt, it is true, but actually I myself looked down on the poor, because they were uneducated and uncouth and filthy.

I know that I was always saying: "The farmers are good. The working class and the poor farmers are the leading classes. All honour to work. All honour to the workers. Physical labour is the highest." I often said that at meetings, but I didn't mean anything by it. I really thought the working class and the poor farmers an uneducated, dirty lot, and even though I did in a way believe what I said – in that I believed in the liberation of the Chinese people – I was only paying lip-service by saying that. I considered it to be our, the intellectuals', job to be the leaders. Which we have always been. I had no contact with working people. As far as I was concerned, this business of class and class struggle was just words.

But after the liberation, I did at least start washing myself. Before, I had had a servant to do that for me. In 1953, when I was twenty, I got married. But I did no housework, and I did not run the house. My mother-in-law did that. When I had my first baby, I just lay in bed. I did not bother about doing anything. My mother-in-law saw to everything and looked after the baby for me.

In 1953, the party exhorted all young intellectuals to do their share of physical labouring and go out among the people. We decided that all the intellectuals in our organization must go and spend a year in the country. I was a town girl and had never lived in the country, nor even been in a village, and I volunteered in 1958. But I wasn't accepted that year. It was not till 1959 that I was selected to go on one year's lao dung, voluntary physical work. I was in the third group to be sent out from our office.

We were to be re-educated and given a proletarian attitude to life. We were to fortify our physique and help the people's commune, to which we were sent, in its work. We were five women and four men. I had discussed all this with my husband. Of course, it was a pity being unable to be together for a year; but we had discussed it all thoroughly and come to the conclusion that one year was not of such great significance in a whole life. It was important to do one's share of physical work and also necessary for me, if I was to be a true revolutionary woman. My mother-in-law promised to look after the baby, which she loves dearly, and my husband said he would write to me often. My husband works at the university. He teaches Russian. He was going to use this year for further study.

My group was attached to Liu Ling People's Commune, [in Yenan district]. The commune decided that we should join Liu Ling Labour Brigade, so all nine of us drove out to Liu Ling. That was on 2 March 1959. It was a warm afternoon, and the Old Secretary, Li Yiu-hua, was sitting outside the cave here, smoking. He gazed at us for a while, then he said: "I know that most of you have never done any real work before in your lives. We will try to help you. You won't have to do too much to begin with. I shall try to find simple jobs for you at first, so that you can accustom yourselves to working with your hands. The best things, perhaps, will be for you to start by trundling up dry dung and helping to carry soil. After that, we shall see." Two in our group had done physical work before, but the other seven of us had never done a thing. The first fortnight was difficult for all of us. We ached all over and fell asleep the moment we lay down. But at least nobody laughed at us. Then, little by little, things began to go better. But even the two who said they had done physical work before were as tired as the rest of us, although we were only doing the lightest jobs, the sort of things that otherwise were only given to the old men, and to the women whose feet had been bound, to do.

We had two caves, one for women, one for men. We had a man who cooked for us. He cooked for his family at the same time. We were still paid by our office and got the same salary as we had had. Twice a week I got a letter from my husband. We helped build the collective dining-hall behind here, which they were going to use at harvest-time. Sometimes we would show a film there in the evening.

In July, I was chosen to lead the women's group. We held the meeting on the open space in front of the cave here. We held meetings once a month to discuss our work and plan the next month's work. The brigade leader had had a talk with me, at which he said: "The women's group needs your help. There are now three work leaders among the women here and not one of them can either read or write. Your job is not only to lead the work, but also to teach the other leaders to read and write. You'll have six months in which to do it." I said to him: "If it really is so that the women are relying on me and have chosen me themselves, of course I shall do my best." At the meeting, I was elected. I was very happy that the women believed in me. That was my first position of trust. At first, I was a bit scared by the job, because, after all, I was a town girl, so how could I take charge of things in the country? Everything there was so different. But after a month I had become one of the group. Well, when I left Liu Ling, at least one of the women labour leaders was able to read and write sufficiently well to be able to keep a work daybook and calculate the day's work. Before, they had to go to the book-keeper every day and ask him to make the entries. That had been a lot of trouble both for him and for them.

Well, after that I worked all the time. I ploughed and I weeded. I dug and I sowed. I had to learn everything. Every Monday and Tuesday evening, I went to the three leaders of the women's group and taught them reading and writing. Otherwise, when off duty, I went around visiting the families. I was supposed to be on the look-out for difficulties, such as a child ill or anything else. Where there were any, I would help the women in the cave or try to find some other woman in the vicinity who could come and help them. But it was out in the fields that I talked most with the women. We have occasional rests, and then the women sit and chat.

At the same time, I worked at my own ideological re-education. I had, you see, to transform myself from a bourgeoise to a human being. This was done partly by physical work and partly by reading. I read a book called *Steel Yourself In the Fight with a Hundred Thousand Difficulties*. I read Liu Shao-chi's *How To Become a Good Communist*. I read a variety of articles. We had a leader of our group. He had been chosen even before we left Sian. At first, we all found it very difficult. Even the two who came of farming stock found everything primitive and difficult, but in our second month we had grown accustomed to the work and had adjusted ourselves. We tried to spend as much time as possible with the people of Liu Ling. We were not going to huddle together or make a sort of urban clique. We were to learn from the people and become one with them.

We paid nine yuan a month for our food. We ate a lot because, of course, we were now doing physical labour. Before we went out to the fields in the morning, we helped the families where the husband was working in the town or elsewhere. The women in such families had a hard time of it. We fetched water from the well for them, and we also swept up outside their caves. We helped the women wash the clothes and make quilted winter coats. We also tried to help the women to learn a few characters. What we did was to draw a picture of something, a pig for example, and write the character for pig beside it. We gave ten such pictures to every woman who was interested, and they put them up on the walls of their caves, so that they should have them in front of their eyes all day long. After a week, they were supposed to exchange pictures with each other. The schoolchildren also helped in this voluntary study. But it did not work as well as we had hoped. There are very few women in the village of Liu Ling who can read or write. It is much more difficult to learn to write our characters than you imagine. It is especially difficult for adults. But it is also true that they are much more beautiful than letters.

After the winter harvest was in, that was December 1959, there was less work in the fields. That is the time of year when life in the country quietens down and people occupy themselves with minor jobs. We then embarked on serious criticism and self-criticism. For two months we kept at this and held discussions about it. We went through each one's faults and judged whether they had corrected them and how. We probed into ourselves and examined each other and tried to get to the bottom of all our personal problems and each of our incorrect attitudes to life and work. Sometimes, these meetings lasted half a day, and we went on day after day. Altogether we had seventy or more meetings. This meant that each of us in the group was analysed and corrected for anything up to fifty hours. These meetings were attended by the different intellectuals in the village. Li Yiu-hua [the Old Secretary] spoke at them, and so did the different leaders of the brigades and the labour groups and the party organizations. Even the villagers got up one after the other and told us what they thought about us and our work.

This was very important. You know that most of us come from non-proletarian background, in which we never come in for harsh criticism. In the old days, one never told people the truth to their faces. In my home we had always to be polite. It was not fitting to criticize another person. It was only servants one could tell off properly. But these farmers spoke frankly to us. Of course, we were doing lao dung in order to be transformed. Often enough this criticism hurt, but it helped. The village women considered that one of the girls in the group was arrogant; but they talked her out of it. You know, the old person has to go, so that the new can emerge and take her place. I was told I had said that I would teach the leaders of the women's group to read and write, but when it came to it, I had only been able to teach one of them to read.

All that winter we went through our work and our behaviour in this way. Afterwards, there was not much left that we had not analysed and criticized. When you go on as long as that, you have no possibility of hiding behind fine phrases. Then, after thirteen months of lao dung the time came for us to go home. I felt torn in two. On the one hand, I was longing dreadfully for my husband, but on the other hand I felt fearfully unhappy at having to leave Liu Ling. I had grown in to the place and become part of it.

I shall never forget the morning we left. People had come down to the flat here to say good-bye. The women and I were in tears. They begged us to stay. Then they gave us eggs and pumpkin seeds, which are lovely. I wept very much. You see, I had been working with the women's group and now I was having to leave them. I knew all the women and had associated with them all the time and knew them better than I had ever known anybody in my life before. I had never been so close to people before. In my home one did not behave like that. Then the car moved off and we drove away from Liu Ling.

I believe I learned a lot during those thirteen months. I became a different person. I had acquired a fundamentally proletarian attitude to life. For example, before, in the summer, if I thought it too hot, I used to hope it would rain, without stopping to think whether the rain would be good for the harvest or not. I can never do that again. Now, I automatically think first how the weather will affect the harvest. That year also gave me self-confidence. I learned to rely on myself and on my own capabilities. I am young and actually rather strong, and always have been; yet, before, I could scarcely even wash myself. When first we were told that we were to break new ground up on the hillside, I stood down there in the valley and looked up and almost burst into tears, because it all seemed so impossible. It was so high up and far away and the ground so hard. But there was nothing else to do but to climb up and start work. There was no way of my getting out of it. It was so hard, and it looked so hopeless. But then I noticed that we were making progress, and that I could work. And in the end I realized that nothing was impossible, and that it had only been my bourgeois up-bringing that had prevented me from relying on myself. The work went ahead quicker than the Old Secretary, Li Yiu-hua, had expected.

Yes, that year gave me the working people's attitude to existence. I became a completely different person. I had learned to work, and, when I returned home to my husband, he too thought I had changed. Since leaving Liu Ling, I have written to them all the time and heard from them too. I have longed for this the whole time. I have put my name down as a volunteer for another year's physical work, but they haven't given me much hope. First, I must do my work in Sian and make use of all the education I have had. And I cannot expect to be sent out for a second year's lao dung until all the others who have not yet been have done their year. Then it is possible that I may. But I'm told that society has invested a lot of money in my education, and that I must exploit it.

3

Mao's Thoughts on School Reform–Put Students to Work

By COLIN McCULLOUGH

PEKING – The long-awaited program for reformation of higher education in China was at last laid down by Mao Tse-tung in a new instruction that breaks the traditional education pattern followed by every other country in the world.

An able graduate of a high school in China apparently will not automatically move on to university to complete his education in science or engineering. Instead, he will go to work in a factory, farm commune, or in whatever job he or the state is able to find.

Only after a period of work will he go to university – if it is agreed that he is qualified to do so. In the simplest terms this means that manual labour will be added to the list of required subjects for entrance to university science and engineering courses.

In addition, university courses will be shortened. Apparently the number of years lopped off the degree program will equal approximately the length of time the student works, so that his age at graduation will be about the same as in the past.

These points were made in a report from workers in a Shanghai machine tools factory which was published in The People's Daily.

Their report said technical personnel of worker origin are far more proficient than most technicians who come to high factory jobs directly from college.

It has been known for some time that one of the objectives of the cultural revolution was the overhauling of higher education. In the past few months, the Chinese press has suggested that courses such as engineering and medicine are too long, and the press has talked about the value of field work and of having older workers doing some teaching (also recommended by the Shanghai workers' report).

The main criticism of the universities was that under the system of education inherited from foreign sources, intellectuals had become divorced from the masses, had succumbed to bourgeois influences and no longer were motivated by the needs of Socialist construction.

The new program is designed to break the academic framework of the past and prevent the growth of an intellectual elite whose views do not reflect those of the workers as expressed by the central leadership of the Chinese Communist Party.

The important question now is who will decide which workers will be allowed to enter university. The answer is not yet known, but the ultimate control will probably rest with the revolutionary committees–the alliances of old and new cadres, army men and workers.

These committees are established not only at the provincial level but also in factories, communes, hospitals, and even primary schools. They are instruments of political power created by the central leadership as a result of the cultural revolution.

To give the committees this new responsibility would not only strengthen their position, but also insure a new set of criteria exercised in the selection of university entrants.

A student aspiring to higher education would have to prove himself a willing and able worker for two or three years, and, perhaps more important, also satisfy the committee he was correctly oriented politically.

What will happen to students already in university and to graduates currently working is also covered in the report of the Shanghai machine tools plant, which is held up as a model in Mao's instruction.

The report said students graduating from university should begin as labourers in the factory or countryside. When they received qualification certificates from workers and peasants, they could take up the technical work for which they were trained but should still do manual labour from time to time.

Those who don't get certificates should remain as workers and peasants.

Graduates working should undergo criticism and repudiation and also be employed in their factory as ordinary workers for specified periods.

How quickly this massive change in the educational system can be made is open to question. The Shanghai newspaper Wen Hui Pao called it an urgent task. Leading Chinese newspapers have been conducting a campaign for several weeks calling on middle school graduates to become ordinary labourers and to work and settle in remote areas of China.

There are only two months before the next school term begins and still unanswered is the question of reform of the disciplines other than science and engineering. Indeed, it is still uncertain what other faculties will continue to operate.

In the first sentence of the new instruction, Mao wrote: "It is necessary to have colleges – here I refer, in the main, to colleges of science and engineering.

"While 'instruction continues, however, the period of schooling should be shortened, education should be revolutionized, proletarian politics be put in command and the road for training technicians from among the workers which the Shanghai plant followed should be taken. Students should be selected from workers and peasants who have practical experience. They should return to production after a few years of schooling."

The Globe and Mail, Toronto
July 24, 1968

Discussion guidelines

1. Assess the extent to which Mao's revolutionary ideas and practices originated from sources outside China.
2. From your own experience, evaluate the claims made for physical labour by Ching Chi.
3. (a) In what ways do you think Mao's educational reforms, as reported, will strengthen or weaken his nation?

   (b) To what degree (if any) could Canadian society benefit from similar educational reforms?

Democracy

PEANUTS
Tm. Reg. U. S. Pat Off.—All rights reserved
Copr. 1958 by United Feature Syndicate, Inc.

SCHULZ
11-24
I SET THEM ALL FREE!

Democracy is great! Why then did it fail in earlier societies? Why are modern youth challenging the leaders of democracy, and is their challenge justified? Has democracy failed its minorities and its poor? Is it dominated by ad-men and image makers? Behind these questions loom larger ones. Is it realistic for democratic citizens to be seeking wider participation in decision-making? In the final analysis, does it really matter if democracy itself, as it has developed in the West, survives?

DEMOCRACY IN CRISIS

Student Rebellion

from *Democracy and the Student Left*
by George F. Kennan

One cannot, on looking at young people in all the glory of their defiant rags and hairdos, always just say, with tears in one's eyes: "There goes a tragically wayward youth, striving to document his rebellion against the hypocrisies of the age." One has sometimes to say, and not without indignation: "There goes a perverted and willful and stony-hearted youth by whose destructiveness we are all, in the end, to be damaged and diminished."

These people also pose a problem in the quality of their citizenship. One thing they all seem to have in common – the angry ones as well as the quiet ones – is a complete rejection of, or indifference to, the political system of this country [the United States]. The quiet ones turn their backs upon it, as though it did not concern them. The angry ones reject it by implication, insofar as they refuse to recognize the validity of its workings or to respect the discipline which, as a system of authority, it unavoidably involves.

I think there is a real error or misunderstanding here. If you accept a democratic system, this means that you are prepared to put up with those of its workings, legislative or administrative, with which you do not agree as well as with those that meet with your approval. This willingness to accept, in principle, the workings of a system based on the will of the majority, even when you yourself are in the minority, is simply the essence of democracy. Without it there could be no system of representative self-government at all. When you attempt to alter the workings of the system by means of violence or civil disobedience, this, it seems to me, can have only one of two implications: either you do not believe in democracy at all and consider that society ought to be governed by enlightened minorities such as the one to which you, of course, belong; or you consider that the present system is so imperfect that it is not truly representative, that it no longer serves adequately as a vehicle for the will of the majority, and that this leaves to the unsatisfied no adequate means of self-expression other than the primitive one of calling attention to themselves and their emotions by mass demonstrations and mass defiance of established authority. It is surely the latter of these two implications which we must read from the overwhelming majority of the demonstrations that have recently taken place.

I would submit that if you find a system inadequate, it is not enough simply to demonstrate indignation and anger over individual workings of it, such as the persistence of the Vietnam war, or individual situations it tolerates or fails to correct, such as the condition of the Negroes in our great cities. If one finds these conditions intolerable, and if one considers that they reflect no adequate expression either of the will of the majority or of that respect for the rights of minorities which is no less essential to the success of any democratic system, then one places upon one's self, it seems to me, the obligation of saying in what way this political system should be modified, or what should be established in the place of it, to assure that its workings would bear a better relationship to people's needs and people's feelings.

If the student left had a program of constitutional amendment or political reform – if it had proposals for the constructive adaptation of this political system to the needs of our age – if it was *this* that it was agitating for, and if its agitation took the form of reasoned argument and discussion, or even peaceful demonstration accompanied by reasoned argument and discussion – then many of us, I am sure, could view its protests with respect, and we would not shirk the obligation either to speak up in defense of

Wide World Photo

A confrontation in 1969 between students and university administrators at the University of California (Berkeley Campus) led to the calling of troops. To what extent can the democratic system tolerate this kind of confrontation?

institutions and national practices which we have tolerated all our lives, or to join these young people in the quest for better ones.

But when we are confronted only with violence for violence's sake, and with attempts to frighten or intimidate an administration into doing things for which it can itself see neither the logic nor the electoral mandate; when we are offered, as the only argument for change, the fact that a number of people are themselves very angry and excited; and when we are presented with a violent objection to what exists, unaccompanied by any constructive concept of what, ideally, ought to exist in its place – then we of my generation can only recognize that such behavior bears a disconcerting resemblance to phenomena we have witnessed within our own time in the origins of totalitarianism in other countries, and then we have no choice but to rally to the defense of a public authority with which we may not be in agreement but which is the only one we've got and with which, in some form or another, we cannot dispense. People should bear in mind that if this – namely noise, violence, and lawlessness – is the way they are going to put their case, then many of us who are no happier than they are about some of the policies that arouse their indignation will have no choice but to place ourselves on the other side of the barricades.

PAST EXPERIENCE

The Greek Example

from *The Ever-Present Past*
by Edith Hamilton

The greatest civilization before ours was the Greek. They challenge us and we need the challenge. They, too, lived in a dangerous world. They were a little, highly civilized people, the only civilized people in the west, surrounded by barbarous tribes and with the greatest Asiatic power, Persia, always threatening them. In the end they succumbed, but the reason they did was not that the enemies outside were so strong, but that their own strength, their spiritual strength, had given way. While they had it they kept Greece unconquered and they left behind a record in art and thought which in all the centuries of human effort since has not been surpassed.

Basic to all the Greek achievement was freedom. The Athenians were the only free people in the world. In the great empires of antiquity – Egypt, Babylon, Assyria, Persia – splendid though they were, with riches beyond reckoning and immense power, freedom was unknown. The idea of it never dawned in any of them. It was born in Greece, a poor little country, but with it able to remain unconquered no matter what manpower and what wealth were arrayed against her. At Marathon and at Salamis overwhelming numbers of Persians had been defeated by small Greek forces. It had been proved that one free man was superior to many submissively obedient subjects of a tyrant. Athens was the leader in that amazing victory, and to the Athenians freedom was their dearest possession. Demosthenes said that they would not think it worth their while to live if they could not do so as free men, and years later a great teacher said, "Athenians, if you deprive them of their liberty, will die."

Athens was not only the first democracy in the world, it was also at its height an almost perfect democracy – that is, for men. There was no part in it for women or foreigners or slaves, but as far as the men were concerned it was more democratic than we are. The governing body was the Assembly, of which all citizens over eighteen were members. The Council of Five Hundred, which prepared business for the Assembly and, if requested, carried out what had been decided there, was made up of citizens who were chosen by lot. The same was true of the juries. Minor officials also were chosen by lot. The chief magistrates and the highest officers in the army were elected by the Assembly. Pericles was a general, very popular, who acted for a long time as if he were head of the state, but he had to be elected every year. Freedom of speech was the right the Athenians prized most and there has never been another state as free in that respect.

There was complete political equality. It was a government of the people, by the people, for the people. An unregenerate old aristocrat in the early fourth century B.C. writes: "If you *must* have a democracy, Athens is the perfect example. I object to it because it is based on the welfare of the lower, not the better, classes. In Athens the people who row the vessels and do the work have the advantage. It is their prosperity that is important." All the same, making the city beautiful was important too, as were also the great performances in the theatre. If, as Plato says, the Assembly was chiefly made up of cobblers and carpenters and smiths and farmers and retail businessmen, they approved the construction of the Parthenon and the other buildings on the Acropolis, and they crowded the theatre when the great tragedies were played. Not only did all free men share in the government; the love of the beautiful and the desire to have a part in creating it were shared by the many, not by a mere chosen few. That has happened in no state except Athens.

But those free Greeks owned slaves. What kind of freedom was that? The question would have been incomprehensible to the ancient world. There had always been slaves; they were a first necessity. The way of life everywhere was based upon them. They were taken for granted; no one ever gave them a thought. The very best Greek minds, the thinkers who discovered freedom and the solar system, had never an idea that slavery was evil. It is true that the greatest thinker of them all, Plato, was made uncomfortable by it. He said that slaves were often good, trustworthy, doing more for a man than his own family would, but he did not follow his thought through. The glory of being the first one to condemn it belongs to a man of the generation before Plato, the poet Euripides. He called it, "That thing of evil," and in several of his tragedies showed its evil for all to see. Greece first saw it for what it is. But the world went on in the same way. The Bible accepts it without comment. Two thousand years after the Stoics, less than a hundred years ago, the American Republic accepted it.

Athens treated her slaves well. A visitor to the city in the early fourth century B.C. wrote: "It is illegal here to deal a slave a blow. In the street he won't step aside to let you pass. Indeed you can't tell a slave by his dress; he looks like all the rest. They can go to the theatre too. Really, Athenians have established a kind of equality between slaves and free men." They were never a possible source of danger to the state as they were in Rome. There were no terrible slave wars and uprisings in Athens. In Rome, crucifixion was called "the slave's punishment". The Athenians did not practice crucifixion, and had no so-called slave's punishment. They were not afraid of their slaves.

In Athens' great prime Athenians were free. No one told them what they must do or what they should think – no church or political party or powerful private interests or labor unions. Greek schools had no donors of endowments they must pay attention to, no government financial backing which must be made secure by acting as the government wanted. To be sure, the result was that they had to take full responsibility, but that is always the price for full freedom. The Athenians were a strong people, they could pay the price. They were a thinking people; they knew what freedom means.

Miller Services, Toronto

This was the setting in which ancient Athenian democracy flourished.

They knew – not that they were free because their country was free – but that their country was free because they were free.

A reflective Roman traveling in Greece in the second century A.D. said, "None ever throve under democracy save the Athenians; *they* had the same self-control and were law-abiding." He spoke truly. That is what Athenian education aimed at, to produce men who would be able to maintain a self-governed state because they were themselves self-governed, self-controlled, self-reliant. Plato speaks of "the education in excellence which makes men long to be perfect citizens, knowing both how to rule and be ruled." "We are a free democracy," Pericles said. "We do not allow absorption in our own affairs to interfere with participation in the city's; we yield to none in independence of spirit and complete self-reliance, but we regard him who holds aloof from public affairs as useless." They called the useless man a "private" citizen, *idiotes*, from which our word "idiot" comes.

They had risen to freedom and to ennoblement from what Gilbert Murray calls "effortless barbarism"; they saw it all around them; they hated its filth and fierceness; nothing effortless was among the good things they wanted.

> Before the gates of Excellence the high
> gods have placed sweat.
> Long is the road thereto and steep and
> rough at the first,
> But when the height is won, then is
> there ease.

When or why the Greeks set themselves to travel on that road we do not know, but it led them away from habits and customs accepted everywhere that kept men down to barbaric filth and fierceness. It led them far. One example is enough to show the way they took. It was the custom – during how many millenniums, who can say? – for a victor to erect a trophy, a monument of his victory. In Egypt, where stone was plentiful, it would be a slab engraved with his glories. Farther east, where the sand took over, it might be a great heap of severed heads, quite permanent objects; bones last a long time. But in Greece, though a man could erect a trophy, it must be made of wood and it could never be repaired. Even as the victor set it up he would see in his mind how soon it would decay and sink into ruin, and there it must be left. The Greeks in their onward pressing along the steep and rough road had learned a great deal. They knew the victor might be the vanquished next time. Pericles said that Athens stood for freedom and for thought and for beauty, but in the Greek way, within limits, without exaggeration. The Athenians loved beauty, he said, but with simplicity; they did not like the extravagances of luxury. They loved the things of the mind, but they did not shrink from hardship. Thought did not cause them to hesitate, it clarified the road to action. If they had riches they did not make a show of them, and no one was ashamed of being poor if he was useful. They were free because of willing obedience to law, not only the written, but still more the unwritten, kindness and compassion and unselfishness and the many qualities which cannot be enforced, which depend on a man's free choice, but without which men cannot live together.

Discussion guidelines

1. "We regard him who holds aloof from public affairs as useless." To what extent do you think this Athenian concept of citizenship is shared by Canadian students? Give specific reasons for your opinion.
2. The Athenians "knew – not that they were free because their country was free – but that their country was free because they were free."
   (a) Explain the meaning of this statement.
   (b) How are truly free citizens created?

3. (a) Edith Hamilton has been criticized by some for idealizing ancient Athenian society. Seek evidence from additional reading to support or refute this criticism.
(b) Is Edith Hamilton right in saying that the Greeks "challenge us and we need the challenge"? Why?

Cross reference

A "Troublemaker", page 159

The Iroquoian Example

from *The Great Tree and the Longhouse*

by Hazel W. Hertzberg

[Although the date for the foundation of the Iroquois Confederacy remains a mystery (1350? 1450? 1550?), archaeologists and historians have been able to piece together a picture of a remarkable political organization – an ancient North American democracy! It is said that Iroquoian political practices provided guidelines for the framers of the American constitution; certainly, they offer a valuable case study for modern political scientists.]

The Confederacy Council consisted of fifty chiefs whose names or titles have come down to us. One title, that of Deganawidah,[1] is always left vacant, making the number of chiefs forty-nine in practice. There were nine each from the Mohawk and Oneida nations, fourteen from the Onondaga, ten from the Cayuga, and eight from the Seneca. We are not sure why the distribution was unequal. The best guess is that each chief originally was the head chief of his village, and the number of villages in a tribe varied. We should not jump to the conclusion that a larger number from a tribe meant it had more power. It did not. Each nation voted as a unit, so it did not matter how many representatives there were in a tribal delegation.

But some of the founding nations were more powerful than others. This was recognized by giving them special rights and responsibilities. The Mohawks, the powerful easternmost nation whose territory bordered on that of the hostile Algonquins, were made the Keepers of the Eastern Door of the great symbolic Longhouse. In recognition of their leading role in forming the Confederacy, the Mohawks were also given special rights. No League meeting was considered legal unless all the Mohawk Confederacy Chiefs were present. Nor could the Council pass a measure if the Mohawks protested.

The westernmost nation and the most populous, the Senecas, were the Keepers of the Western Door. Bordering their territory also were unfriendly tribes. The two War Chiefs of the League were chosen from among the delegates of the warlike Senecas.

The Onondagas, whose lands lay in the middle of Iroquoia, were appointed Keepers of the Central Fire. They held the wampum belonging to the League. They called the meetings and set up the agenda. If they disagreed with a Council decision, they could veto it, but their veto could be overridden, as we shall see. The Onondaga chief, Atotarho, was moderator of the Council, but his power

[1] Deganawidah was one of the two mythical hero founders of the Iroquoian Confederacy.

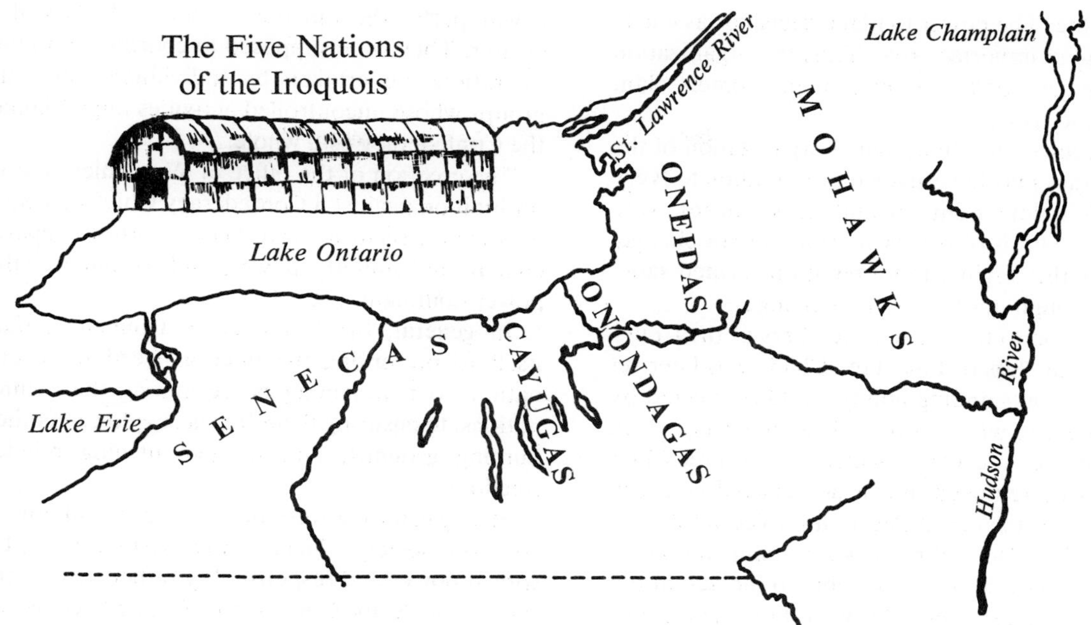

was not really greater than that of the other chiefs. He was a presiding officer rather than a chief with authority over others. In one respect he was given power. No decisions, except very unimportant ones, could be made in his absence. Such an arrangement was characteristic of much of Iroquois political organization: the power to stop something rather than the power to get something done.

Thus the big three – the Mohawks, the Onondagas, and the Senecas – were given special rights and duties. Their titles as Keepers were part of the conception of the League as a Longhouse. . . .

In order to understand how the Confederacy Chiefs were chosen, it is necessary to understand village government. The Confederacy was firmly based on village and clan.

Each village in Iroquoia had its own village council, which looked after village affairs. Members of the council were men – clan representatives chosen by the Clan Matron of each clan in consultation with the other women of the clan. Each village had a head chief, who presided over the village council. Thus village government consisted of men who represented clans and who were chosen by women.

Although the details are not clear, it appears that each nation or tribe had a council made up of these head chiefs of the villages. The tribal council managed tribal affairs.

In turn, the Confederacy Council consisted of the tribal chiefs. We are not sure whether or not this council included all the tribal chiefs, but probably it did in the beginning. In any case, this council of Confederacy Chiefs had jurisdiction over all the member nations in certain matters.

All the Confederacy Chiefs were men, but they were chosen and could be removed by women. The office of Confederacy Chief was hereditary within clans from certain localities. Within each such clan, the Chief Matron, in consultation with other clan women, named a chief from among the clan members. Once elected, a Confederacy Chief held office for life, unless he was removed for a serious offense or became too ill to hold office.

The power to name and remove Confederacy Chiefs gave women an important role in Iroquois political life. The power to make decisions as chiefs gave men an important role. Thus the organization of the League took account of men, women, clan, village, and tribe.

As we have said, the original organization of the Confederacy may have given representation to every village. As time went on and new villages were formed, the basis of representation did not change. Evidently the original representation seemed satisfactory enough not to require a change.

In addition to the regular members of the Council, a special class of Pine Tree Chiefs was later set up. Men of outstanding ability could be elected by the Council, in whose proceedings they were given a voice but no vote. Once elected, a Pine Tree Chief could not be removed, but if he behaved contrary to the laws of the Great Peace, his voice would not be listened to. He had no power to name a successor. By this device it was possible to include in the Council respected men who were not members of clans entitled to name chiefs or who came from clans already represented. Perhaps the class of Pine Tree Chiefs was created to widen the basis of representation to the Council without altering the basic structure of the League.

Members of the Confederacy Council were not permitted to engage in warfare. If a Confederacy Chief wished to go on the warpath, he had to lay aside his horns of office and fight as a common warrior. A temporary chief could be appointed in his place by his clan women. After his war service was done, he might then take up the horns of office again. Apparently it was thought proper to keep the chiefs of the Great Peace from engaging in warfare. Since the Confederacy Chiefs were usually men too old to go on the warpath, this situation probably did not arise too often.

However, the Confederacy itself had two War Chiefs. While they were permitted to go on the warpath, their main duty was not to fight but to command field operations undertaken by the League. If we recall that Iroquois warfare was organized quite informally, and that any warrior could get up a war party, the function of these chiefs will be clearer. They were supposed to coordinate military operations undertaken by individuals and small groups whose uncontrolled activities might damage the Confederacy as a whole.

The creation of the office of War Chief, and the prohibition against a Confederacy Chief's engaging in warfare, seem to have been efforts to separate civilian and military power, and to make civilian power dominant. . . .

In general, the Confederacy Council confined itself to preserving the internal freedom of each nation, to maintaining peace among the member nations, to ensuring them free access to each other's hunting grounds, and to guaranteeing religious freedom.

Strong central government was quite unknown to Iroquois society. Their whole system tended to spread power and responsibility rather than to concentrate it. At the Confederacy Council, a chief was an equal among equals. The Iroquois never concentrated power in one man and gave very little even to a group of men. The word "chief" in our language suggests a figure in command in a way that does not correspond to Iroquois reality. In fact, in historic times the white man often thought that the chief he was dealing with had more power to commit his people than he actually had. The white man was often disappointed in his expectations.

The Confederacy Constitution provided for consultation with the people. On matters of grave importance, the Council members were directed to meet with the people, and abide by their decision. The male or female members of any clan could also meet and bring a matter to the attention of the Council. People had the right to form committees and appoint delegates to bring important matters to the Council for consideration. Such provisions made it possible for the people to bring their views to bear directly on the Council. Because the Iroquois were not very numerous, such devices could work very well.

The Iroquois believed that their Confederacy

might eventually bring into the Great Peace all the nations of the world. But the terms for admission of new members were not such as to make it very attractive for other nations to join unless they needed League protection. On the one hand, new nations were guaranteed freedom in running their own religious and internal affairs. This was, of course, an inducement to join. However, new nations were not given a direct voice in the League Council. Foreign nations had to apply for membership through one of the Five Nations. Their membership was temporary, since they could be expelled for behavior contrary to the rules of the Great Peace. A foreign nation remained under the wing of one of the original five and spoke through it at Council meetings. . . .

The Iroquois wanted to make provision for other nationalities to join, but at the same time, they wanted to protect their own lands and their own domination of the League. They did not want the admission of foreign nations to involve them in foreign quarrels, nor did they want the old enemies of newly admitted nations to become their enemies.

One of the conditions of admission to the League was a pledge that the new nation would do its best to persuade others to join, and would refrain from warfare against other nations.

The Confederacy Constitution actually provided for the conquest of nations which refused to accept the Great Peace. Three councils were to be held with the foreign nation to persuade it to join. If after three councils the effort was unsuccessful, the League might then make war upon it. After the foreign nation was conquered, it could join the Confederacy under terms which were much like those providing for the admission of any foreign nation. In this way the Iroquois tried to relate the purposes of war to the purposes of the Confederacy. . . .

The Confederacy met at least once a year, frequently in late August but sometimes in September or October, in the land of the Onondagas, the Keepers of the Central Fire. Not only were the Confederacy Chiefs in attendance, but also many other people including women and children were seated around the council fire.

The meeting opened with prayer, offered by the Onondaga delegates. Thanks were returned to the Great Creator in a Thanksgiving Address like that used in the Green Corn and Midwinter festivals. Then songs were sung around the fire by each nation in turn.

The chiefs were always seated in a traditional order. On the east side of the fire sat the Elder Brothers, with the Mohawks sitting to the north. On the west side sat the Younger Brothers, the Cayugas to the north. In the center were the Onondagas, seated to the north side of the Council fire. Thus they were grouped into three phratries.

Council debate was carried on across the fire. Debate was frequently very long and drawn out. A proposition offered for Council consideration could not be debated on the same day it was proposed. Nor could the Council meet after nightfall, when men were in the realm of the left-handed twin.

The Council had a number of procedures designed to help the members come to a unanimous decision, for the Iroquois set great store by unanimity. The matter for debate was first discussed separately by each national delegation, which had to come to a unanimous decision. This meant that one strong-minded person in a delegation could block a vote, but strong pressure might be put on that person. A decision once arrived at had the weight of unanimity behind it.

Next, two of the phratries met together to discuss the proposition, the Mohawks with the Senecas, the Cayugas with the Oneidas. When they had agreed to "speak with one voice" – that is, unanimously – the Mohawks, representing the Elder Brothers, announced their decision. If the Younger Brothers agreed, they so notified the Mohawks, who then announced the agreement of both phratries to the Onondagas. Speaking for the third phratry, Atotarho confirmed that the matter was settled.

If the Onondagas, through any misunderstanding or obstinacy, rendered a decision different from that already agreed on by the other phratries, the matter was again considered by the Elder Brothers and the Younger Brothers. If, after reconsideration, these phratries came to the same decision, the Onondagas were compelled to confirm it. Thus the Onondagas had a kind of veto over the decisions of the others, but the veto could be overridden.

What happened if there was disagreement? In such a case, the proposition was returned to the point where the disagreement had developed. If, for instance, the Mohawks and Senecas could not agree, the proposition was returned to them to see if they could work it out. If the Younger Brothers could not agree with the Elder Brothers, they met together to try to resolve the difference. If they still were unable to agree, the Mohawks announced this fact. Then the Onondagas met together and rendered a decision. Their decision was then conveyed to the Mohawks, who announced it to the open Council.

Discussion guidelines

1. By considering both its decision-making procedures and its checks and balances, indicate why the Iroquoian form of government has been hailed as an almost perfect democracy.
2. "The granting of political power to women was not only unique for the times but also for generations thereafter." How do you account for the political role played by Iroquoian women?
3. "Although an interesting experiment, the Iroquoian system of government would simply not work in a modern, industrialized society." In the light of the preceding statement, comment on the value of studying this system.
4. How do you explain the fact that we have heard so much about Greek democracy and so little about Iroquoian democracy?

Cross references

Democracy and Minorities, page 115
Claims Canada Lagging in Promoting Women, page 168

DESPOTISM REJECTED

Leaders Are More Important

from *Democracy and the Student Left*

Any system regardless of its political hue is no better nor worse than those people who run it. I do not believe in American democracy really, I merely accept it. I believe in wise, intelligent, and knowing men. I believe in government by the ablest. I believe in a better life by better minds. American democracy has been able to provide this through the years, and to that extent I wish to congratulate American democracy on its good fortune. But there's nothing inherent in American democracy which preserves government by the best minds. In fact there's a frightening number of forces in the system working in just the contrary direction. And today it seems to me luck is not with us, for those forces are prevailing. Government is not the instrument of enlightened statesmen, but the plaything of ignorant and psychologically torn men. There are few good men in government. And those who are good are relatively without power. This is to say, then, that I'm willing to posit that a single-party authoritarian state can meet the demands of a society every bit as capably as American democracy has met the demands of its society, if its leaders are able and wise. As long as the best men rule, I'd say the product would be more or less beneficial.

CURTIS W. DOWDS, YALE '68

The Ideal State

from *Considerations on Representative Government*

by John Stuart Mill – an abridged text

It has long been said that a despotic monarchy would be the best form of government, if a good despot could be guaranteed. I consider this a dangerous misunderstanding of what good government really is. According to this theory, if you put absolute power into the hands of an outstanding individual, you would be sure to get honest, intelligent government. Under such a government, the theory goes, good laws would be enforced; bad laws would be reformed; the best men would be appointed to positions of trust; justice would be well administered; public burdens would be wisely imposed and as light as possible; and every branch of government would be the best that circumstances allowed.

I am willing, for the sake of argument, to admit all this – but I must point out that the theory contains an essential flaw. This form of government requires not only a good monarch, but an all-seeing one as well. Such a monarch would have to be correctly informed, at all times, and in considerable detail, about the conduct and working of every branch of his administration, in every district of his entire country. He would have to give daily attention, and effective supervision, to every part of this vast field – and he would only have the normal twenty-four hours that are granted to men, whether king or labourer, in which to do all this. If he could not do it, he would at least have to be able to select from among his subjects a large number of honest and talented men who were suited to conduct every branch of public administration, while remaining themselves under effective supervision and control. Our monarch would also need the ability to choose certain outstanding men who could be trusted to do without supervision, and, in fact, be capable of supervising others.

If the situation that I describe were to occur, what should we have then? – One man of superhuman mental activity managing the entire affairs of a mentally passive people. The nation as a whole, and every individual composing it, would be without any voice in their own destiny. They would not be able to make their will felt in matters that were of vital concern to all. Everything would be decided for them by a will that was not their own, and which it was a crime to disobey.

But what sort of human beings could be formed under such a system? How far could the thinking and active capacities of such a people develop? On matters that involved theory only, such beings might perhaps be allowed to speculate, as long as their thoughts did not approach politics, nor have the slightest connection with its practice. At the most, they could only be allowed to make suggestions on practical matters. But even under the most moderate despots, only superior people, who already have a reputation, could hope to have their suggestions heard by the men who administered affairs. And it would be much less certain that even the views of such outstanding individuals would be really considered.

Under such a despotism, moreover, much more would be affected than the people's intelligence. Their moral capacities would be equally stunted. This would arise because a person's feelings are intensified when he can act on them. Let a person have nothing to do for his country, and he will not care for it. Indeed, the ancient saying is true: in a despotism, there is at most but one patriot – the despot himself.

Discussion guidelines

1. "The argument concerning the best form of government boils down to the fact that either man is capable of governing himself or he is not." By citing some examples, defend your opinion of the best form of government.

you're nothing but a punched hole in a computer card and a big machine counts your ballot before you vote —
Macpherson Toronto Star

© *The Toronto Star*, with permission of Duncan Macpherson

2. To what extent do you think the computer will become the despot of modern society?

Cross references

Men Need Rulers, page 14
In Defence of Equality, page 15
Does Dictatorship Create Order?, page 73
The Individual in Society, page 139
The Unknown Citizen, page 142
A "Troublemaker", page 159

HOW FREE ARE WE?

Our "Free Society"

from *The Smug Minority*
by Pierre Berton

The word "freedom" has had such a working-over during two post-war decades that it has become almost meaningless. "Our basic freedoms" . . . "our free way of life" . . . "the freedom we enjoy" . . . who has not heard these phrases rolling glibly from the tongues of politicians and public speakers? And who has not heard that all-encompassing phrase "the free world" – a world which includes such nations as Portugal where freedom is spat upon and trampled? With all this talk of freedom, who can blame the new generation for demanding more? For this is exactly what they are asking for: freedom to dress the way they wish, freedom to use their own brands of intoxicant, freedom to demonstrate in the streets, freedom to speak and read and see without censorship, to spout poetry in the parks, to walk the streets shoeless without police interference, and to question the major values of adult society.

But this is not the kind of freedom the smug minority talks about when its members gather together.

Charles E. Wilson, President of General Motors (U.S.A.), addresses the Empire Club in Toronto in January 1951 and tells it what it wants to hear

"For more than one hundred and fifty years, free men in our countries have had the opportunities to educate themselves, choose their own religions, select their own occupations, accumulate capital and invent better ways of doing things.

"The reason the people of our countries are relatively more prosperous results from the simple fact that, by accepting the challenge of individual competition as a responsibility that comes with personal freedom, we have done a better job of applying our human energy and individual initiative to the improvement, not only of ourselves, but of all. . . . Our political systems that permit and promote individual enterprise, personal responsibility, free competition, respect for the rights of others, freedom of choice and decision, freedom itself, are the final important factors that make the difference between our country and others."

H. Gordon Love, President of the Canadian Chamber of Commerce, speaks to the forty-eighth annual meeting of the U.S. Chamber, attacks the welfare state, and praises "those tried and proved weapons – the resourcefulness of individual freedom and individual enterprise":

"We must cherish freedom, understand it, believe in it, and desire it so strongly that nothing will shake our purpose to maintain it and expand it."

It is quite clear that the freedoms meant here are of a very special kind and have very little to do with the nature of the freedoms upon which the new generation is insisting. When businessmen talk about freedom they mean the freedom to operate with the minimum of government interference, to charge the highest prices the market will bear, to pay the lowest wages they can get away with, and to organize cosy little monopolies without federal snooping. These freedoms include freedom from higher taxation, freedom to choose one's own charities (or none at all), and freedom from government regulation.

Unfair! scream the businessmen. *Untrue! There is government regulation and we don't object to it. There are laws against monopolies and we go along with them. Unions regulate hours and wages and the government sets minimum wages and we accept all that. We simply think things have gone far enough. We don't want further interference. We don't want the welfare state to go any further. If it does, then we say that freedom is in jeopardy.*

Well, all right. And it is also true that all the things the business establishment now says it accepts, from the right to organize to the eight-hour day, it once opposed vehemently as an erosion of freedom or an economic impossibility. It has been dragged kicking and screaming down the road to social progress, crying out at every step that we have gone far enough, that it is time to call a halt, that anything new will wreck the country. And always it has yammered about freedom.

Most of the time when people mouth clichés about our "free society", they mean that we are politically free. And so we are to a considerable extent, more so than most peoples in the world. Yet even in this sense we are not as free as we think or as free as we could be. Westerners are always boasting to Communists about their right to boo their country's leaders. But in the summer of 1967, a young art critic named Barry Lord discovered he wasn't free to utter aloud a dissenting political opinion on Canadian soil. When Lord shouted the words "murderer" and "bloody butcher" at Lyndon Johnson during the United States President's visit to Expo '67, he was immediately seized by four plainclothesmen, manhandled, punched, held for seven hours, and ultimately fined one hundred dollars for disturbing the peace. As Lord remarked later, quoting Bertrand Russell, "I had my freedom until I needed it."

The right to free speech and free expression in Canada is hedged around with a variety of factors, many of them economic. A very large proportion of Canadians are afraid of being outspoken because of the fear – a real one – of losing their jobs if they express unorthodox opinions. When I was a newspaper columnist, I received letters every day expressing views on a variety of subjects from people who asked me not to use their names for that reason.

It is true that in a Communist country any man who publicly expresses consistent capitalist leanings will find himself in trouble and probably in jail. It is equally true that anyone who publicly expresses consistent Communist opinions in Canada will find himself out of a job, socially ostracized, and economically strangled.

Still, we can vote, we can write letters to the press, we can talk and argue freely, we can (if we can afford it) publish and distribute pamphlets, buy radio and newspaper space for unpopular causes, carry signs of protest (as long as we have a permit and don't commit the awful crime of interfering with traffic), and, in one or two places, even stand up on soap boxes and make speeches (as long as we don't cause a riot). And we cannot be jailed for our views.

But there are other freedoms denied to large numbers of Canadians, and to many these freedoms are just as important, perhaps more important, than the periodical freedom to vote or to dissent. When Charles Wilson tells Canadians that free men here have the opportunity to educate themselves, to select their own occupations, and to accumulate capital, he is promoting one of the great myths of the age. The truth is that large numbers of men and women have not had the opportunity to educate themselves to the limits of their mental abilities. The truth is that twenty-five per cent of all adult Canadians have not been able to accumulate any liquid capital at all. The truth is that an army of people are working in jobs which are not really of their own choosing and which can only be described as degrading. None of these people can be said to be free in the proper sense of that overworked and mangled word.

A poor man is not free and a destitute man is as much a prisoner as a convict; indeed a convict generally eats better. A man who can't afford a streetcar ticket, let alone real travel, who can exercise no real choice in matters of food, clothing, and shelter, who cannot follow the siren song of the TV commercials, who can scarcely afford bus fare to the library let alone a proper education for himself or his children – is such a man free in an affluent nation? There are such men and women in Canada and their numbers are legion. Until there is a basic economic floor beneath them, these people cannot begin to participate in the whole range of what we mean when we talk glibly about a free society.

Discussion guidelines

1. "Democracy is a farce, unless it guarantees both economic and political freedom to the citizenry as a whole – not merely to a business élite."
   (a) Is this what Pierre Berton is saying? Explain.
   (b) On the basis of your experience, to what extent do you agree or disagree with this statement?
2. "The basic weakness of democracy has always been what the Greeks called 'stasis', or class war. Given political equality, the lower classes . . . have sooner or later used their vote to [rob] the rich." (C. Northcote Parkinson, *Can Democracy Survive?*)
   To what degree do you think this observation applies to present-day Canada?

Us Too

A Photographic Essay
by Ian MacEachern

Prince Edward Island, June 1968

Trefann Court, Toronto, May 1968

Trefann Court, Toronto, May 1968

North end of Saint John, N.B., May 1966.

MINORITY RIGHTS?

1

Democracy and Minorities

from *Democratic Government*
by R. MacGregor Dawson

Democratic government is more than a form of organization and more than cleverly designed machinery; it is also, as a Canadian Governor-General, Lord Tweedsmuir, once said, "a spiritual testament". It implies a number of vitally important beliefs and traditions which have been woven into the democratic fabric and have become quite inseparable from it. Among these are tolerance or a proper consideration for the opinions of others, freedom of discussion and criticism, freedom of religious beliefs, a respect for law, a regard for the rights of both the majority and the various minority groups into which the people are divided. Thus while it is true that, generally speaking, the wishes of the majority must prevail and the minorities must willingly accept the decisions of the majority, it is equally true that the minority also have certain rights, and there must be a corresponding willingness by the majority to recognize these rights as guaranteed. The degree to which this "willingness" is displayed is one of the distinguishing marks of modern governments.

2

Canadian Sins Against Minorities

from *Why I Am a Separatist*
by Marcel Chaput

You think I am exaggerating, that the Canadian psychological climate has nothing terribly evil about it? Let us examine some of these contradictions, against which any national of a normal state is protected, but with which, on the contrary, every French Canadian must struggle daily.

- He is a Canadian, but he is also a French Canadian.
- His country is the whole of Canada, but he is accepted only in Quebec.
- He is told that he belongs to the great French civilization, but simultaneously he hears someone speak of "those damned Frenchmen".
- He is forced to be bilingual; the others are unilingual.
- He hears nothing but praise at school and elsewhere for the beauty of the French language; he is obliged to learn English.
- He is told that Canada is a country which united two cultures; he has difficulty getting service in west Montreal if he uses French.
- He thinks he speaks an international language; people snarl out "Speak White" in his face.
- He enters the French university only to study from American text-books.
- He is told all about national unity, but is ordered: "Stay in your province."
- He hears people insist that Canada is an independent country: every day he sees another country's queen on his coinage and on his stamps.
- He is told that his province is the most wealthy;

it is always in his province that there is the most unemployment.

- He is told that he is eligible for any position; but he is hampered by the extra obligation of bilingualism.
- He is roused to Canadian patriotism, but all he hears played is God Save the Queen.
- He is incited to rid himself of his inferiority complex; then he hears someone assert that he is not mature enough to govern himself.
- He is urged toward self-respect, and as his emblem he is given a sheep.

And so on down to the last death rattle. Yet people are at a loss to explain why the corner merchant doesn't make it a point of pride to advertise in French, why our young men lack the power to think big, why the pupil who tops his class suddenly loses his enthusiasm.

Anyone who would want a nation to disappear would not act differently.

© *The Toronto Star*, with permission of Duncan Macpherson

Discussion guidelines

1. In a democracy "the minority also have certain rights, and there must be a corresponding willingness by the majority to recognize these rights".
   (a) To what extent has progress been made to meet complaints such as those voiced by Marcel Chaput in 1962 in his book *Why I Am a Separatist*?
   (b) Submit remedies to the grievances outlined by Chaput which you think might be acceptable to others like him, as well as to the majority of Canadians.
   (c) How can the rights of minorities be effectively recognized and protected in a democratic state?
2. "For 100 years, Indians have not controlled, in any meaningful sense, their lands, monies, business transactions, social, community and local government activities." (Peter A. Cumming, *The Globe and Mail*, Toronto, February 24, 1969)
   (a) On the basis of personal research, account for this treatment of Canada's Indian minority group.
   (b) How can Canada claim to be a democratic country, and yet allow conditions as described by Cumming to exist?
   (c) Suggest workable solutions to this problem.

Cross references

My Dungeon Shook, page 165
"Claims Canada Lagging in Promoting Women", page 168
Civil Disobedience: National and International, page 181

Miller Services, Toronto

"They but forget we Indians owned the land
From ocean unto ocean; that they stand
Upon a soil that centuries agone
Was our sole kingdom and our right alone."

Pauline Johnson (1862-1913)

RULE BY AD-MEN AND THE MASS MEDIA?

The Pearson Image

from *The Distemper of Our Times*
by Peter C. Newman

The task of creating a favourable public image for the Pearsons occupied the energies of a long line of earnest and frustrated public relations and television specialists. While in Opposition, Pearson seemed willing to put up with practically any indignity to create some kind of rapport with his television audiences. Expert after expert was given complete freedom to make him look as warm on TV as he was with small groups of friends. A voice coach was brought in from Toronto and writers were hired to remove as many sibilants as possible from his scripts so that he could hide his speech problem. Toronto's MacLaren Advertising Company exhausted its considerable resources trying to improve his television manner. The TV manipulators tried a dozen different settings – intimate soirées, crowd scenes, living-room shots, interviews with academics – but nothing really worked. Lester Pearson emptied many a living room in his time. "They're trying to make me look like 'Danger Man' but I feel more like 'The Fugitive'," Pearson complained to a friend about his TV advisers.

Unfortunately for him, Pearson's political ascendancy coincided with the breakthrough of television as the most important medium through which politicians communicate with the voters. The adroit exploitation of television made it possible to maintain the nation in a constant state of political mobilization. The whole country became a whispering gallery, with political triumphs and errors flashed from coast to coast as they happened. Just as few TV comedians could survive more than two seasons (when they used to go on for twenty years on the vaudeville boards), there was a constant demand for new faces and new ideas in politics. "Television has made democracy workable," wrote Roy Shields, television critic for the *Toronto Daily Star*. "Gone, or going, are the phony rhetoric, the wheeling and dealing, the rule of the oligarchy. To gain power these days, a politician has to present himself to the people through TV, a medium that tears the mask from all who dare to appear before it."

Pearson could not cope with this revolution in communications.

His frantic image-makers recognized the problem but their diagnosis for his failure was shortsighted and inadequate. They blamed his high-pitched voice, his persistent lisp, the total absence in him of a sense of occasion. These were relevant liabilities but the real reason he could not communicate with the people was that fundamentally he didn't wish to do so.

Miller Services, Toronto

2

Trudeau: His Image Has Everything
from *Pendulum of Power*
by J. Murray Beck

On April 6, 1968, Liberals chose as their national leader Pierre Elliott Trudeau, whose very existence had only dawned on English Canadians a few months before. "Never in our history has a man risen from the herd to grasp supreme political power with such dazzling notoriety."[1] Late in 1965, when he decided to give Quebec federalists a stronger voice at Ottawa, he was not even a member of the Liberal party. Not until April 1967 did he enter the cabinet as Minister of Justice. Circumstances and accident had provided him the best possible stage to display "his qualities at a time when the public [was] unimpressed with the familiar faces of the declared candidates" for the leadership.[2] Towards the end of 1967 he caught the eye of English Canada with his proposal to broaden the divorce law and his omnibus bill to liberalize the Criminal Code with respect to homosexuality and abortion. Then, at the constitutional conference of February 1968,

> before a spellbound nation . . . he sparred with steel wits against the member from Bagot, Premier Daniel Johnson . . . [and] burst upon the consciousness of tired, discouraged federalists of every background as a leader to defend the citadel of eroding federal power.[3]

The confrontation between Trudeau and Johnson catered to the Anglo-Saxon backlash everywhere; here was a Frenchman who could put the trouble-making Frenchmen in their place. However, this merit simply reinforced his more intangible qualities of charisma and style. It has been suggested that the mass media produced the Trudeau boom for the leadership. Anthony Westell denies it: "The press and TV began to hear about Mr. Trudeau from the grassroots before they took him seriously as a possible candidate."[4] But once they did he was irresistible. "Through sheer force of personality, the demagogue . . . appropriated the nation's attention for six weeks. . . . One can't deny he got [power] with the eager complicity of nearly all the country's media outside his native province."[5] An avid public got its fill of

> the Mercedes sports car, ascot ties and sandals. The racy reputation as wealthy bachelor surrounded by beautiful women. The academic

[1]Toronto *Globe and Mail*, April 23, 1968.

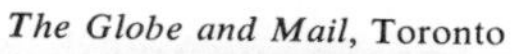
The Globe and Mail, Toronto

[2]Anthony Westell, ibid., February 12, 1968.
[3]Keith Spicer, ibid., April 23, 1968.
[4]Anthony Westell, ibid., February 12, 1968.
[5]Keith Spicer, ibid., April 23, 1968.

> achievements at some of the world's best universities. The judo brown belt, and acquaintance with yoga. . . . The crusading intellectual who campaigned against Duplessis, helped launch Quebec's Quiet Revolution, went to work as a trade union adviser in the struggle for social justice, [and] opposed nuclear arms in 1963.[6]

Only "the chicken syndrome" – as Charles Lynch put it – stood between him and the leadership. Was he too big a gamble for the Liberal establishment? Knowledgeable Conservatives watched their television screens hopefully as the opposition [united] against Trudeau, the only candidate they really feared. But all efforts to stop him were ineffective. Once established as Prime Minister, Pierre Elliott Trudeau was free to pursue his "love-in" with the media and the public. When he presented a makeshift cabinet consisting largely of hold-overs and decided on an immediate dissolution without presenting a program to Parliament, he largely escaped the shellacking that such action would have normally produced.

Just as the Prime Minister dominated the election, so he must dominate any account of it. During his campaign for the leadership he had shown he could "turn the people on"; prior to his formal electioneering he caused "frenzied scenes of clutching, pushing and shouting"[7] wherever he went. As George Bain told an American audience, "Canada has a case of Trudeaumania."[8] All sorts of people succumbed: teeny-boppers, students, young businessmen, working men, elegant women, academics – even older people. But Pied Piper Trudeau aroused most excitement among the young. Kids, it was said, had found a new kick: politics. "It beats LSD, glue-sniffing, Beatles and transcendental meditation, they find."[9] Trudeau told "the young people that politics is more fulfilling than pot, and they seem to agree."[10]

The Liberal organizers, wrote Gary Oakes, would have had to have "rocks in their heads not to capitalize on Mr. Trudeau's greatest asset – the exciting response his presence evokes everywhere".[11] In his first formal campaigning – a swing through metro Toronto – he discovered the ideal forum for what Dalton Camp called "a non-campaign":[12] the shopping plaza. But although his opponents derided him as Pierre de la Plaza, there was nothing wrong in itself in his going where the people were, to plazas, parks, and city hall steps, "finding the people who [were] not committed and [wouldn't] go to a rally in the evening because it [was] miles away from the suburb in which they [lived]". Largely abandoning the concept of the formal meeting, he sped across the country in a DC-9 jet – thus reinforcing his modern, glamorous image – sometimes visiting three provinces in one day. By using helicopters to reach small centres, he created "the anticipatory excitement of a god descending from the sun into the midst of his people. . . . This is the jet age, man. And there is the jet age candidate."[13]

A superb organization masterminded by William Lee ensured that everything went according to plan. Action Trudeau girls in orange and white miniskirted costumes acted as guards of honour. Introductory speeches were short and snappy. There was the ovation as the Prime Minister moved to the podium; he gave a quiet smile, a slow wave, and a few minutes of a soft-toned and usually slight message. He made another surge through the crowds, signed a few autograph books and Trudeau pictures, and went on by jet to the next shopping centre.[14] Reporters said this "mad mod election cam-

[6]Anthony Westell, ibid., February 12, 1968.
[7]Ottawa *Citizen*, May 13, 1968.
[8]*New York Times Magazine*, June 16, 1968.
[9]Toronto *Star*, May 11, 1968.

[10]Ottawa *Citizen*, May 14, 1968.
[11]Gary Oakes, Toronto *Telegram*, May 18, 1968.
[12]Dalton Camp, Toronto *Star*, June 29, 1968.
[13]Anthony Westell, Toronto *Globe and Mail*, June 22, 1968.
[14]Halifax *Chronicle-Herald*, June 5, 1968.

paign with [its] exploding color and excitement" was "like looking at a psychedelic film."[15]

In other respects, too, the Trudeau campaign was unconventional. He declined to lay out a catalogue of specific policies but concentrated on describing and indicating his attitudes towards the problems and challenges he outlined.[16] As George Bain put it, "He has said, in effect, these are the attitudes I bring to public questions, this is the turn of my mind: never mind the specifics, take a chance, we'll deal with the problems as they come up."[17] At places such as Oakville he appealed to Canadians' spirit of adventure. A young, dynamic, progressive people possessing a wealthy country should not be afraid of change. "We don't want to buy back the past like the old parties with old ideas. . . . If [Canadians] want to take a bit of a risk, if they want to take a chance on the future, then we're asking them to vote for us."[18]

This was the man and the stance against which the opposing leaders had to contend. Basically, Robert Stanfield and T. C. Douglas conducted conventional campaigns, although holding the normal type of meeting itself constituted a risk. When projected through the media it might appear to be a failure – "no great crowds, no wild cheering, no color or drama or excitement".[19] Anthony Westell even wondered if Stanfield's reliance on a propeller-driven DC-7C hurt his image. Had Canadian politics "vaulted straight from the train to the jet"?[20]

Newspaper readers must have tired of hearing about the quiet, unassuming person that Stanfield was – a man who conducted a low-key campaign that underwhelmed his listeners, whose "gothic mask of unconcern [hid him] from public scrutiny", and who continued to deliver halting, strained, monotonous speeches "with here a tired joke, there a platitude".[21] Stanfield suffered, of course, from comparison with Trudeau. It might have been better, however, if he had avoided projecting an artificial image on television and had altogether spurned the "sock-it-to-'em" type of oratory. Some thought he needed a communicator to help him project his virtues, and suggested that Dalton Camp would have been ideal if it had not meant reviving the allegations that Stanfield was his puppet.[22] But T. C. Douglas needed no communicator, and he was not being heard either. In this election public and newspapermen alike had eyes for the performance of only one man.

Both Stanfield and Douglas hoped to make the government's record on economic questions a major issue, but failed. According to Douglas, the greatest problem of the election had been to get the Prime Minister to discuss the issues.[23] "Nothing but a theatrical performance . . . contemptuous of the democratic process," said Stanfield.[24] "For the first time in Canadian history a prime minister has asked the people for a blank cheque."[25]

What was the source of enthusiasm for Trudeau? It had much to do with both the mood of the country and the image of the leader. Supposedly, "the Canadian style changed in 1967. The Quiet Canadian became the Confident Canadian during the Centennial."[26] In the mood of 1968 they were not likely to turn to Robert Stanfield whose image, according to Marshall McLuhan, may be "Abe Lincoln", but is also that of "an archaeological exhibit". In contrast, the Trudeau image had everything.[27]

[15]Ottawa *Citizen*, May 31, 1968.
[16]Toronto *Globe and Mail*, May 17, 1968.
[17]George Bain, Toronto *Globe and Mail*, June 22, 1968.
[18]Toronto *Globe and Mail*, June 15, 1968.
[19]Ibid., May 29, 1968.
[20]Anthony Westell, ibid.

[21]Toronto *Star*, May 14, 1968.
[22]Toronto *Globe and Mail*, June 22, 1968.
[23]Montreal *Star*, May 28, 1968.
[24]Toronto *Star*, May 31, 1968.
[25]Halifax *Mail-Star*, June 25, 1968.
[26]Anthony Westell, Toronto *Globe and Mail*, June 22, 1968.
[27]Montreal *Gazette*, June 12, 1968.

3

HOW A HIP PM FILLED THE SQUARE

By JOHN BURNS

If the Liberal strategists who planned yesterday's noon rally for Prime Minister Pierre Trudeau in Toronto's City Hall Square wanted one thing, it was the sharpest possible contrast with Robert Stanfield's anti-climactic election appearance in the city on Monday night.

And contrast they got.

At least 40,000 people – the largest turnout for a Canadian political rally – crammed the square, the parade route, and the windows of surrounding buildings to catch a glimpse of the suntanned bachelor on whose shoulders the Liberal fortunes ride.

Promised tax cut

Two nights before, 4,500 faithful Tories traipsed out to the CNE Coliseum (seating capacity 5,500) to watch a display of ethnic dancing and hear their leader promise income tax deductions on mortgage interest rates. Even Mr. Stanfield's most ardent admirers were hard pushed to rate the evening a success.

The comparison, of course, is invidious – (City Hall Square at lunchtime being a far cry from an evening rally at the CNE) but it will be made.

Paul Goulet, a 28-year-old advertising executive who supervised the promotional activities behind the rally, had the air of a bespectacled Cheshire cat as he sat in his office minutes after it ended.

"When we started our planning three weeks ago, we knew Stanfield would be here some time in the last week of the campaign, and it was a safe bet the Tories would go for the traditional kind of indoor political rally where you pump your people in by the bus-load.

"We decided to forgo all that, and try for something a little more genuine – an open-air event which would draw not only committed Liberals but the uncommitted and the curious – the kind of people who might be swayed just by the sight of the Prime Minister.

"We couldn't count on the Tory show being the debacle it was, but even if they had had a roaring success we thought we could outreach them. . . . We thought the contrast might be interesting, and you saw it – it was."

Conceived by the executive committee for the Liberal campaign in Ontario, the rally scheme was forwarded to the Prime Minister's campaign committee, co-chaired by the president of the Liberal Federation, Senator Richard Stanbury, and his predecessor in the post, Senator John Nichol.

Ottawa gave swift approval, and a three-man team – Mr. Goulet, Colin Vaughan, treasurer of the Toronto and District Liberal Association, and Joseph Potts, Liberal campaign director in the Metro area – buckled down to the detail planning.

Throughout, they were encouraged by the memory of the disastrous rally at the Yorkdale Shopping Plaza which wound up former Prime Minister Lester Pearson's Metro campaign in the 1965 election.

On that occasion, crowd control was non-existent, half a dozen bands played at once, and the public address system went dead before Mr. Pearson had a chance to speak. His attempts to address the crowd of 20,000 with a bull-horn proved futile, and the rally fizzled.

Working on the assumption that they had to fill the square, which they understood to hold 45,000, the organizers made their first priority a Metro-wide publicity blitz.

Liberal Pied Piper

By the time Mr. Trudeau's convertible rolled up Bay Street and into the square, a total of 107,000 handbills ("Come and Greet Pierre Elliott Trudeau"), 10,000 posters, 10,000 Trudeau placards and 10,000 Trudeau buttons had been distributed, and anyone who had seen his office notice board, travelled by subway, or read a newspaper knew that the Liberal Pied Piper was coming to town.

In the interests of spontaneity, Liberal riding associations in Metro were specifically instructed not to pack the rally by bringing in supporters by bus.

Next, Bobby Gimby was hired – at union rates – to lead the parade and inaugurate his latest patriotic theme, Canada Forever, Let's Get Together.

The Travellers, a folk group, and The Other Day, a Toronto pop group, were commissioned to entertain those waiting in the square, and someone collected a handful of small girls from Toronto's ethnic communities to present the Prime Minister with a bouquet. (Red roses, of course.)

Apart from a sound loudspeaker system and the weather – Mr. Goulet conceded they would have been "dead if it rained" – the biggest worry for the Liberals was crowd control, and the associated problem of protecting the Prime Minister.

Sensibly, they decided the most effective and least offensive means of crowd control in the square itself would be young Liberal volunteers, each equipped with a Trudeau-orange armband. About 500 of the volunteers were in the square when Mr. Trudeau arrived, politely remonstrating with the perennial pushers and shovers, and linking arms to form human barriers between the more zealous of the faithful and the dissidents who had come to air their distaste for the Prime Minister and his Government.

150 police in square

For their part, the Metro police assigned a squad of 150 uniformed officers to the square and the parade route (far less than the number needed to protect the Beatles when they performed in the city at the height of their fame, but enough to inhibit potential trouble-makers.)

The RCMP and Metro plainsclothesmen assigned to the Prime Minister whenever he visits the city made themselves as inconspicuous as plainclothesmen can, showing alarm only when Mr. Trudeau stepped down from the podium and advanced to the front row of supporters to begin what the President of the United States likes to call "pressing the flesh".

As always, the great majority of those who held out their hands for the Prime Ministerial touch were from the teenybopper class, though a fair number of enthusiasts old enough to be their grandparents were not behind in seeking the laying on of hands.

The 10 minutes the Prime Minister spent touching hands was the most manifest display of Trudeaumania seen in his 47 minutes in the square, and was a strange contrast with the low-key tenor of his speech.

All in all, it was a thoroughly organized yet spontaneous display of Trudeau popularity, and it cost the Liberals only $8,000. If Mr. Goulet's prognostication is correct, next Tuesday may prove it to have been "money," as he himself put it, "very well spent."

The Globe and Mail, Toronto
June 20, 1968

Discussion guidelines

1. In view of your personal response to advertising, organized rallies, and the mass media, would you consider these forces a threat to democracy? Cite some examples to illustrate your opinion.
2. "Personality rather than philosophy is the key to office. . . . A successful leader becomes the major symbol of his party; the party stands for what he stands for, and his pronouncements become party dogma." (John T. McLeod, *Explanations of Our Party System*)
   (a) Do you agree that personality rather than ideas is more important for the success of a Canadian political leader? Provide historical evidence to support your position.
   (b) If McLeod's analysis is correct, to what extent can ad-men and image makers assume dangerous powers when they package political leaders?
3. In January 1969, while attending a Commonwealth Prime Ministers' conference in London, England, Mr. Trudeau and the press had a "confrontation" over coverage of his social life.
   (a) How much privacy do you think a public figure is entitled to? Suggest guidelines for determining where privacy begins and how it can be safeguarded.
   (b) How important do you think it is that there be a friendly relationship between an elected leader and the media men?

Cross references

The Use of Symbols, page 44
Nazi Rituals, page 46
Propaganda and the Mass Meeting, page 133
Leaders and Followers, page 136

WHAT IS DEMOCRACY?

Definitions by Aristotle, Rousseau, Jefferson, Bentham, Mill, Lincoln, Shaw, Trudeau

"Every citizen, it is said, must have equality, and therefore in a democracy the poor have more power than the rich, because there are more of them, and the will of the majority is supreme."

ARISTOTLE (384-322 B.C.)

"Taking the term in its strict sense, there never has existed, and never will exist, any true democracy. It is contrary to the natural order that the majority should govern and that the minority should be governed."

JEAN-JACQUES ROUSSEAU (1712-1778)

"We hold these truths to be self-evident, That all men are created equal, that they are endowed by their creator with certain inalienable rights; that among these are life, liberty, and the pursuit of happiness; that to secure these rights governments are instituted among men, deriving their just powers from the consent of the governed; that whenever any form of government becomes destructive of these ends, it is the right of the people to alter or to abolish it, and to institute new government, laying its foundation on such principles and organizing its powers in such form, as to them shall seem most likely to effect their safety and happiness."

THOMAS JEFFERSON (1743-1826)

"The aim of government should be the greatest possible happiness of the greatest number; in a word, the common good is the right aim of government, and the proper task of a lawmaker is to discover regulations designed to bring about the greatest good to the greatest number of human beings."

JEREMY BENTHAM (1748-1832)

"The meaning of representative government is, that the whole people, or some numerous portion of them, exercise through deputies periodically elected by themselves the ultimate controlling power, which, in every constitution, must reside somewhere. This ultimate power they must possess in all its completeness. They must be masters, whenever they please, of all the operations of government. Representative government must fulfil three fundamental conditions: 1. That the people should be willing to receive it. 2. That they should be willing and able to do what is necessary for its preservation. 3. That they should be willing and able to fulfil the duties and discharge the functions which it imposes on them."

JOHN STUART MILL (1806-1873)

"It is . . . for us to be here dedicated to the great task . . . before us . . . that this nation, under God, shall have a new birth of freedom – and that government of the people, by the people, for the people, shall not perish from the earth."

ABRAHAM LINCOLN (1809-1865)

"Democracy means the organization of society for the benefit and at the expense of everybody indiscriminately and not for the benefit of a privileged class. A nearly desperate difficulty in the way of its realization is the delusion that the method of securing it is to give votes to everybody, which is the one certain method of killing it. Adult suffrage kills it dead. . . . It takes all sorts to make a world; and to maintain civilization some of these sorts have to be killed like mad dogs whilst others have to be put in command of the state. Until the differences are classified we cannot have a scientific suffrage; and without a scientific suffrage any attempt at democracy will defeat itself as it has already done."

GEORGE BERNARD SHAW (1856-1950)

"Parliamentary democracy I take to be a method of governing free men which operates roughly as follows: organized parties that wish to pursue – by different means – a common end, agree to be bound by certain rules according to which the party with the most support governs on condition that leadership will revert to some other party whenever the latter's means become acceptable to the greater part of the electorate. The common end – the general welfare – which is the aim of all parties . . . may be defined in different ways by different men. Yet it must in some way include equality of opportunity for everyone in all important fields of endeavour. . . . For democracy cannot be made to work in a country where a large part of the citizens are by status condemned to a perpetual state of domination, economic or otherwise. Essentially, a true democracy must permit the periodic transformation of political minorities into majorities."

PIERRE ELLIOTT TRUDEAU (1919-)

Discussion guideline

Select any one of the definitions of democracy given here and weigh democracy as you know it against the definition you have chosen.

DEMOCRACY: ITS FUTURE?

Democracy in the Modern World

from *Can Democracy Survive?*
by C. Northcote Parkinson

The Issue

Are we now quite so certain that democracy must everywhere prevail as not only the best but the final achievement of human wisdom?

There is little in history to show that democracy is much more stable than any other form of rule. What history does show is that people have always inclined to regard their own form of government as perfect. Subjects of, say, a deified emperor have seldom supposed that any other form of rule was worth serious discussion. For most of them, at any period, talk of an alternative scheme would have seemed impracticable, (irreligious) or merely crazy. If we are to defend democracy today, it must not be because it is sacred – but because it produces some good result. If it is good, we should be able to explain why.

Now there are three developments which affect the future of democracy, developments in psychology, communication, and "conventional" war.

Psychology

To deal with psychology first, there was a time when the results of an election or plebiscite were given a sort of religious approval. Victorian editors could announce that the people would oppose the Updrainville irrigation scheme, that the people had rightly demanded the construction of the Moose Canyon Bridge, or that the people had wisely chosen Mr. Clawhammer as governor. In a simply organized agricultural society, the relevant facts could be widely known. Today, however, in a more complicated society, the will of the people breaks

drawing by George Price, copr. © 1938, 1966, The New Yorker Magazine, Inc.

down under psychological analysis, turning out to be ill-informed, emotional, and liable to vary indeed from day to day. Taken apart in this fashion, the will of the people turns out to be a myth. Voting is a more orderly process than rioting, but has only an even chance of producing the right answer.

Communications

As for communications, it must be remembered, first of all, that these have always determined the scale – and to some extent the nature – of political institutions. The earliest civilized states were each based on a river system as their means of communication, the length of the river determining the size of the state. Kingdoms based on the Nile, the Tigris, or the Ganges could be relatively larger; kingdoms based on the Tagus, the Mekong, or the Scheldt had to be relatively small. The Romans and the Chinese broke through these limits by building roads, but the river system scale of political organization lingered on to a surprisingly recent period of history, determining the sizes of, say, Yorkshire, Virginia, Canada, and Venezuela. A single government could stretch its authority only as far as it could reach, the amount of its influence being roughly proportionate to the distances involved.

Today the extent of a government's influence has been at once extended and intensified. Rail, road, telegraph, air, and radio communications have made a distant supervision both effective and continuous. Today the Queen's voice, and even she herself, can come through the air, just as the President's personality can be projected by television or recorded on tape. Communication is no longer in the same sense a problem.

So, far from presenting any technical difficulty, communications now present the government, whatever its character, with almost limitless scope. By means of state-organized schools, newspapers, films, radio, and television, a docile people can be taught practically anything – that all capitalists are wicked, that all Jews are criminals, or that China does not exist. Techniques based on psychology and developed in advertising have already some remarkable achievements to their credit. Mass media of instruction would seem to have endless possibilities. So far the known results include the popular election by enormous majorities of both scoundrels and lunatics. There is nothing to prevent any government from building up for itself a dream world in which dramatized leaders with purely fictitious ability give the appearance of prosperity to lands of which the extent has been exaggerated, reporting triumphs over rival powers which have been invented for the purpose and boasting the success of improbable missions to other and imaginary planets.

NASA

Do the propaganda possibilities of communications satellites pose a threat to democracy?

Conventional War

The world that has seen this revolution in the methods and speed of communication has also seen a transformation in the acts of war. From the time of the French Revolution to the time of the Russian Revolution land campaigns were mostly settled by massed infantry, national strength being roughly measured by the number of bayonets each nation could put in the field. During World War II the massed infantry attack went out of fashion. Now, the potential war strength of a country might be measured by the number of its scientists: it can no longer be measured by the mere number of its people. In general, democracy has best suited societies in which the equal value of votes has been reflected in the roughly equal value of the voters when armed for war. It has flourished less securely in societies where the decisive weapons – whether war chariots or cannons – have been in the hands of a few. For this reason it might be thought that the technical basis for democracy in war, as well as in peace, has by now been weakened.

Prospects for Democracy

From facts such as these it would be natural to conclude that the days of democracy are over. The conclusion would be premature, however, for political systems do not develop as rapidly as that. Where democracy exists, it may well survive for a further period; but there is good reason to question whether it is likely to take root in any soil to which it is new. With a less favourable climate, the transplanting becomes a less hopeful idea and doubtfully worth the effort. What may flourish for a time in the atmosphere of the West has far more dubious prospects in the atmosphere of the East. For there the racial and religious background, the family, caste, and clan relationships, the secret societies and fanaticisms, the illiteracy and ignorance make the voting process seem curiously out of place.

What, by contrast, are the prospects of democracy in the West? Put in the simplest terms, it is now far easier for a government to tell the people what it is to do. But that is not the whole story. In at least one important respect, democracy is being strengthened and it is important to see how this has come about – more especially in the United States,

The basic weakness of democracy has always been what the Greeks called "stasis", or class war. Given political equality, the lower classes, which have always in times past been the more numerous, have sooner or later used their vote to rob the rich. They have voted, in effect, for economic equality – that is, for socialism.

Whatever the result of the battle, freedom has always been the first casualty. In the struggle between capital and labour both sides are driven by exactly the same material motive, and both sides are guilty of exactly the same sin. Neither, of course, is concerned with the welfare of society as a whole.

In trying to translate the Greek theory of class war into the terms of modern industry Karl Marx foretold a process by which the wealthy would become richer and fewer, the poor would become poorer and more numerous until the situation would make revolution inevitable.

However, in twentieth-century industrialized societies, it was not the working class that multiplied in growing poverty but a middle class that multiplied in growing wealth. The future lay not with the skilled worker but with the qualified engineer on the one hand and the unskilled factory worker on the other. These were classes of people of whose existence Marx was only dimly aware. It is upon them, rather than upon the skilled worker, that industry has come to rely.

By a process of technical achievement, rehousing, and education, the middle class came to outweigh the class above and outnumber the class below it. There are depressed classes in the United States, and there are people with a grievance against society: but they are swamped by the masses of people whose fear is that they will lose what they have – namely, a suburban home, garage, car, refrigerator, washing machine, television, telephone, supermarket, and high school. That democracy in the United States should end in class war is now almost unthinkable, for the raw materials do not exist. People are more likely to choke themselves, as in Los Angeles, with the fumes of their own exhaust pipes. It is true that the whole picture could be drastically altered by an industrial depression, but the story, whatever happened, would not conform to either Greek theory or Marxist prediction.

Discussion guidelines

1. "Is a democracy the last improvement possible in government? Is it not possible to take a step further towards recognizing and organizing the rights of man? There never will be a really free and enlightened State until the State comes to recognize the individual as a higher and independent power, from which all its own power and authority are derived, and treats him accordingly." (Henry David Thoreau, *Civil Disobedience)* To what extent do you agree with this proposition?
2. Does it really matter if democracy in the Western tradition survives? Argue your point of view.
3. "The future of democracy, whatever happens, will not conform either to Greek theory or Marxist prediction." What is your prediction of the shape that the future might give to Western democracy?

Cross references

The Aims of the Communists, page 65
The Individual in Society, page 139
The Unknown Citizen, page 142
Controlling the Mind, page 322

The Individual

drawing by Kraus, © 1960, The New Yorker Magazine, Inc.

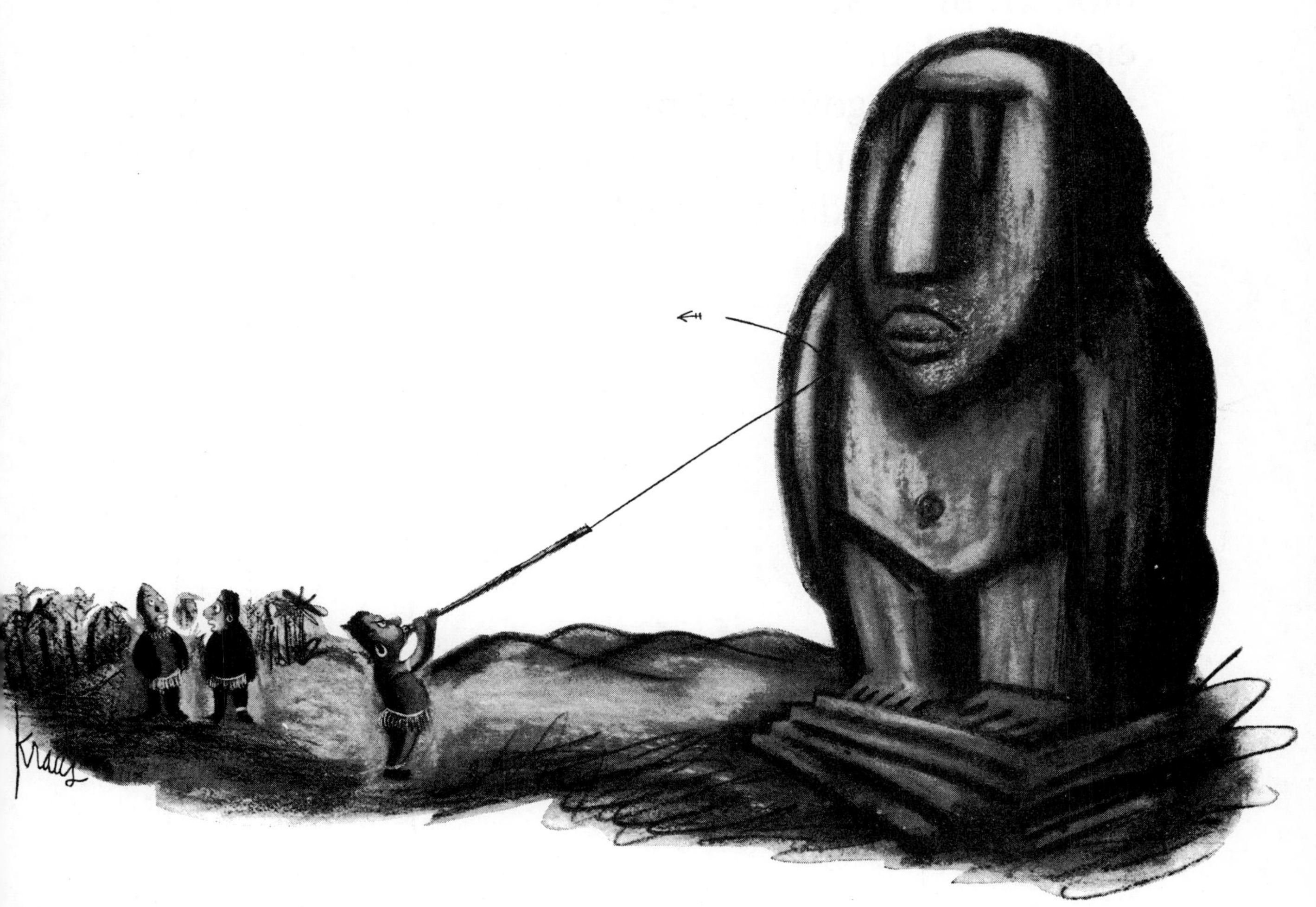

"Pointless rebellion against authority, if you ask me."

An individual! Bombarded by advertisements and political slogans, caught up in a computerized world, driven by emotions and social pressures he vaguely understands, modern man faces an identity crisis. Who is he? Can he claim an identity of his own separate from that of the masses? Is he governed by inherited animal instincts, or by traditions and environment? What role must he play in politics in order to benefit both himself and his society?

SIX VIEWS

Propaganda and the Mass Meeting
from *Mein Kampf*
by Adolf Hitler

Propaganda
The art of propaganda lies in understanding the emotional ideas of the great masses and finding, through a psychologically correct form, the way to the attention and thence to the heart of the broad masses.

Once we understand how necessary it is for propaganda to be adjusted to the broad mass, the following rule results:

It is a mistake to make propaganda many-sided, like scientific instruction, for instance.

The receptivity of the great masses is very limited, their intelligence is small, but their power of forgetting is enormous. In consequence of these facts, all effective propaganda must be limited to a very few points and must harp on these in slogans until the last member of the public understands what you want him to understand by your slogan. As soon as you sacrifice this slogan and try to be many-sided, the effect will piddle away, for the crowd can neither digest nor retain the material offered. In this way the result is weakened and in the end entirely cancelled out.

Thus we see that propaganda must follow a simple line and correspondingly the basic tactics must be psychologically sound.

For instance, it was absolutely wrong to make the enemy ridiculous, as the Austrian and German comic papers did. It was absolutely wrong because actual contact with an enemy soldier was bound to arouse an entirely different conviction, and the results were devastating; for now the German soldier, under the direct impression of the enemy's resistance, felt himself swindled by his propaganda service. His desire to fight, or even to stand firm, was not strengthened, but the opposite occurred. His courage flagged.

By contrast, the war propaganda of the English and Americans was psychologically sound. By representing the Germans to their own people as barbarians and Huns, they prepared the individual soldier for the terrors of war, and thus helped to preserve him from disappointments. After this, the most terrible weapon that was used against him seemed only to confirm what his propagandists had told him; it likewise reinforced his faith in the truth of his government's assertions, while on the other hand it increased his rage and hatred against the vile enemy. For the cruel effects of the weapon, whose use by the enemy he now came to know, gradually came to confirm for him the "Hunnish" brutality of the barbarous enemy, which he had heard all about; and it never dawned on him for a moment that his own weapons possibly, if not probably, might be even more terrible in their effects.

What our authorities least of all understood was

Miller Services, Toronto

An anti-German poster produced in France during World War I

the very first axiom of all propagandist activity: to wit, the basically subjective and one-sided attitude it must take toward every question it deals with.

What, for example, would we say about a poster that was supposed to advertise a new soap and that described other soaps as "good"?

We would only shake our heads.

Exactly the same applies to political advertising.

The broad mass of a nation does not consist of diplomats, or even professors of political law, or even individuals capable of forming a rational opinion; it consists of plain mortals, wavering and inclined to doubt and uncertainty. As soon as our own propaganda admits so much as a glimmer of right on the other side, the foundation for doubt in our own right has been laid.

The people in their overwhelming majority are so feminine by nature and attitude that sober reasoning determines their thoughts and actions far less than emotion and feeling.

And this sentiment is not complicated, but very simple and all of a piece. It does not have multiple shadings; it has a positive and a negative; love or hate, right or wrong, truth or lie, never half this way and half that way, never partially, or that kind of thing.

The purpose of propaganda is not to provide interesting distraction for blasé young gentlemen, but to convince, and what I mean is to convince the masses. But the masses are slow-moving, and they always require a certain time before they are ready even to notice a thing, and only after the simplest ideas are repeated thousands of times will the masses finally remember them.

When there is a change, it must not alter the content of what the propaganda is driving at, but in the end must always say the same thing. For instance, a slogan must be presented from different angles, but the end of all remarks must always and immutably be the slogan itself. Only in this way can the propaganda have a unified and complete effect.

The Mass Meeting

Go to a theater performance and witness a play at three o'clock in the afternoon and the same play with the same actors at eight at night, and you will be amazed at the difference in effect and impression. A man with fine feelings and the power to achieve clarity with regard to this mood will be able to establish at once that the impression made by the performance at three in the afternoon is not as great as that made in the evening. The same applies even to a movie. This is important because in the theater it might be said that perhaps the actor does not take as much pains in the afternoon as at night. But a film is no different in the afternoon than at nine in the evening. No, the *time* itself exerts a definite effect, just as the hall does on me.

In these cases we have to do with an encroachment upon man's freedom of will. This applies most, of course, to meetings attended by people with a contrary attitude of will, who must now be won over to a new will. In the morning and even during the day people's will power seems to struggle with the greatest energy against an attempt to force upon them a strange will and a strange opinion. At night, however, they succumb more easily to the dominating force of a stronger will. For, in truth, every such meeting represents a wrestling bout between two opposing forces. The superior oratorical art of a dominating preacher will succeed more easily in winning to the new will people who have themselves experienced a weakening of their force of resistance in the most natural way than those who are still in full possession of their mental tension and will.

The mass meeting is necessary for the reason that in it the individual, who at first, while becoming a supporter of a young movement, feels lonely and easily succumbs to the fear of being alone, for the first time gets the picture of a larger community, which in most people has a strengthening, encouraging effect. The same man, within a company or a

Miller Services, Toronto

battalion, surrounded by all his comrades, would set out on an attack with a lighter heart than if left entirely on his own. In the crowd he always feels somewhat sheltered, even if a thousand reasons actually argue against it.

But the community of the great demonstration not only strengthens the individual, it also unites and helps to create an *esprit de corps*. The man who is exposed to grave tribulations, as the first advocate of a new doctrine in his factory or workshop, absolutely needs that strengthening which lies in the conviction of being a member and fighter in a great comprehensive body. And he obtains an impression of this body for the first time in the mass demonstration. When from his little workshop or big factory, in which he feels very small, he steps for the first time into a mass meeting and has thousands and thousands of people of the same opinions around him; when, as a seeker, he is swept away by three or four thousand others into the mighty effect of suggestive intoxication and enthusiasm; when the visible success and agreement of thousands confirm to him the rightness of the new doctrine and for the first time arouse doubt in the truth of his previous conviction – then he himself has succumbed to the magic influence of what we designate as "mass suggestion". The will, the longing, and also the power of thousands are accumulated in every individual. The man who enters such a meeting doubting and wavering leaves it inwardly reinforced: he has become a link in the community.

Discussion guidelines

1. Compare the methods of persuasion recommended by Hitler with those practised by our own politicians.
2. Are the masses as gullible as the methods of persuasion suggest? Comment.
3. "Power over opinion is more important to a nation than military hardware or wealth." Cite examples that seem to support this opinion.

Cross references

The Use of Symbols, page 44
Nazi Rituals, page 46
Democracy in the Modern World, page 125
"Daddy, What Did You Do in the Great War?" page 247

2

The Canadian Press

Leaders and Followers
from *The True Believer*
by Eric Hoffer

No matter how vital we think the role of leadership in the rise of a mass movement, there is no doubt that the leader cannot create the conditions which make the rise of a movement possible. He cannot conjure a mass movement out of the void. There has to be an eagerness to follow and obey, and an intense dissatisfaction with things as they are, before movement and leader can make their appearance. When conditions are not ripe, the potential leader, no matter how gifted, and his holy cause, no matter how potent, remain without a following. The First World War and its aftermath readied the ground for the rise of the Bolshevik, Fascist, and Nazi movements. Had the war been averted or postponed a decade or two, the fate of Lenin, Mussolini, and Hitler would not have been different from that of the brilliant plotters and agitators of the nineteenth century who never succeeded in ripening the frequent disorders and crises of their time into full-scale mass movements. Something was lacking. The European masses up to the cataclysmic events of the First World War had not utterly despaired of the present and were, therefore, not willing to sacrifice it for a new life and a new world. Even the nationalist leaders, who fared better than the revolutionists, did not succeed in making of nationalism the popular holy cause it has become since.

Militant nationalism and militant revolutionism seem to be contemporaneous.

In Britain, too, the leader had to wait for the times to ripen before he could play his role. During the 1930's the potential leader (Churchill) was prominent in the eyes of the people and made himself heard, day in, day out. But the will to follow was not there. It was only when disaster shook the country to its foundation and made autonomous individual lives untenable and meaningless that the leader came into his own.

There is a period of waiting in the wings – often a very long period – for all the great leaders whose entrance on the scene seems to us a most crucial point in the course of a mass movement. Accidents and the activities of other men have to set the stage for them before they can enter and start their performance. "The commanding man in a momentous day seems only to be the last accident in a series."

Once the stage is set, the presence of an outstanding leader is indispensable. Without him there will be no movement. The ripeness of the times does not automatically produce a mass movement, nor can elections, laws, and administrative bureaus hatch one. It was Lenin who forced the flow of events into the channels of the Bolshevik revolution. Had he died in Switzerland, or on his way to Russia in 1917, it is almost certain that the other prominent Bolsheviks would have joined a coalition government. The result might have been a more or less liberal republic run chiefly by the bourgeoisie. In the case of Mussolini and Hitler the evidence is even more decisive: without them there would have been neither a Fascist nor a Nazi movement. . . .

The main requirements [for a leader] seem to be: audacity and a joy in defiance; an iron will; a fanatical conviction that he is in possession of the one and only truth; faith in his destiny and luck; a capacity for passionate hatred; contempt for the present; a cunning estimate of human nature; a delight in symbols (spectacles and ceremonials); unbounded brazenness which finds expression in a disregard of consistency and fairness; a recognition that the innermost craving of a following is for communion and that there can never be too much of it; a capacity for winning and holding the utmost loyalty of a group of able lieutenants. This last faculty is one of the most essential and elusive. The uncanny powers of a leader manifest themselves not so much in the hold he has on the masses as in his ability to dominate and almost bewitch a small group of able men. These men must be fearless, proud, intelligent and capable of organizing and running large-scale undertakings, and yet they must submit wholly to the will of the leader, draw their inspiration and driving force from him, and glory in this submission.

Not all the qualities enumerated above are equally essential. The most decisive for the effectiveness of a mass movement leader seem to be audacity, fanatical faith in a holy cause, an awareness of the importance of a close-knit collectivity, and, above all, the ability to evoke fervent devotion in a group of able lieutenants. Trotsky's failure as a leader came from his neglect, or more probably his inability, to create a machine of able and loyal lieutenants. He did not attract personal sympathies, or if he did he could not keep them.

. . . The quality of ideas seems to play a minor role in mass movement leadership. What counts is the arrogant gestures, the complete disregard of the opinion of others, the singlehanded defiance of the world.

Charlatanism of some degree is indispensable to effective leadership. There can be no mass movement without some deliberate misrepresentation of facts. No solid, tangible advantage can hold a following and make it zealous and loyal unto death. The leader has to be practical and a realist, yet must talk the language of the visionary and the idealist.

Originality is not a perquisite of great mass movement leadership. One of the most striking traits of the successful mass movement leader is his readiness to imitate both friends and foe, both past and contemporary models. The daring which is essential to this type of leadership consists as much in the daring to imitate as in the daring to defy the world.

. . . All mass movements rank obedience with the highest virtues and put it on a level with faith:

. . . Obedience is not only the first law of God, but also the first tenet of a revolutionary party and of fervent nationalism. "Not to reason why" is considered by all mass movements the mark of a strong and generous spirit.

The disorder, bloodshed, and destruction which mark the trail of a rising mass movement lead us to think of the followers of the movement as being by nature rowdy and lawless . . . The true believer, no matter how rowdy and violent his acts, is basically an obedient and submissive person. The Christian converts who staged razzias against the University of Alexandria and lynched professors suspected of unorthodoxy were submissive members of a compact church. The Communist rioter is a servile member of a party. Both the Japanese and Nazi rowdies were the most disciplined people the world has seen.

People whose lives are barren and insecure seem to show a greater willingness to obey than people who are self-sufficient and self-confident. To the frustrated, freedom from responsibility is more attractive than freedom from restraint. They are eager to barter their independence for relief from the burdens of willing, deciding, and being responsible for inevitable failure. They willingly abdicate the directing of their lives to those who want to plan, command, and shoulder all responsibility. Moreover, submission by all to a supreme leader is an approach to their ideal of equality.

In time of crisis, during floods, earthquakes, epidemics, depressions, and wars, separate individual effort is of no avail, and people of every condition are ready to obey and follow a leader. To obey is then the only firm point in a chaotic day-by-day existence.

The frustrated are also likely to be the most steadfast followers. It is remarkable, that, in a co-operative effort, the least self-reliant are the least likely to be discouraged by defeat. For they join others in a common undertaking not so much to ensure the success of a cherished project as to avoid an individual shouldering of blame in case of failure. When the common undertaking fails, they are still spared the one thing they fear most, namely, the showing up of their individual shortcomings. Their faith remains unimpaired and they are eager to follow in a new attempt. . . .

There is probably a crucial difference between a mass movement leader and a leader in a free society. In a more or less free society, the leader can retain his hold on the people only when he has blind faith in their wisdom and goodness. A second-rate leader possessed of this faith will outlast a first-rate leader who is without it. This means that in a free society the leader follows the people even as he leads them. He must, as someone said, find out where the people are going so that he may lead them. When the leader in a free society becomes contemptuous of the people, he sooner or later proceeds on the false and fatal theory that all men are fools, and eventually blunders into defeat. Things are different where the leader can employ ruthless coercion. Where, as in an active mass movement, the leader can exact blind obedience, he can operate on the sound theory that all men are cowards, treat them accordingly, and get results.

Discussion guidelines

1. Great leaders, suggests Hoffer, are like actors who must wait for the right moment to step on stage and "strut their stuff". Comment on the adequacy of Hoffer's statement to explain the emergence of any local, national, or international leader you choose.
2. A former Prime Minister of Canada, Mackenzie King, believed that a prime minister should follow the example of the ram in a flock of sheep. "Most of the time the sheep nibble at the grass or rest in the shade and the ram stands by, keeping his eye on them. But every now and then the sheep begin moving to one of the pasture gates. When this happens, the ram trots up to the head of the flock and leads them out." To what extent does Hoffer agree with this explanation of the relationship between a leader and the people of a free society? What is your viewpoint on the matter?

Cross references

The Use of Symbols, page 44
Lenin: Portrait of a Revolutionary, page 67

 a

The Individual in Society
from *The Mass Mind*
by Joyce Cary

Every age, they say, has its special bit of nonsense. The eighteenth century had its noble savage, and the nineteenth, its automatic progress. Now we have this modern nonsense about the "mass man". We are told constantly that people are becoming more and more standardized. That mass education, mass amusements, mass production, ready-made clothes, and a popular press are destroying all individuality – turning civilization into a nice, warmed, sterilized orphan asylum where all the little lost souls wear the same uniforms, eat the same meals, think the same thoughts, and play the same games.

This belief is now so completely accepted that it underlies half the writing and thinking of the time, like chalk under the downs. You don't see it but it gives shape to what you do see. If you deny it you will get exactly the same response as Galileo when he said the earth moved through the sky. You will be told, "Use your eyes. And don't talk nonsense. Look at the crowds in the street or at any football match. Go to the films, read the newspapers. Consider the disappearance of national dress all over the world – the immense development of laws restricting individual liberty, standardizing our lives. Go on a tour to famous sights – year by year there will be bigger crowds of morons gaping at them and listening to the spiel of some bored guide – a piece

Wide World Photo

Are the clothes worn by these hippies in San Francisco, 1967, an expression of individualism or an attempt to be part of a group?

nicely designed to satisfy the mass mind."

And you will be referred to history and old travel accounts to learn how various and delightful the world was, in dress and thought and individuality, one hundred or even fifty years ago.

I was convinced of all this myself till I went to administer the affairs of a primitive tribe in Africa. There I found that the tribal mind was much more truly a mass mind than anything I had known in Europe. The nearest approximation to it was among illiterate peasantry in remote country districts. Tribesmen and primitive peasants are intensely narrow and conservative. Their very simple ideas and reactions guide them in a mysterious and dangerous world.

I found that young chiefs with enterprise and ambition were keen to learn about the world outside the tribe. If they got away from it, they tended to put on European dress. To them, European dress was a mark of the free and independent mind, not of the mass mind.

Likewise, when a European peasantry becomes educated and enterprising, it breaks away from the national dress which seems a badge of servitude and backwardness. To tourists, no doubt, this is a misfortune. As a keen tourist and sight-seer, I wish all Scotsmen would wear the kilt and all Turks the tarboosh. I'm delighted that some are beginning to do so again. But these are individualists, eccentrics, nationalists – national dress is not a tribal uniform to them, but a proclamation of difference, an assertion of self.

Education, contact with other peoples, breaks up tribal uniformity of thought and custom, brings in new ideas. That is, it makes for difference. The celebrated eccentrics of former centuries were either lunatics – or educated men.

New ideas also make for conflict. Old African chiefs hated roads and railways: they said they brought in strangers who corrupted the young people with new ideas and made them rebellious. They were quite right. It is far easier to rule a primitive tribe than a modern democracy where every individual is ready to criticize the government, where everyone has his own ideas about politics and religion, and where dozens of societies, unions, and religious sects claim independence and support ambitious leaders who are ready to fight at any time for their "rights".

The more education a man has the more likely he is to be independent in his views and obstinate in sticking to them. A committee of professors, I can assure you, is much harder to manage than a council of African chiefs.

And this throws light on another argument brought forward to prove that individuality is vanishing from the world – the enormous increase of law and regulation, the growing power of the police. In my primitive African tribe, law enforcement was in the hands of village chiefs. There was little theft. I could leave my bungalow wide open and unguarded for three weeks at a time and nothing was ever taken. We had crimes of passion and crimes of witchcraft, but no criminal class, no crooks as you know them in the big city, no cranks, no anarchists – so we did not require an elaborate structure of law.

You do not need traffic police where there is no wheeled traffic. You do not need postal bylaws where no one knows how to write. But the modern state, simply because of the independence of its citizens, the complication of their demands, needs a huge machine of law and police. This is not a proof of the mass mind but the exact opposite – of a growing number of people who think and act for themselves, and rightly or wrongly, are ready to defy the old simple rules founded on custom.

Thus, the modern state has lost its mass mind in getting education. But, you will say, this education destroys the primitive mass mind only to replace it with a number of mob minds: in the crowds which queue for the films or a match, read the same newspaper, and shout for the same spellbinders. Mass education is driving out the sound, traditional culture to bring in a lot of halfbaked slogans. It produces the shallow brain seeking only to be distracted from serious reflection.

But these "mobs" have no resemblance to those of the tribal world where every individual does the same thing at the same time – hunts, dances, drinks in the mass. Even if he had the will to do anything else, it would not be there to do. The modern individual has an immense choice of occupation and amusement. So that the "mass" of sight-seers at any show place today is actually composed of individuals who have freely chosen to join that crowd and will join a different one tomorrow. What looks like a proof of the mob mind is really evidence of spreading interest among the people and a variety of occupations. And if some of these interests are "popular", aimed at a crowd which is not very critical or reflective, they are a good deal more so than interests which were the only recourse of their ancestors – dog-fighting, bear-baiting, the fit-up melodrama or one-night stand, once a year, and booze.

In the best educated countries, you find the biggest demand for something new in amusement as well as for instruction. Education enlarges all the interests of a man. Apart from what he learns, he acquires a general curiosity and a wider taste.

Compare the press of today with that of a hundred or even fifty years ago. You will find a far greater variety of subjects appealing to a greater variety of tastes. You will find instructive articles on matters formerly dealt with only in the special magazines. Perhaps they don't aim at a learned audience, but they help the general reader to get some idea of what the experts are doing in atomic research or medicine or even astronomy. If you want to write a best seller, your best subject nowadays is probably cosmology.

But if a hundred thousand people are ready to buy a book on the nature of the universe, you have a mass demand at the bookshops. The mass demand is not proof of falling standards: it means that millions are being educated who would formerly have been left in the illiterate mass. There are "masses" reading learned works just as there

Miller Services, Toronto

are other "masses" going to popular films. The number of people with a good university education is many hundred times what it was fifty years ago, and that explains the immense development of arts and literature in experimental forms that would have had no chance of appreciation before. And in the millions in the next category who have just become literate in the last generation, whose reactions to education have given rise to this illusion of an increasing "mass mind", what we are seeing is not a collapse of standards, but a very rapid improvement. The crowds at the cinemas and the bus-loads on the sight-seeing tours are on the way up. They have already left the mass; they are individuals seeking ideas for themselves.

The mass mind idea is not only a bit of nonsense. It leads to a profound defeatism, to the secret and unacknowledged belief that the dictators hold all the trumps.

The reasoning, when you bring it to light, is something like this. There are two kinds of education in the world: the free, which develops the individual according to his nature, and the specialized, which turns out doctors, scientists, mechanics – useful servants of the state or of industry. In a democracy each individual has both types. In the Soviet he gets only the specialized – the whole plan is to make him a state slave.

But it seems that free education merely debases the standards of thought and life by producing mob minds without spiritual strength. Meanwhile the Soviet acquires millions of workers, docile as serfs, yet skilful as our own craftsmen. Aiming deliberately at the creation of a mass mind it will easily defeat the free world, where opinions are shallow and divided.

But this is based on bad psychology. The West is not producing a mass mind, but a variety of strong minds with the richest sense of adventure and will for discovery. The East is not succeeding in obtaining a mass mind either – it is going in the opposite direction. Merely by process of education, it is producing every year people who can at least think a little more freely than illiterate peasants, who are very likely therefore to think critical thoughts, however much they may hide them. That is why the task of the dictatorship becomes constantly more difficult, why it is obliged to stiffen its grip, to hire more police, to bribe more spies, and to purge its own party, every year or so, of "deviators".

What I suggest is that no kind of education, however narrow, can produce the mass mind. The reason is that minds are creative, that thoughts wander by themselves and cannot be controlled by the cleverest police. All education is free in this sense; it cannot be shut up within walls. To teach people to think, if only to make them more useful as soldiers and mechanics, is to open all thoughts to them – a world full of new ideas. And though the dictator may wish to think of them as a proletariat, they have already begun to leave the proletariat.

The "mass mind" is a delusion. How many dictators have been amazed when their rule, which seemed so strong, has collapsed in a few hours without a friend?

b

The Unknown Citizen

(To JS/07/M/378 This Marble Monument
is Erected by the State)

He was found by the Bureau of Statistics to be
One against whom there was no official complaint,
And all the reports on his conduct agree
That, in the modern sense of an old-fashioned
word, he was a saint,

For in everything he did he served the Greater
Community,
Except for the War till the day he retired
He worked in a factory and never got fired,
But satisfied his employers, Fudge Motors Inc.,
Yet he wasn't a scab or odd in his views,
For his Union reports that he paid his dues,
(Our report on his Union shows it was sound)
And our Social Psychology workers found
That he was popular with his mates and liked a
drink.
The press are convinced that he bought a paper
every day
And that his reactions to advertisements were
normal in every way.
Policies taken out in his name prove that he was
fully insured,
And his Health-card shows he was once in hospital
but left it cured,
Both Producers Research and High-Grade Living
declare
He was fully sensible to the advantages of the
Instalment Plan
And had everything necessary to the Modern Man,
A phonograph, a radio, a car and a frigidaire.
Our researchers into Public Opinion are content
That he held the proper opinions for the time of
year;
When there was peace, he was for peace; when
there was war, he went.
He was married and added five children to the
population,
Which our Eugenist says was the right number for
a parent of his generation,
And our teachers report that he never interfered
with their education.
Was he free? Was he happy? The question is
absurd:
Had anything been wrong, we certainly should
have heard.

W. H. AUDEN

Discussion guidelines

1. Do you think Hitler's or Cary's analysis of the mass mind is more realistic? Give evidence from your own experience to support your opinion.
2. (a) "No kind of education . . . can produce the mass mind." With reference to your own school program, support or refute this claim.

   or

   (b) "A high school that treats its senior pupils exactly as it treats its beginners is an abject failure, for the aim of the school is not to train pupils to follow promptly, accurately, and even willingly a prescribed code of behavior. The aim is to develop young adults who may be depended upon to cope courageously with the problems of life as they arise." (Dr. J. G. Althouse, *The Structure and Aims of Canadian Education)* Assess the degree to which your school experience has realized this aim.
3. "Our most notable lack today would seem to be not men of action with their hands on instruments of power; nor calculating geniuses, supported by giant computers; but men of sensibility, gifted to appreciate and value human life." *(Living and Learning, The Report of the Provincial Committee on Aims and Objectives of Education in the Schools of Ontario)*
   (a) Evaluate this claim.
   (b) Suggest some ways by which Canadian educators can encourage the development of "men [and women] of sensibility gifted to appreciate and value human life".

Juvenile Delinquency?
from *African Genesis*
by Robert Ardrey

> What is man, that thou art mindful of him? and the son of man, that thou visitest him?
>
> For thou hast made him a little lower than the angels and hast crowned him with glory and honour.
>
> Psalm 8: 4-5

The delinquent today is an international figure who cannot be identified with any particular social or political system. In New York he is a JD, in London a teddy boy, in Cape Town a tsotsi, in Peking or Moscow a hooligan. Everywhere he is a figure arousing concern, puzzlement, sometimes [condemnation], more often guilt. Nowhere, to my knowledge, is he understood.

In [a report published by Harvard University] the histories, behaviour, and attitudes of five hundred delinquent boys are compared with the histories, behaviour, and attitudes of five hundred non-delinquents, all of comparable backgrounds. And we find the delinquent, by and large, superior to the non-delinquent in energy and physique. We find conforming children with a greater sense of insecurity, of being unloved, unwanted, or rejected, than delinquent children. And among the five hundred boys who had smoked at an early age, kept late hours, played with other delinquents, frequented neighbourhoods far from their homes [continually] and seriously misbehaved at school when they did not persistently and seriously play truant, and who had rolled up a fair record of repeated burglary, larceny, assault, and public disturbance – among the ranks of this inglorious five hundred we find far fewer neurotics than in the ranks of the non-delinquents.

. . . Society flatters itself in thinking that it has rejected the delinquent; the delinquent has rejected society. And in the shadowed byways of his world so consummately free, this ingenious, normal adolescent human creature has created a way of life in perfect image of his animal needs. He has the security of his gang, and finds his rank among its numbers. He has sex, although it does not preoccupy him. Without any learned instruction, he creates directly from his instincts the animal institution of territory. In the defence of that territory his gang evolves a moral code, and his need to love and be loved is fulfilled. In its territorial combats, the gang creates and identifies enemies, and his need to hate and be hated finds institutional expression. Finally, in assault and larceny, the gang and its members enjoy the blood and the loot of the predator. And there is always the weapon, the gleaming switch-blade which the non-delinquent must hide in a closet, or the hissing, flesh-ripping bicycle chain which the family boy can associate only with pedalling to school.

[Another opportunity for observing basic human behaviour was provided by the Hungarian Revolution.]

Had I been a Kremlin master in the autumn of 1956, I presume that I should have regarded the Hungarian uprising as the most appalling outbreak of juvenile delinquency that a civilized society has ever been asked to endure. From start to finish it was a revolution of youth. From start to finish its heroes were children, its most fearsome battalions the armed adolescents, and its most [determined] leaders men little their seniors. Never had west or east anticipated such a situation. We had believed that young people in a closed society could act none but the charades they had been taught, and that

Miller Services, Toronto
Hungarian student rebels paying homage to fallen comrades

only those members old enough to recall the open fields of freedom would be capable of revolution in its name. The east, equally innocent, had presumed that its most trusted citizens were to be found in the ranks of the sheltered young. The Hungarian uprising demonstrated that the opposite was true.

In the aftermath of the revolution I encountered a Hungarian attorney who told a most curious story. On the day of the uprising he had been a prisoner in a vast lodging for the politically restless which the regime provided at Pecs. There he had been for seven years. . . . At the time of the uprising he shared a cell with seventeen other men. Necessarily, he knew them all well. But imprisoned as they were, they knew nothing, saw nothing, heard nothing of the event that was shaking the world. And so, on the fourth day after the outbreak, they sat on their benches and crouched on their floor unaware that Hungary was free. But then an odd thing happened. Their incommunicative jailer entered with food. And something was wrong with his cap.

My attorney friend recalled the moment as something both hazy and terrifying. All eighteen men stared at the jailer's cap, groping to know what was wrong with their world. And only as the jailer left the cell did it come to them – and to all simultaneously. The red star had been torn off. Suddenly madness possessed them and all were screaming and some were breaking benches and pounding on the door of their cell and others were fighting those who screamed for freedom and were trying to restrain them, and from down the corridor all could hear the same madness overtaking cell after cell with the jailer's progress and there were the same screams for freedom, the same shouts of restraint, the same blows between prisoners, the same crashing of broken benches on broken doors. And in a stupendous jail-break the prisoners of Pecs fought their way out of their cells and out of their prison yard, and on the other side of their prison walls found themselves in a free Hungary.

The incident at Pecs was one among thousands – all dramatic, all ironic, and most of them inexplicable – that made up the cryptogram of the Hungarian uprising. What haunted the escaped young attorney, as he recalled his own incident, was a clear recollection for which he had no explanation. In the moment of maniac frenzy that followed the recognition of the missing star, there had been a division among the prisoners. Not one man under forty-five years of age had failed to scream for freedom. Not one man over forty-five had failed to fight for restraint.

The masters of Soviet society have explained the Hungarian uprising as the work of reactionaries and foreign agents; and for all I know they may believe their own lie. But, in truth what they faced was their own total failure to condition the instincts of a subject people; their own fatal ignorance of what those instincts were, and of the shattering power released when animal compulsions throw aside the learned restraints of human experience; and their own incapacity to deal with such power except by the use of superior weapons, and of force bared naked for all to see.

Man is a wild species, and every baby born is a wild young thing. Advancing age, weakening vitality, and a long accumulation of fears and experiences may at last work a general inhibition on certain animal sources of human behaviour. But the dilemma of any society, closed or free, finds its chief place of residence in the birth-rate. Every accouchement delivers to society a creature who somehow must be tamed.

Discussion guidelines

1. To what extent does Robert Ardrey's theory explain the motivating force behind modern motorcycle clubs or street gangs?
2. "The older you get, the more conservative you become." Is Ardrey's explanation of the generation gap adequate? Comment.
3. Is man a wild species, or is he a "little lower than the angels"? Give examples to support your opinion.

Cross references

Men Need Rulers, page 14
A "Troublemaker", page 159
Civil Disobedience: National and International, page 181
Man Is a Killer, page 248

The Culture Concept

from *The Proper Study of Mankind*
by Stuart Chase

George Adams is an imaginary character who run a garage, filling station, and milk bar in Middle burg, Connecticut.

On the Warner and Lunt six-class scale, h would be a member of the lower middle class which when bracketed with the upper middle, contain the most energetic and dependable citizens in th community. He is thirty-seven years old, five fee nine, weighs 158 pounds, and was a bombardie with the 16th Air Force in the war. He is a Legion naire, an Elk, and an active member of the Middle burg Volunteer Fire Company; he goes to the Con gregational Church half a dozen times a year. Jun ior is four, and the baby is eighteen months. Hi wife taught seventh grade in the Hill School befor he married her.

George, a Red Sox fan, likes to watch ball game on TV, and loves to go trout fishing in the spring He is a Republican in town politics, but twice h voted for Franklin Roosevelt. He is well regarde in Middleburg, for at one time or another hi wrecker, a 1930 Pierce Arrow, has pulled nearl everyone in town out of a ditch.

What kind of person is this George Adams? Wha shaped him? How did he get to be what he is? W know that he must be the product of a group an the culture which goes with it. What group an what culture? Here we encounter a hierarchy c attachments and loyalties. George is not the produ of a single culture, as the Greenland Eskimo is (c was), but of a whole ring of cultures, one inside th next. His group, meanwhile, is now so large that covers a continent – though we can also distinguis a number of subgroups to which George belongs.

He identifies himself loyally with Middleburg, with Connecticut, with New England, in a declining scale. His major loyalty, however, is to the United States of America, with its 3,000,000 square miles and 165 million neighbors. This has now become his community, his We-group, in the most binding sense of the term, as it is mine. It is so by the test of a common culture as well as by national sovereignty. The concrete highway, even more than the railroad, has broken up the old local patterns. To many G.I.s overseas, "home" meant a place where you can get a good ice cream soda, decent service at a filling station, beauty shops, ice water, TV, acceptance of a majority vote, sports writers who make sense, and big league baseball.

The nation has also become George's *economic* unit in these days of fresh vegetables from California, lumber from Oregon, and oil from Texas. In the times of Obadiah Adams, deacon of the Methodist Church, blacksmith of Middleburg, and George's great-great-grandfather, loyalty to the town came first; Connecticut also claimed a fierce loyalty, but New York State was practically a foreign country, separated by a tariff wall. America, reaching way out to the wilds of Ohio, was a pretty vague concept to Obadiah. He never went 50 miles from where he was born in all his life. His economic region lay within that radius; even the iron for his horseshoes came from the Connecticut hills. He knew the face and name of everyone in town, and many in the region.

George has heard much about rugged individualism. He may think he is on his own, above the crowd, responsible only to himself and to his God, but the facts do not bear out his assumptions. In Middleburg there are many things he might feel impelled to do, but cannot do, because the folkways forbid it. For instance, he may not talk aloud in church, or grow a beard – unless he is an artist – or strike a woman, or eat with his fingers, or take off all his clothes in public on a hot day, or wear brown shoes with a tuxedo, or bright colors at a funeral, or appear at the Elks' Hall with a patch on his coat. His freedoms are strictly relative. George can choose his necktie from the rack, but he wears a necktie at the appropriate times. Certain foods highly prized among many peoples, such as eels, snails, certain kinds of grubs, he does not think fit to eat. Although his hunger is physical and common to all men, the way he will satisfy it is cultural.

Superstitions have declined somewhat since Obadiah's day, but George still avoids walking under ladders, he would rather not sign a contract on Friday the thirteenth, and wants no black cats to cross in front of him. He is perfectly sure, too, that Ellery Sanford can find water every time with that willow wand.

Where did these codes and beliefs come from? They started coming to George very soon after the doctor slapped him on the back, and he let out his first yell. They came from parents, teachers, schoolmates, relatives, truck drivers, drill sergeants, ministers, policemen, storekeepers, the drug store gang, from nearly everyone who crossed George's path during his impressionable years. Think, for instance, of all the people who taught him to talk, including the voices on the radio.

Where did *they* get the codes? From the generation which inducted them. There was nothing floating in the air; codes always come from people or written records. A few of the simpler habits, like drinking from a cup, or sitting on a chair rather than on the ground, may have been handed down unchanged for 20 generations. Altogether we can identify at least five major cultural rings from which most of George's behavior is derived.

1. To begin with the broadest, he is a product of *civilization*. For more than 6,000 years the group he belongs to has practiced a widespread division of labor and city living, based on the development of a storable grain. This marks off his behavior from nature peoples who never had cities, writing, architecture, or mathematics. At the same time it connects George with the peoples of India, China, Persia, and other areas where civilization as defined has been long in evidence. To him personally it

Miller Services, Toront

These "pushers" are hired by Japanese railroads to cram as many commuters as possible into railway coaches a rush hour. Would a railroad employee in our culture geta punch in the nose if he tried to do this?

neans, among other things, living in a house, going o school, eating cereals, paying taxes, using money.

2. Next comes *Western civilization* as distinct rom other civilizations. From this source George gets the Christian religion, many of his standards of ight and wrong, the decimal system with its priceess zero, nationalism and the sovereign state, modern science and technology, tinkering with machnes, music in the diatonic scale, the free market – ow, alas, much corrupted with monopolies and government control – property rights, pecuniary mulation, and military conscription, to name a few.

3. The next smaller ring is *Anglo-Saxon culture* – hat part of Western civilization in which English is poken. Here George learns his language – *the most nportant single element in his entire cultural ineritance.* Without language the group could not ommunicate and would rapidly break up. Here oo George learns to vote and believe in habeas orpus, the Bill of Rights, political democracy, the dea of progress, and romantic love as the proper asis for marriage. He acquires a streak of Puritansm and the ability to cover up his emotions. He is aught to disapprove of people who shout and weep nd wave their hands. For a grown man to cry in he presence of others is humiliating and disgraceul. George stands nearer the Iroquois than the atin peoples in this respect, but nearer the Latins 1 his public laughter.

4. Next comes *North American culture*, which George shares with most Canadians, somewhat less vith Mexicans. Here he picks up many words and lace names and a few customs – like canoeing and orn roasts – which derive from the Indians. More han half the 48 states have Indian names, including is own Connecticut. He has been heavily influnced by the frontier pattern, for even New England as the frontier a few generations ago.

This pattern helps to reinforce George's indiviualism and a certain social irresponsibility, espeially toward public property and resources. "Cut ut and get out", move on West, was the frontiersnan's idea. The Pacific has long since been reached, but the irresponsibility remains, a cultural lag. It is shown in the fabulous wastes of topsoil, timber, grasslands, natural gas – wastes which mean nothing whatever to George, but which communities in Europe could not tolerate. It is shown in the political immaturity and awkwardness of most Americans when faced with international contacts. There is nothing in their culture to help them cope with such situations.

Other patterns which North America gives to George include: the great motor car complex on which he makes his living, Hollywood, radio and TV habits, the comics; mass production, bathrooms, a sublime belief in education; service clubs, baseball, the success story, the ability to laugh at himself, juke boxes, jazz bands, and a propensity to spoil his children. Notice that we are mixing up material things with customs and attitudes, but so they are mixed in the cultural stream.

5. *New England* is the last ring. Though most of George's habits were learned there, its unique contributions to his way of life are few, far fewer than in grandfather Obadiah's day. George is more tolerant of Negroes, coming from an abolitionist area, than many Americans. New England has given him some favorite dishes, such as clam chowder with milk; a nasal twang to his speech; a disposition to be close-mouthed, to be thrifty and count his pennies, and to be critical of the neighbors; the moral virtue of early rising, hard work, and a full woodpile.

A man brought up in New England usually stands 18 to 20 inches away when talking face to face with a man he has just met. If it is a woman he will back off four inches, making the distance about two feet. If a stranger begins to talk within eight to 13 inches, George's hackles rise, and the stranger should be ready to duck. If George had been reared in Cuba, however, he would feel perfectly comfortable at 13 inches, and uncomfortable at 20. . . . An Arab thinks no more of being 30 minutes late than George does of ten minutes: the time ratio is roughly three to one. "See you later," means nothing to

George beyond a polite good-bye. But if he should say the words to an Iranian and fail to look the gentleman up later, it would be a serious insult. . . .

It is obvious that most of George Adams's habits and systems of belief come from Western civilization, from the Anglo-Saxon culture, and from North America. The first has been in existence at least since Socrates, say for 2,500 years; the second since Chaucer, say 600 years, the third since Captain John Smith, say 300 years. But Indian additions reach back much further; Indian corn probably antedated Homer.

George . . . tries to reconcile these far-flung influences. Wherever he goes he carries this great cultural load – like the Old Man of the Sea. Nobody can get at him, talk to him, tell him anything, except in relation to this burden. When he met Chinese, Burmese, or Dutch during his overseas service, he judged them by these standards, built into his nervous system as the transmission is built into a car. If he happens to take a tourist cruise in the Caribbean, he will judge Haitians, Cubans, Virgin Islanders in a similar way, and unless he is aware of his reaction, it is unlikely that he will judge them fairly. Because their culture rings are somewhat different, many things they do will vary from what he does in similar circumstances, and he will blame them for it. At times the blame may flare into anger. . . . [For example] a United States paymaster dealing with Arabs on a Point Four project of technical assistance in the Near East . . . had been accustomed in previous assignments to pay the help on Friday, and he proposed to keep right on doing so in his new location. Friday, however, is a holy day, when good Moslems are not supposed to touch money. The agent pulled out his .45 and forced some of them to take their pay – holy day or not. Later he complained bitterly because the "lazy beggars" had left the job never to return. Such tragic misunderstandings could not occur if Americans – and Arabs – had a working knowledge of the other fellow's culture.

Discussion guidelines

1. Identify the characteristics of your own culture rings as distinct from those of George Adams.
2. "Centuries ago, mapmakers both in China and in Europe drew ridiculous monsters on the 'unknown lands', which made up the greate part of the world. Today, monsters must be exchanged for genuine cultural understanding if our 'Village Planet' is to survive." From your own experience of "monsters", suggest examples that have contributed to misunderstanding.

Cross references

Government Without Adults, page 5
Revolution? page 217

The Limit of Human Endurance?

from *Into the Whirlwind*
by Evgenia S. Ginzburg

[Imprisoned during the 1937 purges of the Russian Communist party, the author was sentenced to hard labour in the forests of Siberia. After enduring horrifying conditions on the S.S. *Dzhurma* which brought her and her companions to their destination, she faced life at the labour camp.]

Our overseer was a criminal called Kostik, nicknamed "The Actor". He was a man of some education, who at one time in his varied career had worked as a stage-hand in a provincial theatre, where he had added to his otherwise obscene vocabulary such sophisticated words as "*mise en scène*", "farce", and "travesty"; these gave an original turn to his language.

Reviewing the ranks of ragged women, armed with saws and axes, as if he were a commander inspecting his troops before a battle, he looked deeply depressed. Clearly, if he wanted any fun he would have to go to Elgen for it. He didn't care for prostitutes, indeed he had a respectable fear of venereal disease; as for the "believers", they were plainly cracked. That left the politicals, perhaps they had once been women but by now they'd certainly no charm left, they were just walking skeletons. Pushing back his forelock he started to sing:

> Not a blooming one for me,
> Goodness, what a travesty.

When Pavel Keyzin, the timber-procurement officer, appeared, they started to discuss the production situation. "How d'you think we're going to reach the norm with these dregs?"

Keyzin looked with equal dissatisfaction at our persons and our rusty, unset saws. What a squad! He had not developed any sadistic habits but his job, a difficult one, had taught him to consider human beings simply as adjuncts to their tools. It was about two and a half miles to the shanties where we were to live. We trudged along in single file through the virgin forest covered deep in slushy April snow. After the first few steps our feet were soaked, and when the afternoon frost set in our bast sandals were frozen stiff and we could hardly walk for the pain in our frostbitten feet. As soon as the guards had left us, to sit smoking round a bonfire, Kostik came along to give us some perfunctory instruction in the art of tree-felling.

"Ever taken a look at a tree? No? Lord, what a set of mollycoddles. Well, you see the way the snow piles up round the trunk? The first thing you've got to do is to stamp on it till it's firm. Like this."

It was easy enough for him to do it in his strong felt boots with elegantly turned-down tops and his breeches hanging over them in spiv fashion. When Galya and I (we were to work together) tried to imitate his movements, our sandals filled with snow.

"Now make a dint with your axe on the near side – after that you can start sawing. But do you two ladies know how to handle a saw? Lord, what a pantomime!"

"Do you really think that Galya and I can fell a tree that size?"

From Keyzin, who had not yet left the camp, came the curt reply:

"Not just one. Eight cubic metres a day. That's the norm for the two of you."

And Kostik, who until then couldn't have cared less about the trees or about us, chimed in, in a revoltingly boot-licking tone:

"Yes, and you have three days to get your hand in. You'll get full rations for that long. Afterwards it will depend on how much timber you can produce. We can't have any parasites here."

For three days Galya and I struggled to achieve the impossible. Poor trees, how they must have suffered at being mangled by our inexpert hands. Half-dead ourselves, and completely unskilled, we were in no condition to tackle them. The axe would slip and send showers of chips in our faces. We sawed feverishly, jerkily, mentally accusing each other of clumsiness but we knew we couldn't afford the luxury of a quarrel. The most terrifying moment was when the battered tree began to sway and we had no idea which way it would fall. Once Galya got a hard blow on the head, but the medical orderly refused to put iodine on the wound, remarking:

"That's an old trick. You'd like to be put off work from the start."

We watched the "believers" from Voronezh attentively; they seemed to possess some magic secret. How quickly and neatly they made the first cut with the axe. How smoothly and rhythmically they worked the saw. How obediently the tree fell in the required direction at the feet of these women who had been used to manual labour from their childhood.

Perhaps, if we had been allowed to recover and properly fed, we too might one day have achieved the elusive norm?

But during our apprenticeship our head overseer, who by all accounts was not such a bad fellow, exchanged jobs with his counterpart of Kilometre Fourteen. This man was a complete brute; he brought several lesser tormentors with him and instituted a régime of extermination.

"This isn't a rest-house." (We knew this saying all too well.) "You've a norm to fulfil. You'll eat according to your output. If there's any sabotage you'll be for the punishment-cell."

Though he had nothing Caucasian about him – he was tow-haired, and pitted with smallpox – his malignant sneer when he bawled at us recalled the Vulture of Yaroslavl.

"He's the living image of Vulturidze – must be his brother or his cousin." We nicknamed him Cousin.

We were woken at 5 a.m. Our sides ached from the untrimmed logs of which our bunks were made. We felt a devastating sense of emptiness which we had to overcome in order to stagger to the stove to retrieve our puttees and mittens from the stinking heap. This was none too easy because, for the first time since we'd been on the *Dzhurma*, we were sharing quarters with the criminal riff-raff who pinched foot-cloths and sandals, pushed us away from the stove, and were liable to grab a sharp saw out of its owner's hands.

It was no use complaining to "Cousin", who informed us at line-ups and roll-calls that he was only concerned with output and had no intention of wasting government rations on traitors who did not fulfil their norm. When we asked questions about our living conditions he gave a special grimace as he uttered the usual formula: "This isn't a rest-house."

And so, we amateur foresters came to know famine. Kostik might have taken pity on us and lightened our lot in some way, but "Cousin" was inexorable. He took personal care to see that his servitors kept us away from camp-fires, and made certain that his overseers did their duty. When Kostik came with his yard-stick to measure our daily output, a rifleman stood behind watching him, so even if he had wished to show some compassion it would not have been possible.

"Eighteen per cent – that's all today's output," he would say gloomily, with a sidelong glance at his escort. Then he would write down the figure against our names.

After receiving the scrap of bread which corresponded to our performance, we were led out next day literally staggering from weakness to our place of work. We divided the scrap into two parts. One we ate in the morning with boiling water, the other we ate in the forest, sprinkled with snow.

"Galya, don't you think a snow sandwich is much more satisfying than dry bread?"

"Of course it is."

During the first week of starvation rations, we still made occasional jokes. For instance, as we dragged ourselves home in our filthy rags, bent double, with the skin peeling off our weather-beaten faces, we would make up stories about ourselves such as might have appeared in the Society page of a western magazine.

"A gay troup of Amazons returned the other afternoon from a delightful *fête champêtre* in the grounds of the Château d'Elgen, in the valley of Toscana. (Elgen was in the Taskan region.) Shady boskages rang to the ladies' merry chatter. By general consent the most elegant member of the cavalcade was the Russian, Princess Stadnikova. (The patches on Galya Stadnikova's breeches certainly surpassed everyone else's in originality.) Baroness von Axenburg (a portmanteau version of my name) wore a confection inspired by Paquin which will undoubtedly set the trend for the coming season. On returning to the château the ladies partook of an exquisite supper of fresh lobsters under the attentive surveillance of the veteran major-domo, Cousin Vulturidze."

During the first day of our starvation diet, this sort of nonsense helped to keep up our spirits and to remind us that we were human beings. Before long we were in no mood for joking. "Cousin" began to use his second weapon: not only was food related to the fulfilment of the day's norm, which practically all politicals were too weak to achieve, but failure to fulfil it was treated as sabotage and those who had failed were confined to the punishment-cell.

This was a shack resembling a public lavatory. We were not allowed out of it to attend to our natural needs and no bucket was provided. At night we had to take turns sitting on the three logs that served as bunks, so most of the time we had to sleep standing up. At about 8 p.m. we were driven there, wet and hungry, straight from the forest, and were marched back to the forest at 5 a.m.

Now death seemed a certainty. We were so exhausted that it was bound to catch up with us soon. When I saw myself dimly reflected in a piece of looking-glass which Galya had found, I quoted Marina Tsvetayeva's words:

> Such a self I cannot live with,
> Such a self I cannot love.

Surely this couldn't be me?

Galya did not waste time trying to comfort me. Dry-eyed she said: "So long as he doesn't desert the boy."

Her husband had not been arrested.

We tried to find some way out. Kostik, the "Actor", was the first to offer us advice; he wasn't after all such a bad fellow.

"On your uppers, eh?" he said to Galya and me one day when the guards were absent. "If you go on like this you'll end up here, the curtain will fall. Couldn't you find a better *mise en scène*?"

"What else can we do? Just you tell us."

"You need to keep your heads. Kolyma rests on three foundations: threats, intrigue, and graft. Choose the one you want to star in."

This was theory. It was Polina Melnikova who showed us how to apply it. She was one of the few to fulfil her norm, yet she worked alone on a one-handed saw. One afternoon we found ourselves working beside her, that is to say we were working, but she, huddled in her rags, had been resting for an hour on a frozen log, her axe and saw thrown aside.

"Look!" said Galya, "She's like a statue of Gogol."

"It's true."

"How can she fulfil her norm sitting about like that?"

We asked her. She said that she had already reached it. Amazed, we pressed her to tell the secret. Looking around furtively, she explained: "The forest is full of piles of timber cut by our predecessors. No one has ever counted them."

"But anyone can see that they were cut long ago. By the fact that the cross-sections have grown dark in colour."

"If you saw off the slices at the end of each log it looks as though it had just been cut. Then you re-lay the logs in a different place and there's your norm."

This dodge, which we called freshening up the sandwich, gave us a respite. We made some variations in Polina's technique. We used as a nucleus of our pile some trees which we had in fact felled. We left two trees cut down but not yet sawn up as a sign of our assiduous activity. Then we dragged along some old logs and after slicing off their ends, added them to our pile.

Of the three foundations of Kolyma, we had opted for the third, and I may say we felt no compunction. I don't know whether Kostik realized

Miller Services, Toronto

Early in 1968, the American "spy" ship *Pueblo* was captured by North Korea, and its captain and crew were imprisoned. Although he repudiated his confession after his release, the captain is shown here, in captivity, admitting that his ship intruded in North Korean waters. What pressures produce such confessions?

why our output had increased; anyway, he never said anything about it.

Our respite was a short one. We had not yet recovered on our full rations from the punishment-cell, when tractors arrived at Kilometre Seven to cart away the timber. In three days all the reserves which helped us to fulfil the norm had vanished.

"Cousin" got into a rage when our output fell to 18 or 20 per cent. We were hoist with our own petard. Again we were condemned to the punishment-cell for sabotage.

During the eighteen years of our Via Dolorosa I many times found myself face to face with death. I never got used to the experience. Each time I felt the same terror and tried frantically and incoherently to find a way out. And each time my healthy, indestructible organism found a way to survival. I was helped by events which at first sight seemed accidental, but which were in reality manifestations of that Supreme Good which, in spite of everything, rules the world.

At first, escape from death in the forest of Elgen came by way of cranberries. This sour fruit did not ripen here in the summer as it does at home, but came to fruit after its ten months' sleep beneath the snow, when it first saw the pale sunlight.

It was on a May morning, as I was crouching close to the ground by a little spring in order to cut the branches of a felled larch, that I first noticed through the mist that fragile miracle of nature, a sprig of cranberry, emerging from the melting ice. It bore five or six berries of such a deep red that they looked almost black, and they were so tender that the sight of them was deeply moving. Like all over-ripe fruit, they fell at a touch. If you tried to pick them they squashed, but you could lie on the ground and suck them straight through your chapped lips and crush them between your tongue and your palate. They had an indescribable flavour, something like that of old wine. In no way could it be compared to the acid taste of our home bilberries. The intoxicating aroma was that of victory over suffering and winter.

I ate the two sprigs myself and it was only when I saw a third that I remembered my fellow creatures and called excitedly to Galya: "Galya, throw away your axe. I have found 'berries of golden wine'." These words of Severyanin were the only ones I could think of to describe my treasure trove.

From that day forward we went to the forest not in despair but in hope. We observed that the berries grew mostly on hummocks and around tree-stumps. We managed to find some nearly every day.

Discussion guideline

"I believe that man will not merely endure: he will prevail. He is immortal, not because he alone among creatures has an inexhaustible voice, but because he has a soul, a spirit capable of compassion and sacrifice and endurance." (William Faulkner, Address upon receiving the Nobel Prize for Literature)

To what extent does the selection support this quotation?

Protest!

Wide World Photo

If a man disagrees with his government, how far can he go in showing his dissent? Under what circumstances does his protest border on treason? Does he have the right to disagree with the majority? Or must he remain silent, even if he thinks his government is violating his sense of justice and morality? Suppose, however, that the actions he objects to are on the international level. Is effective protest on this level possible? And how can a man protest if he lives under an authoritarian government?

RAISING THE ISSUE

A "Troublemaker"
from *Socrates, His Life*
by Hermann Hagedorn

If your Greek toga had a buttonhole, Socrates' thumb would be through it, holding you pinned in your place while the goggle-eyed and delightful old gentleman asked you exactly how clever you think you are and what in the world, in the first place, makes you think you are clever anyway.

He is the first and greatest of all buttonholers. It makes no difference where you are, or how busy you are. If Socrates fixes his eyes on you, he will come lumbering across the athletic field or the market place, and, smiling most courteously, he will engage you in conversation. Socrates is a glutton for conversation. Money means nothing to him. Fame, power, influence mean nothing. He never knows exactly where the next meal is coming from; but he must have conversation.

It is not that he wishes to hear himself talk; but he does want to hear what you have to say. He does not seek gossip, tips on the races or the discus throwers, or stories of the dancing girls, or wails on the political situation and the state of the war between Athens and Sparta. But he loves talk of fundamental things, of justice and virtue and wisdom and love and death and immortality. He can talk on these matters as no one else in his city – and it is a city of great talkers – and he can make you talk as you have never talked before.

Who is he, this man Socrates? What is his profession, his job? He is the son of a stonemason. For a while he was a stonemason himself. Yes, and he has been a soldier, not from choice, but because Athens needed all her able-bodied men in her wars with Sparta, the physical examination taking no account of height, or of eyes somewhat off center. At thirty-seven he is at the siege of Potidaea, at great risk saving the life of a brilliant young fellow townsman, Alcibiades, who proves, in the end, not to have been worth saving. At forty-five he is in the disastrous defeat at Delium, carrying Xenophon, a young friend of his, who is to make his mark as an historian, off to safety on his broad shoulders. "He stalked along like a pelican," Alcibiades subsequently reports, "glaring around with his projecting crab's eyes, so that none of the enemy dared molest him."

But soldiering is the least important activity of this extraordinary person's life. It is as a conversationalist that Athens knows him – as the man who asks questions. If you enjoy conversation and can answer Socrates' questions with intelligence, you love him and gratefully accept his invitations to walk under the olive trees with him or to spend the night with a few other sympathetic souls, talking about courage or happiness or the ideal republic. But if you don't enjoy high talk, if you think yourself wise and are really dull and Socrates shows you up by a keen question or two, you hate him and talk of him as a public nuisance and go around growling that if the government had any sand in its gizzard it would shut him up.

He is a queer customer, unquestionably. But he has a wise mind, a humble spirit, and a voice within him which he calls his daemon, which lays a check on him, he says, when he is tempted to do wrong or stupid things. His clothes are always shabby. He goes about with bare feet. How he lives no one knows. The truth is that he has a small income, much too small to keep a family on in any style which Athens would approve. But he refuses to increase it, preferring to adjust his needs to his income rather than his income to his supposed needs. His wife, a sharp-tongued lady named Xantippe, rails at him as an irresponsible loafer and gadabout. At home there are arguments in which, it is rumored, all of the questioning and most of the talking is for once done by the other party.

But Socrates is not a philosopher for nothing. When a friend asks him how he happened to marry Xantippe, of all women, he replies, "Those who want to learn to ride well choose restive horses, because, if they can handle these, they can manage any others. I want to learn to associate with all mankind, and I chose Xantippe, knowing that if I could bear her society, I should be able to get along with anyone!" Perhaps he is joking; but it would not be safe to be too sure.

He is not what would be called an established citizen, with a pleasant house to live in and taxes to growl about. He is something rarer, an institution. Everybody knows him. He has nothing to do all day except to ask questions and to talk, and as he does these things invariably in public places, he is as familiar a figure as the town constable. Even the comic writers poke fun at him in their plays. His questions always have point; that is one reason why people find them disturbing.

The oracle at Delphi, consulted by all the Greeks, has told Socrates that he is "the wisest of men". Socrates laughs at the idea. He isn't wise, he knows he isn't; that is all, in fact, that he does know. There are countless men wiser than himself, he is certain, in Athens alone. He sets about to prove it, and that is how the questioning begins. He goes to a statesman with a great reputation and asks for light on the nature of wisdom or happiness, and is most astonished to find that the statesman is as much in the dark as he is, though he thinks that he really knows.

"Well," says Socrates to himself, "I am wiser than this fellow anyway. He thinks that he knows, when he doesn't, and at least I know that I don't know."

Thereupon he calls on a great soldier, a great artist, a great philosopher. In every case his experience is the same. They all think they are wise, but when he pins them down, they do not really know anything at all, not even that they are ignorant. Men of vision, whom he thus questions, gratefully accept the light he throws into their darkness. But the men who are vain and self-important are indignant.

Young men crowd about him, however, fascinated and thrilled. It is a period of change in Athens. Thinking people find it difficult to believe in the old gods as their fathers did. When they look coolly at the stories of Jupiter and his adventures, of Venus and Juno, of Mars and Mercury and the rest, the gods look rather shabby, a little too human in their frailties to be regarded as divine.

The young men are asking, "What is this earth made of; how did it come to be? What are we human beings here for? How can we be happy? What happens when we die?" The old myths give no answers that satisfy these eager questioners.

Socrates says to them, "Do not bother your heads overmuch with problems regarding creation or the substance of things. Here you are, a man, living for awhile in the world with other men. What you must do is to think how you can live and help others to live most nobly and wisely."

They listen, and come day after day to hear his keen questioning and to answer as intelligently as they can. Those are congenial gatherings, for Socrates loves these young men as much as they love him.

"Some men," he has a way of saying, "have a fancy for a fine horse, or a dog, or a bird. What I fancy, and take delight in, is friends of a superior kind. If I know anything, I teach it to them. In common with them I turn over and explore the treasures of the wise men of old which have been left written in books. If we find anything good, we pick it out, and we think it a great gain if we can be beneficial to one another."

Majestic themes are discussed at those gatherings – fundamental questions of right and wrong, of the meaning of justice, the meaning of love. Questions of government are threshed through.

Socrates is outspoken and spares no one. The government of Athens, splendid under the great Pericles, has come to troublous times now that the leader is dead. There are wars without and revolutions within; and now the mob rules, and now a small group of powerful and wealthy citizens. The mob and the oligarchy, as this small group is called, are equally unjust and despotic, and in his quiet way Socrates strikes at them both.

When the Thirty Tyrants, who are now ruling, send for Socrates in anger and forbid him to "discourse with the young", he merely asks them most humbly what they mean by "discourse", and whom exactly would they call "the young"? Can't he even ask directions or buy meat of anyone, say, under thirty? The Tyrants rage and threaten him with death. But Socrates pays no attention whatsoever to their orders, teaching as before.

But the old philosopher does not love a stupid mob any more than a stupid committee of tyrants. He says that democracy, if it is stupid and unjust, is as evil as stupid and cruel tyranny. Forms are comparatively unimportant; the essential thing is that government, whatever form it takes, shall be enlightened and just. It is a dangerous doctrine to preach, for it sets the stupid on both sides against him. When the Thirty Tyrants are overthrown and the popular party comes into control, Socrates is a marked man.

Slowly the feeling against him in Athens takes definite form. The men he has shown up to themselves with his straightforward questions, the ruling classes he has made fun of, the blundering mob he has refused to praise and to bow down to, begin to ask themselves why they have borne with this gadfly so long. He is teaching the young men of the city that in government, majorities are not enough. You must have intelligence also. Dangerous doctrine! He is corrupting the youth!

Socrates smiles and goes quietly on, not teaching any philosophy of his own so much as stimulating his pupils to think out an intelligent way of living for themselves. And then one day, a notice is posted in Athens:

"Meletus, son of Meletus, accuses Socrates, son of Sophroniscus, as is underwritten. Socrates is guilty of crime – first, for neglecting the gods whom the city acknowledges, and setting forth other strange gods; next, for corrupting the youth. Penalty – death."

Meletus is a poet (or thinks he is), but there are other accusers, notably a democratic politician named Anytus, whose son Socrates has persuaded to give up his father's leather trade and devote himself to learning. Anytus feels strongly that to persuade any young man to give up the leather business for the shadowy rewards of scholarship is clear corruption.

Socrates seems to be the only individual in Athens who is not disturbed by the approaching trial. He does not even make any preparations for his speech of defense. All his life has been a preparation for it, he says, having been spent in learning what was right and trying to do it.

The trial is held before a jury of five hundred fifty-seven citizens of Athens. Eloquently, Socrates speaks in his own behalf. He states his case as only he can state it, but his speech is not really a defense, but a lecture. If the jurymen are expecting him to back down in any respect, or to plead for his life, they are doomed to disappointment. On the contrary, he will not accept acquittal if it means that he shall stop his teaching. When he was a soldier and his commander placed him in a post of danger, there he was bound in honor to stay. It is the same now.

"Strange indeed would be my conduct, men of Athens," he insists, "if, now when God orders me, as I believe, to fulfill the philosopher's mission of searching into myself and other men, I were to desert my post through fear of death, or any other fear. Men of Athens, I honor and love you; but I shall obey God rather than you, and while I have life and strength, I shall never cease from the practice and teaching of philosophy."

The court declares him guilty, but only by a majority of five or six. According to ancient custom, he is asked what punishment he would regard as just. Fearlessly he replies that if it is required of him to say how the public in justice ought to treat him, he can only say that he should be recognized as a public benefactor and given a pension for life; but, as an alternative, he proposes a small fine. The court regards his proposal as an insult, and he is condemned to death.

He takes the sentence with perfect calmness. Instead of pleading for mercy or sympathy, in fact, he turns about and encourages the court, as though he suspected that their consciences were pricking them for condemning him, and felt sorry for them.

"O Judges, be of good cheer about death," he says, "and know of a certainty that no evil can happen to a good man, either in life or after. I am not angry with my accusers, or with you, my condemners. The hour of departure is at hand, and we go our ways, I to die, and you to live. Which is better, God alone knows."

For a month he is in prison, with fetters on his ankles, surrounded by his friends; talking, questioning as always; refusing to escape, regretting nothing, fearing nothing. Then, one evening as the sun is setting, the young men gather around him for the last time.

One of them, Apollodorus, is loud in his lamentations. "I grieve most for this, Socrates," he cries, "that I see you about to die undeservedly."

But the old gentleman's sense of humor is as active as ever. With a smile he strokes his pupil's hair. "My dearest Apollodorus," he says, "would you rather see me die deservedly?"

The last scene has all the sad beauty of autumn, or dying day. Minute by minute the shadows deepen. Xantippe, Socrates' wife, is there, wailing. For all that she abused her philosopher these many years, she loves him, and he has to send her away at last because he will have no lamentations when the end comes.

The jailer, in tears, brings him the hemlock, the poison which he is to drink. Holding the cup to his lips he drains it and begins to walk about as the jailer has told him to do. His friends try hard to keep back the tears, but when young Apollodorus gives a sudden exclamation of grief, they lose their grip of themselves for a moment.

Socrates alone remains calm. "What is this strange outcry?" he says. "I sent away the women in order that they might not offend in this way, for I have heard that a man should die in peace. Be quiet then, and have patience."

The poison is working. He can no longer walk; he lies down. They all know the end is near. But once more he uncovers his face, remembering a debt he owes to the temple of the god of medicine. "Crito," he says, turning to one of the young men. "I owe a cock to Aesculapius.[1] Will you remember to pay the debt?"

"The debt shall be paid," Crito answers in low tones. "Is there anything else?"

There is nothing else, no word more. And his friends have, to comfort them, only the words which he spoke in answer to their question what they should do with his body: "You may do with it what you like, provided you do not imagine it to be me."

No, that quiet shape is not Socrates. He is elsewhere, questioning the eternities. And he still halts men in the churches and schools and market places, and on the buzzing highways of the world, asking them what they mean by the words they fling about so lightly; and what do they know – and are they really as wise as they imagine?

Magnificent old questioner that he was! Wisest and noblest of all the Greeks!

[1]When recovering from illness, it was the Greek custom to make an offering to Aesculapius, the Divine Healer.

Discussion guidelines

1. (a) "Socrates was either a fool or truly the 'wisest and noblest of all the Greeks'." Defend your choice of these two evaluations.
   (b) Suggest contemporary individuals who you think are in the tradition of Socrates.
2. "Every society needs troublemakers but few societies tolerate them." Provide some reasons to account for this situation.

   or

   "Why does [society] not cherish its wise minority? Why does it not encourage its citizens to be on the alert to point out its faults and do better than it would have them? Why does it always crucify Christ, and excommunicate Copernicus and Luther and pronounce Washington and Franklin rebels?" (Henry David Thoreau, *Civil Disobedience*)
   How would you answer the questions raised by Thoreau?

Wide World Photo

A modern Greek protester. When the army seized power in Greece in 1968, Melina Mercouri, a well-known Greek actress, led a number of protests against the government of her homeland. Because of this, her Greek citizenship was revoked.

SEVEN VIEWS

The Duty to Conscience

from *A Man for All Seasons*
by Robert Bolt

[When Henry VIII married Catherine, his brother's widow, he had to obtain special permission from the Papacy. Later, when he wished his marriage to Catherine to be dissolved so that he could marry Anne Boleyn, the Pope refused to grant a dissolution. Consequently, Henry VIII broke from the Church of Rome, appointed a co-operative Archbishop of Canterbury, and proceeded with his marriage plans. It was important to Henry for personal, religious, and political reasons that Sir Thomas More, his Lord Chancellor and friend, agree to his actions. More, however, withheld his approval and refused to take the oath, demanded of all Englishmen, that Henry's marriage was legal. As refusal was declared treasonous, More was put on trial. In Act II of *A Man for All Seasons*, Robert Bolt records Sir Thomas More's defence at this trial, which ended with More's condemnation and execution.]

CROMWELL: Now, Sir Thomas, you stand upon your silence.

MORE: I do.

CROMWELL: But, Gentlemen of the Jury, there are many kinds of silence. Consider first the silence of a man when he is dead. Let us say we go into the room where he is lying; and let us say it is in the dead of the night – there's nothing like darkness for sharpening the ear; and we listen. What do we hear? Silence. What does it betoken, this silence? Nothing. This is silence, pure and simple. But consider another case. Suppose I were to draw a dagger from my sleeve and make to kill the prisoner with it, and suppose their lordships there, instead of crying out for me to stop or crying out for help to stop me, maintained their silence. That *would* betoken! It would betoken a willingness that I should do it, and under the law they would be guilty with me. So silence can, according to circumstances, speak. Consider, now, the circumstances of the prisoner's silence. The oath was put to good and faithful subjects up and down the country and they had declared His Grace's Title to be just and good. And when it came to the prisoner he refused. He calls this silence. Yet is there a man in this court, is there a man in this country, who does not *know* Sir Thomas More's opinion of this title? Of

Columbia Pictures

Sir Thomas More before his accusers. This scene is from the movie version of *A Man for All Seasons,* with Paul Scofield playing the role of Sir Thomas More.

course not! But how can that be? Because this silence betokened – nay this silence *was* – not silence at all, but most eloquent denial.

MORE (*with some of the academic's impatience for a shoddy line of reasoning*): Not so, Mr. Secretary, the maxim is "qui tacet consentire". (*Turns to* COMMON MAN.) The maxim of the law is: (*very carefully*) "Silence Gives Consent". If, therefore, you wish to construe what my silence "betokened", you must construe that I consented, not that I denied.

CROMWELL: Is that what the world in fact construes from it? Do you pretend that is what you *wish* the world to construe from it?

MORE: The world must construe according to its wits. This Court must construe according to the law. . . . (*To the* FOREMAN) The law is a causeway upon which so long as he keeps to it a citizen may walk safely. (*Earnestly addressing him.*) In matters of conscience –

CROMWELL (*bitterly smiling*): The conscience, the conscience . . .

MORE (*turning*): The word is not familiar to you?

CROMWELL: By God, too familiar! I am very used to hear it in the mouths of criminals!

MORE: I am used to hear bad men misuse the name of God, yet God exists. (*Turning back.*) In matters of conscience the loyal subject is more bounden to be loyal to his conscience than to any other thing.

Discussion guidelines

1. In the discussion on "silence", explain whether or not you think Sir Thomas More is telling the truth.
2. Do you agree that man's loyalty to his conscience must be placed before his loyalty to the laws of the state? Comment on this statement by citing modern examples.

Cross reference

Alliances Don't Work, page 269

My Dungeon Shook

from *The Fire Next Time*
by James Baldwin

Dear James:

I have begun this letter five times and torn it up five times. I keep seeing your face, which is also the face of your father and my brother. Like him, you are tough, dark, vulnerable, moody – with a very definite tendency to sound truculent because you want no one to think you are soft. You may be like your grandfather in this, I don't know, but certainly both you and your father resemble him very much physically. Well, he is dead, he never saw you, and he had a terrible life; he was defeated long before he died because, at the bottom of his heart, he really believed what white people said about him. This is one of the reasons that he became so holy. I am sure that your father has told you something about all that. Neither you nor your father exhibit any tendency towards holiness: you really are of another era, part of what happened when the Negro left the land and came into what the late E. Franklin Frazier called "the cities of destruction". You can only be destroyed by believing that you really are what the white world calls a nigger. I tell you this because I love you, and please don't you ever forget it.

I have known both of you all your lives, have carried your Daddy in my arms and on my shoulders, kissed and spanked him and watched him learn to walk. I don't know if you've known anybody from that far back; if you've loved anybody that long, first as an infant, then as a child, then as a man, you gain a strange perspective on time and human pain and effort. Other people cannot see what I see whenever I look into your father's face, for behind your father's face as it is today are all those other faces which were his. Let him laugh and I see a cellar your father does not remember and a house he does not remember and I hear in his present laughter his laughter as a child. Let him curse and I remember him falling down the cellar steps, and howling, and I remember, with pain, his tears, which my hand or your grandmother's so easily wiped away. But no one's hand can wipe away those tears he sheds invisibly today, which one hears in his laughter and in his speech and in his songs. I know what the world has done to my brother and how narrowly he has survived it. And I know, which is much worse, and this is the crime of which I accuse my country and my countrymen, and for which neither I nor time nor history will ever forgive them, that they have destroyed and are destroying hundreds of thousands of lives and do not know it and do not want to know it. One can be, indeed one must strive to become, tough and philosophical concerning destruction and death, for this is what most of mankind has been best at since we have heard of man. (But remember: *most* of mankind is not *all* of mankind.) But it is not permissible that the authors of devastation should also be innocent. It is the innocence which constitutes the crime.

Now, my dear namesake, these innocent and well-meaning people, your countrymen, have caused you to be born under conditions not very far removed from those described for us by Charles Dickens in the London of more than a hundred years ago. (I hear the chorus of the innocents screaming, "No! This is not true! How bitter you are!" – but I am writing this letter to you, to try to tell you something about how to handle them, for most of them do not yet really know that you exist. I know the conditions under which you were born, for I was there. Your countrymen were not there, and haven't made it yet. Your grandmother was also there, and no one has ever accused her of being bitter. I suggest that the innocents check with her. She isn't hard to find. Your countrymen don't know that she exists, either, though she has been working for them all their lives.)

Well, you were born, here you came, something like fifteen years ago; and though your father and mother and grandmother, looking about the streets through which they were carrying you, staring at the walls into which they brought you, had every reason to be heavy-hearted, yet they were not. For here you were, Big James, named for me – you were a big baby, I was not – here you were: to be loved. To be loved, baby, hard, at once, and forever, to strengthen you against the loveless world. Remember that: I know how black it looks today, for you. It looked bad that day, too, yes, we were trembling. We have not stopped trembling yet, but if we had not loved each other none of us would have survived. And now you must survive because we love you, and for the sake of your children and your children's children.

This innocent country set you down in a ghetto in which, in fact, it intended that you should perish. Let me spell out precisely what I mean by that, for the heart of the matter is here, and the root of my dispute with my country. You were born where you were born and faced the future that you faced because you were black and *for no other reason*. The limits of your ambition were, thus, expected to be set forever. You were born into a society which spelled out with brutal clarity, and in as many ways as possible, that you were a worthless human being. You were not expected to aspire to excellence: you were expected to make peace with mediocrity. Wherever you have turned, James, in your short time on this earth, you have been told where you could go and what you could do (and *how* you could do it) and where you could live and whom you could marry. I know your countrymen do not agree with me about this, and I hear them saying, "You exaggerate." They do not know Harlem, and I do. So do you. Take no one's word for anything, including mine – but trust your experience. Know whence you came. If you know whence you came, there is really no limit to where you can go. The details and symbols of your life have been deliberately constructed to make you believe what white people say about you. Please try to remember that what they believe, as well as what they do and cause you to endure, does not testify to your inferiority but to their inhumanity and fear. Please try to be clear, dear James, through the storm which rages about your youthful head today, about the reality which lies behind the words acceptance and integration. There is no reason for you to try to become like white people and there is no basis whatever for their impertinent assumption that they must accept *you*. The really terrible thing, old buddy, is that *you* must accept *them*. And I mean that very seriously. You must accept them and accept them with love. For these innocent people have no other hope. They are, in effect, still trapped in a history which they do not understand; and until they understand it, they cannot be released from it. They have had to believe for many years, and for innumerable reasons, that black men are inferior to white men. Many of them, indeed, know better, but, as you will discover, people find it very difficult to act on what they know. To act is to be committed, and to be committed is to be in danger. In this case, the danger, in the minds of most white Americans, is the loss of their identity. Try to imagine how you would feel if you woke up one morning to find the sun shining and all the stars aflame. You would be frightened because it is out of the order of nature. Any upheaval in the universe is terrifying because it so profoundly attacks one's sense of one's own reality. Well, the black man has functioned in the white man's world as a fixed star, as an immovable pillar: and as he moves out of his place, heaven and earth are shaken to their foundations. You, don't be afraid. I said that it was intended that you should perish in the ghetto, perish by never being allowed to go beyond the white man's definitions, by never being allowed to spell your proper name. You have, and many of us have, defeated this intention; and, by a terrible law, a terrible paradox, those innocents who believed that your imprisonment made them safe are losing their grasp of reality. But these men are your brothers – your lost, younger brothers. And if the word integration means anything, this is what it means: that we, with love, shall force our brothers to see themselves as they are, to cease fleeing from reality and begin to change it. For this is your home, my friend, do not be driven from it; great men have done great things here, and will again, and we can make America what America must become. It will be hard, James, but you come from sturdy, peasant stock, men who picked cotton and dammed rivers and built railroads, and, in the teeth of the most terrifying odds, achieved an unassailable and monumental dignity. You come from a long line of great poets, some of the greatest poets since Homer. One of them said,

The very time I thought I was lost,
My dungeon shook and my chains fell off.

You know, and I know, that the country is celebrating one hundred years of freedom one hundred years too soon. We cannot be free until they are free. God bless you, James, and Godspeed.

Your uncle,
James

Discussion guidelines

1. "Kill Whitey." or "You must accept them and accept them with love." Given the history of the American Negro, which reaction is a more realistic approach to attempting to solve the racial problem?
2. "Passive resistance is a weapon of the weak: it implies the obstinate endurance of suffering without giving in . . . whereas Civil Disobedience seeks to take the initiative in exposing and bringing an end to unjust conditions." (George Woodcock, *Civil Disobedience*)
   To what extent can Baldwin's advice be classified in either of these two categories?

Cross reference

In Defence of Equality, page 15

3

by permission of Johnny Hart and Field Enterprises Incorporated

CLAIMS CANADA LAGGING IN PROMOTING WOMEN

Canada trails behind Britain and the United States in promoting women to senior civil servant positions, a group of professional and business women said yesterday.

The Canadian Federation of Business and Professional Women's Clubs, appearing at a hearing of the Royal Commission on the Status of Women in Canada, said the 1960 Glassco Royal Commission reported that 3,041 men and only 32 women received $10,000 or more a year in public service and 586 men and only three women received $14,000 or more.

It urged the Government to provide leadership to business and industry in promoting qualified women to senior positions.

The federation spokesmen said university education is considered desirable for women, providing the course is general arts. But because of pressures of finance, marriage, and lack of job opportunities, they are still discouraged from entering medicine, law, architecture, and engineering.

"At the high school level, counselling often encourages the road to easy success," the federation brief said. Much could be done in school counselling to encourage girls toward their potential goals.

The group said women should have the right to decide whether they want an abortion and that they should be entitled to skilled medical help if they decide to terminate the pregnancy.

It urged that laws forbidding discrimination in employment because of color, race, religion, political opinion or country of origin also include the word sex as stipulated by the International Labor Organization.

Quebec is the only province that includes sex in its anti-discrimination laws.

The federation says many jobs are specified as women's work with lower wages.

Margaret Hyndman, a Toronto lawyer and one of the federation spokesmen, said the old argument that employers do not want to hire women because they don't stay in their jobs, no longer applies.

Men change jobs on their way to the top. They do not stay with one company and wait until someone retires or dies so they can be promoted, she said.

Women accept lower wages because they are in the minority in the work force and may need the jobs. "They take what is dished out to them."

Chatelaine editor Doris Anderson said a survey by her magazine showed women want tighter equal pay laws, more subsidized day-care centres, tax exemptions for household help for working women and a legal penalty for discrimination against women in business, universities, government and the church.

The Globe and Mail, Toronto
June 4, 1968

Discussion guidelines

1. Considering your own school and job experiences, to what extent do you think girls are treated like "second class citizens"?
2. "If the French Canadians can make it, if the Negroes and Indians can make it, then it is likely that women will make it too." (Judy LaMarsh, *Memoirs of a Bird in a Gilded Cage*) Although Canadian women are numerically stronger than the French Canadians, Negroes, and Indians, in Judy LaMarsh's opinion, they have still not "made it". Suggest some reasons to account for this situation.
3. "If, by equality, women mean the right to compete in every sphere of activity with men, then they defy their greatest biological and sociological commitment – namely, to bear and nurture children. The human quality of our society will be the real victim." Discuss.

Cross reference

The Iroquoian Example, page 102

What Would You Have Done?

from *They Thought They Were Free*
by Milton Mayer

[*They Thought They Were Free* concerns the lives of ten law-abiding German citizens during Hitler's Third Reich. A high school student, a teacher, a policeman, and an unemployed salesman are five of the ten representative "ordinary" people who figure in the account.]

None of my ten friends ever encountered anybody connected with the operation of the deportation system or the concentration camps. None of them ever knew, on a personal basis, anybody connected with the Gestapo, the Sicherheitsdienst (Security Services), or the Einsatzgruppen (the Occupation Detachments, which followed the German armies eastward to conduct the mass killing of Jews). None of them ever knew anybody who knew anybody connected with these agencies of atrocity. Even Policeman Hofmeister, who had to arrest Jews for "protective custody" or "resettlement" and who saw nothing wrong in "giving the Jews land, where they could learn to work with their hands instead of with money", never knew anyone whose shame or shamelessness might have reproached him had they stood face to face. The fact that the Police Chief of Kronenberg made him sign the orders to arrest Jews told him only that the Chief himself was afraid of getting into trouble "higher up".

Sixty days before the end of the war, Teacher Hildebrandt, as a first lieutenant in command of a disintegrating Army subpost, was informed by the post doctor that an S.S. man attached to the post was going crazy because of his memories of shooting down Jews "in the East"; this was the closest any of my friends came to knowing of the systematic butchery of National Socialism.

I say none of these ten men knew, and, if none of them, very few of the seventy million Germans. The proportion, which was none out of ten in Kronenberg, would, certainly, have been higher among more intelligent, or among more sensitive or sophisticated, people in, say, Kronenberg University or in the big cities where people circulate more widely and hear more. But I must say what I mean by "know".

By *know* I mean knowledge, binding knowledge. Men who are going to protest or take even stronger forms of action, in a dictatorship more so than in a democracy, want to be sure. When they are sure, they still may not take any form of action. . . . What you hear of individual instances, second or third hand, what you guess as to general conditions, having put half a dozen instances together, what someone tells you he believes is the case – these may, all together, be convincing. You may be "morally certain", satisfied in your own mind. But moral certainty and mental satisfaction are less than binding

Miller Services, Toronto

Jews being herded out of the Warsaw Ghetto, 1943. Most of them were shot.

knowledge. What you and your neighbors don't expect you to know, your neighbors do not expect you to act on, in matters of this sort, and neither do you.

Men who participated in the operation of the atrocity system – would they or wouldn't they tell their wives? The odds are even in Germany, where husbands don't bother to tell their wives as much as we tell ours. But their wives would not tell other people, and neither would they; their jobs were, to put it mildly, of a confidential character. In such work, men, if they talk, lose their jobs. Under Nazism they lost more than their jobs. I am not saying that the men in question, the men who had first hand knowledge, opposed the system in any degree or even resented having to play a role in it; I am saying, in the words of Cabinetmaker Klingelhöfer, that that is the way men are; and the more reprehensible the work in which they are voluntarily or involuntarily engaged, the more that way they are.

I pushed this point with Tailor Marowitz in Kronenberg, the one Jew still there who had come back from Buchenwald. On his release, in 1939, he was forbidden to talk of his experience, and, in case he might become thoughtless, he was compelled to report (simply report) to the police every day. Whom did he tell of his Buchenwald experience? His wife and "a couple of my very closest friends – Jews, of course".

"How widely was the whole thing known in Kronenberg by the end of the war?"

"You mean the rumors?"

"No – how widely was the whole thing, or anything, *known*?"

"Oh. Widely, very widely."

"How?"

"Oh, things seeped through somehow, always quietly, always indirectly. So people heard rumors, and the rest they could guess. Of course, most people did not believe the stories of Jews or other opponents of the regime. It was naturally thought that such persons would all exaggerate."

Miller Services, Toronto

A Jewish survivor of Nazi treatment, April 1945

Rumors, guesses enough to make a man know if he wanted badly to know, or at least to believe, and always involving persons who would be suspected, "naturally", of exaggerating. Goebbels' immediate subordinate in charge of radio in the Propaganda Ministry testified at Nuremberg that he had heard of the gassing of Jews, and went to Goebbels with the report. Goebbels said it was false, "enemy propaganda", and that was the end of it. The Nuremberg tribunal accepted this man's testimony on this point and acquitted him. None of my ten friends in Kronenberg – nor anyone else in Kronenberg – was the immediate subordinate of a cabinet minister. Anti-Nazis no less than Nazis let the rumors pass – if not rejecting them, certainly not accepting them; either they were enemy propaganda or they *sounded* like enemy propaganda, and, with one's country fighting for its life and one's sons and brothers dying in war, who wants to hear, still less repeat, even what *sounds* like enemy propaganda?

Who wants to investigate the reports? Who is "looking for trouble"? Who will be the first to undertake (and how undertake it?) to track down the suspicion of governmental wrongdoing under a governmental dictatorship, to occupy himself, in times of turmoil and in wartime with evils, real or rumored, that are wholly outside his own life, outside his own circle, and, above all, outside his own power? After all, what if one found out?

Suppose you have heard, second hand, or even first hand, of an instance in which a man was abused or tortured by the police in a hypothetical American community. You tell a friend whom you are trying to persuade that the police are rotten. He doesn't believe you. He wants first hand, or if you got it second hand, at least second hand testimony. You go to your original source, who has told you the story only because of his absolute trust in you. You want him now to tell a man he doesn't trust, a friend of the police. He refuses. And he warns you that if you use his name as authority for the story, he will deny it. Then you will be suspect, suspected of spreading false rumors against the police. And, as it happens, the police in this hypothetical American community are rotten, and they'll "get" you somehow.

So, after all, what if one found out in Nazi Germany (which was no hypothetical American community)? What if one came to know? What then?

There was *nichts dagegen zu machen*, "nothing to do about it". Again and again my discussions with each of my friends reached this point, one way or another, and this very expression; again and again this question, put to me with the wide-eyed innocence that always characterizes the guilty when they ask it of the inexperienced: "What would you have done?"

What is the proportion of revolutionary heroes, of saints and martyrs, or, if you will, of troublemakers, in Stockholm, Ankara, El Paso? We in America have not had the German experience, where even private protest was dangerous, where even secret knowledge might be extorted; but what did we expect the good citizen of Minneapolis or Charlotte to do when, in the midst of war, he was told, openly and officially, that 112,000 of his fellow-Americans, those of Japanese ancestry on the American West Coast, had been seized without warrant and sent without due process of law to relocation centers? There was *nichts dagegen zu machen* – not even by the United States Supreme Court, which found that the action was within the Army's power – and, anyway, the good citizen of Minneapolis or Charlotte had his own troubles.[1]

It was this, I think – they had their own troubles – that in the end explained my friends' failure to "do something" or even to know something. A man can carry only so much responsibility. If he

[1]It should be noted that in 1942 the Canadian federal government approved the evacuation of 22,000 persons of Japanese descent from their British Columbian homes. Some were relocated in isolated camps in the interior of the province; some were sent to other Canadian provinces. The question of restitution for the indignities and injustices suffered is still being raised in the courts.

tries to carry more, he collapses; so, to save himself from collapse, he rejects the responsibility that exceeds his capacity.

Discussion guideline

"A man can carry only so much responsibility. If he tries to carry more, he collapses; so, to save himself from collapse, he rejects the responsibility that exceeds his capacity." From your observations, do you think this is a feeble excuse or a valid explanation for an individual's refusal to protest against evil?

Cross reference

The Breakdown of Society, page 48

Miller Services, Toronto

German citizens of the town of Sautau are forced by the Allies to see for themselves the results of Nazi brutality. A trainload of slave workers were unloaded near the town, marched into the adjacent woods, and murdered.

The Right To Resist – Did It Exist?

from *The Burden of Guilt*
by Hannah Vogt

Young people who never experienced terror themselves sometimes ask: "Why did you not kill Hitler in time?" They cannot understand why resistance did not spread widely and why it did not have more success. Others, however, say to this day that no resistance should have been offered while the war lasted, and that Hitler should have been made to account for his crimes afterwards. Both views misrepresent the actual situation. But they reveal also a central problem affecting German resistance.

Today, in the security of a state based on law..., it is simple to [assume] a duty to resist. No doubt, it did exist as long as everybody was still free to defend himself – during the period of the Weimar Republic. It existed also to a large extent during the first few months following the "seizure of power", when Hitler was still feeling his way to see how far he could go. There is no doubt, too, that the first attacks on the institutions of the state based on law should have been more vigorously opposed. . . . Once terror, with all its brutality, had been incorporated in the law, both open and [secret] resistance [threatened] life and limb to such an extent that it took extraordinary courage to risk the consequences. This is all the more true for relatives of resistance fighters, who were also endangered by such action. . . . Everybody had to decide according to his own conscience how much he was prepared to tolerate, and at what point he felt obliged to make his stand. An incessant barrage of propaganda had blunted the consciences of many, and others who had retained a moral standard kept their distance from the N.S.D.A.P.[1] as much as possible and suffered injustices which they were too weak to oppose. Still others chose the way of martyrs and heroes. This is their story.

. . . German resistance fighters had no . . . support. The regime they opposed was created an supported by a sizable section of their own people In addition, they had to face the strong belief from most of their countrymen that their actions [meant] high treason and a disgraceful disloyalty towar their own nation in wartime. This often sharpene conflicts of conscience until they became well-nigh unbearable.

Yet another difficulty to be overcome by Germa resistance fighters was the fact that Germany ha almost no tradition of revolutionary action, of th moral freedom of the individual to oppose those i power, which has occurred on numerous occasion in British and French history. . . .

With the exception of the German Christians, the Protestant as well as the Catholic Church re mained faithful to their calling. . . .

Soon, all Germany knew the names of som members of the resisting churches. Everybody ha heard of Pastor Niemöller who, having been ac quitted by a court, had been arrested by the Ge stapo and taken to a concentration camp as " personal prisoner of the Fuehrer", from where h was not liberated until 1945. Copies of sermon delivered by Bishop Clemens August, Count vo Galen, passed from hand to hand. The fate of other was known only to their congregations; for exam ple, the unspeakable tortures which Pastor Schnei der of Diekenscheid had to endure in Buchenwald or the sentence imposed upon Provost Bernhar Lichtenberg of the Berlin Cathedral. He earne himself a two-year sentence by including a praye

[1]The National Socialist German Workers' Party (Na Party).

[2]A group of Protestants who tried to reconcile the religious beliefs with those of the Nazi state.

for the Jews and the poor inmates of concentration camps in his evening services. . . .

After the fall of the Nazi regime in 1945, many Germans tried to prove that they, too, had offered resistance. It is therefore essential to distinguish between real resistance and "silent opposition". There were different ways by which "co-ordination" could be avoided. Some stiff-necked people refused to give the Hitler salute. Some professors would not be deterred from quoting Jewish scientists with respect. But resistance could be said to exist only where people knew that they risked their lives, and acted in full awareness of this risk.

Some figures testify to the extent of the resistance. The number of *German* concentration camp inmates has been estimated at 500,000 or 600,000, and the number of executions carried out for political crimes at about 12,000. One must remember, of course, that some arrests were made in pursuit of personal vendettas, and that people were sentenced to death merely for re-telling a political joke! Still, these figures give a general idea of the extent of the various resistance organizations deserving of the name. Motives for such action were diverse.

One large group was the Communists, who were driven into resistance from the first days of Hitler's rule. Belonging to an international party which traditionally engaged in illegal activities, they were, so to speak, predestined for planned resistance. Those who did not immediately vanish into concentration camps naturally took to building up illegal cells and cadres on Lenin's prescriptions.

This Communist resistance, however, cannot be grouped with other resistance efforts, because it was directed from Moscow and did not aim at democratic freedom but, instead, at replacing one dictatorship with another. Despite this, however, it must not be forgotten that some of these Communist resistance groups acted independently, as for example the well-known Red Chapel group. . . . There were also some attractive and brave women, two of whom were executed after giving birth to children.

Above all, we must never forget the Communist resistance in the concentration camps, which had to be carried on under absolutely unprecedented conditions. Many of these inmates had been arrested in 1933 or the next few years; some never regained their freedom, others were released for a short time but soon found themselves back in the concentration camp. These people were better acquainted with the appalling conditions of life in the camps than other groups of inmates. They served as office helpers or hospital orderlies, and made great efforts to strengthen the other prisoners' will to resist. They also shed some of their anti-religious prejudices, since they could not help paying their respect to the steadfastness of priests and monks and to the [stubborn] faith of the Jehovah's Witnesses. Never before or since did Christians and Communists come as close to each other as under the terror of the SS.

. . . Another group . . . saved their Jewish fellow-citizens from persecution and extermination by providing them with illegal passports and forged identification papers, or by sheltering them in their own homes. Such aid also included the employment of Jews in their businesses. Oskar Schindler can be cited for his impressive example of an employer who saved more than 1,100 people from extermination by using Jewish labor in his enamel works in Cracow. He also placed on his payroll relatives of his workers who were aged or incapable of work, and provided them with food and hid them every time the SS inspected his plant. When evacuations were about to start, he kept the entire night shift working on some pretext to save them from SS raids. As a last resort, he often used bribes to pry one of his charges from the grip of the Gestapo. Almost his entire fortune was spent on such acts of mercy.

. . . One must remember, too, those students in Munich who ". . . opposed the all-powerful state with their tiny mimeographing machines". Their self-selected password, "White Rose", symbolizes their pure spirits. They were young, believing Christians, who loved everything noble and beautiful and were often exuberant and in high spirits; but they became increasingly conscious of and tortured by the disgrace of what they called the "dictatorship of evil" in Germany. They were convinced that they had no right to keep silent. They knew that it was nearly impossible to "knock down an iron wall of fear and terror". But, nevertheless, they were ready to try. . . . A sentence in the last leaflet which Hans and Sophie Scholl dropped from the top balcony of the inner court of Munich University, and which led to their arrest, reads: "Germany's name will remain disgraced forever unless German youth finally rises up at once, takes revenge and atones, smashes its torturers, and builds a new, spiritual Europe."

They may have believed, for a time, that they would succeed in carrying the torch of revolt from university to university, but they had never seriously calculated the dangers and risks against the chances of success. After their arrest they had no other thought but to incriminate themselves in order to protect their friends. They realized immediately that their lives were forfeit. Sentenced in a quick trial, all six of them mounted the scaffold with matchless courage. . . .

All these resistance groups had very similar motives and attitudes, although they differed in their particular image of a future and better Germany. None was driven by ambition or selfishness. They were guided by their conscience, their sense of justice, their love for Germany. But they could not act alone; Hitler could only be removed by military force. . . .

The army alone was in a position either to imprison Hitler following a *coup d'état*, or to remove him by assassination. This is so obvious that the other difficulties, special to the army, pale by comparison. First, there was its traditional abstention from politics, which allowed many fence-sitters to suppress their moral scruples: "The soldier must fight battles, not determine the war aims." Of greater importance, especially for the enlisted men and younger officers, was the oath of allegiance sworn to Hitler's person. . . . Before Hitler had made himself Supreme Commander of the Armed Forces, a soldier used to swear loyalty to his nation and his fatherland. The new method of swearing unquestioning obedience to Hitler implied a fundamental change and made an attempt on Hitler's life inevitable, because only through Hitler's death could the armed forces be formally released from their oath.

Under the circumstances, only a small group of "intellectual soldiers", after much soul-searching arrived at the conclusion that an oath of allegiance implied a mutual obligation and was to be kept only as long as the "liege lord" kept faith with it on his part. . . . The oath of loyalty ceased to be binding when the Fuehrer to whom it was sworn was prepared to drag nation and fatherland down with him into destruction. To support this view, Hitler, in his own words, could have been quoted as state's evidence, for he had said in *Mein Kampf*: "If through the power of a government a people is led to its own destruction, each member of such a people has not only the right but the duty of rebelling." If one wants to evaluate the opposition within the army one must remember that for moral reasons many military men felt unable to break their oath while others used this merely as an excuse. . . .

Superficial observers of the German resistance don't understand why the resistance failed to remove Hitler; for instance, why no one "simply" shot him. But it was by no means a "simple" matter. During the last years of the war, only a very few people had direct access to Hitler, and these rarely included anyone from the inner circle of the resistance. Each gesture was carefully watched by Hitler's bodyguard. Even a move to the holster aroused suspicion. In order to lower the risk, seven officers f Tresckow's Army Group volunteered to shoot Hitler simultaneously with their revolvers. But no mount of wiles or efforts could persuade Hitler to visit this sector of the front a second time.

Hitler was reputed to have sensed personal danger with the instinct of a beast of prey. It remains n uncanny aspect of the history of these attempts hat he often canceled or cut short visits after all reparations had been made. Accidents, too, played role. Thus, at one point a young captain, Axel on dem Bussche, had volunteered to throw himself pon Hitler and detonate a bomb while modeling ew uniforms. Bussche was among those who had vitnessed the systematic extermination of human eings in Poland and Russia. But shortly before the llotted time, an air raid on Berlin destroyed the emonstration models. Before new ones could arve, Bussche was re-assigned to front duty, where e was gravely wounded soon after. . . .

As early as 1946, Winston Churchill said in the louse of Commons that there had been an opposion in Germany whose strength had been gradually apped through its sacrifices and the degenerating ternational situation, but their achievements anked among the most stirring and greatest deeds ver performed in the political history of any naon. These men, he continued, fought without any elp whatsoever from inside and outside the couny, spurred on solely by their restless consciences. s long as they lived, they remained unseen and nrecognized for they had had to disguise themlves. But, said Churchill, their resistance was vealed in their deaths.

iscussion guidelines

In the excerpt "What Would You Have Done?" an explanation given for non-resistance was that "there was nothing to do about it." Hannah Vogt's evidence indicates that some Germans were prepared to do something, even if it meant death. How do you account for this second reaction?

2. "Totalitarian governments cannot be destroyed from within." Supply examples from your knowledge of history to support or refute this claim.

Cross reference

In Defence of Equality, page 15

A Dialogue on Protest

from *Democracy and the Student Left*
by George F. Kennan

Mr. Kennan States His Case:

The world seems to be full, today, of embattled students. The public prints are seldom devoid of the record of their activities. Photographs of them may be seen daily: screaming, throwing stones, breaking windows, overturning cars, being beaten or dragged about by police and, in the case of those on other continents, burning libraries. That these people are embattled is unquestionable. However, there is doubt whether civil disobedience has any place in a democratic society. But there is one objection I know will be offered to this view. Some people, who accept our political system, believe that they have a right to disregard it and to violate

Miller Services, Toronto

Can protest go too far?

the laws that have flowed from it so long as they are prepared, as a matter of conscience, to accept the penalties established for such behaviour.

I am sorry; I cannot agree. The violation of law is not, in the moral and philosophic sense, a privilege that lies offered for sale with a given price tag, like an object in a supermarket, available to anyone who has the price and is willing to pay for it. It is not like the privilege of breaking crockery in a tent at the county fair for a quarter a shot. Respect for the law is not an obligation which is exhausted or wiped out by willingness to accept the penalty for breaking it.

To hold otherwise would be to place the privilege of lawbreaking preferentially in the hands of the wealthy, to make respect for law a commercial proposition rather than a civic duty and to deny any authority of law independent of the sanctions established against its violation. It would then be all right for a man to create false fire alarms or frivolously to pull the emergency cord on the train, or to do any number of other things that endangered or inconvenienced other people, provided only he was prepared to accept the penalties of so doing. Surely, lawlessness and civil disobedience cannot be condoned or tolerated on this ground; and those of us who care for the good order of society have no choice but to resist attempts at its violation when this is their only justification.

George F. Kennan
Institute for Advanced Studies
Princeton, 1968

One of His Own Generation Replies:

It seems to me, in his discussion of civil disobedience, Mr. Kennan is uncharacteristically bland and cocksure. He is "sorry" but he cannot agree that it "has any place in a democratic society". By this line of reasoning, any appeal from the authority of the state to a higher law of conscience can be admirable only if it took place either in the past or at a safe distance. Thus it may have been admirable in Socrates' Athens, Christ's Palestine, More's England, and Gandhi's British India. It may still be so in the late Chief Luthuli's South Africa and in the Soviet Union of Pavel Litvinov and his friends who have just been tried and convicted in Moscow. But in the United States of America it cannot be tolerated, nor can its roots and meaning be understood. The work of such Americans as Roger Williams, the men who wrote and voted for the Declaration of Independence, Thoreau, and John Brown is entirely done and they have nothing more to say to us. If this is really so, then America is a finished nation in more senses than one.

L. H. Butterfield
Editor-in-Chief
The Adams Papers

Two Students Reply

A:

Regarding the case for civil disobedience, I disagree with you on a vital point. I, too, am against breaking laws with demonstrations to draw attention, simply because I cannot imagine that to be anything but futile. In fact I feel that in almost every case the law should be respected. In the draft law I find a conspicuous exception. I am not against the draft, though I am emphatically against the way it is being presently employed. I view it as a necessity of the world situation, though an odious one. But I do support those who think that the draft, in relation to the war in Vietnam, constitutes a violation of their personal morality. The draft is not a criminal law designed to protect the people from the evils of individuals, nor is it a civil law designed to maintain an economic or political equality. It is a law created solely for providing manpower for enforcing the policies of a government. Much as a tax bill provides money for a war, the draft provides men. In this situation the law is reaching into the personal domain of a man's soul. I think the government can ethically demand that a man offer money for what it considers to be the betterment of society, and time for the same reason. But it is on shaky ground when it asks him to die, and even shakier ground when it asks him to kill. In the end, every individual is responsible to a higher authority than the government and whether it is religious or personal it is sacred. The United States itself held this view in the Nuremberg trials when it found that "following orders" does not excuse one from the consequences of his actions. When one has exhausted all alternatives to fighting and feels definitely that the cause is not just, he is, in my opinion, justified in resisting the government's attempts to subvert his morals, though with full knowledge that he is not exempt from the consequences of that resistance.

David C. King
Harvard '71

B:

As to the question of when civil disobedience is justified in a democratic society, one must ask if this is the right question to ask at all. In any society, democratic or otherwise, when one sees injustice, one must resist. Nor should he get "hung up" in an abstract debate over the issue of civil disobedience violating someone's rights or principles. If I see a woman being murdered on the street, I do not stop to ask if I will be violating her attacker's rights or abstract democratic principles before taking some kind of action.

Lee T. Bridges
Dartmouth '68

Discussion guideline

"In any society, democratic or otherwise, when one sees injustice, one must resist."

or

"If every individual resists injustice according to the dictates of his own conscience, the result will be anarchy." Argue one of these viewpoints.

Cross reference

In Defence of Equality, page 15

 a

The Watts Riot: An Incident

from *Rivers of Blood, Years of Darkness*
by Robert Conot

Gabriel Pope had a sense of grim satisfaction. This was the way he wanted it. He was through with integration. Maybe integration would work one day, but he didn't think he'd live to see it. Integration was the cover the whites used to leach the Negro of his life's blood, the name they gave to taking his money in their stores and restaurants, the excuse by which they could set up their businesses in the ghetto, the way they could keep their police down on his neck to stifle him whenever he cried "Freedom!" He was convinced that all of this police harassment hadn't been haphazard. It had been deliberately planned and carried out to give as many Negroes as possible arrest records, so that they wouldn't be able to compete for jobs with Caucasians.

After he had made up his mind at midnight, Thursday, Gabriel Pope had gone out and burned. He had gotten together with a couple of the blood, and they had taken his car and started on their path of destruction. It was the "Easy Terms, We Carry Our Own Credit" places that he hated most of all. They'd had a disagreement among themselves – one of the guys had said that if they were going to burn it all anyway, they ought to get some stuff first. But Gabriel had said *No*, stealing wasn't his intent. The object was burning.

The object was burning, and when he saw all those people running around with stuff in their hands, Gabriel had the feeling that it was this that had been twisting his guts – he couldn't blame the people for making off with food when all the time they had to count every nickel and dime, he couldn't expect them not to grab what they could while they had a chance to when they'd had such little chance, but it was detracting from what *he* was after. He wanted it to be the Boston Tea Party, and the Civil War, and the Emancipation Proclamation all thrown into one; he wanted to show the white that the Negroes didn't need the big fat liberals throwing them crumbs, that the Negro was a proud man who could stand on his own feet and do his own fighting; he wanted to erase the shame he felt because all the *leaders* of his people had always needed some great white protector; he wanted to wipe out the humiliation that had stained him when he had seen his grandfather humble himself in Mississippi just to protect that little patch of land – a if that was worth living for!

Wide World Photo

Do riots tend to make authorities more rigid and less likely to compromise? The above incident occurred in Chicago in 1968 after rocks were thrown at the police

b

Civil Disobedience: National and International
from *Conscience for Change*
by Dr. Martin Luther King

There is nothing wrong with a traffic law which says you have to stop for a red light. But when a fire is raging, the fire truck goes right through that red light, and normal traffic had better get out of its way. Or, when a man is bleeding to death, the ambulance goes through those red lights at top speed.

There is a fire raging now for the Negroes and the poor of this society. They are living in tragic conditions because of the terrible economic injustices that keep them locked in as an "underclass", as the sociologists are now calling it. Disinherited people all over the world are bleeding to death from deep social and economic wounds. They need brigades of ambulance drivers who will have to ignore the red lights of the present system until the emergency is solved.

Massive civil disobedience is a strategy for social change which is at least as forceful as an ambulance with its siren on full. . . .

The emergency we now face is economic, and it s a desperate and worsening situation. For the 35-million poor people in America – not even to mention, just yet, the poor in the other nations – there s a kind of strangulation in the air. In our society t's murder, psychologically, to deprive a man of a ob or an income. You're in substance saying to that man that he has no right to exist. You're in a real way depriving him of life, liberty, and the pursuit of happiness, denying in his case the very creed of is society. Now, millions of people are being trangled that way. The problem is at least national in fact, it's international) in scope. And it is getng worse, as the gap between the poor and the affluent society" increases.

The question that now divides the people who want radically to change that situation is: can a program of non-violence – even if it envisions massive civil disobedience – realistically expect to meet such an enormous, entrenched evil?

First of all, will non-violence work, psychologically, after the summer of 1967? Many people feel that non-violence as a strategy for social change was cremated in the flames of the urban riots of the last two years. They tell us that Negroes have only now begun to find their true manhood in violence; that the riots prove not only that Negroes hate whites, but that, compulsively, they must destroy them.

This blood lust interpretation ignores one of the most striking features of the city riots. Violent they certainly were. But the violence, to a startling degree, was focussed against property rather than against people. There were very few cases of injury to persons, and the vast majority of the rioters were not involved at all in attacking people. . . .

I am aware that there are many who wince at a distinction between property and persons – who hold both sacrosanct. My views are not so rigid. A life is sacred. Property is intended to serve life, and no matter how much we surround it with rights and respect, it has no personal being. It is part of the earth man walks on; it is not man.

The focus on property in the 1967 riots is not accidental. It has a message; it is saying something.

If hostility to whites were ever going to dominate a Negro's attitude and reach murderous proportions, surely it would be during a riot. . . . Far more rioters took chances with their own lives, in their attacks on property, than threatened the life of anyone else. Why were they so violent with property, then? Because property represents the white-power structure, which they were attacking and trying to destroy. A curious proof of the symbolic aspect of the looting for some who took part in it is the fact that, after the riots, police received hundreds of calls from Negroes trying to return merchandise they had taken. Those people wanted the experience of taking, of redressing the power imbalance that property represents. Possession, afterwards, was secondary.

A deeper level of hostility came out in arson, which was far more dangerous than the looting. But it, too, was a demonstration and a warning. It was directed against symbols of exploitation, and it was designed to express the depth of anger in the community.

What does this restraint in the summer riots mean for our future strategy?

If one can find a core of non-violence towards persons, even during the riots when emotions were exploding, it means that non-violence should not be written off for the future as a force in Negro life. Many people believe that the urban Negro is too angry and too sophisticated to be non-violent. Those same people dismiss the non-violent marches in the south and try to describe them as processions of pious, elderly ladies. The fact is that in all the marches we have organized some men of very violent tendencies have been involved. It was routine for us to collect hundreds of knives from our own ranks before the demonstrations, in case of momentary weakness. And in Chicago last year we saw some of the most violent individuals accepting non-violent discipline. Day after day during those Chicago marches I walked in our lines and I never saw anyone retaliate with violence. There were lots of provocations, not only the screaming white hoodlums lining the sidewalks, but also groups of Negro militants talking about guerrilla warfare. We had some gang leaders and members marching with us. I remember walking with the Blackstone Rangers while bottles were flying from the sidelines, and I saw their noses being broken and blood flowing from their wounds; and I saw them continue and not retaliate, not one of them, with violence. I am convinced that even very violent temperaments can be channelled through non-violent discipline, if the movement is moving; if they can act constructively.

I intend to show that non-violence will be effective; but not until it has achieved the massive dimensions, the disciplined planning, and the intense commitment of a sustained, direct-action movement of civil disobedience on the national scale.

The dispossessed of this nation – the poor, both white and Negro – live in a cruelly unjust society. They must organize a revolution against that injustice, not against the lives of the persons who are their fellow citizens, but against the structures through which the society is refusing to take means which have been called for, and which are at hand to lift the load of poverty.

The only real revolutionary, people say, is a man who has nothing to lose. There are millions of poor people in this country who have very little, or even nothing, to lose. If they can be helped to take action together, they will do so with a freedom and a power that will be a new and unsettling force in our complacent national life.

I have said that the problem, the crisis we face is at least national in scope. In fact, it is inseparable from an international emergency which involves the poor, the dispossessed, and the exploited of the whole world.

Can a non-violent, direct-action movement find application on the international level, to confront economic and political problems? I believe it can. It is clear to me that the next stage of the movement is to become international. National movements within the developed countries – forces that focus on London, or Paris, or Washington, or Ottawa – must help to make it politically feasible for their governments to undertake the kind of massive aid that the developing countries need if they are to break the chains of poverty. We in the West must bear in mind that the poor countries are poor primarily because we have exploited them through political or economic colonialism.

But movements in our countries alone will not be enough. In Latin America, for example, national reform movements have almost despaired of non-violent methods; many young men, even many priests, have joined guerrilla movements in the hills. So many of Latin America's problems have roots in the United States of America that we need to form a solid, united movement, non-violently conceived and carried through, so that pressure can be brought to bear on capital and government power-structures concerned, from both sides of the problem at once. I think that may be the only hope for a non-violent solution in Latin America today.

Even entrenched problems like the South African Government and its racial policies could be tackled on this level. If just two countries, Britain and the United States, could be persuaded to end all economic interaction with the South African regime, they could bring that Government to its knees in a relatively short time. Theoretically, the British and American governments could make that kind of decision; almost every corporation in both countries has economic ties with its government which it could not afford to do without.

In a world facing the revolt of ragged and hungry masses of God's children; in a world torn between the tensions of East and West, white and colored, individualists and collectivists; in a world whose cultural and spiritual power lags so far behind her technological capabilities that we live each day on the verge of nuclear co-annihilation; in this world, non-violence is no longer an option for intellectual analysis, it is an imperative for action.

Discussion guidelines

1. Assess Martin Luther King's formula of non-violent protest as the only alternative to a racial holocaust in the United States. Refer to specific incidents in American race relations to support your evaluation.
2. "Civil Disobedience has no place in a democratic society."

   or

   "In any society, democratic or otherwise, when one sees injustice one must resist." Argue one of these propositions.
3. "Civil Disobedience on an international level is an unrealistic, dead-end and even harmful approach to reform." Discuss.

Cross references

In Defence of Equality, page 15
"Us Too", page 111
Juvenile Delinquency? page 144

THE FREEDOM TO DISSENT

The Dangers of Rejecting Protest

from *On Liberty*
by John Stuart Mill

If all mankind minus one were of one opinion, and only one person were of the contrary opinion, mankind would be no more justified in silencing that one person, than he, if he had the power, would be justified in silencing mankind. The peculiar evil of silencing the expression of an opinion is, that it is robbing the human race; posterity as well as the existing generation; those who dissent from the opinion, still more than those who hold it. If the opinion is right, they are deprived of the opportunity of exchanging error for truth: if wrong, they lose, what is almost as great a benefit, the clearer perception and livelier impression of truth, produced by its collision with error.

We can never be sure that the opinion we are endeavouring to stifle is a false opinion; and if we were sure, stifling it would be an evil still.

PART TWO

INTERNATIONAL AFFAIRS

Issues in Canadian Foreign Policy

In an ever shrinking world, Canadians must face certain foreign policy issues squarely. Does American investment threaten our independence? Do we depend too much on American defence systems? Should the rest of Canada push the panic button over relations between Quebec and France? Should we sell guns while preaching world peace? And can we really play a meaningful role in peacekeeping?

CANADIAN-AMERICAN RELATIONS

Knowing Americans

from *A Change of Pace*
by Bruce West

Not long ago the Canadian ambassador to the United States mentioned during a visit back to this country that Canadians didn't understand the United States as well as they should. The first reaction of many of us to a statement of this kind is, naturally, one of some indignation and vexation. After all, it has been recognized for years that Canadians know much more about the United States than the people of that country know about Canada.

Any Canadian school child, for instance, can name at least 10 states for every Canadian province that can be named by the average American. And 1,000 or maybe even 1,000,000 Canadians can tell you who George Washington or Abe Lincoln or Thomas Jefferson were for every American who can tell you who Sir Wilfrid Laurier or Sir John A. Macdonald were.

And so, in the face of all this, our ambassador tells us we should be making more efforts to understand our United States neighbors! No wonder this statement was greeted by a number of rather angry growls in this country.

But when you come to consider his theory a little more closely, it appears he may not be quite so far off base. It could be that Canadians are burdened with almost as much superficial information about the United States as Americans are about Canada.

At one time it seemed to me that the United States was made up almost exclusively of flag pole sitters, gangsters, marathon dancers, and blustering Senator Foghorns who wanted to take over Canada to settle the British war debt. Later on, however, I had the opportunity of living for almost three years among the Americans, during which time I traveled their vast country from the Canadian border to the Mexican border and from the Atlantic to the Pacific. Sometimes, when I was traveling through their neat little towns and villages full of hard-working and level-headed people, it occurred to me that it was too bad that more Canadians couldn't see this side of United States life.

The great bulk of the nation – the mightiest that has ever existed in all the history of the world – never make the headlines and probably never will. They do their jobs and pay their taxes and raise their families just as quietly and as conscientiously as Canadians do. They have no more designs upon Canada than Canada has upon the United States. As they sit reading or listening to the war news, they feel just as troubled and uneasy as we do.

It seems to me that although many Canadians may be able to tell you that Tallahassee is the capital of Florida, there are not enough who fully appreciate that besides bathing beauties and palm trees there are families called Smith and Jones living in Tallahassee who are God-fearing people who pay their debts promptly and go to church regularly.

Our ambassador suggests that our increased wealth and power of the past few years have not done much to lessen our feeling that we must somehow prove ourselves to Americans. Instead we seem to be growing a little more truculent and touchy toward our United States neighbors as new factory chimneys blossom on our horizons and whenever the exchange rate on the Canadian dollar goes up. He may not be too far wrong on this one, either. In some quarters in Canada, awe of the United States has been replaced by a "we'll show 'em" attitude that's almost as juvenile as our original approach to the matter.

Both of these attitudes are bad, it seems to me. It is not necessary for us to be dazzled and overwhelmed by the wealth and power of the United States. Neither is it necessary for us to look down our noses at our U.S. neighbors with pious expressions of "dear, dear, it couldn't happen here" every time some member of the lunatic fringe down there does something foolish, privately or officially.

It is necessary, however, to remember at all times that the leadership of the world has descended heavily upon our huge neighbor, and that for better or for worse, our fates are tied closely together. Under the circumstances she deserves our friendly sympathy and understanding. And it may well be that this understanding should extend beyond a mental list of the states of the union or even the knowledge that the Mississippi River extends from Little Elk Lake, Minnesota, to the Gulf of Mexico.

Discussion guidelines

1. "It is just as important for Americans to know Canadians as it is for Canadians to know Americans."
   (a) Comment on the validity of this statement.
   (b) How can Americans get to know Canadians in a meaningful way?
2. "Canadians unwisely try to equal the United States and to get the United States to regard them as equals." By citing supporting examples, indicate your agreement or disagreement with this statement.

Cross reference

The Culture Concept, page 146

General Motors of Canada

Assembly line at a Canadian subsidiary plant of an American-owned firm closely to ultimate American military direction. There was really a further question, still debated by Canadians: was anything else possible when the danger was that of nuclear attack and the issue actual survival?

b

The Military Facts of the Case

from "Complications of Defence"
by General Charles Foulkes

There are already signs that the United States plans to become less and less dependent on Canada for the operation of its defence devices; consequently, Canadian claims for participation in the consultation and decision-making process will be less justified.

In order to get some indication of the requirements of joint defence, it is essential to examine defence forecasts. U.S. future requirements for continental defence are indicated in extracts from a statement made by the Secretary of Defense before the House Armed Services Committee in January, 1964.

> In my past appearances before the committee, I noted that the weight of the strategic threat against the United States was steadily shifting from manned bombers to I.C.B.M.s and submarine launched missiles, and as I indicated earlier, the trend is continuing. Therefore the main thrust of our defense effort in the years ahead should be directed to meet this rising threat.
>
> Our present continental air and missile defense forces were designed primarily to defend against the manned bomber threat. As a result, today they provide only a limited capability to reduce damage of a nuclear attack in which long range strategic missiles are used. Clearly we should be recasting our defense programs to recognize the change in the threat.

As the bomber defences diminish, the United States will have less and less need for the use of Canadian territory, and Canadian air space will be of much less importance to the defence of the United States and its retaliatory forces. There are indications already that the United States will be able to provide whatever defence is possible against missile attacks without the use of Canadian territory or air space.

The Nike "X" defence installations are being designed as a point defence system. Several sites will be needed to cover a city or air-field complex, in the same way as groups of anti-aircraft artillery batteries were used to protect important targets from bombing attacks. Unlike the present bomber defences, whereby the U.S. air defence provides protection for certain areas in Canada not covered by Canadian air defences, the adoption of this system of missile defence by the United States will not provide any protection to Canada.

As the proposed missile defences are being designed to deal with attacks on point targets, the control of such defences will become largely a local problem and will not require the extensive continental type of control which has vested in NORAD to deal with a massive bomber attack. This reduction of the control requirements in the missile era will lessen the operational control functions of NORAD. Once the bomber threat has disappeared, the remaining functions of NORAD will be restricted to the operation of the ballistic-missile early-warning system, a bomb-alarm system, a fallout-location device, and a space-surveillance control centre.

These remaining functions of NORAD do not seem

to require Canadian participation to ensure their successful performance. There appears to be little doubt that the United States is able to carry out these remaining defence functions on a national basis, without the frustrating delays and irritations of Canadian participation, as well as pressure for consultation and a share in the decision-making process.

However, Canada will need much of the information and early-warning data provided by the early-warning and reporting systems assembled at NORAD headquarters. This information is necessary in order that arrangements can be made to monitor any fallout drifting into Canada and as a guide to the Canadian authorities in issuing any general warning.

C

On Whom Do We Open Fire?

from testimony before a parliamentary committee

by James Eayrs

The means for deterring a deliberate military attack by the United States upon Canada lie well within Canada's capabilities. Canada could make nuclear weapons if it needed them. Their delivery system poses no problem. It only needs a range of half a mile to take out Detroit. A less implausible type of military incursion from the United States might arise as follows. We are in the early Nineteen Seventies. The Vietnam war is over. But the racial war is worse. Negro Americans, led by well trained veterans of Vietnam, have passed through the Luddite stage of their revolt. They no longer burn down their own ghettos. Instead, they are embarked upon a highly organized campaign of guerrilla and commando warfare. One of their columns has just executed a hit-and-run raid on some target of national significance – a governor's mansion, a missile complex – and turns and runs for Canada, to seek political asylum. Hard on its heels, in hot pursuit, are U.S. army troops. Upon which column, if either, do the armed forces of Canada open fire?

Discussion guidelines

1. "Membership in the NORAD club increases Canadian influence in Washington not only in North American defence but in other matters as well." To what degree do you think this claim justifies continued Canadian participation in NORAD?
2. "Canada must make up its mind whether to part company with its beguiling, star-spangled Devil, or resign itself to increasing subservience leading ultimately to absorption. This is the basic choice which is vital for the defence of Canada as a unit, and decisive for the defence of the continent as a whole." (James M. Minifie, *Peacemaker or Powder-monkey?*)
   Argue this position.
3. "Canada could make nuclear weapons if it needed them."
   (a) Do you think Canada should or should not make nuclear weapons? Defend your opinion.
   (b) How would you answer the military dilemma posed by James Eayrs?

Cross references

Alignment? page 231
Non-alignment? page 232
Alliances Don't Work, page 269
The Munich Agreement, page 269
The Necessities of War, page 273
Spheres of influence and Soviet aggression, page 276
Rigidity "the Most Dangerous Aspect of Two-Bloc System", page 278

4 a

We Need America
from *Hooray for the Scars and Gripes*
by J. M. S. Careless

The United States is Canada's great cliché. Our reactions to the country and its people have all the hard-worn polish of "it's a nice place to visit" or "some of my best friends". This is inevitably so because Canadians have been worrying over and responding to the United States ever since the American Revolution created both countries by running a political boundary across the mass of North America. Since then we have been obsessed with the far greater magnitude of American power and success: fearing it, resisting it, and leaning on it; criticizing, deploring, and imitating it.

Again this is all but inevitable, since to a very large degree the American presence has shaped Canada. It gave French-Canadians a reason for accepting British imperial rule and then for aligning politically with English-Canadian colonists as the best means to ensure survival in the face of huge American power. It gave English-Canadians the War of 1812, the one conflict they have fought on their own soil, with its consequent memories of successful national defence to reinforce the original Loyalists' declaration of independence from the United States. And sharp strains during the American Civil War did much to impel the separate British-American colonies to combine in Confederation in 1867 in order to form a political and economic unit big enough to be workable outside of a notably unfriendly republic. In short, through varied impacts with deep historic effect, the United States has served repeatedly, if unwittingly, as the best friend nationalism could have in a country as culturally and sectionally divided as Canada.

Courtesy Toronto-Dominion Centre Ltd.

Does the skyline of this Canadian city imitate the skyline of New York? Does modern Canadian architecture owe more to American inspiration than to any other source?

The process continued throughout the century after Confederation. American probing into the Northwest, American railroad projects, spurred the building of the C.P.R. The rising wall of the United States tariffs provided justification for the adoption of Canadian policies of economic nationalism. Then the influx of American capital and techniques, from dry-farming in the West to factory industry in the East, gave increasing breadth and substance to the Canadian continental system. And later improved relations with the United States stimulated a sense of North American defensive security, which had its own consequence in the drive to realize full Canadian nationhood. Thus, in striking ways –

though certainly not as the only factor – the United States has worked to build the modern Canadian nation.

Obviously, it has no less helped to hinder it, to offer always the seductive charm of giving up. What country other than Canada exists with the implied assumption that if we can't go home to Mother anymore, Uncle (supposedly) will always take us in?

Again there is the evident fact that the presence of the United States promotes sectional division in Canada. Pulls to the south tie the various Canadian regions with their more powerful American neighbours, thus thwarting the development of strong east-west ties within Canada herself. Through mass media, as in travel, Canadians look south to New York or Hollywood, to Chicago, Boston, or Miami. And the power of American investment may develop our resources and technology, but sap our control and determine our lives within our own country. Everybody has heard about that.

All this indeed is true – but hardly new, dating almost from the time that the two countries first took form. We have both used and had to pay for superior United States development (superior, that is, in terms of time, wealth, and availability) ever since American entrepreneurs opened blast furnaces at Normandale, Ontario, in the 1820s or put the steamboat on the Red River in the 1850s. We see the results of American penetration all around us today. Yet what we need also to observe is how this massive and pervasive force has continually invited reactions which have shaped a separate Canadian entity.

At any rate it is small wonder that Canadians are thoroughly contradictory in their response to the United States. They must be. Throughout their history they have been so constantly helped or hampered by America and the Americans. But they have always been utterly involved. One is tempted to conclude, in fact, that there could not be a Canada without the United States – and may not be a Canada with one.

b

O Canada

Canada could have enjoyed:
English government,
French culture,
and American know-how.

Instead it ended up with:
English know-how,
French government,
and American culture.

JOHN ROBERT COLOMBO

Discussion guidelines

1. "The small next-door neighbour to a giant should be asking how much independence, on what issues and at what price?" Submit some answers to these questions.
2. "There could not be a Canada without the United States – and may not be a Canada with one." Debate this viewpoint.

Cross references

Soviet-Czech Relations – See-Saw Between Pressure and Reconciliation, page 80
The Fears That Spurred the Russians into Action, page 82

A TWO-NATION FOREIGN POLICY?

The Case for Quebec
from "Special International Status for Quebec?"[1]
by Louis Sabourin

The Issue
If many Canadians were not yet aware of Quebec's intentions to look for a distinctive international role, President de Gaulle's 1967 trip to Canada has certainly wakened them up to that new reality. For most of them it was shocking to realize in such a way . . . that Quebec was determined to establish official international activities.

Too few people – including too few French Canadians – have yet understood that this is not a new caprice, but a desire on the part of the Province of Quebec to use fully its legislative [rights], which have many international implications nowadays, in order to assure the continued progress of a French-Canadian society that is open to the world.

Besides, French Canadians have finally realized that, in about thirty years, they will represent less than 20 per cent of the Canadian population; and unless the Government of Quebec undertakes more positive steps in order to assert their identity, the role of the French-speaking Canadians will then become very marginal in almost every field of life in Canada. If French Canadians have survived, it is mainly because it was possible to live (and because they wished to live) in a closed society. . . . But in the era of mass media and the new technology, this is not possible any more. Besides, every small society which refuses to welcome foreign know-how is bound to remain mediocre. French Canada must obviously look for such know-how in countries with a close cultural affinity. . . .

It is therefore necessary for French Canadians to import from France not only literature and songs but French science, technology, research, and administrative methods which will allow them to progress. . . .

Many people will ask why French Canadians – at least those living in Quebec – are not ready to leave such a task to the federal government or to private institutions as it is being done in English-speaking provinces.

The reason is that French Canadians control very few important institutions besides the government of the Province of Quebec. . . .

Secondly, even if Ottawa has established closer ties with [French-speaking states], most Québécois, rightly or wrongly, have second thoughts about these new federal activities and are not ready to forget the past record of neglect. . . . In such circumstances, whatever Ottawa does in order to develop its relations with the [French-speaking world], Quebec will not back down, for it is not only a question of seeing something being undertaken "for Quebec", but of deciding if it can be done "by Quebec".

If Quebec's international activities stem, on the one hand, from a new self-awareness and a better knowledge of the rest of the world, it is undeniable, on the other hand, that foreign countries are now discovering the French-Canadian people. Expo 67 and de Gaulle's controversial visit have been the most important factors in that regard. Besides, there is no doubt that France and the other French-speaking States have been taking a greater interest in French Canada in the last few years.

But above all these factors, two main reasons have [influenced] the behaviour of the government of Quebec. First is its determination to assume all its legislative and administrative responsibilities. In concrete terms this means that the government must

[1]Adapted from *An Independent Foreign Policy for Canada?* edited by Stephen Clarkson for the University League for Social Reform, Toronto, McClelland and Stewart, 1968.

make sure that the million and a half young people who will look for jobs in the next fifteen years will be able to work in their language. . . .

Finally, French Canadians are determined to put an end to their traditional isolation. . . .

At the beginning, Ottawa was quite surprised but not astonished by Quebec's desire to seek closer ties with French-speaking countries. Many other Canadian provinces in the past, especially Ontario, which has signed pacts with a dozen foreign states, had had several dealings with foreign authorities and nobody had protested too loudly.[1] But as more and more initiatives were taken by the government of Quebec and more and more statements of principle were handed out by its leaders, making it clearer every day that the province was truly looking for some sort of "international personality" of its own, the federal government became more suspicious of the province's stands and actions in this field. . . . [At] the end of 1966 Ottawa stated in unmistakable terms that the federal government was the sole authority in the conduct of Canada's international relations and that there was no room for the theory of the dual international personality in Canada.

The Reaction

For a fairly large group of people, Quebec's international activities have been overemphasized and exaggerated. They contend that the press is largely responsible for the misleading of public opinion. They hold the view that Quebec is speaking a lot but not doing much in that field. They assert that Quebec's position is very weak on the world scene and that even if paragraph 132 of the BNA Act is obsolete, the constitutional practice has clearly shown that Ottawa is the only level of government in Canada which is competent to deal with foreign powers. According to them, no country besides France is ready to enter into official relations with Quebec. Ottawa's position is one of strength and as long as the federal government does not wish to "bow" to Quebec's demands in that field, Quebec will not be able to expand its "official external relations" very much: besides Quebec cannot financially afford to compete with Ottawa in the field of international co-operation.

Others maintain that Canada is facing here a political problem only. . . . They conclude that the only important question is to discover if the government of Quebec can really pretend to be a better interpreter of French-Canadian views on the world scene than the federal government. They state that as long as Quebec has not proved such a point, Ottawa has no reason to make any major concession.

Summary

In reality, the main issue should not be to decide whether it is a legal or a political problem (in fact it is both) or to decide if Ottawa is right and Quebec is wrong or vice versa . . . – both Quebec and Ottawa have a strong case.

There is also no doubt that a lot is at stake in this dispute: the image of Canada on the world scene and the very existence of a strong French-Canadian society in North America. . . . Ottawa may have every legal right to "short circuit" Quebec's international programs, but it would be a grave political mistake to try to do so. Unless there is a change of moods in the near future, it is easy to foresee that many people in Quebec will react with impatience, will tend to forget the real issue and will speak only in terms of self-assertion and prestige. In reality, the whole question is so complex and so important that it will take a few years before it can be solved, if indeed it is ever solved! . . .

Quebec's role in international affairs represents both a challenge and an asset to Canadian foreign policy. It will force Ottawa to look for more imaginative programs, while it will oblige the central government to think [beforehand] about French Canada rather than [afterwards] as it did before in

[1]Ontario has offices in London, New York, Düsseldorf, and Milan. Quebec opened an office in Paris (1968), a Délégation générale in London (1962), and an office in Milan (1965).

devising its international policies.

Quebec's international role represents also a definite challenge to Canada's foreign policy and to Canada as such. It is a test case of mutual trust. It all depends on Quebec's restraint in its attitude toward Ottawa and on English-speaking Canadians' sincerity toward Quebec. If Quebec demands too much in the field of international affairs, this cannot but lead to the establishment of a dual image of the country on the world scene which is an inevitable step toward breaking up Canada.

On the other hand, if English-speaking Canadians do not recognize that Quebec has every right to develop international activities which will favour the self-fulfilment of French-Canadian society, this will give ample proof that they do not wish to accept French Canadians as equal partners in Canada. This also may lead to separatism.

Restraint and sincerity are certainly not qualities which all Canadians share but one can hope that a sufficient number of leaders who possess them will be around the negotiation table in the coming years.

2

Quebec and France rebuked by Sharp

By LEWIS SEALE
Globe and Mail Reporter

OTTAWA – External Affairs Minister Mitchell Sharp yesterday rebuked France and Quebec for their exchange of letters concerning the possibility of a joint communications satellite for educational and cultural programs.

In a Commons statement, Mr. Sharp reiterated Ottawa's claim to exclusive jurisdiction over telecommunications and said there should have been prior consultation by Quebec with the federal Government.

In Quebec City, Education Minister Jean-Guy Cardinal, who headed the Quebec delegation to Paris, said he could see no point in consulting Ottawa about the province's satellite plans before going to Paris. Premier Jean-Jacques Bertrand would make no comment.

Ottawa had asked for advance copies of the letters, but got them only after they had been signed. Mr. Cardinal signed three exchanges of letters dealing with communications satellites, French investment in Quebec, and educational assistance.

"It would have been preferable for the Quebec Government to be willing to take into its confidence the Government of the country and to disclose its intentions before making them known . . . to the Government of another country," Mr. Sharp told the Commons.

He said he agreed with the assessment of NDP Parliamentary Leader David Lewis who called the statement a mild reproof and told interviewers he saw no need to escalate the dispute.

Mr. Sharp's statement came a week after the letters of intent were signed in Paris and three days after Mr. Cardinal's return to Canada.

Mr. Sharp issued a statement the day the letters were signed, stating Ottawa's claim to constitutional responsibility for telecommunications. Copies of the letters were delivered to Ottawa last Monday.

Mr. Sharp's statement had some rough edges – for example, his reminder that Canadian communications satellite technology is advanced and that three French engineers have come here for training. But it also reiterated the federal Government's desire to cooperate with France in the satellite field.

Mr. Sharp's views will be passed on to the French Government. The Canadian Ambassador in Paris, Paul Beaulieu, is expected to be instructed to call on the French Foreign Ministry to set out the federal stand orally.

It was not clear how Ottawa's position would be transmitted formally to Quebec City, or even whether it would be.

Mr. Cardinal's comment on Mr Sharp's statement was made through his executive assistant, Jacques Laurent "The Sharp statement in no way changes the position of Quebec," the aide said. "Education is an exclusive provincial jurisdiction.

"Quebec is willing to undertake negotiations with Ottawa on the question of telecommunications, but Quebec maintains that telecommunications i merely a means of education, just a chalk and blackboards are.

"It would have been neither preferable nor useful to consult with Ottawa."

Earlier, a spokesman in Mr. Cardinal's office noted that Mr. Cardinal had said earlier that the question o satellites would be discussed at th federal-provincial constitutional conference to be held in Ottawa from Feb 10 to 12.

He said Mr. Cardinal had maintained that the letter of intent signe in Paris did not engage the province in any program to build satellites o launch them, but was merely a continuation of studies already undertaken

Outside the Commons, Mr. Shar expressed satisfaction with earlier statements by Mr. Cardinal that the exchanges were not intended to be international agreements.

He told interviewers he felt th

General Dynamics

outcry from the powerful aircraft lobbies in Washington. A notable exception is the de Havilland Caribou transport plane. The success of this aircraft led to the development of another of the same general type, the Buffalo, which was jointly financed by Canada and the United States.

The list of items sold by Canadian firms is an eye-opener. It includes jet engines and parts for them; the wing actuator system for the controversial swing-wing F-111 jet; radar and sonar equipment; a system enabling helicopters to land on the decks of small ships in rough seas; bomb fuses; valves for nuclear-powered warships; and radio aerials that unwind like a metal tape measure, which were used on the Canadian Alouette satellites and on the Mercury and Gemini spacecraft.

E. C. Drury, Minister of Industry and Defence Production, stated in the House on June 13, 1967: "It is estimated that the contract received in 1966 resulted in the full-time employment of between 13,000 and 15,000 Canadians. An additional 110,000 persons are estimated to be affected in varying degrees by the many sub-tiers of industrial activity generated by the contracts involved."

T. C. Douglas, leader of the NDP, has said that Canada has the right to tell the Americans: "We are required to supply weapons for defence. However, in our opinion, weapons going to Vietnam are weapons for aggression and, unless we can have an assurance that our weapons are not going to Vietnam, we will not sell you any arms." He urged the government to follow the example of Sweden in not selling arms till peace comes to Vietnam. In his view, the issue is a moral one: "It is the issue of whether I am prepared to sell a revolver to a man when I suspect he is going to use it to rob some old woman of her life savings. You can always argue that if I don't sell the revolver, someone else will, or perhaps he will buy a shotgun, which is more dangerous. But this does not relieve me of my moral responsibility. All you can do is live up to your moral responsibility and hope it has some effect."

L. B. Pearson, former leader of the Liberal Party, argued that:

> Relations between Canada and the U.S.A. regarding the sales of war materials are currently covered by the Defence Production Sharing Agreements (sic) of 1959 and 1963, but in fact they go back much further and find their origins in the Hyde Park Declaration of 1941. During this extended period of co-operation between the two countries, a very close relationship has grown up, not only between the Canadian defence industrial base and its U.S. counterpart, but also between the Canadian and U.S. defence equipment procurement agencies. This relationship is both necessary and logical not only as part of collective defence, but also in order to meet our own national defence commitments effectively and economically.
>
> Equipments required by modern defence forces to meet even limited roles such as peace-keeping are both technically sophisticated and very costly to develop, and because Canada's needs are generally very small, it is not economical for us to meet our total requirements solely from our own resources. Thus, we must take advantage of large scale production in allied countries. As the U.S.A. is the world leader in the advanced technologies involved, and because real advantages can be gained by following common North American design and production standards, the U.S.A. becomes a natural source for much of our defence equipment.
>
> The U.S.-Canadian production sharing arrangements enable the Canadian government to acquire from the U.S.A. a great deal of the nation's essential defence equipment at the lowest possible cost, while at the same time permitting us to offset the resulting drain on the economy by reciprocal sales to the U.S.A. Under these agreements, by reason of longer production runs, Canadian industry is able to participate competitively in U.S. research, development, and production programmes, and is exempted from the "Buy American" Act for these purposes.
>
> From a long-term point of view, another major benefit to Canada is the large contribution which these agreements have made and are continuing to make to Canadian industrial research and development capabilities, which in turn are fundamental to the maintenance of an advanced technology in Canada.
>
> In this connection, I should perhaps point out that the greater part of U.S. military procurement in Canada consists, not of weapons in the conventional sense, but rather of electronic equipment, transport aircraft, and various kinds of components and sub-systems. In many cases the Canadian industries which have developed such products to meet U.S. and continental defence requirements have at the same time been able to develop related products with a civil application, or have been able to use the technology so acquired to advance their general capabilities.
>
> For a broad range of reasons, therefore, it is clear that the imposition of an embargo on the export of military equipment to the U.S.A., and termination of the Production Sharing Agreements, would have far-reaching consequences which no Canadian government could contemplate calmly. It would be interpreted as a notice of withdrawal on our part from continental defence and even from the collective defence arrangements of the Atlantic Alliance.

2

Vhat We Can Do

'rom *Canada as a Peace-keeper*

›y Donald R. Gordon

On the face of it, peace-keeping is enormously attractive. Usually there are four main reasons cited for this.

The first reason for Canadian involvement in U.N. peace-keeping was suggested by Andrew Boyd of *The Economist*, in his book on the United Nations in which he paid great tribute to the "fire brigade" of the U.N. Mr. Boyd made a great fuss about the importance of Canada, the Scandinavian countries, and Ireland, as the firemen who charge from the firehouse whenever an action is deemed to be tolerable to all the major powers and is actually supported by a sufficiently strong coalition of major powers. He argued that middle powers possessed the specialized men and equipment and the political know-how that are necessary. They are felt to be qualified to deal with a brush fire threat which, if unchecked, will either spread into the preserves of the major powers or assume proportions that will involve major powers, whether they like it or not.

Secondly, there is the suggestion that by taking part in peace-keeping Canada raises her influence

Canadian Forces Photo

One of the very few incidents in which Canadian troops opened fire while serving on the U.N. peace-keeping mission in Cyprus. When Turkish Cypriot units refused to obey a local ceasefire ordered by the Canadian commander, warning shots were fired. Although no one was injured, the dangers of such a situation are evident. In enforcing their U.N. mandate, Canadian troops have had to move with both firmness and extreme caution.

and prestige. From a Canadian viewpoint there is the attraction of being able, in an assortment and succession of coalitions of middle and minor powers, to gain the attention of the major powers. A single state power like Canada has one voice of comparable weight to that of, say, Texas. But in coalitions there are that many more Texases involved. And so we can command attention in a way that we might have trouble doing otherwise.

Also, to a degree, we can influence policies and their implementation. If we say we are going to take our peace-keeping baseball and go home, sometimes it matters. When it does matter – as a threat or a negotiating instrument – then we can influence a policy.

And, perhaps as the most important aspect of our strengthened influence and prestige, we can break a log-jam. A coalition of middle and minor powers can gain attention and can suggest the slightly different points of view that can help often to resolve a conflict or issue.

Now, in addition to this, it is often believed that continual activity in such successions of coalition – rubbing shoulders with the Swedes regularly, the Irish occasionally, and so on – serves to increase the confidence, the cooperation, and the information available to us. Thus it becomes possible, in theory, for us to begin to provide a much-needed bridge between major and minor powers.

The third of the four arguments for this peace-keeping idea is the argument that peace-keeping really serves domestic Canadian purposes. This probably is the most defensible point. Apart from the people actually involved in peace-keeping, it seems to me that peace-keeping does feed our fires of nationalism. It provides a certain element contributing to domestic unity and it suits practical partisan political needs.

Peace-keeping has overtones of romance, adventure, and intrigue. It is relatively cheap and simple of operation. Thus, inasmuch as it serves domestic purposes, peace-keeping does have much to be said for it.

And fourthly, it is argued that peace-keeping is an inescapable task, because there are no other practical alternatives available. Thus you get buffer forces providing a physical barrier of man and equipment between potentially warring factions, with the idea that only a neutral U.N. is acceptable for the job and only a middle power is talented enough among the neutrals to be able to do the job.

Discussion guidelines

1. To what extent should Canadians be concerned by a policy that, on the one hand, permits the sale of war materials to the United States while, on the other hand, it promotes peace-keeping operations?
2. Explain how peace-keeping can feed Canadian "fires of nationalism".

Cross references

A Meaningful Voice? page 296
Negotiators at Work, page 304
The Dangers of Present Trends, page 327

̓ANADA –
N THE YEAR 2000?

. Declining Role?

:om *The Year 2000*
y Herman Kahn and
ınthony J. Wiener

Do you agree with the following prediction of ̓anada's position in the year 2000?]

.et us comment briefly on the strange career – a ıarp rise and a sharp fall – of . . . Canada . . . in ıe middle third of the twentieth century. . . . Canada chieved great . . . influence in the decade after Vorld War II. Canada was then perhaps the third r fourth most influential power in the world, having merged from World War II as a major industrial nd agricultural power with large surplus resources f material, men, and energy, which it contributed) reconstruction, rehabilitation, and peace-keep-ıg. It controlled territory essential to the air de-:nse of the United States. It was, effectively, leader f the small powers of NATO, in part because of its ıtimacy and influence with the United States, but lso because it shared the small powers' perspec-ves and interests – or at least the small powers ıought so and thus were almost always greatly ıfluenced by Canadian example. Finally, Canada layed an active and central role in United Nations :tivities generally, and peace-keeping in particular. oday, however, the economic and political recov-·y of the rest of the world, the development of allistic missiles, the erosion of NATO, and the rise : the Afro-Asian bloc in the United Nations have :duced Canada to the least important of the inter-.ediate powers.

What will the international hierarchy of the future look like? . . . Most likely there will be ten "major" powers of which two, the United States and the Soviet Union, will continue to be considered superpowers. Japan, West Germany, France, China, and the United Kingdom are likely to be considered large powers; India, Italy, and Canada intermediate powers; and the next one hundred and twenty nations can be thought of as small powers. The ranking is generally a simple one of estimated GNP [Gross National Product, or the total amount of all goods and services produced by a country] in the mid and late 1970s: the intermediate powers have at least half again the GNP of any of the small powers, the large powers have one-third again the GNP of the intermediate powers, and the superpowers have more than twice the GNP of the large powers; but it should be noted that the grouping is natural.

The Challenge of Underdeveloped Nations

Wide World Photo

A few countries, like Canada and the United States, are prosperous, but most nations are not. What is life like in "underdeveloped" areas? Are underdeveloped countries so weak that they are nothing but pawns in the hands of their rich neighbours – or do they have a significant role to play in world politics? To what extent are developed nations responsible for the backwardness of others? And, when the chips are down, is war the price that must be paid for the gap between the "haves" and the "have-nots"?

THE MEANING OF UNDERDEVELOPMENT

The Facts Are –

from *What It's Like to be "Underdeveloped"*
by Robert L. Heilbroner

To begin to understand economic development we must have a picture of the problem with which it contends. We must conjure up in our mind's eye what underdevelopment means for the two billion human beings for whom it is not a statistic but a living experience of daily life. Unless we can see the Great Ascent from the vantage point of those who must make the climb, we cannot hope to understand the difficulties of the march.

It is not easy to make this mental jump. But let us attempt it by imagining how a typical American family, living in a small suburban house on an income of six or seven thousand dollars, could be transformed into an equally typical family of the underdeveloped world.

We begin by invading the house of our imaginary American family to strip it of its furniture. Everything goes: beds, chairs, lamps, tables, television set. We will leave the family with a few old blankets, a kitchen table, a wooden chair. Along with the bureaus go the clothes. Each member of the family may keep in his "wardrobe" his oldest suit or dress, a shirt or blouse. We will permit a pair of shoes to the head of the family, but none for the wife or children.

We move into the kitchen. The appliances have already been taken out, so we turn to the cupboards and larder. The box of matches may stay, a small bag of flour, some sugar and salt. A few moldy potatoes, already in the garbage can, must be hastily rescued, for they will provide much of tonight's meal. We will leave a handful of onions, and a dish of dried beans. All the rest we take away: the meat, the fresh vegetables, the canned goods, the crackers, the candy.

Now we have stripped the house: the bathroom has been dismantled, the running water shut off, the electric wires taken out. Next we take away the house. The family can move to the toolshed. It is crowded, but much better than the situation in Hong Kong, where (a United Nations report tells us) "it is not uncommon for a family of four or more to live in a bedspace, that is, on a bunk bed and the place it occupies – sometimes in two or three tiers – their only privacy provided by curtains".[1]

But we have only begun. All the other houses in the neighborhood have also been removed; our suburb has become a shantytown. Still, our family is fortunate to have a shelter; 250,000 people in Calcutta have none at all and simply live in the streets. Our family is now about on a par with the city of Cali in Colombia, where, an official of the World Bank writes, "on one hillside alone, the slum population is estimated at 40,000 – without water, sanitation, or electricity. And not all the poor of Cali are as fortunate as that. Others have built their shacks near the city on land which lies beneath the flood mark. To these people the immediate environment is the open sewer of the city, a sewer which flows through their huts when the river rises."[2]

And still we have not reduced our American family to the level at which life is lived in the greatest part of the globe. Communication must go next. No more newspapers, magazines, books – not that they are missed, since we must take away our family's literacy as well. Instead, in our shantytown we will allow one radio. In India the national average of radio ownership is one per 250 people, but since the majority of radios is owned by city

[1] *Social Aspects of Urban Development*, Committee on Information from Non-Self-Governing Territories, March 10, 1961, p. 129.

[2] "The Cauca Valley", unpublished World Bank memo by George Young.

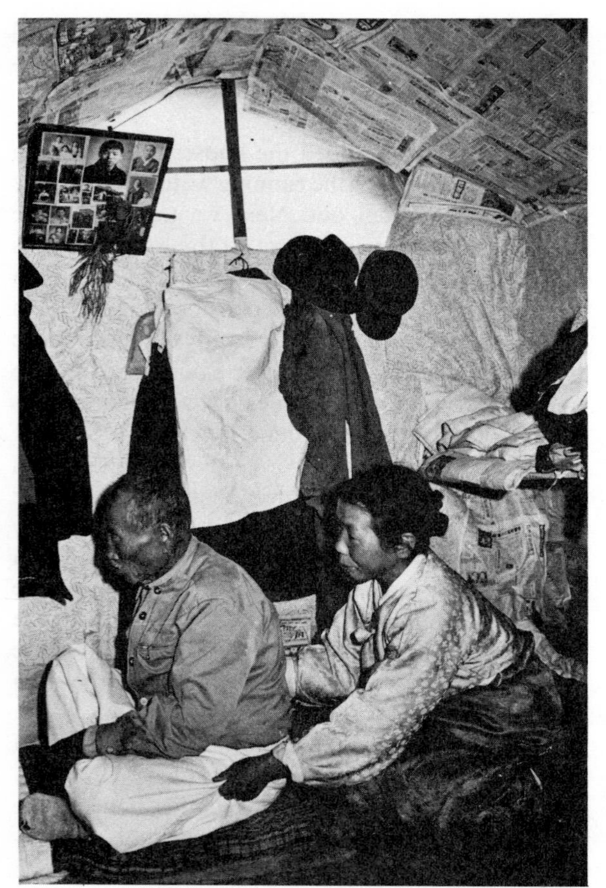

Miller Services, Toronto

Interior of a shanty in South Korea

dwellers, our allowance is fairly generous.

Now government services must go. No more postman, no more fireman. There is a school, but it is three miles away and consists of two classrooms. They are not too over-crowded since only half the children in the neighborhood go to school. There are, of course, no hospitals or doctors nearby. The nearest clinic is ten miles away and is tended by a midwife. It can be reached by bicycle, provided that the family has a bicycle, which is unlikely. Or one can go by bus – not always inside, but there is usually room on top.

Finally, money. We will allow our family a cash hoard of five dollars. This will prevent our breadwinner from experiencing the tragedy of an Iranian peasant who went blind because he could not raise the $3.94 which he mistakenly thought he needed to secure admission to a hospital where he could have been cured.

Meanwhile the head of our family must earn his keep. As a peasant cultivator with three acres to tend, he may raise the equivalent of $100 to $300 worth of crops a year. If he is a tenant farmer, which is more than likely, a third or so of his crop will go to his landlord, and probably another 10 per cent to the local moneylender. But there will be enough to eat. Or almost enough. The human body requires an input of at least 2,000 calories to replenish the energy consumed by its living cells. If our misplaced American fares no better than an Indian peasant, he will average a replenishment of no more than 1,700–1,900 calories. His body, like any insufficiently fueled machine, will run down. That is one reason why life expectancy at birth in India today averages less than forty years.

But the children may help. If they are fortunate, they may find work, and thus earn some cash to supplement the family's income. For example, they may be employed as are children in Hyderabad, Pakistan, sealing the ends of bangles over a small kerosene flame, a simple task which can be done at home. To be sure, the pay is small: eight annas – ten cents – for sealing bangles. That is, eight annas per gross of bangles. And if they cannot find work? Well, they can scavenge, as do the children in Iran who in times of hunger search for the undigested oats in the droppings of horses.

And so we have brought our typical American family down to the very bottom of the human scale. It is, however, a bottom in which we can find, give or take a hundred million souls, at least a billion people. Of the remaining billion in the backward areas, most are slightly better off, but not much so; a few are comfortable; a handful rich.

Of course, this is only an impression of life in the

underdeveloped lands. It is not life itself. There is still lacking the things that underdevelopment gives as well as those it takes away: the urinous smell of poverty, the display of disease, the flies, the open sewers. And there is lacking, too, a softening sense of familiarity. Even in a charnel house life has its passions and pleasures. A tableau, shocking to American eyes, is less shocking to eyes that have never known any other. But it gives one a general idea. It begins to add pictures of reality to the statistics by which underdevelopment is ordinarily measured. When we are told that half the world's population enjoys a standard of living "less than $100 a year", this is what the figures mean.

Discussion guidelines

1. "Although both self interest and humanitarianism demand that the wealthy nations of the western world understand the meaning of underdevelopment, they cannot do so." Suggest some ways by which the West might close this "understanding gap".
2. Is North America totally free of the blight of underdevelopment? Discuss with reference to specific situations.

Cross references

Our "Free Society", page 108
"Us Too", page 111

The Psychology of Poverty
from *The Underdeveloped Country*
by J. Kenneth Galbraith

The first and most elementary effect of poverty is to enforce attitudes and behavior that make it self perpetuating. Similarly the first effect of wealth is to allow the freedom of action that permits of the creation of more wealth. It has often been observed that very poor communities are intensely conservative – that, far more than the more fortunate, these people resist the change that is in their own interest. Illiteracy, and the limited horizons it implies, is a partial cause of this; so is the inertia resulting from poor health and malnutrition. But poverty is an even more direct cause of conservatism. If there is no margin to spare, there is no margin for risk. One cannot try a new variety of wheat or rice that promises an additional twenty per cent yield if there is any chance that it is vulnerable to insect pests, disease, or drought, and thus in an occasional year might fail altogether. However welcome the extra twenty per cent, it is not worth the risk of not eating for a whole season, the consequences of which tend to be both painful and irreversible. Since there is a measure of risk in anything that is untried, it is better to stick with the proven methods – the methods that have justified themselves by the survival of the family to this time. The well-to-do farmer, by contrast, can accept some risk of loss if the prospect is for a greater gain. He is in no danger of starving whatever happens. Even within India the comparatively well-to-do Punjabis in the north are far more inclined to try new crops and new methods than the villagers in the poorer regions who live closer to subsistence. Needless to say, in the firm tradition of the fortunate, they attribute their progressiveness not to higher income but to higher intelligence.

But fear of loss is not the only cause of conservatism among the very poor. Any change is regarded with uneasiness – and also with reason. In our world, change is identified with new and better ways of producing things or of organizing production; it is an article of faith that the whole community benefits from the advance. If someone loses his job, he is told with great unction and some truth that his sacrifice is for the greater good of the greater number. As a result, to be against change is like being against God and perhaps worse, for, of late, we have been more tolerant of religious than of economic heresy.

The experience of the poor community is with a very different kind of change. Technical innovation is unknown; change when it has occurred has usually meant that some rascal more powerful, more ruthless, or more devious than the rest has succeeded in enriching himself at the public expense. Change is associated with someone seizing land, exacting rents, levying taxes, provisioning an army, or exacting tribute for his own benefit. . . . This being the view of change, the instinct of the community is to resist it and to suspect even beneficial change.

Discussion guideline

"If the poor are too stupid to change their ways and do what's best for them, we must make them. The only way to break down their resistance to change is by force." From your own observations, comment on the validity of this solution.

Cross reference

A Case in Point, page 291

EXTENT AND TYPES OF UNDERDEVELOPMENT

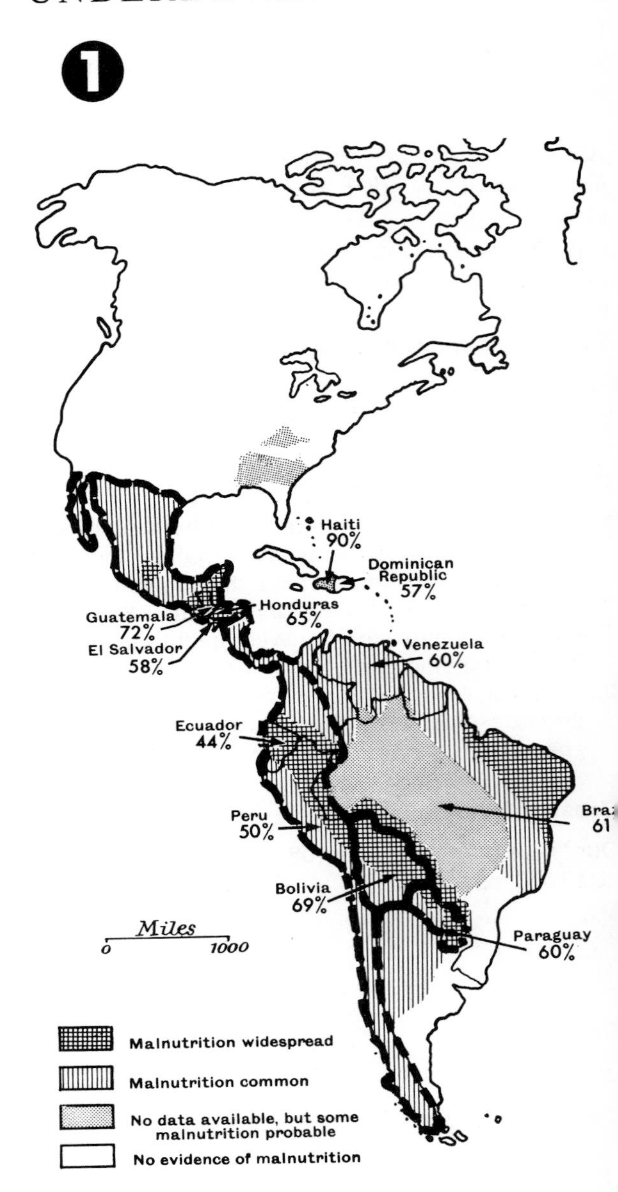

from *Recent History Atlas*, by Martin Gilbert and John Flower, by permission of Weidenfeld and Nicolson

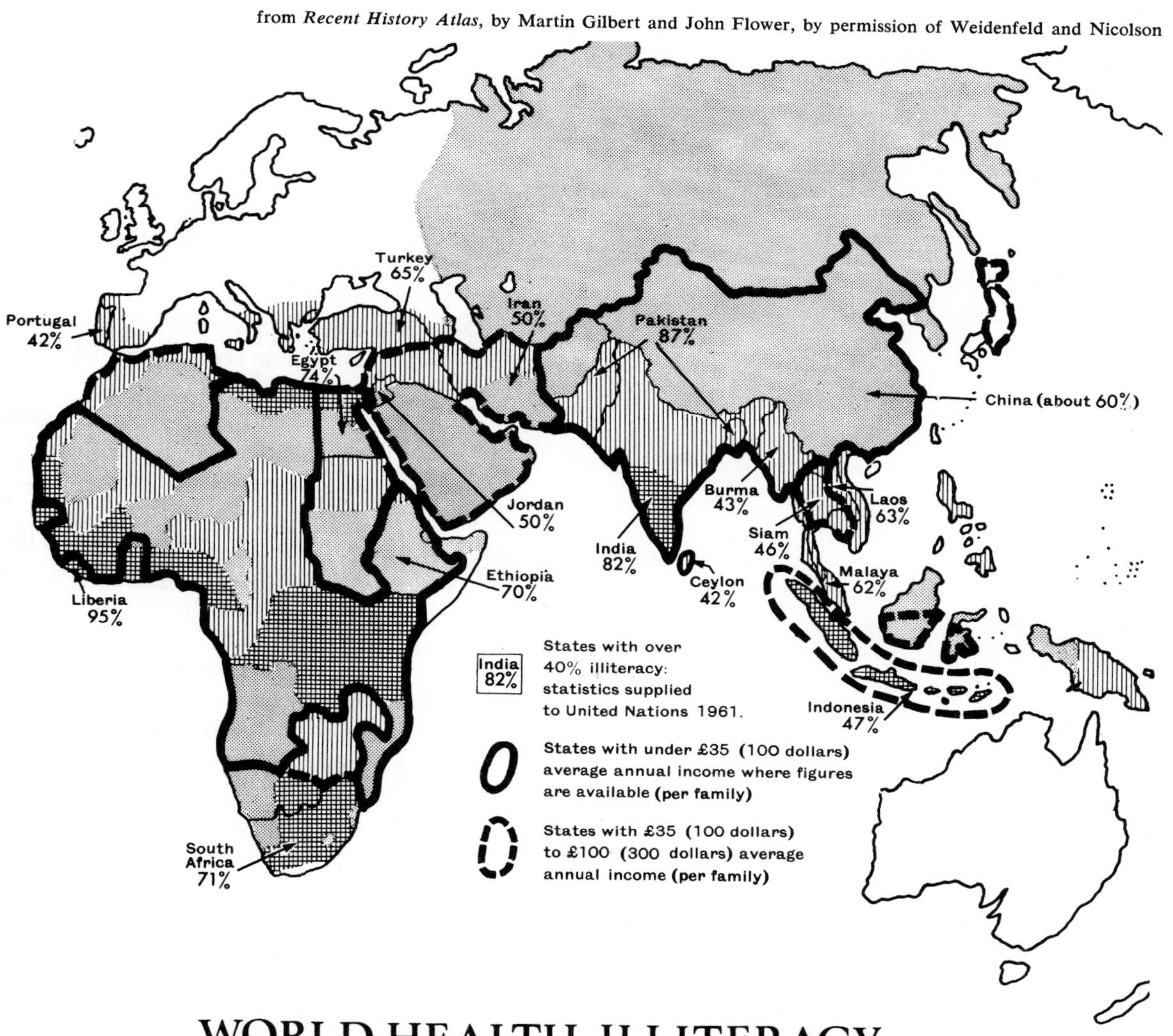

WORLD HEALTH, ILLITERACY
and INCOMES since 1960

An Overview

Chart based on information in
The Underdeveloped Country
by J. Kenneth Galbraith

TYPES OF UNDERDEVELOPMENT		
MODEL	*LIMITING CHARACTERISTIC*	*ELABORATION*
I. SUB-SAHARA (for example, The Republic of Congo)	AN INADEQUATE CULTURE BASE	– recent emergence from colonial rule – insufficient trained personnel – mismanagement of public funds – unstable government – unreliable law enforcement – minimum public services – restricted opportunities for large-scale commerce and industry – inadequate educational system
II. LATIN AMERICA (except Mexico and Costa Rica)	A RIGID SOCIAL STRUCTURE	– social position dependent on land ownership, business, government employment, and position in the armed forces – large rural mass dependent on the produce of small plots of land – unskilled, semi-employed urban population – government in the interest of the economically unproductive élite
III. SOUTH ASIA (for example, India and Pakistan)	POOR DISTRIBUTION OF THE FACTORS OF PRODUCTION	– large and dense population – shortage of arable land – limited savings – retarded industrial development – shortage of capital – limited effective employment – risk-taking prohibitive

Miller Services, Toronto

A Guatemalan peasant carrying goods to market

Discussion guideline

Given the information on the map and chart, submit proposals which you think might contribute to overcoming the development problems of each of the following models: (a) the Sub-Sahara, (b) Latin America, (c) South Asia.

OVERCOMING THE PROBLEMS OF UNDERDEVELOPMENT

Revolution?

from "The Uprooted: A Guatemala Sketch" by Richard F. Behrendt

Esteban Pazuj was an Indian carpenter in Guatemala. He made chairs and tables from a poor type of pine, fitted together without nails. In order to find customers, he had to take them from Totonicapan to Guatemala City, one hundred and twenty miles of mountain road at altitudes ranging down from eight thousand to four thousand feet. He carried on his shoulders and back the table and six chairs suspended from a tump-strap pressed against his forehead. He had to take his food along and would spend the nights in caves or under trees near the road. It took him eight days to reach the capital, several days to sell his goods on a special market, and another week to return home. He used to get three dollars for the table and the chairs or forty cents for each chair if sold separately. He charged for the lumber and his work only, not for the time spent en route. When he returned home, he had usually just enough left to buy more lumber and sustain himself and his family until his next sale.

During a few weeks every year, Esteban and his family used to go down to the western slopes of the volcanic mountain range, at about 3,000 feet altitude, to pick coffee beans on a large plantation owned by Germans. He received twenty cents a day and his children, who were working with him in the field, ten cents a day. They lived in a large shack together with the dozens of other families of seasonal workers. Each family prepared its meals, consisting mostly of corn and beans, over open fires inside the building. They slept on homemade woolen blankets spread on the dirt floors. There was no furniture of any kind. The women got their water from a brook half a mile away. Nature served as an open-air toilet. The Indian workers greeted the German administrators and their families, when these happened to cross their path, with bare heads and folded arms. If the workers broke any of the rules they were denied payment or put in the stocks.

Four years ago, an agent of the United Fruit Company came to Esteban's home town near Totonicapan to hire workers for the banana plantations around Tiquisate, in the lowlands of the west coast. He offered seventy cents a day, free housing, food at lower prices than it could be had in the stores, and the use of a plot of land for any worker who wanted to grow food on his own. It sounded fantastic to Esteban, but he accepted.

Now he loads banana stems on railway lorries from six o'clock in the morning to two o'clock in the afternoon. Sometimes he works overtime and is paid fifty per cent extra. In the afternoon he works for a few hours on his lot, if he feels like it. He and his family occupy a medium-sized room in a low, long wooden building housing several families. They have a kitchen of their own and share a toilet with their neighbors. They have electric light. They can buy rations of staple foods in the company commissary, at prices lower than those in regular stores. Their children go to a near-by school provided by the company, as required by the law of the country. The company fights the malaria-carrying mosquitoes and provides safe water supply. The company hospital, the second largest in the country, gives free service to the workers and their families.

But Esteban is not happy. For one thing, he and his family have never liked the hot, humid climate of the lowlands. He knows that he, his wife, and his children have more things to eat and a better place to live than before. However, to get these things he had to leave his village where generations of his family had spent their lives. His neighbors are comparative strangers, not related to him by blood, custom, or even language. Esteban does not speak Spanish very well and his neighbors, having come from other parts of the country, do not speak his language, which is Quiche. He had to discard his aboriginal dress, with its patterns and colors distinctive of his native village. He now lives in an outlying finca, very different from his old, tight little home town whose people had been organized for centuries in kinships, cofradias (civic hereditary fraternities), and parishes. There everybody knew – although not necessarily spoke to – everybody else, and there everyone's position in the community was strictly defined by tradition.

Tiquisate is very different indeed from those parts of Guatemala where Esteban spent his earlier life. There are no old buildings; everything seems to him too new. In fact, the entire town and the outlying plantations were established only fifteen years ago when the fruit company shifted part of its operations from the Atlantic to the Pacific coast because of plant diseases and soil exhaustion. There was then very little population and very little of anything – except climate and soil. Workers like Esteban had to be hired in the highlands where too many people try to eke out a living from thin soil on steep hillsides. Housing, transportation, communications, sanitation, irrigation, schools, hospital, entertainment had to be provided by the company. People from various countries, speaking different languages, professing even different religions, having different traditions and customs – and very different living standards – came to live here.

Esteban, and some ten thousand workers like him, with their families, changed from a form of life which had remained essentially fixed for centuries, almost unaffected by outside influences, in which people had obeyed traditional institutions and leaders, to a new planned form of life which was organized by a foreign corporation for the one purpose of producing and marketing a profitable commodity. . . . They know nothing (of the company) except that it is controlled by an indefinite number of foreigners, somewhere in the United States, nobody knows exactly how. They have never seen those people and never will. Some foreigners they do see: the North Americans who manage and supervise local operations. The Guatemalan workers do not bow with folded arms to them. Nor are they put in the stocks for infractions. Still they are not closer to them than they were to their German bosses. The americanos live in a small town of their own, divided from the "native" town by a barbed wire fence. They have their own school, commissary, club house, swimming pool, and pleasant one-family bungalows on well-kept grounds. Esteban and most of his fellow workers do not see much of the americanos, because the time keepers and foremen are Guatemalans; but they know that those americanos are the bosses. Or, rather, that they represent the real bosses who live in a faraway country where everything seems to be plentiful, and whence they send orders which may mean great changes for every one of the thirty thousand or more people of Tiquisate, even the loss of their jobs. Formerly, Esteban had lived in his own house, poor as it was, and most of the time he had been his own boss, engaged in a fairly steady trade, even if it paid him only a barest living.

Thus, Esteban is torn between gratification and dissatisfaction. He is bewildered. He is not sure that the advantages of his new life outweigh its disadvantages. In spite of the fact that he earns more than he ever did before, he sometimes feels that he is not paid enough. He knows of neighbors who earn as much as one quetzal (equal to a dollar) or one quetzal and forty cents a day. They are skilled workers: sprayers, or banana pickers, or mechanics, or drivers. They have mastered certain techniques and know how to handle some of the innumerable tools and machines which were unknown to them and most of their fellows until they came to work for the North Americans. These better paid skilled workers have gone to school and can read, write, and use elementary arithmetic. Their number is increasing steadily, as more efficient, more highly mechanized methods of production and transportation are being introduced and elementary school instruction is becoming more common. Esteban's children will probably belong to them.

Strangely enough, the skilled workers are more dissatisfied than Esteban. It is they who are most active in the labor unions which were founded during the last few years, taking advantage of the liberal laws adopted after the overthrow of the dictatorship in 1944. It is they who demand higher wages, better working conditions, free transportation on vacation trips, more school facilities, and many other things of which Esteban would never have dreamed a few years ago in his highland village. Some of these people have even learned English so that they can read the company's reports on its earnings. They now claim that the foreign owners of the company are taking too much money out of the country and they should be forced to leave greater benefits to the nationals, by paying higher wages and offering more social services of all kinds. They are not impressed with the arguments that the company already pays the best wages in the country, and that Esteban and his fellows would still be living the miserable, unhealthy, undernourished, and illiterate life of the past if it had not been for the many millions of dollars of North American capital invested by the company's stockholders. Some of the leaders of the union of which Esteban is a member, though not a very active one, even say that they, the Guatemalans, can take over the banana industry if the North Americans want to pull out of the country – just as the Guatemalans have taken charge of the German coffee and sugar plantations since the last war.

Esteban and his fellow workers have moved from a stationary way of life to a way of life where change – technological, economic, social, geographic – is the rule. They are not yet adjusted to it, but they are becoming accustomed to change. In fact, they may want to operate changes of their own, against the powerful corporation which has exposed them to this new way of life. Up to now, change has been planned and administered by the businessmen and engineers from the United States. New techniques, machinery, and skills were taught by these people to the natives of an economically backward country. Material inducements were offered to them for working in new places and unaccustomed enterprises. Now the principle of change is going farther than its original sponsors had intended. Social status and income are no longer determined by tradition and the accident of birth and, therefore, no longer accepted without criticism or ambition for improvement, as they were for centuries. On the other hand, the new factors on which one's place in life now depends are uncertain and not clearly understood.

If ambition and change are good and should take the place of conformity and tradition, for the sake of progress and a better life, why not push change until Esteban and all Guatemalans will enjoy the good things which are now reserved to the gringos and a few Guatemalans? If children of illiterate Guatemalan peasants can learn how to operate a railway engine, repair a truck, service an airplane, and do double-entry bookkeeping, things which only foreigners did thirty years ago, why can't they also learn to run all of Tiquisate – for their own benefit? And if the ability to operate machines and to plan and administer the work of many men is not limited to the members of certain master races or superior nations or ruling classes – why not change the traditional division of property under which a few families have owned most of the good lands and exploited the majority of the landless people who have had to work for them? Why put up any longer with the rule of privileged cliques in politics and public administration? If Esteban's children can learn things he never learned, as they do right now in school and shops, things which until recently were considered the prerogative of the overlords, what will stop them, or their children, from taking the place of those overlords?

Esteban Pazuj is representative not only of some thousands of fellow workers on the banana plantations of Guatemala but of millions of people working in many parts of the world. They are all going through essentially the same experience. Soon there will be even more Estebans.

Someone in a discussion of the evils of cultural displacement uttered this baroque epigram which sums up aptly the risks of the situation: "The uprooted and the roots of the uprooted are roots of revolution."

Discussion guidelines

1. How could Esteban's problems of adjustment have been overcome?
2. "North American capital has been both a blessing and a curse to areas such as Guatemala." To illustrate this claim, suggest further examples.
3. "The uprooted and the roots of the uprooted are roots of revolution." To what extent is this an adequate explanation of the causes of revolution?
4. " 'Yankee Go Home' is an understandable reaction to American influence abroad." By referring to current events, argue this viewpoint.

Cross references

Adapting Communism to China, page 86
The Culture Concept, page 146
The New Nationalism? page 266

2

The Challenge

from "Tom Dooley Writes to a Young Doctor"
by Tom Dooley

Tom Dooley

Wide World Photo

Village of Muong Sing
Kingdom of Laos

Dear Bart:

It is far past midnight. I am sitting in my house at Muong Sing, high in the foothills of the Himalayas in northern Laos. The kerosene pressure lamps overhead are hissing at me, and the wind is lashing down my valley. It whips the palm and frangipani. All the earth on this sad cut of the world seems flooded in the monsoon rains. This is the season of the crashing violence of the tropical storm. The crickets, frogs and wilder jungle animals screech and scream. The high Lao night land is not calm.

But I feel calm in writing you. I feel as though I have just met you outside the medical-school auditorium. May I thrust my hand out and say, "Congratulations, Bart. Congratulations on your graduation from medical school. Congratulations on being a doctor." But along with my congratulations, I also want to offer you some thoughts to mull over during your coming year of internship.

As a doctor, you have glorious things ahead of you. I am going to presume that you will choose the life of a general practitioner. There is a place in the world for specialists, but this battered world of ours needs more country doctors. As a general practitioner, where will you practice? The world is lopsided in its distribution of doctors. Almost all corners of America have available doctors. With veterans' benefits, industrial group health plans, labor-union programs and all the others, there is hardly a citizen who cannot find medical attention if he is willing to make some effort.

This valley in Laos, prior to our Medico hospital, had nothing to offer the sick but black magic, necromancy, witchcraft, clay images, sorcery and betel juice. The villagers wallowed in monkeys' blood, cobwebs, tigers' teeth and incantations. You know the world's statistics. The Congo, 13 million people and not one native doctor. South Vietnam, 11 million people, about 180 doctors. Cambodia, five million people, seven doctors. Here in Laos, there are three million people and only one Lao doctor. Other nations' statistics are equally staggering.

Though this is sometimes called "the age of the shrug", I do not believe you would say, as some do, "So what, it's not my problem." You and I, Bart, are the heirs of all ages. We have been born and raised in freedom. We have justice, law and equality. But we have overlooked another side of our inheritance. We have also the legacy of hatred, bred by careless men before us. We have the legacy of abuse, degradation and the inhumanity of men blinded by prejudice and ignorance. To people like you and me, richer in educational opportunities than many, this is a challenge. To accept it is a privilege and a responsibility.

I believe that the unique aspect of this challenge to young doctors demands that we invest some of our lives in the practice of medicine in foreign fields. I say "some", not a lifetime. This is not expected of us. But we can give a year or two. It can be part of the maturation of a man, the metamorphosis of a doctor.

Your internship lies ahead, maybe residency, and then – come out to the developing nations of the world for a while, Bart. Bring your gadgets and the armamentarium of drugs, to be sure, but most of all bring your human spirit! Bring your youthful enthusiasm, your drive, your energy, your dedication to help the sick. Bring your belief in the good and the right. Bring along a sense of humor; you'll need it when the roof leaks, the patients eat all the pills the first dosage and the witch doctors put cow dung over your sterile compresses.

Bring also the spirit of adventure that our founding fathers possessed. Spend some time in valleys like Muong Sing. Splash some of your human warmth and goodness on people who heretofore have received few of these elements from Western man. You will find that just by being a doctor with qualities of the human heart you will help to unify men.

You are probably thinking, "But, Tom, what's in it for me? We are all a little selfish, you know." There is a great deal in it for you, Bart. By investing a portion of your life in work here, you will take back with you into private practice accomplishments beyond the narrow confines of continent and custom. Your accomplishments will be along the broad horizons of peace for the whole world.

Doctors know the alikeness of all human beings, and the world today demands a deeper emphasis on the brotherhood of man. This should be a force to unite men – as men. We young Americans must take the heritage of our freedoms, from disease as well as from tyranny, and project it into the future – for other men. We who have it must help those who do not have it.

The kerosene is running out, and the lamps are sputtering and flickering. I'll continue the letter tomorrow.

A day has passed since I began this letter. At clinic this morning we had 78 patients. Everything from a blazing malaria to a man who brought his donkey, requesting that we suture a laceration in its flank. Some children had diarrhea and eye inflammations, and one had head lice. My American corpsmen pulled some teeth. The kids howled, just like they do in America. The old gals complained about having to wait in line, just like they do in America. A few of the older gents wanted some "vigor pills", just like . . . well, anyway, there are no really deep differences between people. I have spent six years of my life among different men, and always, I find that the similarities out-weigh the differences. Each life is infinitely precious as a life. Everywhere.

To recapitulate, Bart, I believe that you should use your profession and your heart as a cable to bind men together. Kindness and gentleness, daily instruments of the doctor, can be potent weapons against the anger of the world. Bring your talents, and the spirituality of your heart, to distant valleys like mine. And take back with you a rich, rich reward.

So, along with my congratulations on your graduation, I send my wish that you will know the happiness that comes of serving others who have nothing.

Sincere best wishes always,
Tom

Discussion guidelines

1. "Bring your gadgets . . . but most of all bring your human spirit." What qualities of the human spirit does a member of the Company of Young Canadians or of the American Peace Corps need? Why?
2. "To people like you and me, richer in educational opportunities than many, this is a challenge. To accept it is a privilege and a responsibility." What kind of person would be inclined to accept this challenge?
3. "Resolved that: Efforts such as those suggested by Tom Dooley do not get to the roots of underdevelopment; they are only 'drops in the bucket' which our governments support as an excuse for doing nothing more." Debate this resolution.

Cross references

Working with the Masses: A Case Study, page 88
A Case in Point, page 291

 a

The Food Crisis

from "The Promise of Agriculture in the Less Developed Lands"
by Walter C. Lowdermilk

Civilization is running a race with famine and the outcome is in doubt. Some two thirds of the peoples of our world are undernourished, poorly clothed, and inadequately housed, yet demographers tell us that world population will reach 6 billion souls by the end of the century.

It is among lesser developed countries, least prepared to increase food production with their traditional farming and reactionary customs, that population pressures are fast building up into a dangerous and explosive situation as they double their numbers in 25–35 years. The problems of each country stand out against a world crisis in food.

Land is the foundation on which nations and peoples rise or fall. If productivity is improved and maintained, peoples may grow in prosperity, providing there is social justice and freedom from aggression. If lands are damaged or devastated and farmers are exploited as is done in much of the less developed regions, then malnutrition, unrest, riots, and eventual revolution and wars are in store.

Land that grows food sustains the entire social structure and is the hope of the future. Efficiency of farmers in growing food determines the number of others who may be released for various divisions of labor in a developing society. The farmer is the key to progress. His ability to double food production as populations double is all-important to the nation.

My thirty-nine years as technical assistant in agriculture, in the United States, and in countries of the Far East, Middle East, and Africa, has let me observe the effects of population pressures under varying conditions.

China

The Chinese make up about one fourth of the human race and three fourths of them are farmers. Much can be learned from their experiences under varying population pressures during a recorded history of 4,000 years. I cannot speak for conditions under the present regime, but I spent the years 1922–27 and 1942–43 in programs of famine prevention, north of the Yangtze and west to Tibet. I

Miller Services, Toronto

Chinese farming

learned to know firsthand the Chinese farmer and his problems and have a high regard for his splendid qualities. He is individualistic, industrious, self-reliant, intelligent, and reverent. These sturdy farmers fed the Chinese people under annual cropping of fields for forty centuries. Now they cannot grow enough food for exploding populations.

My former experiences with famines in overpopulated areas of China present a terrifying picture of what many less developed or backward countries face as populations double without a proportionate increase of food production. There is nothing more terrifying than food riots, and there is no more terrible way to reduce population than by starvation.

In famines, the frail structure of civilization falls apart. People will sell their liberty and their all for food when faced with a choice between food and starvation. A starving man knows no God and no country. I have found that hungry people do not keep their treaties, neither will they keep the peace, nor will they stay within their own boundaries. There is no substitute for food.

Africa, South of the Sahara

Today, the eyes of the world are on Africa as never before. Africa, with its vast resources, harbors forces of instability that may affect the peace of the world. Millions of people, unlearned and unskilled, are being given freedom and self-government. In past years the white man in Africa generally failed to train the African in fundamental skills for economic independence or to demonstrate the dignity of labor.

While serving as consultant to the British Colonial Office and to missions in Africa, I spoke to many thousands of African students in high school and junior college assemblies. In each place I asked for a showing of hands of those who were training for different lines of work. Many were preparing to be clerks or schoolteachers, some to be lawyers, doctors, and politicians. Not one of these thousands announced that he was preparing to be a skilled mechanic, and none to be mechanical, civil, electrical, or agricultural engineers or modern farmers. I said, "Now you want self-government, but no one of you is preparing to carry on the basic and productive works of a self-governing state."

As these new states attain self-government, they are finding that they lack trained personnel for productive enterprises and are frantically calling for technical assistance from the United Nations or from whatever country will supply experts. A most urgent problem is to step up production of foodstuffs sufficient for rapidly increasing populations from lands badly damaged and deteriorating under primitive farming.

Present leaders in Africa, ambitious to establish prosperous new nations, face tremendous problems in overcoming deep-seated resistance of farmers to adopt improved conservation farming. Old-fashioned African chiefs, with few exceptions, have been a powerful reactionary force with arbitrary powers, especially in customs controlling the tenure of tribal land. Chiefs suspect educated Africans and fear any competitor in leadership.

African farmers live from day to day and crop to crop. They eat when they have food and starve when they do not. They give little thought for the future; if they have a surplus, others would likely take it from them or live with them as long as it lasts. Colonial governments helped certain farmers carry out demonstration plots with composting, fertilizers, improved seeds, and with soil conservation, beside plots of traditional farming – which increased production manyfold. But few if any farmers carried out these practices on their own initiative, and they dropped the demonstration plots immediately when white supervision was removed. As colonial administrations come to an end, only time will reveal what progress the African will make to increase food production.

Millions of people, living in tropical Africa, the "hot-house" of the world, practise an early Iron

Miller Services, Toronto

The women shown at work here are members of the Watusi tribe and are cultivating fields owned by members of the Bantu tribe. The relation between owner and worker is much like that between the medieval serf and his lord.

Age agriculture. Vast regions have not reached the plow stage. Farmers practise "shifting cultivation" wherein they use fire as a tool, along with a stubby ax and a shorthandled hoe, and move to a new patch of "bush" after two or three crops. But now population pressure has reduced the former cycle of twenty years until in many localities farmers must cultivate the same impoverished ground, year after year.

Technical problems for development of the vast resources of Africa are more easily solved than human.

With energetic programs and skilled people, Africa can be made to supply local needs in a more prosperous society and export sufficient to supply all Europe with such products as rice, paper pulp, palm and peanut oils, cocoa, tropical fruits, cabinet woods, rubber, tobacco, copper, iron, chrome, diamonds, and other things in quantity. It is a pity that in the midst of such potentialities, I found people undernourished, sometimes suffering famine, yet resisting progress.

Birth control to limit populations is a touchy matter across international boundaries. At an International Conference in Israel in 1960, representatives of Afro-Asian states rejected such a suggestion as a "trick of white men to keep down black populations". "No," they said emphatically, "we want to increase our populations rapidly to become strong, with a voice in world affairs." This touchy problem can only be handled by the country concerned, as Japan is doing.

This oncoming population explosion must also stimulate foresight and collaboration among nations, in the development of works worthy of the human spirit. This calls for productive economies that enable peoples to *earn* security in the good things of life. This is a challenge greater than war and would cost burdened taxpayers less. In my view, the potentialities of the "Good Earth" are so great, under the new and enlarged powers that the modern scientific and technological revolution puts into our hands, that we have a fighting chance to win this race with famine.

b

The Surprising Food Increase That's Fighting Famine

By BRUCE MACDONALD

WASHINGTON – It is almost as miraculous as the biblical account of the loaves and the fishes. A year or two ago, alarmed authorities in many quarters were warning about the extreme danger of world-wide famine by the mid-Nineteen Seventies as the population explosion outstripped food supplies.

Now the outlook appears to have changed with dramatic suddenness. In part it is due to vastly improved weather conditions, particularly the ending of drought in India and Pakistan. But the most important new element for the long term is an agricultural revolution that has been taking place around the globe and resulting in staggering increases in food production.

Iowa speech

"Time is the critical new dimension in the world food problem," Lester R. Brown, administrator of the International Agricultural Development Service in the U.S. Department of Agriculture, told an audience in Ames, Iowa, on Nov. 8, 1966.

"The world is now adding a million more people each week – most of them in the less-developed countries. This flood of people is washing away the benefits of millions of man-years of effort and billions of dollars in foreign aid," he declared. In that year, he noted, the global production of food was no greater than in the year before, but there were 65 million more mouths to feed.

Addressing the United Nations in New York the year before, Pope Paul VI spoke against the already massive effort that even then was being mobilized to meet the danger of impending food shortages by promoting intensified use of birth control to dampen the population explosion.

"Respect for life, even with regard to the great problem of birth, must find here in your assembly its highest affirmation and its most reasoned defense," the Pope asserted.

Pope's advice

"You must strive to multiply bread so that it suffices for the tables of mankind, and not rather favor an artificial control of birth, which would be irrational, in order to diminish the number of guests at the banquet of life," he declared.

But many outstanding authorities were highly dubious about man's ability to multiply the output of bread sufficiently to keep pace with the growing number of "guests at the banquet of life".

"The reason for growing food shortages can be simply stated," Mr. Brown said in the course of his Ames speech a year after the Pope's address to the United Nations. "There is little new land that can readily be brought under the plow and many of the less developed countries are not able to raise yield per acre in a rapid, sustained fashion."

Mr. Brown was wrong, as he is the first to acknowledge. "For those whose thinking of Asia is conditioned by the food crises of 1965 and 1966, the news of an agricultural revolution may come as a surprise," he wrote in the July issue of *Foreign Affairs* magazine. "As of mid 1968, both the food situation and the food production prospects in Asia have changed almost beyond belief."

Was Pope Paul then right all along in contending that all that was required was for mankind to find ways of increasing the output of food, rather than limiting the growth of population? Not in the opinion of Mr. Brown. "This agricultural revolution is not the ultimate solution to the food-population problem, but it does buy much needed additional time in which to mount effective family-planning programs," he contended in the *Foreign Affairs* article.

Elaborating in a recent interview, the economist estimated the massive breakthrough that had been achieved in the production of food had bought the world another 10 to 15 years. But that means only that the time when the world might be confronted by the spectre of widespread famine has been put back from the mid-Nineteen Seventies to the latter half of the Nineteen Eighties unless an equally dramatic breakthrough is made in curbing the growth of population during the interval. . . .

The agricultural revolution, which was on the verge of beginning even at the time when widespread and prolonged drought in India and Pakistan was aggravating fears about the long-term crisis that lay ahead, is the product of many factors.

In part it stems from the new awareness by governments of the necessity of concentrating resources on increasing food production through a wide variety of means. This includes raising prices for farm products and thus increasing the return to the farmer, providing new sources of credit, improving irrigation facilities, and actively encouraging farmers to break with the old ways to adopt new techniques and new equipment.

In part, it is the result of the increasing availability of fertilizer at lower cost than in the past, a growing awareness on the part of farmers of what it can do to increase their production, and the fact that higher prices have enhanced their ability to buy it.

Most important

But in the opinion of Mr. Brown, by far the most important element has been the development and incredibly swift adoption of new types of wheat, rice, and corn that are capable of producing a phenomenal increase in output under widely varying conditions of soil, climate, and available sunlight.

Ordinarily, most varieties of cereals have to be especially adapted to the conditions prevailing in a relatively limited area. But a new type of rice developed in the Philippines and wheat developed in Mexico by the Rockefeller Foundation after 20 years of experimentation have produced varieties that can readily be grown in most of the developing countries.

The new varieties of rice mature in around 120 to 125 days, Mr. Brown pointed out, compared with up to 180 days for older varieties. The result is that in many areas farmers are now getting high yields of two or even three crops in a year, where before they obtained only one low-yielding crop.

"Triple-cropping of rice, or rice in combination with sorghum or corn, is resulting in yields under field conditions as high as eight tons of grain an acre a calendar year," Mr. Brown reported. "This contrasts with average yearly rice yields in Japan of just over two tons per acre and wheat yields in Europe of less than two tons per acre."

Increased yields

Substantial increases in yields have also been achieved with the Mexican wheats, which have the added advantage of being short-stemmed and capable of absorbing large quantities of fertilizer to increase the amount of grain produced on each plant without encountering the problem on longer-stemmed varieties of becoming top heavy and collapsing.

What is equally phenomenal is the rapidity with which these new cereal strains have been adopted. Mr. Brown points out that it took 25 years before hybrid corn was planted throughout the United States. It was only in 1967 that Pakistan first imported the new wheat seed from Mexico, 42,000 tons. With the output from that planting it secured sufficient new seed to cover almost its entire wheat acreage this year, with some left over for milling. Less remarkable but still very large strides have been made in the use of the new seed in India and Turkey.

40 per cent rise

An indication of the results achieved from the new wheat, together with the other factors that have contributed to the agricultural revolution, is evident in the fact that Pakistan's production in the crop year ending in April was 40 per cent above the previous record.

Higher yield and higher prices have meant more money for the farmers of the developing nations, which in turn have provided them with the means and the incentive to adopt new technologies and acquire new equipment. And because agriculture is of such dominant importance in so many of these countries, what is good for the farmer is bound to be good for the rest of the populace, since the man on the land has more money with which to buy the output of the man in the towns and cities.

Providing the sharp increase in population can be checked, Mr. Brown is convinced many of the less-developed countries can become not only self-sufficient in food, but even net exporters. In fact, he foresees the day when they will join with Canada and the United States to press the European Common Market countries and Japan to dismantle the walls they have erected to protect their own farmers.

The Globe and Mail, Toronto, July 15, 1968

Miller Services, Toronto

Government-sponsored advertisement in India

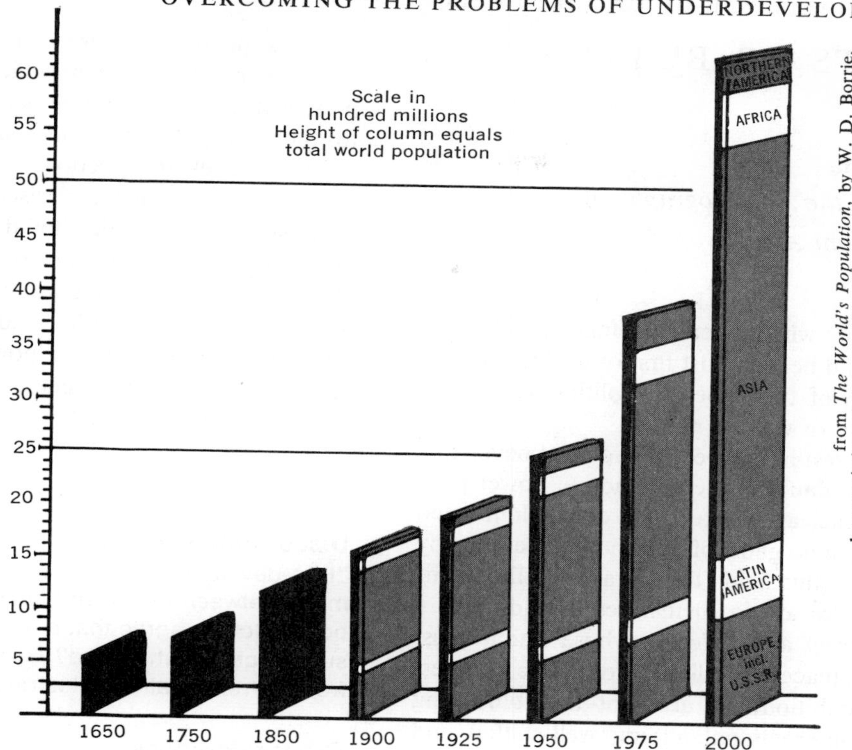

Patterns and Rates of Growth

from *The World's Population*, by W. D. Borrie,
by permission of Canadian Institute of International Affairs

Discussion guidelines

1. "If for no other reason than self interest, Canada must increase her support of all types of foreign aid."
   (a) Defend this position.
   (b) What factors in recipient countries can frustrate the proper use of such aid?
   (c) How might these difficulties be overcome?
2. "The world is faced with a choice between population control or mass starvation." Considering the viewpoints expressed in the resources, what is your assessment of this issue?
3. "Hungry people do not keep their treaties, neither will they keep the peace, nor will they stay within their own boundaries. . . . There is no substitute for food." Are the hungry really such a threat to world order? Discuss with reference to specific illustrations from past history or current affairs.

BULLETS OR BUTTER?

The Dilemma

from *AWO, the Autobiography of Chief Obafemi Awolowo*

In determining what Nigeria's defence and foreign policies should be, we must first of all settle in our minds which of two types of politics we prefer: power politics or welfare politics.

In the interest of our people, we must never cast as much as a glance in the direction of power politics. In this nuclear-, rocket-, and dollar-dominated world we have no ghost of a chance of making any mark at all in this field. The paraphernalia of this type of politics are in themselves bewildering: a mighty array of armed forces whose claims must take pride of place in the disposal of public finances; territorial ambition; an arrogant and blustering attitude in international affairs; well-staffed and luxurious embassies in the more important countries of the world; a foreign policy that is motivated by cunning, trickery, and bad faith; an overpowering desire to outwit, outshine, or humiliate the other nations of the world; and so on and so forth. This kind of politics will not do Nigeria any good. It would bring miseries to our people at home, and notoriety to our nation abroad. Monies which could have been spent in catering for the welfare and prosperity of our people would have to be diverted to devilish and fruitless channels. In any case, we are too late in the race and we just have not got the resources to indulge in it.

We have all heard a good deal of that summit where Britain, the U.S., Russia, and France love to meet. From all accounts, it is a very chilly and precarious rendezvous. The foothills of the summit are comparatively obscure; but there is no doubt that it is quieter and safer there. "He that is down need fear no fall." Nations which indulge in power politics have brought perpetual fear and heartache to their people. The underdeveloped ones like Egypt have left their people to wallow in the mire of poverty, ignorance, and disease as well. It is my submission that Nigeria should regard power politics as a poison, and should avoid it as such. If we choose welfare politics it will be well with us. In a developing country with slender means, such as ours, welfare politics and power politics do not mix. A choice must be made between butter and bullets: we cannot have both.

Discussion guideline

"In a developing country . . . [a] choice must be made between butter and bullets: we cannot have both." Do you agree that a developing country has such a clear-cut choice? Give specific examples from current affairs to illustrate your viewpoint.

Cross references

What We Can Do, page 205
A Meaningful Voice? page 296

ALIGNMENT OR NON-ALIGNMENT?

Alignment?

from *AWO, the Autobiography of Chief Obafemi Awolowo*

There are two distinct ideological camps in the world today: the Western democracies and the Communist bloc. For reasons which I will presently give, my preference is unhesitatingly for the Western democracies. No nation in the world is absolutely good or absolutely evil. There is still a colour-bar in the Western democracies. Negroes in America are still being discriminated against, and can still be lynched. For her part Britain is still guilty, as before, though in a decreasing order of magnitude, of injustice to the black peoples in East and Central Africa. But such evils as are committed in the countries of the Western democracies towards the weaker peoples of the world are not only fast diminishing, but are being constantly subjected to strong and sharp criticisms in those countries by their nationals, without any risk to their lives or personal freedom. If you did likewise behind the iron curtain you would not live to fight another day.

The world in which we live is still very far from perfection. We have got to take it as we find it and, like conscientious and honest people, strive to contribute towards its peace, progress, and happiness. From time to time, things will happen which in his judgment one individual considers to be wrong. Whether the individual is right or wrong in his judgment, he has an inherent and inalienable right to entertain such opinion and to express it. The question is where, as between the Western bloc and the Eastern bloc, can a man freely exercise his natural right to hold and express any opinion, subject to such restrictions as may be laid down by laws enacted by the freely elected parliament of the land? The answer is obvious: it is in the Western bloc. As has been abundantly shown, we in Nigeria have won our freedom mainly as a result of unrestrained organized public opinion against the continuance of British rule. In our struggles against British rule we have enjoyed the support of many Britons as well. Besides, in the Commonwealth of Nations a member nation could hold and express any views it likes. But that is not the way it is done in the Communist community of nations.

In the present world situation, when godless materialism is threatening to destroy or stifle all that is best and noblest in man, neutrality in international affairs is a disservice to humanity. My own analysis has led me to the conclusion that neutrality, as the basis of the foreign policy of certain nations, is no more and no less than the extension, conscious or unconscious, of the deep-seated prejudices which those nations have had towards some of the countries of the Western democracies. But I must urge that in our foreign relations, we must forget the past and work for the future – the great future of our land and of mankind. As between opposing forces, we should have enough courage to make up our minds, independently of any outside influence, as to which side is relatively right and which side is relatively wrong. Having made up our minds, we should have the honesty to pronounce our view and stand. To pretend that neither of two opposite sides is right or wrong, especially if we occupy an influential position in the assembly of nations, is to encourage evil-doing, and to damp the ardour for well-doing.

There is a policy which appears to be in vogue amongst some of the developing countries of the world. In their quest for financial and technical assistance, they adopt the tactics of wooing the

Miller Services, Toronto

Miller Services, Toronto

nations of the two blocs at the same time, in the hope that in the anxious bid for new supporters or converts, they (the developing countries) would get the best of two worlds. I consider these tactics to be both disreputable and dangerous. Disreputable in the sense that it amounts in my view to diplomatic double-dealing. If we want help from more than one nation, by all means let us seek it. But it is immoral to play two opposing forces against each other in the process. It is this kind of diplomacy that is responsible for the fall of many nations in the past; for the many wars and incalculable miseries which have afflicted mankind; and for the tormenting fears and distrust among nations, which the world is now witnessing. The tactics are dangerous because acts of double-dealing – whether diplomatic or otherwise – never pay in the end. There are times when even the greatest expert in diplomatic cunning is outclassed in his own game. It is then that he discovers that all that he thought he had gained is but loss, and that what is left of national honour and dignity is but the shadow of a glorious past that is gone for ever, or of a great future that will never come.

While he was alive, Nehru was the most influential exponent of non-alignment. In the above set of pictures he is shown with the Russian Premier, Bulganin, and the American President, Eisenhower.

Non-alignment?

from *Independence and After*

by Jawaharlal Nehru

Our general policy has been to try to cultivate friendly relations with all countries, but that is something which anyone can say. It is not a very helpful thought. It is almost outside, if I may say so of politics. . . . Nevertheless, something can be said for it even on the political plane. We cannot perhaps be friendly always with every country. The alternative is to become very friendly with some and hostile to others. That is the normal foreign policy of a country. . . . Fortunately, India has in herited no past hostility to any country. Why should we then start this train of hostility to any country? . . . Naturally . . . we are likely to be more friendly to some countries than to others, because this may be to our mutual advantage. . . . But even so, our friendship with [some] countries should not, as far as possible, be such as brings us inevitably into conflict with some other country. Now, some people may think that this is a policy of hedging or just avoiding pitfalls, a middle-of-the-road policy. As I conceive it, it is nothing of the kind. It is not a middle-of-the-road policy. It is a positive, constructive policy deliberately aiming at something and deliberately trying to avoid hostility to other countries, to any country as far as possible.

How can we achieve this? Obviously, there are risks and dangers, and the first duty of every country is to protect itself. Protecting oneself unfortunately means relying on the armed forces and the like and so we build up, where necessity arises, our defence apparatus. We cannot take the risk of not doing so . . . [but] in protecting oneself, we should do so in such a way as not to antagonize others and also so as not to appear to aim at the freedom of others. That is important. Also we should avoid in speech or writing anything which worsens the relationship of nations. Now, the urge to do or say things against countries, against their policies, and sometimes against their statesmen is very great, because other people are very offensive at times; they are very aggressive at times. If they are aggressive we have to protect ourselves against their aggression. If there is fear of future aggression we have to protect ourselves against that. That I can understand, but there is a distinct difference between that and shouting loudly from the house tops all the time [–] attacking this country or that – even though that country may deserve to be criticized or attacked. It does not help – this shouting business; it only makes matters worse. . . . In the shouting that takes place on either side, logic and reason disappear, because people's passions are roused and ultimately they land themselves in war. . . .

Now, can any country, can India succeed in preventing this kind of mutual [accusation]? Can we succeed, as we want to, in dealing with every question on its merits? Today international questions are looked upon from the point of view of how they will affect some future conflict, with the result that you find groupings on either side forgetful of the actual merits of the case. And a country like India which talks in a different language is looked upon as a nuisance . . . ; unfortunately, not only as a nuisance, but every group suspects it of joining hands with the opposite group. But now, I think, there is a certain amount of realization by other countries that we really mean what we say. It is not some deep game or plot and we mean to consider these questions on their merits. . . .

May I say that I do not for an instant claim any superior vantage point for India to advise or criticize the rest of the world? I think we are merely trying not to get excited about these problems and anyhow there is no reason why we should not try. It follows, therefore, that we should not align ourselves with what are called power blocs. We can be of far more service without doing so and I think there is just a possibility – and I shall not put it higher than that – that at a moment of crisis our peaceful and friendly efforts might make a difference and avert that crisis.

Discussion guideline

"A [ruler] is . . . esteemed when he is a true friend or a true enemy, when, that is, he declares himself without reserve in favour of some one or against another. This policy is always more useful than remaining neutral." (Niccolo Machiavelli, *The Prince*)

Assess the merits of this recommendation for a developing country.

Cross references

Alliances Don't Work, page 269
A Meaningful Voice? page 296

The Meaning of War

"YOUR COUNTRY NEEDS
YOU"
ALFRED LEETE

Miller Services, Toronto

What is war? Is it a product of politics – of man's inborn savagery – of man's stupidity? How is it fought? How is it used? Are international affairs nothing more than wars and the intervals between? Can war ever be ended, or will man finally destroy himself?

EIGHT VIEWS

1

What Is War?

from *On War*

by General Karl von Clausewitz –
a condensed and modernized version

The Two Kinds of War

The first type of war has for its object the overthrow of the enemy, either to destroy him politically, or to merely disarm him and force him to conclude peace on our terms. The second kind aims at making some conquests on the frontiers of the enemy's country, either for the purpose of keeping them permanently, or of using them for exchange in the settlement of a peace.

War Is an Act of Violence

War is nothing but a duel on a vast scale, and we can understand this best by considering the contest of two wrestlers. Each strives by physical force to compel the other to submit to his will: each tries to throw his opponent, and thus make him incapable of further resistance. War, therefore, is an act of violence aimed at forcing our opponent to do what we want.

In order to meet violence with violence, war arms itself with the inventions of art and science. It is accompanied, moreover, by minor, unimportant restrictions which it places upon itself and which are called international law. In reality, he who uses physical force ruthlessly, without consideration of the bloodshed involved, will gain an advantage over an enemy who is less ruthless. He thereby forces his opponent's hand and thus both opponents are pushed to extremes which are limited only by their mutual powers of resistance.

Miller Services, Toronto

Now do-gooders may easily imagine that there is a skilful method of disarming and overcoming an enemy without causing great bloodshed. However, in things as dangerous as war, this is an error: and in war, errors which proceed from a spirit of kindliness are the worst.

War Is a Gamble

There is no human affair which is so closely connected with chance as war. As soon as it starts, there is a play of possibilities and probabilities, of good and bad luck, which spreads about like a web, and thus makes war, of all branches of human activity, the most like a gambling game.

But, should our theory leave off here in order to make smug conclusions and absolute rules? This would not be practical. Theory must also take into account the human element; it must allow a place for courage, boldness, even rashness. The art of war has to deal with living beings and moral forces, and the result is that it can never achieve absolute rules. There must be a margin for the accidental, in great issues as in small. And, we must also allot room for courage and self-reliance – just as much room, in fact, as we allot to the accidental. And if the qualities mentioned emerge in a high degree, the margin we allow for them must be as great. Courage and self-reliance are, therefore, principles that are quite essential to war.

But war is no pastime, no mere passion for taking chances and winning: it is a serious instrument for a serious purpose.

War Is a Political Instrument

In drawing up plans for a war it is essential to ask if the political point of view should give way to the military point of view, or whether the opposite should be the case. Indeed, the only possible situation in which political considerations could be left out would be in a war of life and death, a war of pure hatred. In reality, though, wars are only the expressions of political policy.

It would be contrary to common sense to make the political point of view subordinate to the military, since it is political policy that has declared war. Politics is the brains, and war is only its instrument. It follows, therefore, that the military point of view must be subordinate to the political.

Accordingly, purely military judgments and decisions cannot be allowed to determine the conduct of war; indeed, it is irrational to consult professional soldiers on the plan of a war, since they will give only a military opinion of what the cabinet should do. Experience shows that, despite the high degree of skill and science evident in the conduct of modern war, the outlines of any conflict are decided by the cabinet – that is, by the political branch, not the military branch, of government. This is perfectly natural, for none of the major plans required for a war can be made without an understanding of political relations. When people speak of politicians harming a war effort, what they really mean is that the political policy is wrong, not that the influence of politics is wrong. If the political policy is right, that is, if it achieves its objective, it can only help the war effort.

Summary

War is, therefore, a wonderful trinity, composed of violence, chance, and politics.

The first of these concerns the people most; the second concerns the general and his army most; the third concerns the government most. The passions which break forth in war must already have their roots in the people. The opportunity for the display of courage and talents depends on the nature of the general and his army. But the political objects of war are determined by the government alone.

Discussion guidelines

1. "Violence, policy, chance. And the greatest of these is chance." In the light of your study of history, discuss this interpretation of the chief characteristics of war.
2. "Good guys finish last." Is this what Clausewitz is saying?

Cross references

The Fears That Spurred the Russians into Action, page 82
Juvenile Delinquency? page 144
The Necessities of War, page 273
The Confrontation in Cuba, page 281
"Was no other choice", page 285

A Soldier's First Experience

from *The Wheatley Diary*
edited by Christopher Hibbert

[Edmund Wheatley, a twenty-one-year-old foot soldier with Wellington's army, kept a diary of his experiences from October 7, 1813, until the defeat of Napoleon at Waterloo two years later. His account opens with a description of his first battle which took place near the Bidassoa River on the Spanish-French frontier.]

7 October – At one o'clock this morning the dead silence of the Camp was suddenly changed to a scene of hurry and commotion. A passe-parole ordered the Companies instantly under arms; and the rattling of artillery passing soon shook off every drowsy sensation. All was conjecture and expectation. We supposed the forcing of the river to be the object.

We remained till daybreak in a field to the left – the Guards in our rear on the right. The morning was cloudy with a sharp hoar-frost.

About seven o'clock the cry was "Fall in!" We ran to the river side and dashed into it, up to our arm-pits in water, through a shower of musketry from the French. On reaching the opposite shore, my Company and the 2nd ran to cover the riflemen. But to make it more clear, I'll endeavour to sketch the attack.

The Bidassoa is very rapid at the place where I crossed and so very strong was the current that we were constrained to take each other by the arm holding our swords and muskets in the air, the water being up to the arm-pits and knee deep in mud. The French were stationed in the houses opposite, behind the hedges and in the ditches keeping up a regular fire upon us as we struggled through the cold river. Many fell wounded and were drowned through the rapidity of the element. The balls splashed around us like a shower of rain. But the water was so excessively cold and strong that I was insensible to the splashing of the musketry around my chest and I struggled through mechanically, without even reflecting that I was walking to fight a few thousand devils before breakfast.

On reaching the opposite shore we cleared the houses of the French and recovered breath for a few minutes. My company and the 1st under Major Gerber then sallied out. We dived into a wood on the slope of a hill behind every tree of which stood a Frenchman, distraction in his eye and death in his hand, popping from the ditches, between the thickets, and among the bushes.

And now I first heard that hissing and plaintive whistling from the balls around me. The hiss is caused by the wind but when [a ball passes] close to you a strong shrill whistle tells you of your escape. I felt no tremor or cold sensation whatever. I walked without thought or reflection.

We soon gained the outside of the wood, the French scampering like rabbits in a warren. On ascending [higher up the hill] a 9 lb. shot from [our own] artillery [across the river] fell short and nearly cut off half of us. We jumped down a ditch to escape its range and, creeping along a hedge, we gained a field which we had to cross to take a small farmhouse.

On the edge of the field we became exposed to an elevated battery. A heavy shot fell two yards to my left and covered me with mud and slime. The noise was so great and the splash into the earth so violent that I mechanically jumped against a tall Polack who, good-naturedly smiling, pushed me back saying, "Don't flinch, Ensign." Little hump-backed Bacmeister behind me also said, "Vall, Veatley, how you like dat?"

"Not good for the kidneys," I said.

That very moment another volley came and cut a fellow to pieces before my face.

I looked up at the battery and fancied every mouth pointed at me alone, and I moved on expecting my two legs off every moment. The idea of flight never entered my mind but the hotter the fire the stronger I felt myself urged to advance. And in spite of the cannon shot, we gained the farmhouse with the loss of one killed and two wounded.

We remained in this house until that accursed battery destroyed it about our ears, and after some consultation we resolved to rush up and endeavour to storm it. This was the hottest part of the action for it was literally rushing into the cannon's mouth. The balls dashed the earth into my eyes. The wind of the shot was sensibly felt. But we panted up the hill, jumped into the ditch, climbed the mud walls. Away ran the French, and thus fell the battery into our hands containing the 10 pounders, plenty of onions, rotten biscuit and hay.

Thank God for this escape, for my pantaloons were simply torn at the right knee, and the flesh blackened by the wind of the ball.

I cannot refrain noticing one circumstance which occurred during this my first battle. While standing in a ditch with my men, popping through the hedges at the enemy as they ran from field to field, the fellow who stood on my left set up a most lamentable roar and, on turning, I found his cheek swelled up like a currant pudding from a ball which, passing downwards, had shattered his jaw and had lodged in his throat. I, like a novice, took out my handkerchief and endeavoured to staunch the blood. But my bullying Captain Nötting bellowed out, "Wheatley! Mind your duty and leave the man alone."

Experience afterwards convinced me how unwise was the action, but the sudden impulse of human feeling in the breast of a young soldier was the only answer I could return to the jokes and merriment afterwards practiced on me.

Colonel Ompteda with the rest of the regiment stormed the other battery at the same time; and the army on our right and left were equally successful excepting the 95th Regiment which did not succeed until the whole day's fighting enabled them to gain their point.

Thus we entered the French Empire, October the 7th, 1813, about seven o'clock in the morning; and after fighting until four in the afternoon we encamped on the hills where I now write this.

Must not forget to write to Henry to-morrow. I've just returned from burying the dead. How it rains! Poor fellows! No more colds for them.

Discussion guidelines

1. What factors do you think influence a man's reaction to front-line combat? In addition to the evidence in Wheatley's diary, illustrate your opinion by referring to other sources such as poetry, films, biographies, and interviews.
2. To what extent does the Wheatley excerpt illustrate Clausewitz's explanation of war?

Miller Services, Toronto

Compare the relationship between front-line soldiers in this 1968 scene in Viet Nam with that described by Edmund Wheatley in 1813.

The Compensations of War

from *My Early Life*
by Winston Churchill

[The three-minute cavalry charge of 300 lancers against 3,000 Dervishes at Omdurman has been called the last classic cavalry charge in the history of war – and Churchill was there. Having tasted war in Cuba and India, he determined to join Kitchener's forces in the Sudan in 1898. Consequently, he arranged appointments as a lieutenant in the 21st Lancers and as a news correspondent for London's *Morning Post*. The excerpt recounts the impressions gained from his scouting excursion just prior to the cavalry attack.]

Long before dawn we were astir, and by five o'clock the 21st Lancers were drawn up mounted outside the zeriba. My squadron-leader Major Finn, an Australian by birth, had promised me some days before that he would give me "a show". When the time came, I was afraid that he would count my mission to Lord Kitchener the day before as a quittance; but I was now called out from my troop to advance with a patrol and reconnoitre the ridge between the rocky peak of Jebel Surgham and the river. Other patrols from our squadron and from the Egyptian cavalry were also sent hurrying forward in the darkness. I took six men and a corporal. We trotted fast over the plain and soon began to breast the unknown slopes of the ridge. There is nothing like the dawn. The quarter of an hour before the curtain is lifted upon an unknowable situation is an intense experience of war. Was the ridge held by the enemy or not? Were we riding through the gloom into thousands of ferocious savages? Every step might be deadly; yet there was no time for overmuch precaution. The regiment was coming on behind us, and dawn was breaking. It was already half light as we climbed the slope. What should we find at the summit? For cool, tense excitement I commend such moments.

Now we are near the top of the ridge. I make one man follow a hundred yards behind, so that whatever happens, he may tell the tale. There is no sound but our own clatter. We have reached the crest line. We rein in our horses. Every minute the horizon extends; we can already see 200 yards. Now we can see perhaps a quarter of a mile. All is quiet; no life but our own breathes among the rocks and sand hummocks of the ridge. No ambuscade, no occupation in force! The farther plain is bare below us: we can now see more than half a mile.

So they have all decamped! Just what we said! All bolted off to Kordofan; no battle! But wait! The dawn is growing fast. Veil after veil is lifted from the landscape. What is this shimmering in the distant plain? Nay – it is lighter now – what are these dark markings beneath the shimmer? *They are there!* These enormous black smears are thousands of men; the shimmering is the glinting of their weapons. It is now daylight. I slip off my horse; I write in my field service notebook "The Dervish army is still in position a mile and a half south-west of Jebel Surgham". I send this message by the corporal direct as ordered to the Commander-in-Chief. I mark it XXX. In the words of the drill book "with all despatch" or as one would say "Hell for leather".

A glorious sunrise is taking place behind us; but we are admiring something else. It is already light enough to use field-glasses. The dark masses are changing their values. They are already becoming lighter than the plain; they are fawn-coloured. Now they are a kind of white, while the plain is dun. In front of us is a vast array four or five miles long.

Miller Services, Toronto

Omdurman. This sketch appeared in the *London Illustrated News* in 1898.

It fills the horizon till it is blocked out on our right by the serrated silhouette of Surgham Peak. This is an hour to live. We mount again, and suddenly new impressions strike the eye and mind. These masses are not stationary. They are advancing, and they are advancing fast. A tide is coming in. But what is this sound which we hear: A deadened roar coming up to us in waves? They are cheering for God, his Prophet and his holy Khalifa. They think they are going to win. We shall see about that presently. Still I must admit that we check our horses and hang upon the crest of the ridge for a few moments before advancing down its slopes.

But now it is broad morning and the slanting sun adds brilliant colour to the scene. The masses have defined themselves into swarms of men, in ordered ranks bright with glittering weapons, and above them dance a multitude of gorgeous flags. We see for ourselves what the Crusaders saw. We must see more of it. I trot briskly forward to somewhere near the sandhills where the 21st Lancers had halted the day before. Here we are scarcely 400 yards away from the great masses. We halt again and I make four troopers fire upon them, while the other two hold their horses. The enemy come on like the sea. A crackle of musketry breaks out on our front and to our left. Dust spurts rise among the sandhills. This is no place for Christians. We scamper off; and luckily no man nor horse is hurt. We climb back on to the ridge, and almost at this moment there returns the corporal on a panting horse. He comes direct from Kitchener with an order signed by the Chief of Staff. "Remain as long as possible, and report how the masses of attack are moving." Talk of Fun! Where will you beat this! On horseback, at daybreak, within shot of an advancing army, seeing everything, and corresponding direct with Headquarters.

Discussion guidelines

1. "I would that it were in my power to convey to the reader who has not had the fortune to live with troops on service, some just appreciation of the compensations of war." (Winston Churchill, *Frontiers and Wars*)
   By referring to your reading and association with those who have been "on service", discuss war's compensations.
2. " . . . there is no one who has been six months on active service, who is not delighted to get safe home again to the comfortable monotonies of peace." (Winston Churchill, *Frontiers and Wars*)
   How do you reconcile this viewpoint of Churchill's with his enthusiasm for the rewards of war?
3. Explain whether or not you think Churchill was still saying "Talk of Fun!" when the grey shadows of the German Luftwaffe appeared over England in 1940.

Statecraft

from *The Man and the Statesman*
by Prince Otto von Bismarck

> It can therefore be said that politics is war without bloodshed, while war is politics with bloodshed.
>
> MAO TSE-TUNG

[In 1866 Prussia defeated Austria in a whirlwind seven-weeks' campaign. The king and his military advisers were anxious to seize every possible military advantage from the situation. Minister-President Bismarck of Prussia disagreed, and his reasoning prevailed. His explanation reveals the political factors that motivated his successful recommendations.]

It was my object, in view of our subsequent relations with Austria, as far as possible to avoid cause for mortifying memories, if it could be managed without prejudice to our German policy. A triumphant entry of the Prussian army into the hostile capital [Vienna] would naturally have been a gratifying recollection for our soldiers, but it was not necessary to our policy. It would have left behind it, as also any surrender of ancient possessions to us must have done, a wound to the pride of Austria, which, without being a pressing necessity for us, would have unnecessarily increased the difficulty of our future mutual relations. It was already quite clear to me that we should have to defend the conquests of the campaign in further wars. That a war with France would succeed that with Austria, lay in the logic of history, even had we been able to allow the Emperor Napoleon the petty expenses which he looked for from us as a reward for his neutrality. As regards Russia, too, it is doubtful what would happen if it were then made clear to her what increase of strength the national development of Germany would bring to us. We could not foresee how far the later wars would make for the maintenance of what had already been won; but in any case it would be of great importance whether the wounds we had inflicted upon our opponents and their self-respect were incurable. Moved by this consideration, I had a political motive for avoiding, rather than bringing about, a triumphal entry into Vienna in the Napoleonic style. In positions such as ours was then, it is a political maxim after a victory not to enquire how much you can squeeze out of your opponent, but only to consider what is politically necessary. The ill-feeling which my attitude earned for me in military circles I considered was the result of a military departmental policy to which I could not concede a decisive influence on the policy of the state and its future.

On July 23, under the presidency of the King, a council of war was held, in which the question to be decided was whether we should make peace under the conditions offered or continue the war. A painful illness from which I was suffering made it necessary that the council should be held in my room. On this occasion I was the only civilian in uniform. I declared it to be my conviction that peace must be concluded on the Austrian terms, but remained alone in my opinion; the King supported the military majority. My nerves could not stand the strain which had been put upon them day and night; I got up in silence, walked into my adjoining bedchamber, and was there overcome by a violent seizure of tears. Meanwhile, I heard the council dispersing in the next room. I thereupon set to work to commit to paper the reasons which in my opinion spoke for the conclusion of peace; and begged the King, in the event of his not accepting the advice for which I was responsible, to relieve me of my functions as minister if the war were continued. On the following day, armed with my document I unfolded to the King the political reasons which opposed the continuation of the war.

We had to avoid wounding Austria too severely; we had to avoid leaving behind in her any unnecessary bitterness of feeling or desire for revenge; we ought rather to reserve the possibility of becoming friends again with our adversary of the moment, and in any case to regard the Austrian state as a piece on the European chessboard and the renewal of friendly relations with her as a move open to us. If Austria were severely injured, she would become the ally of France and of every other opponent of ours; she would even sacrifice her anti-Russian interests for the sake of revenge on Prussia.

Austria's conflict in rivalry with us was no more open to criticism than ours with her; *our task was the establishment or initiation of German national unity under the leadership of the King of Prussia*

Discussion guideline

"In practice [war's] fury is modified by political considerations, so that it becomes an instrument of policy." (Karl von Clausewitz, *On War*)

(a) To what extent does Bismarck's explanation support Clausewitz's statement?

(b) Suggest specific examples from recent history which support or refute the view that war is an instrument of policy.

Cross references

German Response to Versailles, page 28
The Confrontation in Cuba, page 281
"Was no other choice", page 285

5 a

CANADA SHOULD SECURE BUSINESS

The war and its conditions have made industrial Canada sit up, and while at first it looked as if this country was to be ruined by the conflict, later it became evident that Canada, either on the farm or in the shop, is able to hold her own, and more too with all comers. Little, if any, credit is due the government for this awakening of the Canadian people. When war broke out, and for months afterwards, orders for supplies for the Allies headed straight for the United States, and little or no effort was made by the Canadian Government to divert any portion of the orders to Canada. The middlemen got next the European Governments and in their anxiety to secure these supplies quickly, and with no person in authority. Speaking on behalf of this country, the war departments of Great Britain, as well as of the Allies, handed the orders to the middlemen, who never saw this country in their calculations, but rushed to the United States with them.

Canadian manufacturers began to be aroused, and they wanted to know why this part of the Empire was getting only spasmodic and fragmentary orders – the fragments and remnants that foreign manufacturers could not well handle or did not want. To the surprise of the manufacturers of Canada, they found that the rake-off chaps were in possession, and that if any sales were to be made, even for the equipment of the Canadian soldiers, these interlopers had to be squared. The secretary of the manufacturers' association protested to the Prime Minister, but although many letters passed to and fro, the Government afforded no satisfaction.

It is true that many millions of dollars went to the United States that should have and would have come to Canada had the Canadian Government been fully alive to the situation.

This all leads up to a discussion which took place in the House on Monday, and while there was little recrimination, but a great deal of horse sense, which ought to produce good results. It must be remembered that Canada supports several offices in London, Eng., including that of the High Commissioner, which is now occupied by Sir George Perley, who is also a member of the Canadian Government, though without portfolio.

As a social and diplomatic office it is, and has been, a great success, but no specialty has been made of real, up-to-the-minute business effort. Whatever may have been thought of this condition in the past, it is all wrong now. Canada needs a live, up-to-the-minute, fully equipped business office in London, so that whether in peace or war, the country shall be in a position to secure all the business that ought to come this way. True, after the orders got under full speed for the United States, Sir Robert Borden started for England to see if something could not be done for Canadians. He helped some, but had there been adequate business machinery in London in connection with the High Commissioner's office, the order would have come to Canada as a matter of course and through channels prepared by the Government.

Sir Wilfrid, E. M. Macdonald, Hon. Wm. Pugsley, Hon. Frank Oliver, George P. Graham, and others took part in this debate, and the government knows full well that the criticism was just, and the business interests of Canada will demand that the government bestir itself and make its offices in both London and Paris useful as well as ornamental.

Brockville Evening Recorder,
February 25, 1916

b

The Aftermath of War

from *The World since 1919*
by Walter C. Langsam

The monetary costs of the combat and the destruction of property on land and sea were staggering. The average daily cost to all belligerents of the war in the first three years was $123,000,000. In 1918 the average daily cost was $244,000,000, that is, more than $10,000,000 per hour. The total net direct cost of conducting the war thus was $186,000,000,000, the Allies expending $126,000,000,000, and the Central Powers, $60,000,000,000. To this sum must be added property damage on land to the extent of almost $30,000,000,000; damage on sea aggregating $7,000,000,000; production losses of about $45,000,000,000; and war relief and losses to neutrals of more than $2,000,000,000. The total real economic cost amounted to $270,000,000,000.

When to this figure was added the $67,000,000,000 generally estimated as the capitalized value of the human lives lost as a direct consequence of the war, the total reached $337,000,000,000. This sum did not take into account the additional economic loss caused by the crippling and devitalization of soldiers and civilians, the billions of dollars of interest due on the debts contracted by the fighting powers, or the vast sums which continued to be appropriated as pension money. And yet it represented five and a half times as many dollars as the number of seconds which have elapsed since the birth of Christ.

Discussion guidelines

1. If the Atlantic Ocean had not separated Canada from the Western Front, would the tone of the Brockville *Evening Recorder*'s editorial have been different? Discuss.
2. Explain the implications of the contrasting evidence in the two articles, "Canada Needs Business" and "The Aftermath of War".
3. From your observations, to what degree is economic prosperity in North America dependent upon war or the possibility of war?

Miller Services, Toronto

Shell production in Britain during World War I. This was a small part of the cost of the war.

What Will You Say When Your Child or Grandchild Asks :

"Daddy, What Did You Do In the Great War"

What answer can you make; where will you hide your shame, if you were able to take a mans' part in 1916 and failed in your duty ? Will your kiddie be proud or ashamed of his father ?

The 156th (Leeds and Grenville) Battalion needs 700 more men at once. The call has gone forth to the young men of Brockville and of these two grand old counties to come to the rescue. The 156th will be a special battalion of picked men, splendidly equipped through the generosity of the citizens and Counties Council, and will be commanded by a gallant officer who has faced and fought the Hun and has come back to recruit and lead a regiment from his home counties.

MEN OF LEEDS AND GRENVILLE, your opportunity is here and now. Prove yourself a true son of your brave and loyal ancestry. Answer the call and help to crush the tyrannic Teuton, and "do your bit" to save the British Empire from being crushed by its treacherous, hate - crazed, blood - lusty enemies.

Others are enlisting; your chums are going along, but what are YOU doing ? Your conscience tells you you are not doing the right thing by hanging back. Then hurry to the nearest recruiting depot and enlist. You'll then feel like a man doing a manly duty. Your pay will begin immediately. Your 156th uniform is ready for you.

"COME ON BOYS"

Free Trip To Germany

Courtesy of *The Recorder and Times*

Discussion guidelines

1. (a) To what extent has patriotism become a weapon of modern war?
   (b) Comment on the advantages and/or dangers of this trend.
2. What techniques of persuasion do you think would be required to persuade young men of today to go to war?

Cross reference

Propaganda and the Mass Meeting, page 133

 a

Man Is a Killer
from *African Genesis*
by Robert Ardrey

Man emerged from the anthropoid background for one reason only: because he was a killer. Long ago, perhaps many millions of years ago, a line of killer apes branched off from the non-aggressive primate background. For reasons of environmental necessity, the line adopted the predatory way. For reasons of predatory necessity the line advanced. We learned to stand erect in the first place as a necessity of the hunting life. We learned to run in our pursuit of game across the yellowing African savannah. Our hands freed for the mauling and the hauling, we had no further use for a snout; and so it retreated. And lacking fighting teeth or claws, we took recourse by necessity to the weapon.

A rock, a stick, a heavy bone – to our ancestral killer ape it meant the margin of survival. But the use of the weapon meant new and multiplying demands on the nervous system for the co-ordination of muscle and touch and sight. And so at last came the enlarged brain; so at last came man.

Far from the truth lay the antique assumption that man had fathered the weapon. The weapon, instead, had fathered man. The mightiest of predators had come about as the logical conclusion to an evolutionary transition. With his big brain and his stone handaxes, man annihilated a predecessor who fought only with bones. And if all human history from that date has turned on the development of superior weapons, then it is for [a] very sound reason. It is for genetic necessity. We design and compete with our weapons as birds build distinctive nests.

b

by permission of *The Globe and Mail*, cartoon by Reidford

When this cartoon was drawn, thousands of Biafran children were starving to death while the opponents in the Nigerian civil war argued over how relief supplies could be sent to them.

C

from *Recent History Atlas*, by Martin Gilbert and John Flower, by permission of Weidenfeld and Nicolson

Discussion guidelines

1. "War has been the most natural mode of human expression since the beginning of recorded history." (Robert Ardrey, *African Genesis*)

   or

   "Aggressiveness is learned rather than inherited."

   Defend the viewpoint of your choice.
2. The anthropologist Margaret Mead has suggested that if wars between nations become increasingly impractical, riots and similar disturbances will be more frequent in order to satisfy man's desire for violence. To what extent do you agree with this assessment? Why?

Cross references

Men Need Rulers, page 14
Juvenile Delinquency? page 144

Is Man Really a Killer?
from *Execution*
by Colin McDougall

[This section from the novel *Execution* concerns Canadian army operations in Sicily in 1943. With the enemy resisting the Americans to the east and the British to the west, the Canadians seize the chance to smash through the enemy centre. As the advance develops, Italian units of the enemy forces break up and desertions mount. At the same time, because sniping attacks on the Canadian forces become serious, orders are issued to shoot enemy deserters as suspected snipers. Contrary to these orders, Lieutenant John Adam, of Number Ten Platoon, adopts two Italian soldiers. Having discovered this breach of discipline, Adam's commanding officer, Major Bazin, orders the Lieutenant, Sergeant Mitchell, and Private Jones to escort the prisoners to Battalion Headquarters.]

Battalion Headquarters was in a stone farm-house. Major Bazin went inside to find Lieutenant-Colonel Dodd, and left Adam standing in a sprawling, cobble-stoned courtyard, crowded with men and vehicles. At one end a picket gate led into a barnyard; from there a pungency of fresh manure flowed forth to flavour the afternoon air. The sun felt like a flat weight, heavy and pressing.

Adam watched while his two charges sat on the cobble-stones, leaned their backs against a wall and lighted cigarettes which Jonesy – for whom this had turned out to be a wonderfully exciting outing – was quick to provide. Adam kept one eye cocked on the door which Major Bazin had entered, and strolled round the courtyard looking for any news which might affect Ten Platoon's immediate fortunes. He picked his way between parked trucks and carriers until he came to a stop beside the Signals jeep. He knew this would be the likeliest place to wait. He nodded to the sergeant who was listening on the Brigade net.

In this courtyard there was no urgency of time: instead there was a sense of lazy well-being and relaxation. In one corner some men brewed a steaming tin of tea. A few yards away from Adam a hairy sergeant, stripped to his underwear shorts, was sitting down to shave; between scrapes of his razor he hummed a tune in complete self-absorption. Adam could not put a name to the tune, but the melody was one that he knew well and it eddied through his mind.

Across the courtyard Adam saw that his two Italians had become the centre of attraction. Men crowded round curiously, staring, pressing on them cigarettes and chocolate bars. Jonesy was a proud master of ceremonies; he was explaining how the two had been named big Jim and little Joe.

"Well, Joe – wadda ya know?" called one of the soldiers.

Little Joe rolled his eyes comically; he made a quick circling gesture with thumb and forefinger. Both of them were sitting erect now, alert, laughing, smiles flashing from their teeth; anxious to please in any way they could. They understood and would go right along with this kidding. It was the same in any army, they knew: there were always the jokes which were not so much intended to be funny as to serve as a kind of greeting, or a wry acknowledgement of shared discomfort. There was always the incessant marching and countermarching, then the waiting while one of the officer-gods decided what to do with them next. They were thoroughly familiar with all this. They much preferred their young Tenente to the horse-faced Maggiore who had brought them here; they would much rather be back eating "M and V" with Ten Platoon; but for the present it was pleasant to sit here in the sunshine and smoke tailor-made cigarettes, and talk and laugh a little. Their little suit-case lay on the cobble-stones before them; soon they would be told to pick it up and go to some other place, and in due course – if God was willing – they would even reach their distant homes in Italy one day.

Now it was big Jim's turn to vie for the onlookers' approval. He thumped his balled fists hard upon his chest. "Canadese – buona!" he declaimed, and he made as though to stuff a chocolate bar, paper wrapping and all, down his throat.

Adam saw that Sergeant Krebs of the Regimental Police had strolled over and was now looking down at the pair. Krebs was a big man, almost too fat to ride his motor cycle; and he had no friend in the Battalion. He stood watching the two Italians sourly and his glance fastened on big Jim's chocolate bar. "Yeah," Sergeant Krebs observed. "Better eat it while you can."

"Cut it out, Krebs – they're my prisoners."

Sergeant Mitchell elbowed his way into the group, his glance cold and hard on Krebs' fat face.

Adam clambered to his feet; but before he could move toward the prisoners the lean, agitated form of Padre Doorn was bustling round him. The Padre's gaunt face was filled with immense concern. He plucked at his friend's arm. "I just heard about this, John," he said. "Is it serious? Is there anything I can do?"

"Hell, no," Adam replied. "All I want to do is get rid of these two goons and get back to my platoon."

Sergeant Mitchell now had a space cleared round the prisoners. As soon as Adam approached the two Italian youths jumped to their feet and stood at quivering positions of attention. Jonesy stood up with them, but as usual several seconds too late. Brooding, Adam regarded his three charges. "Oh, sit down," he said at last. "Every damn one of you is more trouble than you're worth."

Then he heard his name called. He turned and saw Captain Ramsay, the Adjutant, standing by the Signals. As he started back he heard the Padre open a laboured conversation in Italian while more chocolate bars appeared in his hand. But Adam's main concern at the moment was how his platoon was faring with only Corporal Fowler in charge. He wanted to get back to them.

Since Major Bazin was still inside the farm-house with the C.O. he asked Captain Ramsay about this. "You'd better wait," Ramsay replied. "The C.O. is sending your two Wop friends to Brigade. I've just put the message on the air –"

"Sir!" The Signals Sergeant had his earphones off; his voice crackled with urgency. "Bring Sunray to set!"

"Hell," said Ramsay. He wheeled about and started to run toward the farm-house door.

"Sunray" was the code name for a unit commander. This meant that the next highest Sunray – the Brigadier – wanted to speak to Colonel Dodd personally. Adam walked round to the far side of the jeep. He stationed himself as close to the crackling earphones as he could get.

Colonel Dodd emerged from the house at a slow march of dignity; he made a point of not hurrying his pace. He wore a studious, concentrated look on his face, as though to denote he was only temporarily coming away from more urgent business to which he would presently return. At last he came to a halt at the jeep, adjusted the earphones on his head, and picked up the microphone. "Sunray Two Baker on set," Colonel Dodd announced firmly, after clearing his throat.

Adam was close enough to see the flecks in Colonel Dodd's eyes, to observe the vertical bob of his prominent Adam's apple. He was close enough also to hear the powerful voice which now rattled the diaphragms. "I do not choose," this voice crackled loudly, "to be bothered with administrative detail when I am fighting a battle. Shoot these deserters at once. And bloody well smarten up if you wish to keep your command. Report when my order is carried out."

The Brigadier had violated wireless security. An enemy monitoring set would recognize this message at once as an order from Brigadier to Battalion

Commander. The Brigadier considered, of course, that wireless, like other procedures, was devised for him, and not the reverse.

Colonel Dodd stood with the microphone in his hand as though he was holding a deadly serpent. "Wilco" was the only answer allowed him; after gulping for several seconds he forced his words out, and made the breach of security complete. "Wilco, sir," Colonel Dodd replied.

With exaggerated care the Colonel placed the microphone down on the hood of the jeep. He walked on stiff legs round the front of the jeep where he paused, as though surprised to see so many soldiers filling the courtyard. Everyone at once looked away from him; each person pretended to be busy with whatever he had been doing before. Even the Sergeant who had been shaving picked up his razor again, although this time he hummed no tune. The Colonel had his own lips puckered slightly as though he might take up humming himself. He rocked back and forth on his heels, looking at everything and everybody. His glance passed over the two prisoners, still grouped with the Padre and Jonesy, touched momentarily upon Major Bazin, Sergeant Mitchell, Lieutenant Adam, and all the others in the courtyard, continuing panoramically, without pause and without recognition. The sun was even hotter now, pressing flatly on the cobble-stones, expanding upward and outward, to fill the space with thick humid silence. Lieutenant-Colonel Charley Dodd, the insurance broker from Toronto, looked around the Sicilian courtyard for an eternal moment of silence. Then his heels came flat on the ground. He cleared his throat with great vigour.

"Mister Adam." The Colonel's voice undoubtedly sounded louder than he had intended.

"Sir?"

Adam stepped forward, tommy-gun still slung at his shoulder.

"These two deserters you captured – you made a mistake which you will now remedy. Shoot them at once!"

The silence became hollow, like a huge emptiness waiting to be filled. For this moment Adam could not speak, nor could anyone else. The glance of every man in the courtyard flashed instinctively to the two Italians, still sitting on the cobble-stones. Both now leaned alertly forward, the smiles fallen from their olive-soft faces; they knew that something important concerning themselves was under discussion.

Adam flashed a glance of wild appeal toward Major Bazin. "Sir?" he stammered; and Major Bazin stepped forward to his side. "Sir!" he protested angrily.

But Colonel Dodd looked at a point somewhere between their shoulders. There was no bottom to the depth of silence which overflowed the farmyard. A tremendous weight of reluctance, a slow heavy burden of unwillingness settled down on each person's shoulders. It had now penetrated to every soldier in that place, with the possible exception of Rifleman Jones, that the two Italians were going to be executed, and that within a matter of minutes. And this thought required some preparation in their minds. Perhaps this was a reasonable and not unusual demand in war, perhaps the same thing was happening all along the front. But they were still new to war – this was something new in their experience. They had seen some of their friends die, of course, but that had been in the midst of explosions or the angry lash of machine-gun fire – not in a lazy, sun-filled courtyard. This might be a matter of military necessity, this farm-yard affair might have to be done; but they did not like it: their unwillingness was almost palpable in the sun-drunk silence. Big Jim and little Joe sat nervously on the cobblestones; the worst part for them must have been the way no one would meet their questing glances.

The first look of shock had passed from Adam's face. He stood, white and trembling, at attention before Colonel Dodd. Full cognizance of the order he had received cleaved him, and left him incapacitated like a gigantic wound. He watched with dream-like fascination while Major Bazin spoke in the Colonel's ear. Ramsay too had stepped forward and the three of them whispered together urgently. He watched each one glance at him in turn as the discussion went on. Adam was thinking, with desperation: Is there any way out? Have I the guts to refuse the order? Or – he was shameless now – is there anyone else I could stick with the job? Mitchell? Could I ever look Mitchell in the face again?

The discussion ended; the three officers drew themselves up. Then Sergeant Krebs was standing before them. Adam's presence seemed to be forgotten. He swayed slightly and he closed his eyes.

"Listen, Krebs," Colonel Dodd was saying, "I want to get this thing over with as quickly as possible. March them into the barn-yard and do it there."

"Yes, sir."

Sergeant Krebs saluted. There was no change of expression on his beefy jowels. It was as though this was the sort of normal order which he might expect to receive in the course of the day. He wheeled about and started across the cobble-stones toward the two prisoners. The fingernails of his right hand scratched lightly against the revolver case strapped to his side.

There was a sudden flurry of motion. The lean, agitated figure of Padre Doorn came bounding past Krebs, to halt impetuously before the Colonel. The Padre's face was alive with his feeling; all that he had ever been, or ever might be, was posted on his face as though affixed to a bulletin-board, and subject to the same public injury. The Padre was open and defenceless; he looked fragile, as though his being might easily shatter into nothingness.

"Sir," the Padre said, his eyes burning candles on the Colonel's face. "Are you really going to shoot these two boys?"

"Yes," said Colonel Dodd, looking beyond him. "Do you wish to provide spiritual assistance?"

Padre Doorn choked with the force of his outrage. "That would be mockery –"

"In that case, Padre – kindly get the hell out of the way!"

The Padre stood in anguish, his fists balled at his side. Then he turned his head slightly and saw his friend Adam. Their glances locked: they shared a long, aching moment of examination. Then the Padre's gaze dropped to the ground. He looked at the ground as though he would never again wish to look toward heaven.

Sergeant Krebs had the prisoners on their feet now; he forced them before him over the cobble-stones. The two boys looked frightened; their feet were clumsy and uncertain as they walked. Little Joe held the suit-case clenched tightly in both fists. They cast quick glances behind them; once big Jim stumbled and almost fell. The most frightening part must have been the grim faces everywhere they turned, the glances that slid away and refused recognition. Sergeant Krebs prodded them on, and now he had his revolver drawn.

When they came abreast with the officers in the centre of the farm-yard a voice spoke. It was Colonel Dodd, the insurance broker from Toronto, trying to reduce the affair to a mere matter of soldierly toughness, to inject a note of hard-boiled humour. His voice sounded hoarse, and intolerably ugly.

"You can put the suit-case down, bud," the Colonel said. "You won't need it where you're going."

Little Joe, knowing no English, glanced once toward the voice, clutched the suit-case more tightly to him, and scurried ahead. There was not the least stir of response in the farm-yard. It was as though there had been no interruption to the silence; as though the remark had never been made. Colonel

Dodd flushed deeper red, his teeth bit into his lip. Adam felt strong fingers grip his arm; it was Sergeant Mitchell who stood beside him.

As soon as they passed through the picket gate Sergeant Krebs fired a shot which hit little Joe in the back. Little Joe squealed with pain. He fell forward onto the manure, the suit-case flew from his hands, and its meagre contents scattered all around him. Big Jim turned about; he went down on his knees, his hands came together beneath his chin as though he would pray – not to his executioner, but, for a moment, to God. Sergeant Krebs fired again and shot him in the shoulder. Then both men were squealing at once; Sergeant Krebs fired his remaining four rounds into their bodies. But they were both still alive, both flopping despairingly in the manure. Sergeant Krebs broke his pistol and began, laboriously, to load another six rounds in the cylinder.

"For Christ's sake."

It was a cry torn from Adam's throat and being. He started to run; as he ran he ripped the tommy-gun from his shoulder with painful force. He went plunging forward, through the picket gate and into the barn-yard. Half a second behind Sergeant Mitchell came charging after him. Mitchell jostled Sergeant Krebs to one side; his hands reached out towards his platoon commander's weapon. But then the summer afternoon was perforated by sharp, surgical bursts of sub-machine-gun fire. Adam emptied his magazine. In the barn-yard there were floating wisps of smoke, then silence again. Adam turned about. He tramped back, his boots heavy with manure; Sergeant Mitchell came plodding behind. They halted in front of the waiting officers. For several seconds the entire group remained locked in the same attitude: heavy, immovable, borne down with the weight of sun and thick silence. Colonel Dodd's glance was still fixed blankly on the barn-yard.

Adam pulled at the sling on his shoulder and addressed his request jointly to Colonel Dodd and Major Bazin. "Permission to rejoin my platoon, sir?"

Colonel Dodd made no answer. His eyes were glazed, his breath laboured. At his side Padre Doorn's glance was lowered; he held one hand as a shield over his face. Major Bazin made a silent gesture then. Go on, this gesture and the whole weary length of his face seemed to say: Yes, go on – get the hell back and rejoin your platoon.

Adam and Mitchell about-turned and marched in step across the cobble-stones. Jonesy was waiting for them, his face working with violent emotion; he opened his mouth to speak.

"Come on, Jones," Mitchell ordered quickly. "Fall in behind." Rifleman Jones obeyed. Their boots rang a metal tune on the cobble-stones as the three men marched out of the farm-yard.

Out on the road the sun was still shining. Somewhere ahead of them, from the direction of the cemetery, there came the hollow crump of mortar bombs, the uninterrupted lashing of German machine-guns; it sounded like a counter-attack in force. They marched toward this sound, and toward the approaching night and the German infantry, now attacking.

It was not cold in this sunlight, but Adam began to shiver. He had the impression that formless shapes grouped and squatted and disported themselves at the roadside; and as he saw them the fear came. This was the real fear, quite unlike the momentary pang of terror he had known in the assault boat. This was the sick, vulture fear which chained itself to one's shoulder for ever.

Adam felt violated; as he walked he wanted to cry out for his lost innocence. Fear was wanton at the roadside; and now there was certainly no exhilaration in war. There was only this marching, ever closer, toward fear in the night.

The three men walked on in silence. The battle noises became louder as they drew close to the platoon position.

Jonesy felt saddened and disturbed; but he was

ıot sure why, and he translated his worry into one ıe could readily understand. "Say," Jonesy re-ıarked. "I hope the boys haven't gone and eaten ıll that 'M and V'!"

For an instant Adam could actually see the full ıess-tin of meat and vegetable stew he had held in ıis hands a short time before. The thick, meaty ıaste came like grease to his mouth.

"Shut your stupid trap, Jones." But Sergeant ⁄litchell did not look his way. Instead, he was vatching Adam anxiously. He held one hand below ıis elbow; he marched close beside him.

They walked on a few more steps before they had to halt. Then Adam left them. He moved away and vomited at the roadside.

Discussion guidelines

1. How does Adam's reaction tally with Ardrey's opinion that man is naturally a killer?
2. If you had had Colonel Dodd's authority, would you have obeyed the Brigadier's orders? Defend your position on both legal and moral grounds.

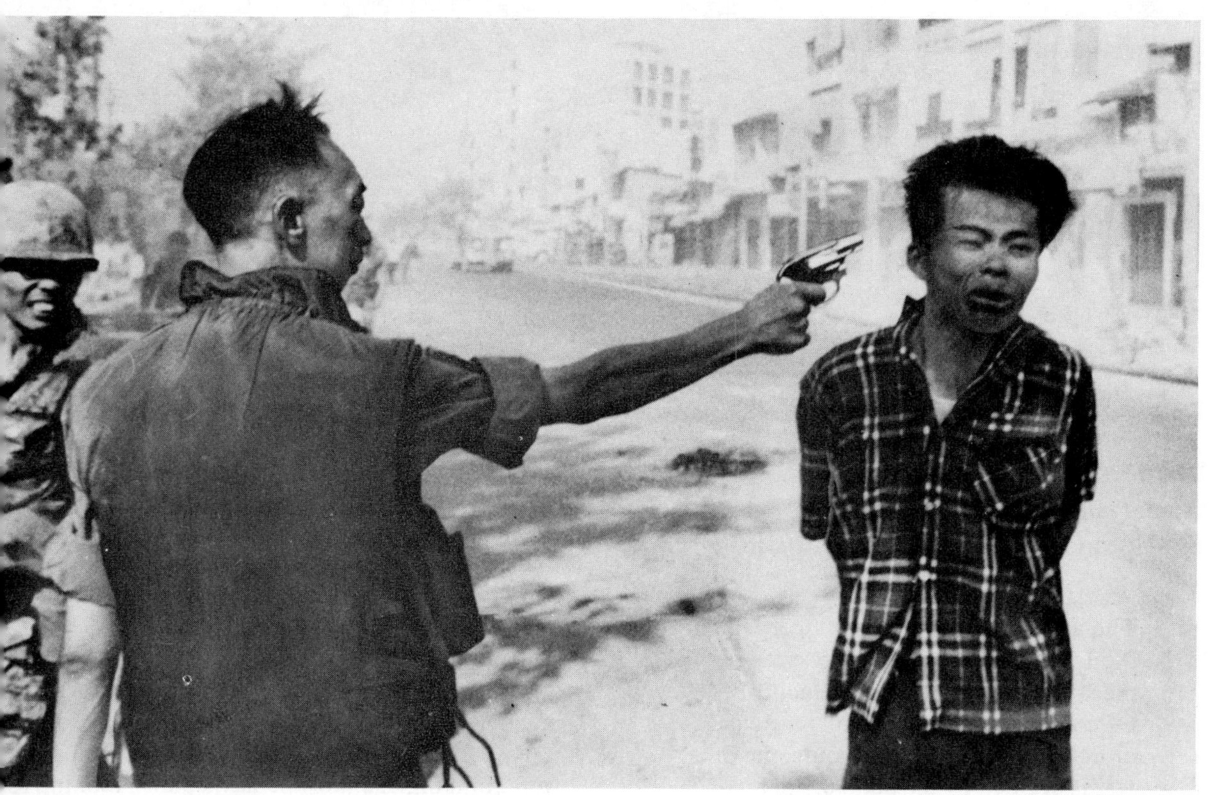

Wide World Photo

/hen Saigon was attacked by bands of Viet Cong guerillas in January 1968, a Viet Cong commander was captured ı civilian dress and brought to the police chief of the city. This picture shows the police chief executing him on ıe spot. When he was asked why he did so, the chief said that many of his own people had been killed by the 'iet Cong. How similar is this situation to that described in the story? Can either execution be justified?

THE NUCLEAR DIMENSION

Miller Services, Toron

Nagasaki after the dropping of the atomic bomb

The First Atomic Bombing
from *That Day at Hiroshima*
by Alexander Leighton

> The atom bomb is a paper tiger which the U.S. reactionaries use to scare people. It looks terrible, but in fact it isn't. Of course, the atom bomb is a weapon of mass slaughter, but the outcome of a war is decided by the people, not by one or two new types of weapon.
>
> MAO TSE-TUNG

About seven o'clock on the morning of August 6, 1945, there was an air-raid warning and three planes were reported in the vicinity. No one wa much disturbed. For a long time B-29s flying ove in small numbers had been a common sight. A some future date, Hiroshima might suffer an incen diary raid from masses of planes such as had deva tated other Japanese cities. With this possibility i mind there had been evacuations, and firebreak were being prepared. But on this particular morn ing there could be no disaster from just three plane

By 7.30 the "all clear" had sounded and peop were thinking again of the day's plans, looking fo ward to their affairs and engagements of the morn ing and afternoon. . . . Children bathed in the rive Farmers labored in the fields and fishermen on th water. City stores and factories got under way wit their businesses.

In the heart of the city near the buildings of the Prefectural Government and at the intersection of the busiest streets, everybody had stopped and stood in a crowd gazing up at three parachutes floating down through the blue air.

The bomb exploded several hundred feet above their heads.

The people for miles around Hiroshima, in the fields, in the mountains, and on the bay, saw a light that was brilliant even in the sun, and felt heat. A countrywoman was going out to her farm when suddenly, "I saw a light reflected on the mountain and then a streak just like lightning came."

A town official was crossing a bridge on his bicycle about ten miles from the heart of the city when he felt the right side of his face seared, and thinking that he had sunstroke, he jumped to the ground.

A woman who was washing dishes noticed that she felt "very warm on the side of my face next the wall. I looked out the window toward the city and saw something like a sun in bright color."

At a slower pace, after the flash, came the sound of the explosion, which some people have no recollection of hearing, while others described it as an earth-shaking roar, like thunder or a big wind. A black smoky mass, lit up with color, ascended into the sky and impressed beholders with its beauty. Red, gold, blue, orange, and many other shades mingled with the black.

Nearer to the city and at its edges, the explosion made a more direct and individual impact on people. Almost everyone thought that an ordinary bomb had landed very close to him, and only later realized the extent of the damage.

A man who was oiling the machinery in a factory saw the lights go out and thought that something must be wrong with the electricity. "But when the roof started crumbling down, I was in a daze, wondering what was happening. Then I noticed my hands and feet were bleeding. I don't know how I hurt myself."

Another, who was putting points on needles, was knocked unconscious, and when he came to, found "all my surroundings burned to the ground and flames raging here and there. I ran home for my family without knowing I was burned around my head. When I arrived home, our house was devastated and destroyed by flames. I ran to the neighbors and inquired about my family and learned that they had all been taken to safety across the river."

An invalid who was drinking tea said, "The tin roof sidings came swirling into my room and everything was black. Rubble and glass and everything you can think of was blasted into my house."

Said a woman, "I was in the back of the house doing the washing. All of a sudden, the bomb exploded. My clothes were burned off and I received burns on my legs, arms, and back. The skin was just hanging loose. The first thing I did was run in the air-raid shelter and lie there exhausted. Then I thought of my baby in the house and ran back to it. The whole house was knocked down and was burning. My mother and father came crawling out of the debris, their faces and arms just black. I heard the baby crying, and crawled in and dug it out from under the burning embers. It was pretty badly burned. My mother carried it to the shelter."

In the heart of the city death prevailed and few were left to tell us about it. That part of the picture has to be reconstructed, as in archeology, from the remains.

The crowd that stood gazing upward at the parachutes went down withered and black, like a burned-out patch of weeds. Flames shot out of the castle keep. Trolleys bulging with passengers stopped, and all died at once, leaving burned figures still standing supporting each other and fingers fused to the straps. The military at their barracks and offices were wiped out. So too were factories full of workers, including students from schools, volunteers from neighboring towns working on the firebreaks, children scavenging for wood, the Mayor's staff, and the units for air-raid precaution, fire, welfare, and relief. The larger war industries, since they were on the fringe of the city, were for the most part not seriously damaged. Most of the personnel in the Prefectural Government offices were killed, though the Governor himself happened to be in Tokyo. In hospitals and clinics, patients, doctors, and nurses all died together, as did the priests and pastors of the temples and the churches. Of 1,780 nurses, 1,651 were killed, and 90 per cent of the doctors in Hiroshima were casualties.

People who were in buildings that sheltered them from the instantaneous effects that accompanied the flash were moments later decapitated or cut to ribbons by flying glass. Others were crushed as walls and floors gave way even in buildings that maintained their outer shells erect. In the thousands of houses that fell, people were pinned below the wreckage, not killed in many cases, but held there till the fire that swept the city caught up with them and put an end to their screams.

A doctor who was at a military hospital outside Hiroshima said that about an hour after the bomb went off, "many, many people came rushing to my clinic. They were rushing in all directions of the compass from the city. Many were stretcher cases. Some had their hair burned off, were injured in the back, had broken legs, arms, and thighs. The majority of the cases were those injured from glass; many had glass imbedded in the body. Next to the glass injuries, the most frequent were those who had their faces and hands burned, and also the chest and back. Most of the people arrived barefooted; many had their clothes burned off. Women were wearing men's clothing and men were wearing women's. They had put on anything they could pick up along the way.

"On the first day about 250 came, who were so injured they had to stay in the hospital, and we also attended about 500 others. Of all of these about 100 died."

A talkative man in a newspaper office said that the most severely burned people looked like red shrimps. Some had "skin which still burned sagging from the face and body with a reddish-white skin underneath showing".

A reporter who was outside the city at the time of the explosion, but came in immediately afterward, noticed among the dead a mother with a baby held tightly in her arms. Many people climbed into water tanks kept for putting out fires and there died. "The most pathetic cases were the small children looking for their parents. There was one child about eleven with a four-year-old on his back, looking, looking for his mother in vain."

Shortly after the bomb fell, there was a high wind, or "fire storm" engendered by the heat, that tore up trees and, whirling over the river, made waterspouts. In some areas rain fell.

The severely burned woman who had been washing when the bomb fell said that she went down to the river, where "there were many people just dripping from their burns. Many of them were so badly burned that you could see the meat. By this time it was raining pretty badly. I could not walk or lie down or do anything. Water poured into the shelter and I received water blisters as well as blisters from the burns. It rained a lot right after the bomb."

Although the fire burned for days, the major destruction did not take very long. A fisherman out on the bay said, "I saw suddenly a flash of light. I thought something burned my face. I hid in the boat face down. When I looked up later, Hiroshima was completely burned."[1]

[1]The population of Hiroshima was given as well over 300,000 before the war, but this was reduced by evacuation, before the atomic bomb fell, probably to about 245,000. It is still not certain how many the bomb killed, but the best estimate is from 70,000 to 80,000.

Discussion guidelines

1. Do you think the Americans were right to initiate nuclear warfare?
2. How has the meaning of war changed from the Napoleonic period to the present day? How has

it remained the same?

3. Is there value in requiring the periodic viewing of film or written evidence of the destruction at Hiroshima? Argue your viewpoint.
4. In August, 1963, the major nuclear powers signed a ban on all but underground nuclear tests. China and France refused to sign. In the light of subsequent military developments, estimate the value of such pacts.

by permission of *Nashville Tennessean*, cartoon by Bissell

"Let's talk about not watering them."

5. (a) Which of the following is the most realistic solution to the threat of a nuclear holocaust: (i) graduated deterrence, (ii) conventional forces, (iii) disarmament? Why?
   (b) Suggest other alternatives.

Cross references

A Meaningful Voice? page 296
The Dangers of Present Trends, page 327

IN PERSPECTIVE

The Conquerors

It seems vainglorious and proud
Of Atom-man to boast aloud
His prowess homicidal
When one remembers how for years
With their rude stones and humble spears
Our sires, at wiping out their peers,
Were almost never idle.

Despite his under-fissioned art
The Hittite made a splendid start
Toward smiting lesser nations;
While Tamerlane, it's widely known,
Without a bomb to call his own
Destroyed whole populations.

Nor did the ancient Persian need
Uranium to kill his Mede,
The Viking earl, his foeman.
The Greeks got excellent results
With swords and engined catapults.
A chariot served the Romans.

Mere cannon garnered quite a yield
On Waterloo's tempestuous field.
At Hastings and at Flodden
Stout countrymen, with just a bow
And arrow, laid their thousands low
And Gettysburg was sodden.

Though doubtless now our shrewd machines
Can blow the world to smithereens
More tidily and so on.
Let's give our ancestors their due
Their ways were coarse, their weapons few.
But ah! how wondrously they slew
With what they had to go on.

PHYLLIS MCGINLEY

Nationalism in World Affairs

Miller Services, Toronto

NASA

What is there about this thing called nationalism that men are willing to die for? Why has it held the world in its grip for generations? To what extent is it connected with race, language, emotions, and history? Is it a political ideology? The actions of politicians on the international scene, it is claimed, are basically decided by nationalist ambitions. How true is this? Will we see our world incinerated for the sake of nationalism – or can it be replaced by something called internationalism?

ITS MEANING AND GROWTH

 a

France

The emotional side of me tends to imagine France as dedicated to an exalted and exceptional destiny. But the positive side of my mind also assures me that France is not really herself unless in the front rank; that only vast enterprises are capable of counterbalancing the divisive ferments that are inherent in her people. In short, to my mind, France cannot be France – without greatness.

CHARLES DE GAULLE

b

Canada – a centennial song

CA-NA-DA – We love thee –
CA-NA-DA – Proud and free –
North, South, East, West
There'll be Happy Times,
Church bells will Ring, Ring, Ring,
It's the hundredth anniversary of
  Confederation,
Everybody Sing together
CA-NA-DA – Notre pays –
CA-NA-DA – Longue vie –
Hurrah, Vive le Canada! Three Cheers,
  Hip, Hip, Hooray!
Le Centenaire! That's the order of the day
Frère Jacques, Frère Jacques, Merrily we
  roll along
Together, all the way.

BOBBY GIMBY

2

The Historical View

from *The Meaning of Nationalism*
by Louis L. Snyder

> By nationalism I mean first of all the habit of assuming that human beings can be classified like insects and that whole blocks of millions or tens of millions of people can be confidently labelled "good" or "bad". But secondly – and this is much more important – I mean the habit of identifying oneself with a single nation or other unit, placing it beyond good or evil and recognizing no other duty than that of advancing its interests.
>
> GEORGE ORWELL[1]

The central fact of modern history, most observers agree, is the existence of the sovereign nation-state as the unit of political organization. Nationalism is a powerful emotion that has dominated the political thought and actions of most peoples since the time of the French Revolution. It is not a natural, but an historic phenomenon, that has emerged as a response to special political, economic, and social conditions.

Nationalism has had its own peculiar historical development. Not the least significant factor in its rise was the tendency of the group, from the small group to the community of the nation, to act in common. The historian H. A. L. Fisher believes that an understanding of nationalism hinges upon this word, common. "What is essential," he says, "to the growth of the national spirit is a common

[1]*Such, Such Were the Joys* (New York, 1953), pp. 73-4.

history – common sufferings, common triumphs, common achievements, common memories, and, it may be added, common aspirations."[2]

Among primitive peoples ancient tribal instincts centered on fear of and hostility to the stranger. In the Middle Ages this same sentiment of suspicion of the outsider existed in the small, localized communities. But nationalism as we know it today was unknown to the ancient and medieval worlds. Certain of its elements appeared during the Renaissance and were strengthened during the Reformation.

Modern nationalism, however, was the product of the late eighteenth-century revolutionary era, "a child of the French Revolution". The state of nature, the new ideal of society, was made the basis of the nation. The earlier provincialism was revived on a grand scale, this time with the nation demanding the supreme loyalty of men. All men, not merely certain individuals or classes, were drawn into the new common loyalty, into the new supreme group consciousness. Inspired by the cry of *fraternité*, the revolutionists arose as a nation in arms to defend their newly won liberties against the Old Régime. "By the French idea of *fraternité* every European country was soon affected, so that formerly latent sympathies were galvanized into a most lively sentiment, and theorists from the domain of history or philosophy or even of economics could find popular approval for their solemn pronouncements that 'people speaking the same language and sharing the same general customs should be politically united as nations'."[3] Formerly Louis XIV could say, it has been asserted, without challenge, "*L'Etat, c'est moi!*" but now the new powerful bourgeoisie was insisting that the French nation had an existence quite apart from the king.

The revolutionary sentiment of nationalism was spread from France to other parts of Europe from 1792 to 1815, and some countries saw a transformation from autocratic rule to a more popular form. This may be attributed not so much to the French Revolution itself as to a kind of defense reaction against the conquests of Napoleon.

> The French Revolution began, it is true, in a period of philosophic cosmopolitanism, since that was the tradition of the *philosophes*, and the French armies undertook to liberate other peoples from their tyrants in the name of the rights of *man*, not of *nations*. But Napoleon, in a somewhat incidental and left-handed fashion, did so much to promote the progress both of democratic institutions and of nationality in Western Europe that he may, in a sense, be regarded as the father of them both. His plebiscites were empty things in practice, but they loudly acknowledged the rights of people to decide on vital matters. He was a friend of constitutions – so long as he himself made them. He is the founder of modern Germany.[4]

Following these initial impulses came the profound stimulus of the Industrial Revolution. From England to all corners of the world, the new means of transportation and communication (the steamship, the railroad) eliminated the old isolation and made possible a new psychological unity within each nation. Huge quantities of printed matter appeared, national armies were raised, great systems of free schools arose, all connected with the new economic nationalism. The old blind and unreasoning attitudes of love for the nation and hatred for the outsider were solidified on a national scale. The implications were dangerous, for the new nationalism was subject to sudden and hysterical explosion.

Since technological advances were no more favorable to one than to the other, either nationalism or internationalism might have won dominance in

[2] *The Common Weal* (London, 1924), p. 195.

[3] Carlton J. H. Hayes, "The War of the Nations", *Political Science Quarterly*, XXIX (1914), pp. 687-8.

[4] James Harvey Robinson, "What Is National Spirit?", *Century Magazine*, XCIII (1916), p. 61.

Miller Services, Toronto

A street scene in Prague during the 1968 invasion of Czechoslovakia. The Czechoslovakian youth is standing on top of a Russian tank while a bus burns in the background. To what extent does the photo indicate the strength of nationalist sentiment in Czechoslovakia?

the new machine age. It is a fact, however, that such technological advances have been used primarily for nationalistic ends. Economic developments of recent times seem to have stimulated nationalistic development, rather than the reverse. The internationalism of Europe's crowned heads and liberal parties, which had been so conspicuous in the 1850s, began to fade rather quickly. But nationalism persisted as a major historical force, the most powerful in modern times. After both World Wars, it took on increasing strength and vigor.

Discussion guidelines

1. From your own experience with school "nationalism", suggest some reasons why an individual gets "caught up" in the promotion of such a feeling.
2. Why did powers such as Britain, France, and the Netherlands lose some of their nationalistic fervour with the loss of colonies after World War I?
3. How do you account for the continued efforts of established countries to promote national feeling by such means as symbols, songs, expositions, war, or threats of war?

Cross references

The Use of Symbols, page 44
Nazi Rituals, page 46

The New Nationalism?

from *African Nationalism: The Cracked Myth*
by Ndabanigi Sithole

We may define African nationalism as a feeling. Unless it is a feeling, then it cannot be identified. But it is not a general feeling, like the feeling we have for water or our friends or enemies. It is a special feeling of a political nature. . . . African nationalism is a political feeling manifesting itself against European rule in favour of African rule. The first time he ever came into contact with the white man the African was overwhelmed, overawed, puzzled, perplexed, mystified, and dazzled. The white man's "houses that move on the water", his "bird that is not like other birds", his "monster that spits fire and smoke and swallows people and spits them out alive", his ability to "kill" a man and again raise him from the dead (anaesthesia), his big massive and impressive house that has many other houses in it, and many new things introduced by the white man, amazed the African. Motor cars, motor cycles, bicycles, gramophones, telegraphy, the telephone, glittering Western clothes, new ways of ploughing and planting, added to the African's sense of curiosity and novelty. Never before had the African seen such things. They were beyond his comprehension; they were outside the realm of his experience. He saw. He wondered. He mused. Here then the African came into contact with two-legged gods who chose to dwell among people instead of in the distant mountains. For the first time he came in contact with gods who had wives and children, and who kept dogs and cats.

These white gods were conscious of the magic spell they had cast over the Africans, and they did everything to maintain it. They demonstrated their control of the lightning by firing their guns regularly, which to the ears of Africans sounded lik thunder in the sky. There was hardly anythin which the white man did which had no god-lik aspects. The African, who never argues with hi gods lest their wrath visit him, adopted the sam attitude to the white man. And so the Africans sub mitted themselves to the rule of the white ma without question. The white man became master i a house that was not his. He ordered the Africa right and left and the African was only too read to please his white god. And the white man saw tha it was good, and he smiled with deep satisfactio and said "Africa, the white man's Paradise". An other race of human beings could have done th same thing under similar circumstances.

World Wars I and II helped to widen the crack of the white myth. Thousands of African soldier went abroad on active service. The English stree girls of London, the French street girls of Paris and the Italian street girls of Naples did not help t preserve the white myth. Drinking white soldier still added their contribution to its annihilation White commanders ordered African soldiers to ki white enemy soldiers. African soldiers from South ern and Northern Rhodesia, Nyasaland, Tangan yika, Kenya, North Africa, French West Africa French Equatorial Africa, the Gold Coast, an Nigeria found themselves at the front-line war wit one purpose in view – to kill every white soldie enemy they could get hold of. Many German an Italian soldiers were shot by African soldiers.

African soldiers saw white soldiers wounded, dy ing, and dead. Bullets had the same effect on blac and white. This had a very powerful psychologica impact on the African. He saw what he used to cal his betters suffer defeat (though not conquest) a the hands of Germans and Japanese, and once mor he was impressed by the fact that it was not the fac of being black or white that mattered. After suffer ing side by side with his white fellow soldiers th African never again regarded them in the sam light. After spending four years hunting the whit enemy soldiers the African never regarded them again as gods.

But what has this to do with the problem of the rise of African nationalism? African nationalism, in many ways, represented the degree to which the white man's magic spell had worn off. As long as this myth was thick and impenetrable the African adjusted himself as well as he could to what he thought were gods, though gods that ate corn. But the externals had had their day and reality had taken their place, though few white people in Africa realized this extremely important change.

There were certain basic facts that these white people who wanted to be regarded by Africans as myth forgot. The generations of Africans who first came into contact with the white man and his wonders were overwhelmed in the sheer novelty of the white man and the new things he had brought to Africa. But numbers of the later generation, born in modern hospitals, raised in modern towns and cities, educated in modern schools, travelling by land, air, and sea, trained in modern arts and skills, employed in modern factories and mines, rubbing shoulders daily with white people in towns, cities, schools, and on the battlefield, took the white man as a matter of course, just as they took another African. The white man could no longer cast his spell over them by a simple trick of showing them the train, or an automobile, or reading them a story book, or cracking his gun, because many an African then knew how to do these things. It pained the white man to realize that the African was regarding him as an ordinary human being. To him the new African generation was all degenerate. It had no proper respect for the white man, not so much because he was human, but because he was white. The white man failed to draw a distinction between what had been and what then was, let alone what had to be in a matter of a few decades.

How African was the African of that time? There was a world of difference between the African before the coming of the white man and the African afterwards. The interaction between the West and Africa was producing a new brand of African. That is, it was pushing the white-man-worshipping African into the background, and bringing into the foreground the African who did not worship the white man. The proud and arrogant African might have thought he was 100 per cent African because both

Miller Services, Toronto

his mother and father were African, just as the proud and arrogant white man born in Africa might have thought he was 100 per cent European. The truth was that there was no such thing in this Africa as 100 per cent this or that race.

Take an African who had been to school. He might have thought that he was 100 per cent African. Physically this might have been true, but an examination of the content of his consciousness even on a superficial level disclosed that his mathematical thought, his legal training, his theological views, his commercial and industrial undertakings, his economic theories, the themes of his conversation, his aspirations and hopes, to quote only a few, were radically different from those of an African who lived before the advent of European powers. The African of the post-European period had new eyes, as it were. He saw new things that he never saw before European rule came. He had new ears. He heard new things that he never heard before European rule came. He had come to possess a new sensibility. He felt things that he never felt before. He did not quite see what his forefathers saw. He did not quite hear what his forefathers had heard. He did not quite feel what his forefathers had felt. He ceased to see the white myth which his forefathers had seen, for the simple reason that he had ceased in many ways to be the African that his forefathers used to be.

But in what way was this African different from his forefathers? The answer is simple: his forefathers were vaguely conscious of the country in which they lived. They were not conscious of the rest of Africa – certainly not of the countries outside Africa. They spent most of their time looking after their livestock, hunting, and trapping game. Their eyes never saw the large cities and towns whose buildings now soar to the sky. They never travelled on bicycles, motor cars, trains, and they never flew. They never went to school. That is, they never learned how to read and write. They never built themselves modern houses and schools.

The African of the post-European period lived in an environment that in many instances was different from that in which his forefathers lived. He was not only conscious of the country in which he lived, but also of Africa as a whole and of the world. Unlike his forefathers' environment that hummed with bees, that was enlivened with singing birds, disturbed by wild animals, and moved at nature's pace, the African of the European period lived in an environment where the mechanical bird had superseded the bird, where automobiles, trains, and tractors had pushed the ox, the donkey, and the horse into the background. If the African forefathers had come back to life and beheld their own descendants on the modern scene, they would have mistaken their own children for gods.

Discussion guidelines

1. "The belief that Canadians defeated the Americans in the War of 1812 is one myth that has had a unifying effect on Canada."
   (a) Check out the historical facts of the case.
   (b) Account for the emergence and survival of national folk myths.
   (c) Identify myths that have retarded or promoted a feeling of unity in the community where you live.
2. Do you think Sithole is describing racism or nationalism; or are they synonymous? Supply evidence from *The Cracked Myth* to defend your position.
3. Give examples from current affairs to explain how the nationalism of new nations has affected (a) the British Commonwealth, (b) the United Nations, (c) relations between the superpowers.

Cross references

My Dungeon Shook, page 165
Alignment? page 231
Non-alignment? page 232

ALLIANCES AND COLLECTIVE SECURITY IN THE NATIONAL INTEREST

Alliances Don't Work
from *Utopia*
by Thomas More

[Sir Thomas More (1478–1535) imagines a perfect society, Utopia, in which the follies of his generation are corrected. In the following excerpt, he uses the term "league" much as we today use the term "alliance".]

Howbeit, the Utopians think that even when leagues are ever so faithfully observed and kept, yet the custom of making leagues was very evilly begun. For it causes men to think themselves born adversaries and enemies one to another, and that it is lawful for one to seek the death and destruction of the other, unless there is a league. Yea, and after the leagues are entered into, friendship does not grow and increase. But the Utopians believe that no man ought to be counted an enemy who has done no injury. And that the fellowship of nature is a strong league; and that men are better and more surely knit together by love and benevolence than by covenants of leagues; by hearty affection of mind rather than by words.

Discussion guideline
"Men are better and more surely knit together by love and benevolence than by covenants of leagues; by hearty affection of mind rather than by words."
(a) By means of examples, defend this principle.
(b) With reference to organizations such as NATO, NORAD, or the Warsaw Pact, indicate the degree to which you think More's advice is practical.

Cross references
North American Defence: Its Background, page 192
The Military Facts of the Case, page 193

The Munich Agreement
from *House of Commons Parliamentary Debates*
a speech by Clement Attlee

[On September 30, 1938, the Munich Pact was signed. This agreement granted important parts of Czechoslovakia to Germany and opened the way to the later conquest of the whole country. In spite of Czech objections, Britain and France had agreed to the pact, and the British Prime Minister, Neville Chamberlain, triumphantly claimed that "peace in our time" had been won. In the House of Commons debate which followed the signing of the agreement, Clement Attlee, the Leader of the Opposition, took issue with Chamberlain's claim. He then examined the problem of alliances and collective security as it applied at that moment.]

We have all been living through difficult and dangerous times and we are living to-day in difficult and dangerous times. The Prime Minister at the close of his speech said that we must continue to arm. It was a comment on his other statement that we have peace for our generation.

We all feel relief that war has not come this time. Every one of us has been passing through days of anxiety; we cannot, however, feel that peace has been established, but that we have nothing but an armistice in a state of war.

The events of these last few days constitute one of the greatest diplomatic defeats that this country and France have ever sustained. There can be no doubt that it is a tremendous victory for Herr Hitler. Without firing a shot, by the mere display of military force, he has achieved a dominating position in Europe which Germany failed to win after four years of war. He has overturned the balance of power in Europe. He has destroyed the last fortress of democracy in Eastern Europe which stood in the way of his ambition. He has opened his way to the food, the oil, and the resources which he requires in order to consolidate his military power, and he has successfully defeated and reduced to impotence the forces that might have stood against the rule of violence.

I fear that the House is faced with this, that the real outstanding problem in this business is that the map of Europe has been forcibly altered by the threat of war. Herr Hitler has successfully asserted the law of the jungle. He has claimed to do what he will by force and in doing so has struck at the roots of the life of civilised peoples. In doing this to one nation he threatens all, and if he does this, there is no longer any peace in the world even although there may be a pause in actual warfare.

The history of the last seven years is the background of this crisis, and the first point I must make to the Government is this. This crisis did not come unexpectedly. It was obvious to any intelligent student of foreign affairs that this attack would come. The immediate signal was given by the Prime Minister himself on 7th March of this year when he said: "What country in Europe today if threatened by a larger Power can rely upon the League for protection? None." It was at once an invitation to Herr Hitler and a confession of the failure of the Government. The invitation was accepted a few days later by the Anschluss in Austria. Then our Government and the French Government could have faced the consequences. They could have told Czechoslovakia, "We cannot any longer defend you. You had better now make the best terms you can with Germany, enter her political orbit and give her anything to escape before the wrath comes upon you." But they did nothing of the sort. Czechoslovakia continued under the supposed shelter of these treaties.

I compared the Prime Minister to the captain of a ship not taking any steps until the eleventh hour. If it had been decided to stand by Czechoslovakia steps should have been taken at once, as has been urged in this House very often by the right hon Gentleman the Member for Epping (Mr. Churchill), to build up the forces that would stand against aggression. After the events of 21st May two things were obvious – the designs of Herr Hitler and also the fact that they could be stopped, because they were stopped then by the resolution of the Czech Government. The prime weakness throughout the whole business has been that the Government have never tried to get together the Powers that might stop it.

I heard a suggestion from the benches opposite "What about the U.S.S.R.?" Throughout the whole of these proceedings the U.S.S.R. has stood by its pledges and its declarations. But there you get th weakness of this Government and at the same time of France – and I say the weakness of France is even greater. At no time did they make up their minds whether they were going to stand or to tell Czechoslovakia to make its own terms.

The real pith of it is that, having decided to leave the League system which we practised and in which we believed, and to embark on a policy of alliances and power politics, instead of strengthening the people whose natural interests were with ours, we have had nothing but constant flirtations with this and that dictator. The Prime Minister has been the dupe of the dictators, and I say that to-day we are in a dangerous position.

And what have we got in place of the alliances and covenants and collective security and all the rest of it which buttressed this country in the past? We are left with two promises, one from Signor Mussolini and one from Herr Hitler. That is really all that we have got. We have to walk by faith – the faith of the Prime Minister in Signor Mussolini and his faith in Herr Hitler. The Prime Minister has said how difficult it was for Herr Hitler to recede from a statement which he had once made. I have five pages of statements made by Herr Hitler, from every one of which he has receded, but the Prime Minister says against all experience that he has faith in Herr Hitler's promise, grounded on two or three interviews – a pretty flimsy support for this country.

I ask, what is to happen next? What reason have we to think that Herr Hitler will stop now? Suppose he does not. What will happen? Suppose he now says that he wants colonies, what will the Prime Minister say when he asks the people of this country for them? But suppose he does not ask for British colonies at all; suppose he only asks for the Belgian Congo, or supposing he asks from Holland Sumatra or Java, what is the position? Czechoslovakia has gone. If there were any doubt about our ability to stand against these armed forces, there is far less now. That is the position in which we have been placed.

The suggestion is made in some quarters that we may now have a Four-Power Pact of the great Powers. I think that would be enormously dangerous at the present time. In any such pact this country will be definitely the junior partner. It will be a pact against liberty. If the Prime Minister wants to walk with the dictators, he will have to conform to their wishes. The moral of this is that the day when our policy changed, when we left the path of collective security in the League of Nations, when we abandoned the attempt to make peace through the League and under collective security, that day we took a step towards war. What are we offered now? All we are offered now by the Prime Minister is to push on with rearmament. Well, the people have seen the gas masks, they have seen the trenches. They have fear in their hearts, and as long as you follow this hopeless policy of power politics, you will never lift this fear of war from the people. I pleaded many months ago in this House that we wanted a peace conference before the next war, but then I did not assume that the next war would be complete defeat, and that is why the Munich Conference was not a real peace conference. It was only the delivery of an armistice.

I want a real conference, a peace conference to which people will not come merely to rattle the sabre. I want a peace conference which will endeavour to deal with the causes of war that are affecting this world, the wrongs of the Versailles Treaty, the wrongs of minorities, to deal with the colonial question, to deal with the question of raw materials, to deal, above all, with the great economic question, the condition-of-the-people question. We desire that from this country there should go forth a demand for a real, new effort to try and rid the world of war, an effort to settle those questions without which you cannot get disarmament, without which you cannot get security. The real question that faces us is not just a review of the past, not just our apprehensions of the present; it is, What can we do for the future of the human race?

The Munich Pact 30 Years Later

Miller Services, Toronto

Chamberlain holding the agreement signed by Hitler

MUNICH – Walter Warlimont, 73, a former Wehrmacht general, is convinced that had Britain and France gone to war to defend Czechoslovakia 30 years ago instead of signing the Munich agreement it would have meant military disaster for Adolf Hitler's armies.

General Warlimont, appointed head of the general staff, territorial defense department of the Wermacht supreme command in September, 1938, is one of the men with long memories in Europe wondering what might have been had the Munich conference failed to satisfy Hitler's claim to the Sudetenland.

The Munich agreement, signed 30 years ago yesterday by Germany, Italy, Britain, and France, ceded the Sudetenland to Germany and led to the complete dismemberment of Czechoslovakia a few months later.

General Warlimont, now living in retirement in the Bavarian mountains, believes that the Wehrmacht could not have beaten Czechoslovakia quickly in 1938 and was at the mercy of the French Army on the Western Front.

Today, Czechoslovakia is again under occupation.

The Munich agreement also remains a bitter memory in Britain. Political observers concluded in weekend articles that while former Prime Minister Neville Chamberlain, who yielded to Hitler's demands, must bear the main responsibility for Britain's involvement he had little choice but to sign the agreement.

Sir Alex Douglas-Home, former British Prime Minister who was parliamentary secretary to Mr. Chamberlain from 1936 to 1939, said: "The main lesson of Munich is that one should never go into negotiation with a dictator without the backing for physical strength."

Two French statesmen, Edouard Daladier, Prime Minister at the time of Munich, and Georges Bonnet, his Foreign Minister, said there was no alternative to signing the agreement. They blamed Munich and its effects on the Western failure to form an anti-Hitler alliance at the time.

Reuters News Agency,
September 30, 1968

Discussion guidelines

1. Does the news article "The Munich Pact 30 Years Later" support Mr. Attlee's view that political power backed by military might (power politics) would have been a hopeless policy in 1938? Comment.
2. "The day when we left the path of collective security in the League of Nations . . . that day we took a step towards war." To what extent do you think faith in collective security is justified today, in the nuclear age? Argue your position by referring to Canada's present day "collective security" arrangements.

Cross reference

The Dangers of Present Trends, page 327

The Necessities of War

from *The Grand Alliance*
by Winston Churchill

[Churchill explains why he, an anti-Communist, declared an alliance with Communist Russia in June, 1941.]

When I awoke on the morning of Sunday, June 22, the news was brought to me of Hitler's invasion of Russia. This changed conviction into certainty. I had not the slightest doubt where our duty and our policy lay. Nor indeed what to say. There only remained the task of composing it. I asked that notice should immediately be given that I would broadcast at nine o'clock that night. Presently General Dill, who had hastened down from London, came into my bedroom with detailed news. The Germans had invaded Russia on an enormous front, had surprised a large portion of the Soviet Air Force grounded on the airfields, and seemed to be driving forward with great rapidity and violence. The Chief of the Imperial General Staff added, "I suppose they will be rounded up in hordes."

I spent the day composing my statement. There was not time to consult the War Cabinet; nor was it necessary. I knew that we all felt the same on this issue. Mr. Eden, Lord Beaverbrook, and Sir Stafford Cripps – he had left Moscow on the tenth – were also with me during the day.

The following account of this Sunday at Chequers by my private secretary, Mr. Colville, who was on duty this weekend, may be of interest:

On Saturday, June 21, I went down to Chequers just before dinner. Mr. and Mrs. Winant, Mr. and Mrs. Eden, and Edward Bridges were staying. During dinner Mr. Churchill said that a German attack on Russia was now certain, and he thought that Hitler was counting on enlisting capitalist and Right Wing sympathies in this country and the U.S.A. Hitler was, however, wrong and we should go all out to help Russia. Winant said the same would be true of the U.S.A.

After dinner, when I was walking on the croquet lawn with Mr. Churchill, he reverted to this theme, and I asked whether for him, the arch anti-Communist, this was [not] bowing down in the House of Rimmon? Mr. Churchill replied, "Not at all, I have only one purpose, the destruction of Hitler, and my life is much simplified thereby. If Hitler invaded Hell I would make at least a favourable reference to the Devil in the House of Commons."

I was awoken at 4 a.m. the following morning by a telephone message from the F.O. to the effect that Germany had attacked Russia. The P.M. had always said that he was never to be woken up for anything but invasion [of England]. I therefore postponed telling him till 8 a.m. His only comment was, "Tell the B.B.C. I will broadcast at nine tonight." He began to prepare the speech at 11 a.m., and except for luncheon, at which Sir Stafford Cripps, Lord Cranborne, and Lord Beaverbrook were present, he devoted the whole day to it. The speech was only ready at twenty minutes to nine.

In this broadcast I [Churchill] said:

The Nazi régime is indistinguishable from the worst features of Communism. It is devoid of all theme and principle except appetite and racial domination. It excels all forms of human wickedness in the efficiency of its cruelty and ferocious aggression. No one has been a more consistent opponent of Communism than I have for the last twenty-five years. I will unsay no word that I have spoken about it. But all this fades away before the spectacle which is now unfolding. The past, with its crimes, its follies, and its tragedies,

Miller Services, Toronto

Winston Churchill in 1940

flashes away. I see the Russian soldiers standing on the threshold of their native land, guarding the fields which their fathers have tilled from time immemorial. I see them guarding their homes where mothers and wives pray – ah, yes, fo there are times when all pray – for the safety c their loved ones, the return of the bread-winne of their champion, of their protector. I see th ten thousand villages of Russia where the means of existence is wrung so hardly from the soil, but where there are still primitive human joys, where maidens laugh and children play. I see advancing upon all this in hideous onslaught the Nazi war machine, with its clanking, heel-clicking, dandified Prussian officers, its crafty expert agents fresh from the cowing and tying-down of a dozen countries. I see also the dull, drilled, docile, brutish masses of the Hun soldiery plodding on like a swarm of crawling locusts. I see the German bombers and fighters in the sky, still smarting from many a British whipping, delighted to find what they believe is an easier and a safer prey.

I have to declare the decision of His Majesty's Government – and I feel sure it is a decision in which the great Dominions will in due course concur – for we must speak out now at once, without a day's delay. I have to make the declaration, but can you doubt what our policy will be? We have but one aim and one single, irrevocable purpose. We are resolved to destroy Hitler and every vestige of the Nazi régime. From this nothing will turn us – nothing. We will never parley, we will never negotiate with Hitler or any of his gang. We shall fight him by land, we shall fight him by sea, we shall fight him in the air, until, with God's help, we have rid the earth of his shadow and liberated its peoples from his yoke. Any man or state who fights on against Nazidom will have our aid. Any man or state who marches with Hitler is our foe. That is our policy and that is our declaration. It follows, therefore, that we shall give whatever help we can to Russia and the Russian people. We shall appeal to all our friends and allies in every part of the world to take the same course and pursue it, as we shall faithfully and steadfastly to the end.

When I spoke a few minutes ago of Hitler's blood-lust and the hateful appetites which have impelled or lured him on his Russian adventure, I said there was one deeper motive behind his outrage. He wishes to destroy the Russian power because he hopes that if he succeeds in this he will be able to bring back the main strength of his army and air force from the East and hurl it upon this island, which he knows he must conquer or suffer the penalty of his crimes. His invasion of Russia is no more than a prelude to an attempted invasion of the British Isles. He hopes, no doubt, that all this may be accomplished before the winter comes, and that he can overwhelm Great Britain before the Fleet and air power of the United States may intervene. He hopes that he may once again repeat, upon a greater scale than ever before, that process of destroying his enemies one by one by which he has so long thrived and prospered, and that then the scene will be clear for the final act, without which all his conquests would be in vain – namely, the subjugation of the Western Hemisphere to his will and to his system.

The Russian danger is, therefore, our danger and the danger of the United States, just as the cause of any Russian fighting for his hearth and home is the cause of free men and free peoples in every quarter of the globe. Let us learn the lessons already taught by such cruel experience. Let us redouble our exertions, and strike with united strength while life and power remain.

Discussion guidelines

1. "Any man or state who fights on against Nazidom will have our aid. . . . It follows, therefore, that we shall give whatever help we can to Russia and the Russian people." To what extent do the necessities of war make "unnatural" alliances valid? Provide illustrations from history in support of your opinion.
2. How fair is it to judge Churchill's defence of England's alliance with Russia in the light of events since 1941?

Cross reference

What is War? page 237

POWER BALANCES AMONG NATIONS

1

Spheres of influence and Soviet aggression

By MAX FRANKEL

WASHINGTON – The hardest fact of all behind the events in Czechoslovakia is that here and there around the globe, and nowhere more firmly than in Central Europe, there exists a line beyond which neither of the two great nuclear nations dares apply its power even for causes and people that it holds dear.

Behind that line on each side, from Ulan Bator to Prague, from Saigon to Santo Domingo, there have been profound and revolutionary stirrings that persistently challenge the giant powers within their realms of influence.

But in the heart of Europe, where the risks of nuclear war have always been greatest, the line itself has held. This week, for the third time in 12 years, a U.S. president has reaffirmed and thus reinforced the bargain that it defines.

When President Dwight D. Eisenhower asked the Russians to withdraw their troops from Hungary in 1956, as President Lyndon Johnson asked them to withdraw from Czechoslovakia on Wednesday, he was told in diplomatic language that the disposition of Soviet forces in Eastern Europe was none of his business.

Gen. Eisenhower, commenting on a note from Premier Nikolai A. Bulganin of the Soviet Union, wrote in his memoir: "This note from Bulganin, written of course in the knowledge that Hungary was, in the circumstances, as inaccessible to us as Tibet, was almost the last provocation that my temper could stand." But it did stand it, and the judgment that Eastern Europe was as inaccessible to U.S. power as Tibet stood, too.

In August, 1961, when the Russians appeared hard-pressed to do something drastic to halt the flight of East German refugees to West Berlin, President John F. Kennedy walked in the White House rose garden with his aide, Walter W. Rostow, and remarked that there was nothing he could do about it. To Moscow, he said, Eastern Europe was a vital interest that could not be allowed to "trickle away". But it was not vital to the United States. "I can get the alliance to move if he tries to do anything about West Berlin," Mr. Kennedy added, according to his biographer, Arthur M. Schlesinger, "but not if he just does something about East Berlin".

And when the wall was built a few days later, Mr. Kennedy wrote to West Berlin's Mayor, Willy Brandt, that the "brutal border-closing" was a Soviet decision that only war could reverse and no one supposes "that we should go to war on this point".

From time to time, Americans have questioned whether U.S. diplomatic and economic power might not have been used more effectively to inhibit Soviet force, even in Eastern Europe. And in slowly evolving situations, such non-military power has been applied to sustain or encourage the Yugoslavs, the Poles and the Romanians in their efforts to win varying degrees of freedom from Soviet control. But in periods of crisis, when Moscow felt its most vital interests threatened, the fear of nuclear war has stayed Washington's hand, despite the Eisenhower rhetoric about the "liberation" of East Europeans or the Kennedy pledge to "pay any price, bear any burden, meet any hardship, support any friend, oppose any foe, to assure the survival and the success of liberty".

What the French scholar Raymond Aron has called the Soviet-U.S. alliance against war has depended primarily upon this belief for vital spheres of interest.

The United States has staked out its own spheres with a series of mutual-security treaties covering Western Europe, Latin America, Japan, South Korea, and Southeast Asia. It had to reassert the sanctity of the line through Korea in blood in the Nineteen Fifties and is attempting to reassert it militarily in Vietnam with the explicit argument that respect for the line through Germany requires its defense in Asia. Administration officials reject these comparisons, on the ground that the United States respects the sovereignty and independence of its allies and employs its power to protect their freedom rather than to curb it.

As the French rebellion against the North Atlantic Treaty Organization shows, this is true in most cases. But the threat of a Communist takeover in the U.S. sphere has usually provoked Washington as much as the threat of a drift away from orthodox communism has provoked Moscow. President Eisenhower rushed troops to Lebanon in 1958, felt justified in organizing an invasion of Cuba in 1961 and Kennedy threatened war to force Soviet missiles out of Cuba in 1962. President Johnson, almost simultaneously in 1965, poured troops into South Vietnam and the Dominican Republic to prevent what he thought were imminent, even though indigenous, Communist seizures.

The Dominican affair, in fact, bore at least some superficial resemblance to the Czechoslovak invasion that toppled the regime of Alexander Dubcek. Though the chaos that provoked it was unlike anything in Prague, the invasion was justified by the arranged invitation of a rump junta and explained with references to an unproved danger of takeover by agents of Moscow. The United States, too, pressed some of its allies into joining the intervention. Its troops departed only after U.S. officials had arranged an election that yielded a moderate regime.

It is not just the arbitrary drawing of a line that has created spheres of big-power interest, but the mutual respect of such lines as they evolved, by design or accident, over the years.

Moscow has let down good Communists in France and Guatemala as Washington has let down liberty – leaving men in Budapest and Prague because survival is ultimately a higher value than any ideology.

The New York Times,
August 24, 1968

Miller Services, Toronto

Dwight D. Eisenhower

Miller Services, Toronto

John F. Kennedy

2

Rigidity 'the Most Dangerous Aspect of Two-Bloc System'

Text in part of Lester Pearson's address over the B.B.C. in London last night in the Reith lectures series:

From the London Bureau of The Globe and Mail

Today, instead of a pluralistic, conventional, balance of power world, we have a bi-polar nuclear world. Most of the powerful, though not necessarily the most populous, nations of the world are grouped in two blocs, centred around two super-powers. The forces of balance that made for at least some degree of peace and order no longer operate. We are now groping for other forces to take their place and which will be adequate to keep the peace. All we can be certain of at the moment is a balance of mutual, nuclear deterrence.

Threat of force

If we want a good illustration of the nature of the bi-polar system as it is constituted today, and of the relationship between and within the two blocs, we can look at the position of two countries: one in the Warsaw Pact, the other in NATO – Czechoslovakia and Greece.

Let us suppose – this is purely hypothetical, of course – that there were a successful Communist coup in Greece, and that the new Greek Government wanted to align itself with the Warsaw Pact. Greece is now in the American, or, if you want to make it more acceptable, the NATO sphere of influence. If Greece, or indeed any other of the smaller NATO nations, tried to withdraw from NATO, not by a free vote of the people, but by a coup d'état, the United States might feel its interests sufficiently affected by this move to warrant a threat of force to stop it; as it did in Cuba, a country much closer to home.

But any threat of force would have to include the possible use of nuclear force, because that is the only way in which it could have the desired deterrent effect on the other bloc so much stronger in conventional forces.

Moscow, on the other hand, would have conventional forces strong enough for effective use against any conventional army that might be opposed to it. It is in a position to impose its will on any or all of the non-nuclear nations by conventional force alone; even if the U.S.A. helped in a conventional way.

If NATO wished to defend itself against aggression from Eastern Europe, it could not do so successfully at present by the use of conventional forces against the same kind of attack. It could only make its collective will prevail by the threat or the use of nuclear force, which would mean taking the responsibility for beginning a nuclear war and destroying both sides in the process. . . .

The most dangerous aspect of the two-bloc system is its rigidity. The old political alliances, because they were alliances between governments, were flexible arrangements. Nations could escape from them quite easily. New leaders would emerge, and the groupings were constantly shifting. Now, because there are only two powers that have the capacity to destroy the world and destroy themselves, the others circle uneasily around them, as satellites or allies.

No mobility

The peripheral members haven't the mobility to play a game of shifts and balances even if they wished to. This kind of relationship may be inevitable in a bi-polar world of the kind we live in but it does not constitute the most solid foundation for a genuinely collective international security organization. . . .

Does Communist imperialism repre sent primarily a messianic urge t spread a new religion, or a Russia desire to win dominance for a natio state? Or is it simply a defensiv conviction that the capitalist state unless they are faced with uncor querable military power, will plot t destroy the Communist states, and i particular the Socialist fatherland? O balance, I find it difficult now to mak up my own mind whether the compu sion is more offensive than defensiv I didn't have so much difficulty 15 yea ago. I was satisfied it really was offe

Discussion guidelines

1. "There are at the present time two great nations in the world, . . . I allude to the Russians and the Americans. . . . The Anglo-American relies upon personal interest to accomplish his ends and gives free scope to the unguided strength and common sense of the people; the Russian centres all the authority of society in a single arm. . . . Their starting-point is different and their courses are not the same; yet each seems marked out by the will of Heaven to sway the destinies of half the globe." (Alexis de Tocqueville, *Democracy in America,* 1835) Considering the current position of the United States and Russia in global affairs, evaluate the accuracy of de Tocqueville's 1835 prophecy.
2. How much truth do you credit to Raymond Aron's statement that there is a "Soviet-U.S. alliance against war when vital spheres of interest are involved"? Refer to current events to illustrate your judgment.
3. "A dewey-eyed optimist or a down-to-earth realist" – in which category would you place L. B. Pearson in the light of his assessment of the world's power balances? Argue your point of view.

Cross references

Soviet-Czech Relations – See-Saw Between Pressure and Reconciliation, page 80
The Fears That Spurred the Russians into Action, page 82
A Meaningful Voice? page 296
Political Idealism! page 319

DECISION-MAKING AND NATIONAL SELF-INTEREST

The Confrontation in Cuba

from *Kennedy*
by Theodore C. Sorensen

[In October 1962, American photo reconnaissance planes discovered evidence of a sudden build-up of Russian Intermediate Range Ballistic Missile sites in Cuba, well within range of major American cities and military installations. President John F. Kennedy was thus faced with a momentous decision, for one false step could begin a disastrous world war. What should the American reply be?]

In our earlier sessions that day [Thursday, October 18, 1962] the President had requested a 9 p.m. conference at the White House. While we had been meeting for only three days (that seemed like thirty), time was running out. Massive U.S. military movements had thus far been explained by long-planned Naval exercises in the Caribbean and an earlier announced build-up in Castro's air force. But the secret would soon be out, said the President, and the missiles would soon be operational.

The blockade course – to stop all further Russian missile shipments into Cuba by a naval blockade – was now advocated by a majority. We were prepared to present the full range of choices and questions to the President. George Ball had earlier directed that the official cars conspicuously gathered by the front door of the State Department be dispersed to avoid suspicion. With the exception of

United States Information Servic

This was one of the photos taken by American reconnaissance planes and released for publication during th Cuban crisis.

Martin, who preferred to walk, we all piled into the Attorney General's [Robert Kennedy's] limousine, some seated on laps, for the short ride over to the White House. "It will be some story if this car is in an accident," someone quipped.

In the Oval Room on the second floor of the Mansion, the alternatives were discussed. Both the case for the blockade and the case for simply living with this threat were presented. The President had already moved from the air-strike to the blockade camp. He liked the idea of leaving Khrushchev a way out, of beginning at a low level that could then be stepped up, and the other choices had too many insuperable difficulties. Blockade, he indicated, was his tentative decision.

But it was not a final decision; and on Friday morning, October 19, it seemed even more remote. Preparing to leave as agreed for weekend campaigning in the Midwest and West, the President called me in, a bit disgusted. He had just met with the Joint Chiefs [the top military command], who preferred an air strike or invasion, and other advisers were expressing doubts. In retrospect it is clear that this delay enabled us all to think through the blockade route much more thoroughly, but at the time the President was impatient and discouraged. He was counting on the Attorney General and me, he said, to pull the group together quickly – otherwise more delays and disagreement would plague whatever decision he took. He wanted to act soon, Sunday if possible – and Bob Kennedy was to call him back when we were ready.

Our meetings that morning largely repeated the same arguments. The objections to the blockade were listed, then the objections to the air strike. Those who had not been present the previous evening or days went through the same processes the rest of us had gone through earlier. I commented somewhat ungraciously that we were not serving the President well, and that my recently healed ulcer didn't like it much either. Yet it was true that the blockade approach remained somewhat vague, and I agreed to write the first rough draft of a blockade speech as a means of focusing on specifics.

At 9 a.m. Saturday morning my draft was reviewed, amended, and generally approved – and, a little after 10 a.m. our time, the President was called back to Washington.

"The President has a cold," announced Pierre Salinger to the White House pressmen who had accompanied them to Chicago. He did have a cold, but it was not a factor in his decision. Before boarding his plane, he called his wife at Glen Ora and asked her and the children to return to the White House. No other decision in his lifetime would equal this, and he wanted his family nearby. (Once the decision was made he asked Jacqueline if she would not prefer to leave Washington, as some did, and stay nearer the underground shelter to which the First Family was to be evacuated, if there was time, in case of attack. She told him no, that if an attack came she preferred to come over to his office and share whatever happened to him.)

The President's helicopter landed on the South Lawn a little after 1.30. After he had read the draft speech, we chatted in a relaxed fashion in his office before the decisive meeting scheduled for 2.30. I gave him my view of the key arguments: air strike no – because it could not be surgical [wipe out all the missile bases completely in one surprise attack] but would lead to invasion, because the world would neither understand nor forget an attack without warning and because Khrushchev could outmaneuver any form of warning; and blockade yes – because it was a flexible, less aggressive beginning, least likely to bring about war and most likely to cause the Soviets to back down.

Our meeting at 2.30 p.m. was held once again in the Oval Room upstairs. For the first time we were convened formally as the 505th meeting of the National Security Council. We arrived at different

Wide World Photo

Not all Americans agreed with Kennedy's actions during the crisis. This demonstration was held in San Francisco while the blockade was still being enforced. What alternative proposals are the demonstrators suggesting?

gates at different times to dampen the now growing suspicion among the press. The President asked John McCone to lead off with the latest photographic and other intelligence. Then the full ramifications of the two basic tracks were set before the President: either to begin with a blockade and move up from there as necessary or to begin with a full air strike moving in all likelihood to an invasion. The spokesman for the blockade emphasized that a "cost" would be incurred for whatever action we took, a cost in terms of Communist retaliation. The blockade route, he said, appeared most likely to secure our limited objective – the removal of the missiles – at the lowest cost. Another member presented the case for an air strike leading to Castro's overthrow as the most direct and effective means of removing the problem.

At the conclusion of the presentations there was a brief, awkward silence. It was the most difficult and dangerous decision any President could make, and only he could make it. No one else bore his burdens or had his perspective. Then Gilpatric, who was normally a man of few words in meetings with the President when the Defense Secretary was present, spoke up. "Essentially, Mr. President," he said, "this is a choice between limited action and unlimited action; and most of us think that it's better to start with limited action."

The President nodded his agreement. Before his decision became final, he wanted to talk directly with the Air Force Tactical Bombing Command to make certain that the truly limited air strike was not possible. But he wanted to start with limited action, he said, and a blockade was the place to start. The advocates of air strike and invasion should understand, he went on, that those options were by no means ruled out for the future. The combination of approaches contained in the draft speech anticipated not only a halt of the build-up but a removal of the missiles by the Soviets – or by us. The blockade route had the advantage, however, of preserving his options and leaving some for Khrushchev, too. That was important between nuclear powers, and he wanted our action directed against the other nuclear power, not Castro. "Above all," he would say later at American University, in drawing the moral of this crisis, "while defending our own vital interests, nuclear powers must avert those confrontations which bring an adversary to a choice of either a humiliating retreat or a nuclear war." Khrushchev had launched this crisis, but a blockade might slow down the escalation instead of rushing him into some irreversible position. It applied enough military pressure to make our will clear but not so much as to make a peaceful solution impossible.

2

'Was no other choice'

WASHINGTON – "It looks really mean, doesn't it? But then, really there was no other choice. If they get this mean on this one in our part of the world, what will they do on the next?"

That was what Robert Kennedy remembered his brother, the President, as having said as they both waited, extremely tense, to see whether the Soviet Union chose to pull its offensive missiles out of Cuba as President John F. Kennedy had demanded, or would risk a world war with the United States.

"I just don't think there was any choice, and not only that, if you hadn't acted, you would have been impeached," Robert Kennedy – who was Attorney-General at the time of the 1962 crisis – said he told the worried President.

President Kennedy thought for a moment, according to his brother, and said, "That's what I think – I would have been impeached."

The agony, the doubts, and the quiet triumph of those critical days were told by Robert Kennedy in a lengthy article written last year and published posthumously today by McCall's under the title Thirteen Days.

The publication takes place on the eve of the sixth anniversary of the speech in which President Kennedy informed the United States and the world that Soviet offensive missiles had been detected in Cuba and that the United States was prepared to go to war to make sure that the missiles were removed.

The New York Senator wrote the article for publication in The New York Times Magazine to commemorate the fifth anniversary of the crisis last October. But he had decided against publication then because he did not want it alleged that he was trying to use the article out of political motives.

After Senator Kennedy's assassination in June, the 25,000-word manuscript was purchased by McCall's for an advance of $1-million, probably the largest sum ever paid for a manuscript of that length.

Senator Kennedy gave details of the crisis from the time he was informed on Oct. 16, 1962, that missile sites had been discovered by a U-2 reconnaissance plane flying over Cuba until the denouement on Oct. 28, when Soviet Premier Nikita Khrushchev agreed to withdraw the missiles.

The crisis actually had two distinct phases. The first was from Oct. 16 to Oct. 21 when President Kennedy and his advisers worked in extreme secrecy to devise their course of action. The second was from Oct. 22 until Oct. 28, when the entire world wondered whether the crisis would be resolved short of war.

The President decided against an immediate military strike at the island's missile bases – an action, Robert Kennedy wrote, that was advocated by the military leaders including the then Chief of Staff of the U.S. Air Force, Gen. Curtis LeMay, now the American Independent Party's candidate for vice-president. Instead, the President adopted as a first step a plan for a quarantine of Cuba.

The blockade, aimed at giving Mr. Khrushchev time to withdraw the missiles without Soviet humiliation, was seen as a means of showing U.S. determination to force the missiles out while stopping short of actual military action. However, in the event the Russians tried to run the blockade, the United States was prepared to go to war, the article asserts.

The blockade was scheduled to go into effect on Wednesday morning, Oct. 24. A few minutes after 10 a.m. an intelligence report stated that two Soviet ships, accompanied by a submarine, were approaching the 500-mile blockade barrier. They were due to be intercepted in the next hour if they tried to enter the forbidden area.

"I think these few minutes were the time of gravest concern for the President," the senator wrote. Was the world on the brink of a holocaust? Was it our error? A mistake? Was there something further that should have been done? Or not done? "His hand went up to his face and covered his mouth. He opened and closed his fist. His face seemed drawn, his eyes pained, almost gray. We stared at each other across the table."

The tension was broken when a messenger brought a note disclosing that some of the Soviet ships had stopped dead in the water, an indication that Moscow did not want a confrontation.

Robert Kennedy wrote that the President had given orders to all his officials never to claim a victory over the Soviet Union.

The lessons from the crisis, the senator wrote, were that it was vital that a variety of opinions be available to the President and that sufficient time be allotted to making critical decisions, if possible.

With Vietnam in mind, Senator Kennedy also asserted that the missile crisis was proof of how vital it was to have allies and friends. Unlike the Vietnam situation, the missile crisis found the United States solidly supported by all its allies, he said.

The New York Times,
October 21, 1968

Discussion guidelines

1. "Where it is an absolute question of the welfare of our country, we must admit of no consideration of justice or injustice, of mercy or cruelty, of praise or [dishonour], but putting all else aside must adopt whatever course will save its existence and preserve its liberty." (Machiavelli, *The Prince*)
   On the evidence available, to what extent do you think American decision-making in the Cuban crisis reflected Machiavelli's statement?
2. "The foreign policy of a country is limited not only by its aims, but also by its military strength, or, more accurately, by the ratio of its military strength to that of other countries." (E. H. Carr, *The Twenty-Years' Crisis 1919–1939*)
   Illustrate Carr's statement by referring to the Cuban crisis.

Cross references

What Is War? page 237
The Case for Internationalism, page 312

NATIONALISM OR INTERNATIONALISM?

The Never-Ending Circle of Nationalism

from *Nationalism: Interpreters and Interpretation*
by Boyd C. Shafer

The fact is that over the world men have become increasingly national-minded. When the Negro in the United States wants equality, he asks action by the national government because he thinks that he cannot get this equality through any other agency. When the Hungarians want rights, they believe that they must throw off Russian domination and obtain Hungarian independence. They know no other way. For the achievement of needs and desires, for order and safety, the nation seems to be the modern means.

Everything the citizen hears and sees seems to reinforce this observation. The radio is national, television is national. The schools teach national citizenship. The historians chiefly teach and write national histories. Literature and cooking and sports are judged on national criteria. Even science and music, written in international notation and symbol, become Russian, German, French, or American rather than just science and music. To make certain that national values rather than others prevail, patriotic societies in every country demand with some success that foreign influences be rooted out, that only good national or "one hundred per cent" ideas be encouraged.

The nation-state has hence often become an end in itself, the one end, indeed, socially approved for the supreme sacrifice. It can and often does, in our contemporary world, control everything a man does or thinks, especially in times of national emergencies. The most extreme nationalisms of our time, those of Hitler and Mussolini, grew out of war, lived on war or probability of war, and themselves made war. Here we see each nationalism living and growing in imitation and in fear of other nationalisms. To beat Nazism and Fascism, as Goebbels and the Nazis predicted, other nations unfortunately had to become somewhat like them. "The true nationalist," the French newspaper *L'Action Française* once declared, "places the fatherland above everything." Not all men in the twentieth century were "true nationalists" in this ultimate sense, but the pressures which conditioned them were relentlessly pushing them in that direction.

Is there no way out of this never-ending circle, whether it is vicious or not? I am a historian. I cannot predict. If we are to have, at any future time, a truly international order above the nations, or if we are to have a world state, the international or world government will have to grow as national governments did, and if indeed it is to exist, it will have to touch the vital interests of each world citizen. It, too, will have to grow, as nationalism did, out of the concrete fears and hopes, desires and actions of people who are passionately interested in its maintenance for their own freedom and safety. It will, too, have to afford the promise of a better life and, at the same time, protect man in the ways national governments have. But whether this can or will happen, whether or not we have time in this age of national hydrogen bombs, I do not know.

The reality of nationalism is the feeling of people, a feeling based upon each people's historical myths and realities. The reality of the nation lies in the hope and freedom, the protection and security it affords. If nationalism is to be succeeded by some new loyalty, to a world religion or world state, some other realities, some new myths will have to provide as much and touch the citizens of the present nations as deeply.

Canadian National

Discussion guideline

Having considered historian Boyd C. Shafer's views, propose concrete ways of breaking what he believes to be a "never-ending circle of nationalism".

Cross references

Civil Disobedience: National and International, page 181
The Case for Internationalism, page 312

Internationalism

"Joe, these people say they want flesh-colored Band-Aids."

Today, newer nations are clamouring for recognition, and established powers are trying to consolidate their spheres of influence. The question arises, therefore, whether nationalism can ever give way to enduring international co-operation. Can smaller and newer nations have a meaningful role in world affairs? Are existing international organizations any more than gestures towards peace, tolerated by the major powers for their own political ends? And what part does the individual play – or can he play – in promoting international understanding?

GRASS-ROOTS INTERNATIONALISM

A Case in Point

from *Operation Crossroads Africa*
by Clarence W. Hall

One summer night in 1965, the village of Mpeseduadze, deep in the bush country of Ghana, was aburst with whooping jubilation. To the throb of jungle drums, chanting Africans swirled around a huge bonfire. At a gesture from the chief, the drums fell silent, the dancing stopped, and a gray-haired American Negro was led forward. Rising from his throne, the chief threw a brilliantly colored toga over the American's shoulders. "I name you Robinson Tekyi III, Honorary Paramount Chief of the Fanti tribe," he said. "We know you cannot stay to rule over us, for you belong to many tribes, many places. But you and the young people you brought shall reign in our hearts forever. You have not only built us a beautiful school; you have also shown us the dignity of labor. You have taught us how to get for ourselves the things we need to take our rightful place in the new Africa."

The American with the grand new title was the Rev. James H. Robinson, founder and director of "Operation Crossroads Africa", a private, non-government, voluntary summer work-camp program that was hailed by President Kennedy as "the progenitor of the Peace Corps". Since its founding in 1958, Operation Crossroads has induced more than 2,300 carefully picked American and Canadian college youths to give up summer vacations, pay a part of their own way to some 30 African nations and, together with African counterparts, engage in work-camp projects that have dotted the continent with new schools and community centers, village clinics and libraries, and have laced the areas with market-access roads, irrigation, and water-supply systems.

Up from "The Bottoms". Jim Robinson's personal history is inspiring proof that, given the right spirit, greatness can arise from the most discouraging surroundings. The grandson of a slave, Robinson spent his boyhood in the Knoxville, Tenn., shantytown known as "The Bottoms". Setting foot outside The Bottoms to deliver the wash done for "white folks" by his mother was always risky. Often clobbered by white boys along the way, he accumulated cuts and bruises – and deep hatred for his tormentors. This hatred for whites might have scarred Jim Robinson's life permanently, had it not been for his mother. She taught him that the achievement of human dignity depends on the set of the heart and not on the color of the skin; that equality, like freedom – while an inherent right – must be earned. "There is kindness and helpfulness everywhere, Jim," she told him again and again. "In white hearts as well as black. All you need to do is find it."

Jim Robinson finally found it, in heaping measure, in the person of a white retired schoolteacher named Lorraine Miller, who pledged part of her life savings to help him get through Pennsylvania's Lincoln University. Having decided on the Christian ministry as the best place to help himself and his people toward dignity and equality, Robinson went on to New York City's Union Theological Seminary. Possessed of a restless, bubbling nature plus fierce determination, he was elected class president and graduated with honors.

Then, eager to tackle the toughest job around, he moved into Harlem and started a new parish, the Church of the Master, as well as the Morningside Community Center, to meet both religious and welfare needs. His congregation and social-welfare program, begun with four Negro adults and six children, within a few years expanded to more than

James Robinson arriving in Senegal

Operation Crossroads Africa, Inc.

3,000 members of all races. Among them were hundreds of college students, white and black, who helped him turn his church and center into a beehive of projects aimed at removing some of Harlem's bleaker aspects.

From Rabbit Hollow to Africa. In 1941, when Robinson was offered the use of a 470-acre farm in Winchester, N.H., he began "Camp Rabbit Hollow" with 87 youngsters picked off Harlem's troubled streets – and a $400 deficit. One day he described to some college students his dreams for making Rabbit Hollow one answer to Harlem's delinquency problem. They promptly volunteered to help construct the needed buildings. Since then, some 20,000 students have had a part in building and improving Rabbit Hollow, now rated one of the finest interracial camps in the country.

This stunning response gave Robinson his idea: Why not utilize this youthful idealism and eagerness for service *on an international scale*? Leaders of his denomination, the United Presbyterian Church in the U.S.A., agreed, and he was dispatched on an exploratory tour of Europe, Asia, and Africa. Of all places, Africa seemed the neediest – and the most neglected by Americans. "The darkest thing about Africa is America's ignorance of it," he reported. With new African countries emerging, and with color rapidly becoming a divisive factor in both international and domestic relations, Robinson became obsessed with the conviction that ways must be found for the white and colored races to know each other better.

But how? The surest route seemed to be through young people. "My mind kept coming back to what those students had done at Rabbit Hollow," Robinson says, and by the end of 1954 he had created the outlines of "Operation Crossroads Africa". It took him three years to sell the project. While students were eager, financial backing was hard to find. Finally, in May 1957, Jim Robinson got his breakthrough. After hearing him lecture on "Commitment", a group of students at Los Angeles' Occidental College met at midnight, wound up pledging to raise $15,000 to send ten of their members to Africa the next year.

Elated, Robinson redoubled his fund-raising efforts, by the next summer had almost enough money to send a contingent of 60 pick-and-shovel Samaritans, divided into five groups, to French Cameroons, Liberia, Sierra Leone, Nigeria, and Ghana. The impact of this pilot experiment, on North Americans and Africans alike, was so impressive that its fundamental procedures of Crossroader enlistment and screening, choice of countries and projects have been followed each year since.

No Joyride. Jim Robinson has never camouflaged either the hazards or the hardships of a summer in Crossroads. "Make it plain," he tells the recruiters, "that Crossroads is neither a tourist joyride nor a safari, and that only the tough-minded, serious, and dedicated need apply." The applicants are told that they will live like the Africans. There will be adventure, of course, but adventure salted with backbreaking labor, the risk of malaria and dysentery, the culture shock of transfer from a college dorm to an African mud hut, from modern plumbing to outhouses and the bush, from rich American food to manioc and plantain.

Despite this stark picture – "or perhaps because of it," says Robinson – Crossroads has experienced no shortage of volunteers. This year, for example, there were 3,500 applicants, from whom Robinson could choose only 226. Though the task of selecting the most promising students is painstaking, he gives even greater care to his choice of group leaders, having proved that "the quality of the leader is crucial to the group's success". Paid only $200 a summer, leaders are usually chaplains of campus religious organizations or college teachers of education and international relations.

If the picture of conditions to be met by Crossroaders proves no deterrent to enlistment, neither is the requirement that each must somehow provide $1,100 of the $1,950 cost of sending him to Africa. Church groups and social service clubs often help sponsor an applicant. At many of Crossroads' 118 participating colleges and universities in the United States and Canada, students band together to help an accepted applicant, using ingenious money-raising schemes: concerts and stage productions, dances, cake sales and raffles, baby-sitting and secretarial pools. To raise money to help meet Crossroads' annual half-million-dollar budget, Jim Robinson ceaselessly travels the country, making speeches, enlisting supporters. He resolutely refuses all offers of government money for programs abroad, for he believes that to accept "would compromise Crossroads' private, person-to-person character".

Requirements for the host countries are also strict. "Crossroaders go nowhere they are not invited" is Robinson's first rule. Others are: each country must pick its own project – one that will meet a real need. It must supply materials and, since every project emphasizes self-help, recruit an equal number of African counterparts, preferably college students, who will work along with the Crossroaders. Firm in the Robinson philosophy is the conviction that "self-respect is the most vital element in any aid program; you can't implant it by doing *for* people, only by doing *with* them. It is any people's willingness to share in their own uplift that separates the sincere from the suppliant."

Proof of Friendship. Suspicion of American motives tops the list of obstacles every team has to overcome. Typical was one Ghanaian village headman who at first refused to let his people co-operate in building a badly needed schoolhouse. While American college youths were putting in 14-hour days at the school site, they were harangued constantly by the chief and his elders: "How do we know you are our friends?" Only after the Crossroads leader laid down his shovel and, wiping the sweat from his brow, demanded, "Aren't these calluses proof enough?" did the chief finally extend his hand – and his help.

A similar suspension of suspicion came from a village chief in Dahomey who confessed to Crossroaders at the dedication of a new school: "When you first came, we thought you represented just another colonial power bent on stealing our country. But all you've stolen is our hearts."

Once confidence is established, the innate African friendliness and generosity gush like a blocked spring suddenly unstopped. In many recent instances, as Crossroaders entered into the rhythm of village life, the villagers entertained them in their homes and invited them to take part in tribal ceremonies usually closed to outsiders. Counterpart student-workers dropped their touchiness, entered heartily into the work, spent long after-work hours sharing their inmost aspirations, questioned Crossroaders about America.

Crossroaders never try to gloss over U.S. racial troubles, another source of initial hostility. In discussions with their African counterparts, they seek – usually with outstanding success – to set the U.S. problem in historic perspective, pointing out that the United States, unlike many countries, is officially committed to solving the problem by all legal and human means, and that Crossroads itself, with its integration of black and white, represents most Americans' sincere desire to do so.

Soiled Hands. Second only to the impact on Africans of Crossroaders' color-blindness is that made by their attitude toward manual labor, traditionally regarded as beneath the dignity of the educated African. At the start of almost any project, African villagers gasp in disbelief as they watch American collegians enthusiastically tackling the most menial of hand-soiling tasks. Robinson's aphorism, "No man ever soiled his soul by soiling his hands," has been repeated by Crossroaders to tens of thousands of young Africans during the past ten years. Claims Robinson, "This selling to Africans of the dignity of labor must rate among our most important accomplishments."

The chain-reactive power of the self-help spirit was dramatically evident at Safo, in Ghana, where, after seeing their brand-new cement-block school, the people raised $2,000 for material to enlarge the school – with their own hands – from two to seven rooms, then fell to planning a new post office, a community center, a church. Said the village chief, "We never did anything for ourselves before. Now see what we have!" In Ghana, Kenya, and Togo, the Crossroads example has led directly to the formation of voluntary work-camp associations which now enroll thousands of local university and high-school students in community-improvement projects.

In addition to his work-campers, Robinson began recruiting small teams of experts in various fields where service was requested by African leaders. In Liberia, Crossroads organized in 1961 the first in-service teacher-training program for hundreds of under-educated African teachers. The following year, special teams of physicians and nurses, agriculturalists and rural-development specialists were sent over to share their knowledge with Africans.

But even more important than the boons brought to Africa by the various Crossroads projects are the friendship and trust created between future leaders of Africa and North America. Said the leader of one large African nation: "In the 33 countries where Crossroads has been received during this decade, ties of understanding and mutual respect have been forged that will require something stronger than communist propaganda to break." To further strengthen these ties, Robinson, in co-operation with the State Department's Bureau of Educational and Cultural Affairs, in 1964 introduced a "reverse Crossroads" project known as the African Youth Leadership Program. Under the AYLP, some 35 of Africa's most promising youth leaders are brought to the United States each summer for intensive exposure to American life and mores.

One of Jim Robinson's chief dreams, when first shaping the outlines of his program, was that the Crossroads experience would awaken young Americans and Canadians to the desirability of service careers. That this dream has had substance is seen in the fact that a full third of Crossroads alumni are already either back in Africa – in U.S. or Canadian foreign service, technical-assistance programs, educational, medical, or religious work – or are in graduate schools of African studies, preparing for service in or related to Africa.

Of even greater significance, however, is Crossroads' confirmation of Robinson's formula for dissipating discords between whites and blacks, at home and abroad: *"Get them together – not to debate and argue, but to work on projects they both deem important. Then watch the animosities fade away!"*

Discussion guidelines

1. (a) What does being a "Good Samaritan" really mean?
   (b) To what degree is "Good Samaritanism" a temporary "craze" confined to idealistic youth? Cite examples to reinforce your opinion.
2. "All cynicism aside, individuals can and are 'moving mountains' of misunderstanding, and in so doing are contributing significantly to world peace." Argue this claim.

Cross references

World Health, Illiteracy and Incomes since 1960, page 214
An Overview, page 216
The Challenge, page 221

Select Samaritan

We think we might adopt two children and
The problem is to know which kind we want.
Not Canadians. Refugees. But they can't
Be Jewish. A couple of Spaniards would be grand
If they were fair. My husband hates dark hair.
Afraid they are mostly dark in any case.
Germans would do, we don't care about race,
Except Chinese, must draw the line somewhere.

So would you let us know soon as you could
What sort's available? We have a car
And would be glad to come and look them over
Whatever time you say. Poles might be good,
Of the right type. Fussy? Perhaps we are
But any kids we take will be in clover.

ROBERT FINCH

THE SMALL POWERS – AN INTERNATIONAL ROLE?

A Meaningful Voice?

from *Fate and Will in Foreign Policy*
by James Eayrs

> Long ago, the mice had a general council to consider what measures they could take to outwit their common enemy, the Cat. Some said this, and some said that; but at last a young mouse got up and said he had a proposal to make, which he thought would meet the case. "You will all agree," said he, "that our chief danger consists in the sly and treacherous manner in which the enemy approaches us. Now, if we could receive some signal of her approach, we could easily escape from her. I venture, therefore, to propose that a small bell be procured, and attached by a ribbon round the neck of the Cat. By this means we should always know when she was about, and could easily retire while she was in the neighbourhood."
>
> This proposal met with general applause, until an old mouse got up and said: "That is all very well, but who is to bell the Cat?" The mice looked at one another and nobody spoke. Then the old mouse said:
>
> "IT IS EASY TO PROPOSE IMPOSSIBLE REMEDIES."
>
> AESOP'S FABLES

Force is the monopoly of the Great Powers, for all the good it does them. But Great Powers enjoy no monopoly over ideas. The foreign minister of a small state may not be able to summon a gunboat in aid of his diplomacy, to carry a big stick let alone to brandish it. But he can carry a briefcase well enough, and stock it with proposals.

Even more than Great Powers, small states may exploit this source of power. Great Powers, just because they have more than their fair share of the wealth of this world, are not inclined to innovation except to protect and add to what is already theirs. They are fearful of change, which for them is for the worse. Opportunities for progress are best ignored, temptations to try new ways are best resisted. The known present, unsatisfactory as it may be, seems preferable to a future filled with uncertainty. They are solaced by the *status quo*.

For small states it is all very different, or ought to be. They have no vested interest save in changing the system that treats them so shabbily. Change for them is for the better. Opportunities for progress are to be seized, temptations to try new ways to be yielded to. An uncertain future, uncertain as it may be, seems preferable to the present so unsatisfactory for them. They are solaced by the prospect of change.

Having little to lose, and much to gain, the small states of the states-system are the natural innovators within the states-system. The smaller the state, the more acceptable its innovation, for its suggestions more than those of greater powers are likely to be disinterested and directed towards the general welfare. This point was made by Pope Paul VI when he addressed the General Assembly of the United Nations in his capacity as temporal leader of Vatican City, the tiniest state of all. "We have nothing to ask for," he told his fellow delegates. "We have at most a desire to express and a permission to request: namely, that of serving you in so far as lies within Our competence, with disinterest, humility, and love. That," added the Pontiff, with exquisite irony, "is so simple that it may seem insignificant to this Assembly, which is accustomed to dealing with most important and most difficult matters." No message could have been more significant – except perhaps that which Paul proceeded

Some representatives of small powers at the U.N. General Assembly

United Nations

to place before its members. "If you wish to be brothers," he told them, "lay down your weapons."

Left to their own devices, Great Powers will never accept this advice. A Great Power never goes into a disarmament conference intending to lay down its weapons. It goes there intending to increase its armed force *vis-à-vis* that of its rivals. The gap between their preaching and their practice, between their declared purpose and their real purpose, has grown so wide and persisted for so long that today their governments sometimes don't even bother to conceal their cynicism and their insincerity. "It's gotten to the point," Dean Rusk has conceded, "where, in our conversations, we've been able to refer to the arguments by the numbers. He would make an argument – the [Soviet] Ambassador or Foreign Minister – and I can say: 'Well, you know our position on that. This is Argument Number Five. Shall I repeat it, or shall we save time and go on?' and they'll smile and say: 'Well, we'll perhaps go on to some other subject.' "

It lies within the power of small states to prevent Great Powers going on to some other subject. They can compel them to stick with the subject at hand, whatever it may be – the spread of nuclear weapons, the testing of nuclear weapons, the demilitarization of outer space. They can compel them to negotiate seriously, rather than by rote and ritual. If serious negotiation on Plan A produces no agreement, they can compel them to consider Plans B and C. The methods by which the small powers may hope to coerce the great consist in their persistence and determination, their fertility of device and idea, and their readiness to invoke the sanction of public opinion. The motive for the small powers wanting to compel the great is the motive of self-interest, than which none is more effective. So long as the Great Powers remain deadlocked on disarmament, the interests of small powers are bound to suffer. Stalemate may suit the strong but it is intolerable for the weak. It perpetuates their misery, it intensifies their danger. "Those terrible weapons that modern science has given you," Pope Paul reminded their custodians, "long before they produce victims and ruins, cause bad dreams, foster bad feelings, create nightmares, distrust, and sombre resolves; they demand enormous expenditures; they obstruct projects of solidarity and useful work. They falsify the very psychology of peoples."

The responsibility borne by small states for the peace and prosperity of the states-system, so far from being small, is really very great. There is much for them to do, much which only they can do. And it is not unrealistic to expect them to be equal to the challenge. They have not done too badly in the recent past, for it is out of the briefcases of the foreign ministers of smaller powers that many of its significant initiatives originate. It was Lester Pearson of Canada who contrived the United Nations Emergency Force; Adam Rapacki of Poland who developed the idea of disengagement in Central Europe; Frank Aitken of Ireland who first proposed a non-proliferation treaty; Östen Undén of Sweden who first suggested the formation of a non-nuclear club; Per Haekkerup of Denmark who first exposed, like the child in the fable of his countryman, the nudity of NATO doctrine.

All this being so, the foreign ministers of smaller countries have little to excuse them when they tell us, as they often do, that their hands are tied by Fate, that nothing can be done. Either they deceive themselves, or they deceive us, or they disclose by their admission that they do not understand what makes the modern world go round.

Discussion guideline

"The view that small powers with original ideas, determination, and the support of public opinion can alter the policies of major powers falls into the realm of 'impossible remedies'."
Argue this opinion.

Cross references

Alignment? page 231
Non-alignment? page 232
Spheres of influence and Soviet aggression, page 276
Rigidity "the Most Dangerous Aspect of Two-Bloc System", page 278

AN EFFECTIVE UNITED NATIONS?

Miller Services, Toronto

Operation Humanity

from *Mankind's Children: The Story of* UNICEF

by Robert L. Heilbroner

> The Twentieth Century will probably be remembered, not as the one in which we had two world wars, or even as the one in which the hydrogen bomb was invented, but as the one in which the idea that it was common sense for the nations of the world to use new inventions to help raise the standard of health and living throughout the world was first accepted as a matter of course.
>
> ARNOLD TOYNBEE

The Problem

Into the vast family of mankind three children are born every second: in the brief moment since you began this sentence six new lives have been added to humanity's billion children. By the time you finish this paragraph another thirty will have come into being; by the end of today, 260,000 more; by the end of the year, 30,000,000. The statistics of newborn life are torrential.

So are the statistics of young death, for in most of the families of mankind, childhood is not a time of play and preparation. It is a time of premature suffering and dying. Of the flood of children everywhere adding to mankind's ranks, a quarter will die before they have left their mother's breast; two-thirds of the remainder never see adolescence; and only one in four goes on into old age – that is, into "old age" as the world measures it: thirty-eight years of life.

Of course, not all the children in the world are exposed to this terrible elimination. The child born in the United States runs only a 3 per cent risk of dying in his first year. Thereafter, except for accident, up to the age of forty his risk of death is close to statistical zero. In all likelihood he will never know what it is to go a whole day without food. Of the most common scourges of his siblings in other parts of the world – the diseases of malaria, yaws, TB, leprosy, trachoma – he is exposed to only one, TB, and that on an already minute scale. With any kind of luck an American child should live into his late sixties or early seventies. A Swedish or a New Zealander baby should do even better.

But most babies are not American, or European, or, for that matter, white. The cataract of births runs swiftest in the continents and subcontinents to the south and east: India, Southeast Asia, South America, Africa. It is here that the statistics of the childhood of mankind are given their tragic weighting.

For a baby born into the villages of Iraq or Pakistan or Indonesia does not face a 3 per cent risk of mortality during his first year. He often begins with a risk of 33 to 50 per cent.

Nor does he then pass, as does the Western child, into a long period of safe growth. Instead, childhood presents itself as a gamut of fearful risks. If he lives in North Africa, for example, it is more than likely that he will contract trachoma – a painful eye infection which frequently leads to blindness. In areas of Asia which are as large as all of Europe, a tremendous proportion of the children have – or have had – malaria. In some parts of Central Africa the percentage of children who have leprosy is greater than the percentage of American children who at any one time are suffering from sore throat.

Some years ago an Indian demographer sought to reduce this fierce contrast of health and death to a single graphic comparison. It was this: *Of a hundred Indian and a hundred American children, more American children would live to be sixty-five than Indian children to five.*

An Answer

UNICEF is the story of a 20th century crusade – a crusade in which scores of governments, hundreds of organizations, thousands of individuals are fighting for the cause of all the children of mankind. It is a crusade which depends on the efforts of overworked and underpaid staffs of doctors and government administrators in a hundred countries. It draws strength from the contributions of many great private philanthropies and of civic and religious groups. It involves the functions of so august and seemingly remote an institution as the World Bank. It leans directly on the work of many United Nations agencies, such as the World Health Organization (WHO), the Food and Agriculture Organization (FAO), and the United Nations Bureau of Social Affairs; also the U.S. Technical Assistance Administration.

But as its very name indicates, in the United Nations Children's Fund the crusade finds its most direct expression, for this is an organization which exists *only* because the nations of the world have begun to wage their common fight for all their children.

Major UNICEF *Programs*

1. Assistance to governments in planning for the needs of new generations
2. Efforts to reduce infant mortality
   (a) provides equipment and supplies for maternal and child health centres
   (b) provides teaching materials and stipends to train midwives and nurses

3. Campaigns against major communicable diseases
   (a) provides insecticides and sprayers
   (b) provides drugs and antibiotics
   (c) provides laboratory and clinical supplies
   (d) provides vaccines
   (e) provides health education materials
4. Efforts to increase production and consumption of protective foods
   (a) provides skim milk powder for distribution in schools and health centres
   (b) assists countries in milk pasteurization, drying, and sterilizing projects
   (c) helps to develop new high-protein foods such as fish flour, soy milk, and various vegetable protein mixtures
5. Support for programs to keep family units together, and to improve care given in the child's home
   (a) stresses day care centres for children of working parents
   (b) assists training of child and family welfare workers
6. Assistance to educational and vocational training projects
   (a) provides stipends for trainees and experts
   (b) provides vehicles to transport supervisors
   (c) provides supplies for production of teacher materials
   (d) provides equipment for vocational workshops
   (e) subsidizes vocational instructors and counsellors

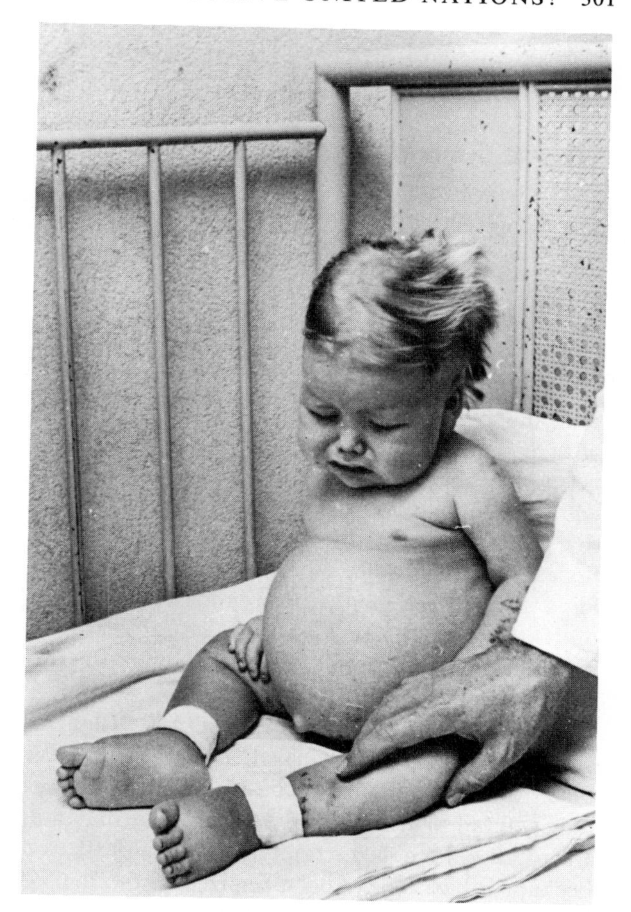

UNICEF Photos, by Nagata

A child in Guatemala suffering from malnutrition. UNICEF programs are aimed, in part, at improving nutrition for mankind's children.

Discussion guidelines

1. Considering the other economic and social agencies of the United Nations, how do you account for the particular appeal of UNICEF?
2. To what extent do you think the non-political bodies of the U.N. can prevent war?
3. "Poverty in Canada is real. Its numbers are not in the thousands, but the millions. There is more of it than our society can tolerate, more than our economy can afford, and far more than existing measures and efforts can cope with. Its persistence, at a time when the bulk of Canadians enjoy one of the highest standards of living in the world, is a disgrace." (Economic Council of Canada, *Fifth Annual Review, 1968*) Debate the viewpoint, sometimes expressed in opposing international aid schemes such as UNICEF, that "charity begins at home".

Cross references

Our "Free Society", page 108
The Dangers of Present Trends, page 327

b

A World Symbol?

from *Democracy in World Politics*
by Lester B. Pearson

To make a true assessment of the value of the United Nations it should be considered primarily as a symbol of the community of nations and peoples, and as an attempt to work out the implications of their interdependence. This world community is yet a very shadowy thing, but it is a goal toward which we may work. Like all the best symbols of the greatest truths, the United Nations is not a lifeless thing, a badge or a flag; it is human, and alive, made up of men. It is only in the first stages of its growth, certainly, but it has at least the possibility of progressive development into a real community.

Tennyson's "Parliament of Man" is a vision for which many men have worked, and not a few have died, to bring to reality in the United Nations. We may still fail to achieve this vision; but we may not. In any case, we have no right to abandon the dream because it has not *yet* been realized in the United Nations glass palace on Manhattan.

Apologists for the United Nations occasionally ask critics to reduce their fire, by recalling that the United Nations is still young. If they refer to the youth of the organization itself, I have little sympathy with this plea. It is not a matter of years. The United Nations is as weak – but also as strong – as the recognition in this new era by the majority of men of the demands of world community, and their devotion to that ideal. It is the intellectual and moral maturity of men and nations throughout the earth that matters, not the chronology of an organization in Manhattan.

In addition to this living symbol, the United Nations provides in its Charter a set of principles or code of ethics which member governments have promised to observe. This code is not perfect, but it is good. Like most ethical systems, it is observed only in part and its violations command more attention than its observances.

Furthermore, the Charter establishes certain representative institutions. These have the power to set up other machinery, so that what we have is a living constitution, a social organism with possibilities that, if not infinite, are great. There is very little in the political field that men could not do through the Charter, if enough men wished to do it.

These representative organs – the General Assembly, the Security Council, the Trusteeship Council, and ECOSOC [Economic and Social Council] – are, as I have suggested, more similar to a parliament than to a diplomatic negotiating conference. A substantial part of their value, like that of national parliaments, lies precisely in the ability to mobilize and focus opinions, to encourage the formulation, expression, and dramatic confrontation of major viewpoints. By bringing issues out into the public, and ventilating them, throwing light into dark places, and thereby encouraging more care and responsibility by administrative authorities who hesitate to do things of which they would be ashamed if they were publicly examined in a searching forum; by doing all this, the United Nations tends to improve the working of governments. Its function in this respect is similar to that of a free and outspoken parliament or congress.

Legislatures in the national domains also perform the function of educating the man in the street about national issues, by dramatizing them in public debate. These debates, in the history of states, have performed invaluable services in extending the awareness of national interests and the feeling of national community. In their way, debates in the General Assembly – or in other agencies of the

United Nations – can perform a similar role on a world scale and have indeed begun to do so.

There is another point. What Sir Harold Nicholson calls "diplomacy by loudspeaker" and "diplomacy by insult" is indeed, as he puts it, "a contradiction in terms" in the context of strict negotiation. But these phrases suggest lively and vigorous debate in a healthy parliament. The unending "propaganda speeches addressed not to those with whom the delegate is supposed to be negotiating but to his own public at home" can certainly be exhausting and at times maddening. But they are something with which I suspect any American Congressman or Senator, or any member of a British or a Canadian Parliament, or any French Deputé will be as familiar as those who have to suffer from them in the committee rooms of the United Nations. It is part of the price of democracy – even, or perhaps especially, of democracy in international infancy.

Within the machinery of any democratic national government there are negotiations aplenty, carried on confidentially before or in connection with public debate. Government would be entirely impossible without them. These negotiations by discussion, exploration, and compromise take place in offices, between officials in different sections of a department of government, and at meetings of inter-departmental committees. They take place over the lunch table, between individuals each expert in, or responsible for, some field. They take place within party caucuses. Above all, they take place at meetings of national cabinets.

All these gatherings have one thing in common: they are private. The privacy is not sinister, it is merely sensible. But neither this principle nor this process . . . makes less necessary the very different role of Parliament or Congress. Indeed it would be meaningless, or fatal to representative government, if it all did not end in the "hurly-burly" and the "cut and thrust" of legislative talk and turbulence.

There is a parallel to this – though not, of course, an exact one – in the debates of the United Nations. Most of the decisions that are taken after these debates in United Nations bodies are either "recommendations" which can nevertheless carry great weight with the more responsible governments of the world – or they are decisions to set up some machinery, temporary or permanent, in which a certain number of governments participate voluntarily for limited purposes.

Now the governments which wished to create and participate in some such special body could, of course, just as easily do so without going to the trouble of having the body established by a resolution, adopted after debate, in the United Nations. The only question is whether or not to put a United Nations hat on the whole thing. What are the advantages of doing this? Essentially, the explanation lies in the primary function of the United Nations, that of acting as a living symbol of a world-wide community which it is our interest to deepen and make more real.

Discussion guidelines

1. To what degree do you consider the symbolic value of the United Nations justifies its existence?
2. Churchill once said that international politics needed "more jaw-jaw and less war-war". How would Pearson's evaluation of the United Nations compare with Churchill's judgment?

Cross references

Peaceful Stalemate! page 324
The Dangers of Present Trends, page 327

C

Negotiators at Work

from *Crisis*

by Terence Robertson

[When Egypt seized control of the Suez Canal in July 1956, Britain and France decided to invade and capture the vital waterway. Russia and the United States, who had interests in the Middle East, opposed these plans. Thus, while British bombs fell on Cairo, and French naval forces assisted Israel in an attack on Egypt, the Russians and Americans united in a U.N. resolution calling for a cease-fire. It appeared, as well, that they would unite for a further vote of condemnation.

Canada, with no vital interests in the area, but with special ties to the United States, Britain, and France, was horrified at the divisions among her allies. Her Minister of External Affairs, Lester B. Pearson, worked to avoid a condemnation of Anglo-French actions and to find a device that would allow a retreat with honour. At the same time, his efforts had to be acceptable to the Americans, and had to promise a solution to the problems of the Middle East.

On November 2, 1956, a dramatic session of the U.N. General Assembly was held. While it met, British and French ground troops were sailing towards Egypt to support the actions of their navies and air units. Meanwhile, despite a world-wide chorus of protest, Russian troops moved to crush a rebellion in Hungary. The fear that either conflict could grow into world war weighed heavily on the Assembly as it met to deliberate the situation.]

Miller Services, Toronto

Photo taken from a British bomber during the attack on Port Said, 1956

The special session of the Assembly had resumed, the crescendo of debate was rising as one delegate after another vehemently condemned Britain and France; the hall was, if anything, even more crowded than on Thursday night. Public spectators as well as delegates were now aware that an invasion fleet was somewhere at sea, that the British and French were making acceptance of the cease-fire conditional upon creation of an international force, that there was precious little time in which to do it. They wondered if Red China would really send the three hundred thousand volunteers it claimed had registered for service in Egypt, whether the Soviet Union would intervene in the Middle East, and whether the United States, the United Nations, or NATO would intervene in Hungary.

The mood was sombre, heavily laden with anxiety and expectancy. Anglo-French attempts to dictate the terms of the cease-fire were bitterly resented; the bombing of Egypt, seemingly endless, aroused severe condemnation. The brutally worded leaflets dropped on Egyptian cities shocked and appalled everyone no less than the frightening broadcasts beamed at Egypt from Cyprus Radio, now calling itself "The Voice of Britain". The accused governments needed friendly witnesses in New York that night, but their actions made friendship difficult to sustain or justify.

The Australian delegate, desperately trying to divert the flow and force of the prosecution, interrupted proceedings to read a bulletin from Vienna, which said, "Premier Imre Nagy, speaking in English over Budapest Radio, today announced: 'In the early hours of this morning Soviet troops started to attack the Hungarian capital with the apparent purpose of overthrowing the democratic government of the Hungarian People's Republic. Our troops are in battle with Soviet forces. The Hungarian army is in position. This is my message to the Hungarian people and to the world.' "

Stung into angry retort, the Russian delegate condemned Anglo-French "hypocrisy" and "barbaric bombing"; and Cabot Lodge [of the United States] in a moment of anguished fury, cried out, "God knows I want to see the bloodshed in Egypt stopped. But there is cynicism in the Soviet representative's words while his army is spilling blood in Budapest."

Like two wounded beasts, the United States and the Soviet Union snarled their rage at each other as events beyond their control continued to pull them closer together.

These flashes of sudden lightning in so thunderous an atmosphere served to aggravate the deepening sense of gravity in man's affairs. For Pearson, shrewd and calculating behind a disconcertingly habitual expression of open, boyish naïveté, it would be a long, decisive night, with his political future suspended in the interim hours until the vote on the Canadian resolution was taken.

The essential first step was to enlist co-sponsors [for a Canadian resolution to set up a peace-keeping force]. Engen [the Norwegian representative] had already agreed to approach Colombia, and while Pearson would have liked to include India, that country was in the forefront of a new move to bring about immediate withdrawal and therefore its support did not seem [possible] then.

The next stage was to mobilize votes, the three co-sponsors – Canada, Norway, and Colombia – had to make the best possible use of their respective contacts among the delegations, and from the moment Pearson took his seat in the Assembly hall at roughly 6.00 p.m. the Canadian desk became the focal point for intensive consultations, with one delegate after another arriving to inquire as to the nature of the anticipated Canadian move.

Pearson and his advisers had to refer constantly to the draft resolution, answering each inquiry with an explanation of its purpose and meaning. When opportunities arose Pearson instructed his advisers to seek out the views of other delegations in the hall. This [involved] a constant movement to and from the Canadian desk, all under the surveillance of batteries of television cameras, and if they looked, as one announcer commented, "gravely concerned", it was because, of all the language in the resolution, the phrase "consent of the parties concerned" was proving the most difficult to explain as its ambiguity aroused persistent suspicion.

Murray [one of Pearson's advisers] has recalled: "This phrase meant different things to different people. To the United Kingdom, France, and Israel it referred to themselves. But the Egyptians thought it should refer to Egypt. Others interpreted it as referring to those countries which might eventually make up the international force. We allowed these varying interpretations to stand, mainly because we were not terribly sure ourselves of who it should refer to.

"This is how United Nations resolutions are made. Ambiguity and vague terminology are often deliberate, because lack of precision permits governments which have to deal with public opinion to place their own positions in the best possible light."

During the preceding year, events at the United Nations had given the Canadians a solid opportunity to exert wide influence in the Assembly. The delegation had sparked a move that eventually led to the addition of some sixteen new members, and in pursuing this earlier initiative Canada had worked closely with at least a third of the existing membership, and had earned the acclaim of the Assembly and the gratitude of the incoming nations. Close and useful contacts had been cemented.

But, despite this influence and concentrated effort, the advisers had to concede before the police force resolution was submitted that the outcome would depend largely upon broad support from the Arab-Asians, as without it the necessary two-thirds majority would not be forthcoming.

The Indian Ambassador, Arthur Lall, was organizing a resolution giving the British, French, and Israelis twelve hours in which to comply with the cease-fire call. Nineteen Arab-Asian countries – including Egypt – were sponsoring it, countries which Pearson now needed desperately to support his own draft resolution. As he had agreed to insert the proviso that intervention would depend upon the "consent of the parties concerned", he wanted Egypt to vote for it on the ground that Nasser could not then refuse to accept a police force. Lall might hold the key to the two-thirds majority which the resolution required.

When he discussed the problem with the Indian Ambassador, he discovered that Lall was also concerned that the Arab-Asian resolution would not command a two-thirds majority, that he was anxious to avoid obtaining so slender a margin of victory that his resolution would lack weight and substance. To give it moral force he needed the thirty or so votes committed to the Canadian resolution.

They made their deal. Pearson would deliver the votes of his supporters to the Arab-Asian resolution, while Lall would deliver the nineteen Arab-Asian countries to the support of the Canadian resolution.

Pearson's next concern was uncertainty about the British and French positions. He was by no means sure that the British and French governments would accept the amended resolution [which would cut British and French troops from a U.N. Emergency Force; this had been done on the insistence of the United States].

Dixon [the British representative] crossed the floor to speak with him, saying: "The text doesn't agree with the one I understand you sent to London. I'm not sure they'll like it."

"The substance is the same," said Pearson. "In any case the main thing is that you and the French should not oppose it. Your abstention would be good enough."

"I may get instructions to oppose it," said Dixon. "If the vote is taken soon enough, I can abstain through lack of instructions. I'll try working toward a snap vote if you will help me prevent this Indian resolution being passed unanimously or by a huge majority."

Another deal was made. In return for Dixon's promise that France and Britain would abstain rather than oppose the Canadian resolution, Pearson would try to persuade the Scandinavian countries to abstain on the Indian resolution, for which the Danes and Norwegians at least had little sympathy. His next step was to insure against the mercurial Afro-Asians changing their minds about supporting Canada. Murray met Lall in the corridor outside the hall, and after twenty minutes of persuasive talking returned with the Indian's agreement that the Canadian resolution should be voted on before the Afro-Asian draft. Pearson and most of the delegates supporting him had no real liking for the Indian resolution with its twelve-hour time limit on the cease-fire expressed in strong and condemnatory language. They considered support for it, however, a small price to pay for the votes needed to ensure approval for a United Nations force. If Lall failed to deliver all nineteen of them, Pearson's supporters would thwart the Indian resolution by abstaining.

Abba Eban, leading the Israeli delegation, confronted Pearson on the floor to suggest bluntly that the Canadian resolution invited the United Nations to intrude upon Israel's sovereignty. Eban made it clear that unless Israel was included among the "parties concerned" there would be no United Nations force on Israeli soil. Pearson ruefully noted later: "The Israelis are obviously in a confident mood and unlikely to co-operate with us unless they are forced to do so. With the United States, Britain, and France so bitterly divided, it is going to be difficult to apply the necessary pressure."

Throughout these manoeuvrings, the speeches from the rostrum droned on above the . . . whispering of delegates, one speaker after another pressing home charges against the three governments no one had yet managed to brand as aggressors.

The time was rapidly approaching when the draft resolution would have to be presented to the Assembly. Pearson, feeling that [Dag] Hammarskjold [Secretary General of the U.N.] should be aware of its contents in advance, as it laid a unique, heavy, and urgent responsibility upon his shoulders, sent Murray behind the dais to deliver a copy of it to the Secretary General. Attached was a note which said: "In a few minutes I shall be proposing this resolution. But before I do, could we discuss it?"

Hammarskjold, frowning as he read the text, left the rostrum. Pearson met him in the small office behind it.

Revealing resignation and depression, Hammarskjold said, "It won't work. We'll never get a force going in time to stop the British and the French. They'll attack Egypt, people will get killed, and what can we really do about it? People will say what use is the United Nations? We can't keep the peace in Egypt, we can't keep the peace in Hungary, and all our diplomats do is condemn each other."

It was so unlike Hammarskjold that Pearson spoke quickly, urgently.

"We may not be able to do much about the Soviet moves in Hungary," he said, "but we can do a lot about Egypt in the next forty-eight hours. Canada will give you troops, so will Norway and Colombia. There are British and French detachments in the area already, and there's the [American] Sixth Fleet. We can impress the lot into United Nations service if necessary."

"How are we going to get them into Egypt if Nasser won't have them?"

"He will. Arthur Lall just told me he's willing to accept American and Canadian troops as well as Scandinavian."

Hammarskjold was suddenly alert. "I wonder if Eisenhower will let us use some people from the Sixth Fleet?"

"I don't know yet," said Pearson. "But if it is really necessary, we'll do our best to persuade him."

The final step in these preparations was taken

when Pearson left the hall to telephone Ottawa and speak with Prime Minister St. Laurent. After reporting on the situation in the Assembly, Pearson mentioned that the British would hold off their landings at least until Monday night. St. Laurent agreed that this information was sufficiently important for [Arnold] Heeney [Canadian Ambassador to the United States] to deliver direct to the White House.

Shortly before midnight, Pearson walked to the rostrum, betraying none of the anxiety he felt, and began his address.

". . . My delegation would like to submit to the Assembly a very short draft resolution, which I venture to read at this time. It is as follows:

> *The General Assembly,*
> *Bearing* in mind the urgent necessity of facilitating compliance with the resolution of 2 November 1956,
> *Requests*, as a matter of priority, the Secretary General to submit to it within forty-eight hours a plan for the setting up, with the consent of the nations concerned, of an emergency international United Nations force to secure and supervise the cessation of hostilities in accordance with the terms of the aforementioned resolution.

"I would assume that during this short period the Secretary General would get in touch with the parties concerned and endeavour to secure their cooperation. . . ."

Cabot Lodge claimed the floor to say, "The United States likes this Canadian draft resolution very much. We have presented two draft resolutions dealing with the long-range questions . . . and we are not pressing them for a vote tonight. We do think the draft resolution submitted by the Canadian Secretary of State for External Affairs is one that should be acted on promptly . . . because it contains a real hope of meeting the very grave emergency that confronts the world."

At 2.00 A.M. Sunday, November 4, before the British and French governments could send instructions to their delegates, the Assembly voted unexpectedly. Nineteen nations abstained for lack of instructions, and the remaining fifty-seven nations voted in favour. Not one vote was cast against it, not even that of the Soviet Union, which has since sought to evade its financial responsibilities by claiming that it had opposed UNEF [the United Nations Emergency Force]. Arthur Lall delivered all nineteen of his promised votes; but more significantly, the Communist bloc abstained, and for the first time in the crisis the Soviet Union was split from the Afro-Asians. Delegate after delegate walked across the hall to congratulate Pearson, and in the corridors the vote was referred to as one of the most skilfully organized coups in United Nations history.

Discussion guidelines

1. "The negotiations to avert a war at the time of the Suez Crisis in 1956 revealed clearly the national interests and diplomatic skill involved in international diplomacy." Comment.
2. "Canada reached its peak as a peace-keeper in the 1956 Suez drama." How do you account for the decline of Canada's influence as an "honest broker" in international affairs since 1956?
3. When the "crunch" comes, to what extent do you think U.N. negotiations can affect major power decisions? Cite some examples as evidence for your point of view.

Cross references

Soviet-Czech Relations – See-Saw Between Pressure and Reconciliation, page 80
The Fears That Spurred the Russians into Action, page 82
Spheres of influence and Soviet aggression, page 276
Rigidity "the Most Dangerous Aspect of Two-Bloc System", page 278
Peaceful Stalemate! page 324

2

A Powerless U.N.?
from *This Kind of Peace*
by T. R. Fehrenbach

During the first twenty years of its life, the United Nations was never a single being. There were really three different U.N.s, each operating on different planes.

The first U.N. was the order-keeping apparatus designed at Dumbarton Oaks. This was the Security Council and General Assembly, one to provide a form of collective security for free nations, the other a forum against injustice.

It had its teeth drawn almost at once by the Cold War.

The greatest handicap this U.N. suffered from was the determination of many U.N. supporters to saddle it with goals utterly beyond the reach of its vital machinery. It could not arbitrate the Cold War, nor could it prevent American-Soviet conflict if either power were bent upon it. There was no apparatus known or designable by man that could. Nations and peoples and powers exist; they go their own ways; they can sometimes be tempered by reason; but they can be cured of evil spirits only by fire and blood. Recognition of that fact to start with would have been all to the good.

Those who questioned the value of the U.N. as a whole because it could not prevent a major war never understood Dumbarton Oaks or the facts of life. The U.N. could not force the retreat of Communist power a single inch. But then it had never been intended as a Communist-control organization.

The U.N. did not assure collective security. As the British government suggested during the war, and as Churchill pointed out in his great speech at Fulton, security for nations rested upon regional groupings and alliances, NATO, Rio, the Warsaw Pact, and others. The U.N. started as such a grouping, and could have remained one.

When the concept of a United Nations was extended to include most of the nations of the world, collective security within the body became impossible. When, by 1945, the U.N. had ceased to be an alliance, the real alliances that tried to stabilize the world had to move outside it.

There is no such thing as a true balance in nature, and such balances as exist are always changing. The so-called "balance of nature" is always in flux. So is the balance of national power. The balance of power is a basically unstable system, but over the past three hundred years the mind of man has been able to devise nothing better. If Richelieu, Pitt, Metternich, and Talleyrand sought a balance of power, so did Harry Truman and John Kennedy.

In the light of all the above, the U.N. was a failure. But it was still not a total loss. The U.N. could not enforce its will, because it had a divided will built into it. But it could focus attention on dangerous matters. It could, and perhaps at times did, provide a sounding board to prevent a blind stumbling into war. It furnished, as in the Berlin crisis, the faceless, antiseptic rooms in which coldly sensible men could sit together and accomplish face-saving devices.

The first U.N. was worth the dough. It was dangerous only if men put too much faith in it or expected it to bring a millennium or the jubilee.

The second U.N. was the apparatus of the Economic and Social Council. The additions to this Council began during the Second World War, as wartime measures. They continued into the peace and Cold War as international humanitarian programs.

UNESCO, the World Health Organization, the Farm and Agricultural Administration – these were

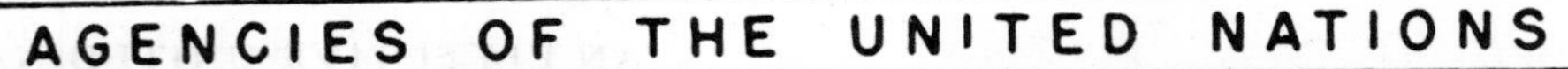

Each country may have 5 delegates, but only 1 vote.

Debates world issues and makes recommendations.

Has 5 permanent members — U.S., Britain, Russia, France, China, plus 10 members elected by Assembly for 2-year terms.

Investigates threats to peace, and can call on UN members to take forceful action against aggressors.

Has 27 members elected by Assembly for 3-year terms.

Works through numerous agencies in effort to improve world living conditions.

Representatives from Big Five nations, plus member countries that govern lands under U.N. control, plus other members elected by Assembly for 3-year terms.

Directs areas under U.N. supervision.

Has 15 judges, all from different countries, elected by Security Council and Assembly for 9-year terms.

Can decide only cases voluntarily submitted to it by nations involved in disputes.

Secretary-General appointed by Assembly, with large staff.

Does office work and makes reports for U.N.

American Observer, Civic Education Service, Washington, D.C.

general wars against poverty, disease, and ignorance. This U.N. carried far more of the seeds of international co-operation than all the lawyers' words in the Charter. It was the only U.N. that could stand proudly and entirely on its own.

This U.N. was hampered and restricted by the Cold War, but had nothing to do with it. It was and is important mainly to the non-European world. It has saved the lives of millions of men, women, and children who would never hear of Berlin.

Noticeably, as the first U.N. seemed to fail its function, the attention of more and more decent men centered on the second. Some came to think and say that this was the real United Nations. It was the one most likely to survive in one form or another.

Yet it was overrated. It could not make decisive change. It could not alter the circumstances, domestic, geographical, cultural, or climatic, that created and continued world poverty or suffering. It could not relieve basic problems; it would never have enough money, men, or, for that matter, the know-how. It treated symptoms. It was a relief program, and it suffered from all the ugly defects a relief program always has. It was almost wholly one-way in direction, from the North Atlantic nations to the others.

The preamble of this U.N. stated, "Wars begin in the minds of men," but its supporters seemed ignorant of the fact that serious wars always have been and always will be beyond the reach of the desperately poor. The poor cannot afford guns. They cannot even afford butter. They are a fester on civilization, but they rarely threaten it. The Germans were rich people. The Soviets, when they began to build rockets, were rich people. The Chinese will be very dangerous only when they have riches, too.

The second U.N. was of enormous humanitarian value; but it could not attack the real sources from which the ills of mankind spring.

The third U.N. was less spectacular than the other two. Yet this last U.N. was the one that over the years would prove most valuable. It was a U.N. that provided a mechanism for settling disputes in the non-Communist world. The East-West argument was not open to negotiation. Most other conflicts were.

This was the U.N. that guaranteed against a stale and sterile world, or the status quo. This U.N. gave the stamp of approval to the changing colonial order.

Before the twentieth century, all nations were born in blood and iron. The existence of the third U.N. could give new and emerging nations certain legal status and approval; membership, not victory in war, was their birth certificate.

The decisions, of course, were not made in New York. They were made in London, Paris, or in the government houses of Africa. But the U.N. helped. In a new and peculiarly effective way, so effective it went almost unnoticed, the apparatus in New York could ratify the outside decisions, by the admission of new states to membership.

This third U.N., also, was the one that provided special military forces for inflamed areas, to stop small wars before the great powers were sucked in.

The ratification and the damping were not always easy. Both always needed the support of at least one of the great powers. When there were emotional factors and indecision, as in Palestine, this third U.N. failed. The one requirement for effectiveness of this third U.N. was that in its functions the great powers never come into confrontation. When they did, as in the first U.N., the mechanism soon broke down.

This was still a U.N. that, even when it worked, could not bring the millennium. It could ratify the orderly removal of power from London to Accra, but it could not make the British go.

Nor could it cure emotional disorders like Egypt's dream of an Arab empire, or Indonesian insistence upon a place in the shade, or the chaos in the Congo.

But without this U.N., the enormous amount of peaceful change that altered the postwar world would have been more difficult.

With the collapse of the European state system and the failure of the projected United Nations, the world was really ruled by three new regional Romes

Miller Services, Toronto

U.N. peace-keeping force policing the ceasefire in the Suez, 1956

(Moscow, Peking, Washington). The agreements at the end of World War II could not prevent each Rome from wanting to be first. Khrushchev dreamed of the Third Rome, and called it Moscow. Mao Tse-tung and Chou En-lai, brooding with the sullen weight of centuries, believed it eventually must be Peking. America's empire was the glittering spread of Western civilization, defended from the capital on the Potomac. America's destiny, which Kennedy said, and Johnson saw, was to mount the Western guard.

In 1965, no single power unit of sufficient strength had emerged. The world went back to empires, and regional solutions, whatever they were called. The U.N. never had a chance to order the world; the U.N. was made meaningless at the start.

Discussion guideline

The United Nations has been referred to as both a "lame duck" and a "dead duck" in an age of rampant nationalism and super power. Considering the opinions expressed in the four excerpts, would you subscribe to either of these labels? Why?

Cross references

The Never-Ending Circle of Nationalism, page 286
Peaceful Stalemate! page 324
The Dangers of Present Trends, page 327

NATIONALISM AND INTERNATIONALISM

The Case for Internationalism

from *Five Ideas That Change the World*
by Barbara Ward

The great contradiction of this century is that we have reached an extreme pitch of national feeling all around the world just at the moment when, from every rational point of view, we have to find ways of progressing beyond nationalism. This point needs great emphasis because, in this field, our reason and our emotion probably do not work in the same direction.

Rationally, we can add up all the reasons why we should be looking towards the creation of a genuine international society, but every single one of us feels the tug of separateness, of nationalism, of ultimate loyalties devoted exclusively to our own community and not concerned with that wider, larger, and admittedly vaguer community of mankind. The natural instinct is to feel united and identified with one's own group, and to forget any wider kinship. We have therefore to rally all that we have of reason and clarity and common sense and look at our world not through a haze of national emotions but see it as it is, in cold, hard reality.

The first fact about our world is that owing to the activities of the scientist, the industrialist, and the technician, it is, in a very real sense, physically one world. We can travel round it in many ways more quickly than our forefathers could travel, say, in Europe or the United States a hundred years ago. We have seen the conquest of space; the airplane is a commonplace, and more and more people are using this means of transport. Yet it is in itself undergoing radical change and the speeds of today

NASA

"When you look down from space, you don't see the boundaries of nations, all you can see are the boundaries between land and water. It is really and truly one world." – James McDivitt, Astronaut are nothing to the supersonic speeds of tomorrow. With each thrust of the new jet engines, our physical closeness is increasing.

And as aircraft increase in size, the cost of travel diminishes. Millions use the air today. Millions more will use it tomorrow. Mobility and accessibility are replacing the old rooted, isolated existence of mankind from one end of the globe to the other.

We are also drawn together by the interconnectedness of our world economy. I need hardly point out that in Ghana the great works of development which we all hope to see accomplished – and which include such promising institutions as the new University – depend directly upon the movements of the world market for cocoa, and on the promise but also on the uncertainties of the export trade.

This is true of Ghana; it is also becoming true of every nation in the world.

To this new proximity we must now add a new and appalling dimension. Even if it is a commonplace, we must try by all means to keep our sense of shock and dismay, for here at least is one idea to which mankind must never become reconciled. This new fact is, of course, that we can destroy ourselves utterly and completely, that we can, by launching a hydrogen war, in all probability put an end to the human species.

This is a totally new risk. Wars in the past have been terrible and wasteful, they have led to the wiping-out of whole civilizations, to the ruin and annihilation of peoples, to destruction beyond name. Yet never, never before could it even be thought that from a war no remnant of humanity would survive. Today, the ending of the human experiment is one of the possibilities of life before us and petty indeed should all our local differences seem compared with the basic challenge of human survival. To the community of conquered space and economic interdependence we have thus added a community of potential destruction. Color, race, class, ideology – these differences vanish as we all stand in our stark, basic equality as mortal men facing the risk of extinction.

These are the realities of our world which no amount of thinking or hoping or believing can turn aside. They are with us; they are the daily bread of our international affairs. Surely it is no more than reasonable to say that priority over every other problem in the world must now be given to achieving the minimum institutions which will enable us not to encompass our own destruction.

But having agreed so far, we have also to admit that the record of humanity thus far is hardly encouraging. Throughout man's checkered history, one common feature has been revealed from his tribal origins down to the present day: that men fight each other, and that war is the oldest, as well as the most savage, institution of mankind. Therefore – and here is another paradox of our century – we have to do away with our oldest institution because of the newest of our discoveries.

Yet the old is rooted in our deepest instincts; above all, in the belief that each group has the right to have its own way. If you do not think that this instinct is deeply rooted, I would implore you to observe any child between the ages of six months and four years, and see the absolute determination with which it pursues its own desires. Those bashings on the nursery floor are the first early signs of the instinct we carry right on into the organization of our adult society – the instinct to have our own way with the things we most want. Organized at the state level with the passion of nationalism behind it – and possibly the ideology as well – we have not a rational institution but a battering-ram of disorderly desires.

In fact, it can be argued that nationalism is to communities what egoism is to human beings. It may destroy us but we cling to it as to our last defense. In our world society we cherish the idea that our own group, our own nation shall be able, in the last resort, to have its own way. Since every other group has the same determination, the ultimate clash is pretty well unavoidable. There is unhappily a certain basic, dreary simplicity about the fact of war, and we can pursue it back to its roots in human nature.

Nevertheless, one of the encouraging signs in the evolution of civilized societies over the last two or three thousand years is that we have, within our domestic society, reached some conclusions about the best methods of preventing lawless violence – which, after all, is what war is. We prevent this violence inside the state by two or three crucial acts of policy. First of all, we give up the right to settle our own disputes by force. Whatever we may think of the rights and the wrongs of our disagreements, we settle them by nonviolent means – by arbitration or through law.

Yet because human nature is frail, and the temptation to knock the other fellow on the head remains very strong, we also accept the necessity of a police force to ensure that neither we nor others revert to private violence in pursuit of our own ends. A force independent of individual influences and desires, linked to the system of judicial control, reinforces our sometimes wavering decision not to take the law into our own hands. It also protects us from anyone else who might succumb to the temptation. These are key institutions in the prevention of private violence within domestic society, and perhaps the greatest effort of imagination we have to make today, when we stand face to face with the risk of possible destruction, is to see that war, too, is private violence – private violence committed on the body of the human race.

In the last hundred years, I would say that one of the great insights of free society in the West has been to realize that there is little hope of a peaceful society if it is not a just and progressive society as well. We have seen that welfare is the prop of justice and that those societies in which civil peace can best be maintained are those in which there is reasonable hope, reasonable stability, and in which parents can look forward to giving their children at least as good a life as they have had themselves or possibly better. In short, a community of well-being within domestic society is one of the soundest underpinnings of social peace.

If, now, we judge our need for international institutions on the basis of domestic experience, it would seem that three kinds of institutions are indispensable – the first to assure peaceful methods of settling disputes, the second to police the legal, peaceful solutions thus obtained and to avert fresh violence, the third to secure minimum conditions of economic well-being. The fact that we do, in some measure, admit the necessity of these institutions is shown by our hesitant steps toward their achievement. We have a United Nations, even though the great Powers' veto enshrines absolutely the principle that "beyond a certain point, I intend to have my way". We have made a first few . . . experiments in international policing, and at least we talk of disarmament, inspection, and control. We have set up a number of international organizations – the World Bank, for instance, or the Children's Fund – which recognize economic problems common to all humanity, irrespective of nationality or culture or race.

These are pointers. They show, perhaps, the direction of our rational convictions.

Discussion guidelines

1. "Internationalism begins at home." Propose some imaginative and practical ways by which you and your fellow students can promote international goodwill.
2. In the light of your reading, how optimistic are you that internationalism will eventually replace nationalism as the chief characteristic of our "Village Planet"? Suggest some reasons to support your opinion.

Cross references

The Never-Ending Circle of Nationalism, page 286
Peaceful Stalemate! page 324

Future Prospects!

"All right, but don't let me catch you around here tomorrow."

What of the future? Are we destined to live in a peaceful world which values humanity and the principles of social democracy? Or are we slipping into a nightmare in which technocratic "Big Brothers" will manipulate human behaviour for their own purposes? Is human society, as we know it, to be ended amid a profusion of mushroom clouds, or to die amid an onslaught of deadly biological weapons? Obviously, no one can be certain of the future; men can only be guided by what they know and sense. Thus, your predictions are valuable if based on a sound assessment of the history of human behaviour. Indeed, your own insight into the future prospects of man will influence your personal political commitment. What kind of world do you want, and what political means will you choose to achieve it?

A POLITICAL LEADER'S VIEWPOINT

Wide World Photo

Political Idealism!

from the Inaugural Address
of John F. Kennedy

[In November 1960, Democratic Senator John F. Kennedy became the youngest President of the United States. Following the example of Franklin D. Roosevelt, he immediately gathered a team of experts (economists, professors, administrators) to help him launch "the new frontier". His inaugural address, given in January 1961, set forth the "new frontier" goals for the United States. The idealism, optimism, and inspirational quality of the address were a reflection of the youthful president as he stepped into office.]

My fellow citizens:

We observe today not a victory of a party but a celebration of freedom – symbolizing an end as well as a beginning – signifying renewal as well as change. For I have sworn before you and Almighty God the same solemn oath our forebears prescribed nearly a century and three quarters ago.

The world is very different now. For man holds in his mortal hands the power to abolish all forms of human poverty and to abolish all forms of human life. And yet the same revolutionary beliefs for which our forebears fought are still at issue around the globe – the beliefs that the rights of man come not from the generosity of the state but from the hand of God.

We dare not forget today that we are the heirs of

the first revolution. Let the word go forth from this time and place, to friend and foe alike, that the torch has been passed to a new generation of Americans – born in this century, tempered by war, disciplined by a hard and bitter peace, proud of our ancient heritage – and unwilling to witness or permit the slow undoing of those human rights to which this nation has always been committed, and to which we are committed today at home and around the world.

Let every nation know, whether it wish us well or ill, that we shall pay any price, bear any burden, meet any hardship, support any friend, or oppose any foe in order to assure the survival and success of liberty.

This much we pledge – and more.

To those old allies whose cultural and spiritual origins we share, we pledge the loyalty of faithful friends. United, there is little we cannot do in a host of new co-operative ventures. Divided, there is little we can do – for we dare not meet a powerful challenge at odds and split asunder.

To those new states whom we now welcome to the ranks of the free, we pledge our word that one form of colonial control shall not have passed away merely to be replaced by a far more iron tyranny. We shall not always expect to find them supporting our view. But we shall always hope to find them strongly supporting their own freedom – and to remember that, in the past, those who foolishly sought to find power by riding on the tiger's back ended up inside.

To those peoples in the huts and villages of half the globe struggling to break the bonds of mass misery, we pledge our best efforts to help them help themselves, for whatever period is required – not because the Communists may be doing it, not because we seek their votes, but because it is right. If the free society cannot help the many who are poor, it cannot save the few who are rich.

To our sister republics south of our border, we offer a special pledge – to convert our good words into good deeds – in a new alliance for progress – to assist free men and free governments in casting off the chains of poverty. But this peaceful revolution of hope cannot become the prey of hostile powers. Let all our neighbors know that we shall join with them to oppose aggression or subversion anywhere in the Americas. And let every other power know that this hemisphere intends to remain the master of its own house.

To that world assembly of sovereign states, the United Nations, our last best hope in an age where the instruments of war have far outpaced the instruments of peace, we renew our pledge of support – to prevent its becoming merely a forum for invective – to strengthen its shield of the new and the weak – and to enlarge the area in which its writ may run.

Finally, to those nations who would make themselves our adversary, we offer not a pledge but a request: that both sides begin anew the quest for peace, before the dark powers of destruction unleashed by science engulf all humanity in planned or accidental self-destruction.

We dare not tempt them with weakness. For only when our arms are sufficient beyond doubt can we be certain beyond doubt that they will never be employed.

But neither can two great and powerful groups of nations take comfort from their present course – both sides overburdened by the cost of modern weapons, both rightly alarmed by the steady spread of the deadly atom, yet both racing to alter that uncertain balance of terror that stays the hand of mankind's final war.

So let us begin anew – remembering on both sides that civility is not a sign of weakness, and sincerity is always subject to proof. Let us never negotiate out of fear. But let us never fear to negotiate

Let both sides explore what problems unite us instead of belaboring those which divide us.

Let both sides, for the first time, formulate serious and precise proposals for the inspection and control of arms – and bring the absolute power to destroy other nations under the absolute control of all nations.

Let both sides join to invoke the wonders of science instead of its terrors. Together let us explore the stars, conquer the deserts, eradicate disease, tap the ocean depths, and encourage the arts and commerce.

Let both sides unite to heed in all corners of the earth the command of Isaiah – to "undo the heavy burdens and to let the oppressed go free".

And if a beachhead of co-operation can be made in the jungles of suspicion, let both sides join in the next task; creating, not a new balance of power, but a new world of law, where the strong are just and the weak secure and the peace preserved forever.

All this will not be finished in the first one hundred days. Nor will it be finished in the first one thousand days, not in the life of this administration, nor even perhaps in our lifetime on this planet. But let us begin.

In your hands, my fellow citizens, more than in mine, will rest the final success or failure of our course. Since this country was founded, each generation of Americans has been summoned to give testimony to its national loyalty. The graves of young Americans who answered the call to service surround the globe.

Now the trumpet summons us again – not as a call to bear arms, though arms we need – not as a call to battle, though embattled we are – but a call to bear the burden of a long twilight struggle, year in and year out, "rejoicing in hope, patient in tribulation" – a struggle against the common enemies of man: tyranny, poverty, disease, and war itself.

Can we forge against these enemies a grand and global alliance, north and south, east and west, that can assure a more fruitful life for all mankind? Will you join in that historic effort?

In the long history of the world, only a few generations have been granted the role of defending freedom in its hour of maximum danger. I do not shrink from this responsibility – I welcome it. I do not believe that any of us would exchange places with any other people or any other generation. The energy, the faith, and the devotion which we bring to this endeavor will light our country and all who serve it – and the glow from that fire can truly light the world.

And so, my fellow Americans: ask not what your country can do for you – ask what you can do for your country.

My fellow citizens of the world: ask not what America will do for you, but what together we can do for the freedom of man.

Finally, whether you are citizens of America or of the world, ask of us here the same high standards of strength and sacrifice that we shall ask of you. With a good conscience our only sure reward, with history the final judge of our deeds, let us go forth to lead the land we love, asking His blessing and His help, but knowing that here on earth God's work must truly be our own.

Discussion guidelines

1. "Kennedy's inaugural address heralded a break with traditional diplomacy in settling international affairs." Suggest specific examples of subsequent American diplomacy to support this statement.
2. "Actions speak louder than words." Did Kennedy's record as a political leader indicate a genuine attempt to realize the goals he eloquently outlined in his address? Cite some evidence from his political record to defend your viewpoint.

Cross references

Spheres of influence and Soviet aggression, page 276
Rigidity "the Most Dangerous Aspect of Two-Bloc System", page 278
The Confrontation in Cuba, page 281
"Was no other choice", page 285

A NOVELIST'S VIEWPOINT

Controlling the Mind

from *Brave New World*
by Aldous Huxley

[First published in 1932, *Brave New World* was one of a number of prophetic novels written before World War II which offered a picture of man's future world. The excerpt from the novel describes a tour through one section of the Central London Hatchery and Conditioning Centre.]

Fifty yards of tiptoeing brought them to a door which the Director cautiously opened. They stepped over the threshold into the twilight of a shuttered dormitory. Eighty cots stood in a row against the wall. There was a sound of light regular breathing and a continuous murmur, as of very faint voices remotely whispering.

A nurse rose as they entered and came to attention before the Director.

"What's the lesson this afternoon?" he asked.

"We had Elementary Sex for the first forty minutes," she answered. "But now it's switched over to Elementary Class Consciousness."

The Director walked slowly down the long line of cots. Rosy and relaxed with sleep, eighty little boys and girls lay softly breathing. There was a whisper under every pillow. The D.H.C. halted and, bending over one of the little beds, listened attentively.

"Elementary Class Consciousness, did you say? Let's have it repeated a little louder by the trumpet."

At the end of the room a loud-speaker projected from the wall. The Director walked up to it and pressed a switch.

". . . all wear green," said a soft but very distinct voice, beginning in the middle of a sentence, "and Delta children wear khaki. Oh no, I don't want to play with Delta children. And Epsilons are still worse. They're too stupid to be able to read or write. Besides, they wear black, which is such a beastly colour. I'm so glad I'm a Beta."

There was a pause; then the voice began again.

"Alpha children wear grey. They work much harder than we do, because they're so frightfully clever. I'm really awfully glad I'm a Beta, because I don't work so hard. And then we are much better than the Gammas and Deltas. Gammas are stupid. They all wear green, and Delta children wear khaki. Oh no, I *don't* want to play with Delta children. And Epsilons are still worse. They're too stupid to be able . . ."

The Director pushed back the switch. The voice was silent. Only its thin ghost continued to mutter from beneath the eighty pillows.

"They'll have that repeated forty or fifty times more before they wake; then again on Thursday, and again on Saturday. A hundred and twenty times three times a week for thirty months. After which they go on to a more advanced lesson."

Roses and electric shocks, the Khaki of Deltas and a whiff of asafœtida – wedded indissolubly before the child can speak. But wordless conditioning is crude and wholesale; cannot bring home the finer distinctions, cannot inculcate the more complex courses of behaviour. For that there must be words, but words without reason. In brief, hypnopædia.

"The greatest moralizing and socializing force of all time."

The students took it down in their little books. Straight from the horse's mouth.

Once more the Director touched the switch.

". . . so frightfully clever," the soft, insinuating, indefatigable voice was saying. "I'm really awfully glad I'm a Beta, because . . ."

Not so much like drops of water, though water, it is true, can wear holes in the hardest granite; rather, drops of liquid sealing-wax, drops that adhere, incrust, incorporate themselves with what they fall on, till finally the rock is all one scarlet blob.

"Till at last the child's mind *is* these suggestions, and the sum of the suggestions *is* the child's mind. And not the child's mind only. The adult's mind too – all his life long. The mind that judges and desires and decides – made up of these suggestions. But all these suggestions are *our* suggestions!" The Director almost shouted in his triumph. "Suggestions from the State."

Discussion guideline

(a) Present evidence from the current scene that confirms Aldous Huxley's 1932 predictions.
(b) Should, and can, these tendencies be resisted? Support your viewpoint by supplying specific illustrations.

Cross references

Men Need Rulers, page 14
Democracy in the Modern World, page 125
The Individual (the entire section), page 131

A POET'S VIEWPOINT

And It Shall Come to Pass . . .

And it shall come to pass in the last days, that the mountain of the LORD's house shall be established in the top of the mountains, and shall be exalted above the hills; and all nations shall flow unto it.

And many people shall go and say, Come ye, and let us go up to the mountain of the LORD, to the house of the God of Jacob; and he will teach us of his ways, and we will walk in his paths: for out of Zion shall go forth the law, and the word of the LORD from Jerusalem.

And he shall judge among the nations, and shall rebuke many people: and they shall beat their swords into plowshares, and their spears into pruning hooks: nation shall not lift up sword against nation, neither shall they learn war any more.

Isaiah 2: 2-4

The Hydrogen Dog and the Cobalt Cat

The Hydrogen Dog and the Cobalt Cat
Side by side in the Armory sat.
Nobody thought about fusion or fission,
Everyone spoke of their peacetime mission,
Till somebody came and opened the door.
There they were, in a neutron fog,
The Codrogen Cat and the Hybalt Dog;
They mushroomed up with a terrible roar –
And Nobody Never was there – Nomore.

FREDERICK WINSOR

AN ECONOMIST'S VIEWPOINT

Peaceful Stalemate!
from *The Village Planet*
by Barbara Ward

There are rather more possibilities for the future than might appear just on the record of where we are. And I would like to take examples from the three fields of the rule of law, the general welfare, and this question of the acceptance of diversity within unity. Now in each of these three fields, tentatively, uncertainly, but nonetheless clearly, there are examples of the human race behaving a little more sensibly than it did at the beginning of this century.

You may say this is odd, when you think of the possibility of wars of national liberation in heaven knows how many places. How on earth can you say that on the question of the rule of law we are doing rather better? As always, we must remember that there is the United Nations. It is at the moment no more, possibly, than the tribute which vice pays to virtue. In other words, it is there because the states uneasily know that sovereignty is not enough, even though they have not quite gone so far as to give that sovereignty up in any measure. But nonetheless it is there – an instrument working better than the League of Nations it superseded.

The mere fact of the atomic risk is producing a new moderation and new sense that ultimately things can no longer be changed by successful violence. That, I think, is the meaning of the twenty-year stalemate within which we are operating now. I think the point at which it began was in Berlin, because in the Berlin airlift which countered Stalin's Berlin blockade, you have the working of a new approach to international politics. . . . What I think it really meant was that people suddenly realized as they looked over that ghastly abyss on the margins of a nuclear Armageddon that you could not go on in the old way. I think Berlin is a very interesting example of this. You had at the time what we would now call "hawks" saying, "Stalin has thrown down the gauntlet. Send in a western division! Blast your way into Berlin." Then you had what I now suppose would be called the "doves" say, "Tricky. No, no. Berlin is much too exposed. We had better withdraw."

What was the solution? The solution in fact was a middle of the road solution, the airlift which, while not doing open challenge, also suggested that the Western powers were going to stay firm. After it had gone on for eighteen months, with a couple of whispered conversations in the corridors of the U.N., a negotiated stalemate was worked out.

And the point is that everybody got back to exactly where they were before. There was no change whatsoever, and there isn't to this day. If you look at every one of the major crises that have emerged since that airlift, they have always ended where they started. Like Cuba, for instance, where you end up with Russian missiles out but Castro is still there and that was exactly as it was before. You fight a war for two years in Korea, you end up with everybody on exactly the same line as they were before. And I think the logic of the Viet-nam war, provided it can be de-escalated, is exactly the same, and that is to end up on the seventeenth parallel with two separate states, which is exactly where you were before. And again similarly in the Middle East if you can get a situation in which the Arabs will accept that they do not change the status quo by force, which means giving up continual belligerency, then an Israel withdrawal to the frontiers they had before and an Arab's acceptance of the fact of Israel will be merely a reinforcement of where it all started.

Now the reason for the stalemate is quite simply that no one can afford to change anything finally by violence in a world which includes the nuclear weapon. You may say the stalemate does not amount to a peace. But consider the alternative. It is very much better than escalating war, and conceivably it can be the basis upon which something nearer to an international rule of law can in fact be based.

Let us for one moment push some of these situations further forward. It is perfectly conceivable that if you can get a stalemate established between the two Vietnams, you could combine it, long term, with an internationalization and a neutralization of this whole area which inevitably is in dispute between great powers, simply because this is the nature of great powers' influence. You could place this area under some kind of international policing and international control (at which we nibble, you know, with our control commission of which Canada is a member, at which we nibble with the idea of the international development of the Mekong River, at which we nibble again with suggestions that if the status quo could be preserved and neutralized then there would be great funds for development). We

Miller Services, Toronto

In 1968, in retaliation for the sinking of an Israeli warship, Israel destroyed an Egyptian refinery. An Israeli officer is shown here looking across the Suez Canal while the refinery burns. Is a stalemate possible in this sort of situation?

are feeling our way around this situation. Certainly the stalemate is a position from which you can begin, whereas an escalating war is one from which you cannot begin.

Or take again the Middle East. If you could get an acceptance of the existence of Israel and at the same time, an acceptance by Israel that these are the frontiers she must abide by, a neutralization of this area where already there is an element of U.N. control is not inconceivable. If you could get this acceptance formalized into a large neutralization of this area, so that neither for the great powers – nor indeed for any of other powers – was it an area in which people fished in troubled waters, but on the contrary recognized it as an international area under international supervision, once again you would have edged human society a little further towards a situation in which disputes are not settled by violence.

If you think that taking out these areas of maximum disturbance and trying to put in some structure of international policing is a very moderate way of beginning the rule of law, I would remind you that this is how the rule of law actually began. One of the first societies in the semi-modern world to create this kind of structure was Britain under the Plantagenets. How did they begin? They did not begin with an absolutely full-scale legal system, telling the barons to behave. They knew at that time you could not tell the barons to behave, any more than at this moment we could tell our two biggest barons in America and Russia to behave. But what they did establish under King Henry II was the concept of the "King's peace" which applied to certain trading routes, to certain areas of asylum.

Maybe we could establish the King's peace in those areas of maximum disturbance and hope that the areas of created peace spread little by little by way of disarmament, by way of limited agreements gradually spreading to wider ones, the kind of agreement which has already been reached on Antarctica, that no one will use it for warlike purposes. Another area where we might get agreement is the sea – that it shall remain international and, as we begin to farm fish, we will not push our territorial limits out two hundred miles and begin creating territorial sovereignties on this so-far free and open element. This is another field in which we could organize a legal structure for mankind. Another whole field is outer space. There is already an Outer Space Convention and Treaty by which we do not use it to shoot each other up. Maybe having decided not to shoot each other up in outer space, we might apply this very same idea to inner space.

In other words, do not let us despair of the possibility of using beginnings of order to extend to wider areas until finally we even bring into the net the biggest of all the bull elephants, which are those vast societies Russia, America, in the future possibly China and possibly India. It is not a totally despairing situation. Over the last twenty years there is some evidence of tremendous restraint springing from fear of the atom bomb and a certain underlying pressure towards organizing the areas of maximum pressure and bringing them under some kind of international control.

I can't say that this is going to go rapidly. In fact I might be completely wrong – we may indeed be going to blow ourselves up. But I do nonetheless discern certain changes in the way great powers look at their relationships which seem to me at least reasonable to throw in on the side of a moderate optimism.

Discussion guidelines

1. Why are stalemates important? Give specific illustrations as evidence.
2. "In this century, the policy of containment has had one major flaw: its aim has been stalemate. To keep the game going has demanded that no one win big, but history has proven that stalemates are not the answer to peace." Argue this point of view.

Cross references

A Meaningful Voice? page 296
Negotiators at Work, page 304
The Case for Internationalism, page 312

SCIENTIFIC AND MILITARY VIEWPOINTS

The Dangers of Present Trends

from *Unless Peace Comes*
edited by Nigel Calder

[This selection summarizes the views of fifteen internationally known scientific and military experts on new possibilities for waging war. These range from the weapons and strategies we now have, to devices like psychic poisons and environment controls which seem just as improbable today as jet planes would have seemed sixty years ago. And yet, are they really so far-fetched?]

The weapons discussed range from some that exist already, through others under development or plainly [possible], to some that may seem far-fetched. Right or wrong, these last must represent the weapons of the more distant future about which we can only guess – knowing that unforeseeable discoveries or inventions are likely to generate even stranger military applications. For each weapon that seems familiar and containable, others rise up threatening to defy [control]; for every problem, generated by the military rivalries between nations, that attracts the attention of statesmen, others are looming scarcely noticed.

Even without the introduction of novel scientific principles or devices into warfare, technical improvement of "conventional" weapons, using projectiles, high-explosives, and armour, is increasing their power to kill and to devastate. The chief reason is that the use of radar and other target sensors, of proximity fuses and of computers for fire control, greatly enhances the accuracy of each gun shot or missile round. Such techniques can probably deny a battlefield to infantry, deny the air to manned aircraft, and deny the sea to surface ships – unless counter-measures can frustrate the electronic systems. No one knows just how effective the competing techniques will be and, if a conventional "great war" were to break out between well-equipped nations in the future, it would be what General Beaufre calls a "truly enormous experiment". It could easily degenerate into bloody attrition worse than that of the two World Wars.

Such a major conventional war is in any case made improbable by the existence of nuclear weapons. Swift attacks, [begun] by greatly superior forces and achieving their purpose within a few days, seem to be politically and militarily the only effective style remaining for conventional war. Against poorly equipped but well-organized guerrillas, on the other hand, the most sophisticated weapons systems may succeed only in "hitting air", and serve merely to postpone an [unavoidable] political settlement.

Professor Dedijer takes the view that new weapons scarcely affect the principles of guerrilla warfare: guerrillas have always been at a disadvantage in firepower and they make it their business to be absent when a massive attack is launched against them. Dedijer characterizes guerrilla warfare as a politically motivated form of resistance in under-developed countries, nationalistic in nature and directed against foreign influences in the rule of the guerrilla's own country. If it matches the aspirations of the general population, it will tend to prosper and the only plausible strategy against well-organized guerrillas involves long and costly attrition in infantry engagements – destroying an idea by killing all those who hold it.

Here is the "poor man's power", the means by which under-privileged people can, when they feel driven to it, confront modern military forces with a good chance of success. With the poor of the under-developed countries tending to become poorer as populations explode, and with continuing interference by great powers in the affairs of nations within their "spheres of influence", the prospect is of an endless series of guerrilla wars, particularly in Latin America, Southeast Asia, and parts of

Africa. The only way of averting such an appalling future, in Dedijer's view, is to remove the causes of social unrest, by massive aid and political reform.

The trend with which Sir John Cockcroft is chiefly concerned is the acquisition of nuclear weapons by countries not already possessing them – leading to greater likelihood of nuclear war breaking out, somewhere, between a pair of nations. The development of usable nuclear weapons and of their means of delivery is an expensive business, but within the resources of several nations, at least. For the manufacture of A-bombs, the cost of plutonium is really very low and the construction of nuclear power stations in many countries provides a ready-made source of nuclear explosive if international safeguards should fail or be disregarded.

Besides the existing nuclear powers, seven nations (Canada, West Germany, India, Italy, Japan, Spain, and Sweden) will have the potential to produce more than 100 kilograms of plutonium per year, by 1971. Cockcroft expresses anxiety about a possible chain reaction, in which the acquisition of nuclear weapons by one new country would provoke other nations to follow suit. For example, if three nations made nuclear weapons for the first time in the 1970s, ten might do so in the 1980s and thirty in the 1990s.

At present, the construction of H-bombs, rather than A-bombs, depends on uranium-235 as the triggering explosive, and the preparation of this material involves very costly and cumbersome gas diffusion plants. As Dr. Inglis points out, the development of ways of obtaining uranium-235 more easily, or of using plutonium as a trigger, could greatly [increase] the problem of nuclear proliferation.

The laws of physics being what they are, Inglis believes with some confidence that there is no radically new principle for nuclear weapons, to supplement the existing choice of fission and fusion bombs. Nor does he think that there is likely to be much extension of the choice of the materials used

Miller Services, Toronto

The nuclear reactor at Trombay, India, was built with the help of Canadian engineers, and Canada contributed $9,400,000 to its construction. To what degree can Canada be held responsible for giving India the ability to produce atom bombs?

as nuclear explosives – for example, he dismisses the idea of a californium bullet as a "confusing fantasy". Existing nuclear weapons are as destructive as any military man could ask for. Variations and technical improvements are possible, of course, and even the hypothetical "doomsday machine", which would obliterate all life on Earth, is not technically absurd – although it is almost certainly strategically absurd. A doomsday machine could plausibly be a series of extremely dirty H-bombs, primed with cobalt. On the other hand, attempts will no doubt continue to make very "clean" H-bombs, which do not rely for detonation on the explosion of a fission bomb – fission products being the major source of fall-out. But on the basis of present-day physics Inglis is sceptical about the practicability of a fission-free H-bomb.

The threat that Inglis sees comes not from new kinds of nuclear weapons but from a multiplication of the existing types of weapons, so that the world's nuclear arsenals will reach a fantastic level of destructive potential. Here he sees the chief risk in a U.S.-Soviet missile race, following the current development of tolerably practicable anti-ballistic missiles (ABMs). This anxiety is shared by Cockcroft, who points out that, at the present time when efforts are being made to limit the spread of nuclear weapons, a responsibility falls upon "nuclear powers" to [cut back] their own armaments.

The ABM will use a nuclear explosion to destroy an oncoming ballistic missile. Professor Stratton discusses the ABM from a technical viewpoint and emphasizes both the very great cost of even a partially effective system and also the very fast response it would need.

If developments in anti-aircraft missiles go as Stratton thinks they may, manned strike aircraft will be kept so far from their targets that they may be effective only as carriers of "stand-off" bombs; in that case, the advantages of pilot judgment in tactical situations would be severely [limited]. The development of aircraft, missiles, and spacecraft for military purposes may be subject to important changes in guidance systems, using the laser. There may also be novel means of destruction; Stratton does not rule out the development of a laser "death ray" and he speculates about an explosive agent intermediate in force between high-explosive and nuclear weapons.

The possibilities for satellites carrying H-bombs, for surveillance satellites, and for satellite interception imply a serious risk of a complex and expensive arms race in space, involving unmanned satellites and manned spacecraft. The fact that bombs parked in orbit will be very difficult to intercept, once they have been "called down" to their targets, gives a strong incentive for the development of systems for inspecting and destroying hostile satellites while they remain in their predictable orbits.

Stratton is alarmed by the way automatic systems designed and programmed by engineers may replace the political and military judgment of national leaders. He also emphasizes the great scope for error and false assumption that exists in the complicated studies needed to choose aerospace weapons a decade in advance of their deployment in service.

The ways in which the use of computers in intelligence and control systems is revolutionizing the character of international relations and of war provide the main theme of Professor Wheeler's [views]. Already the Commander-in-Chief of a super-power can – indeed, is required to – monitor events in all troubled areas of the world. Because of the speed and sensitivity of the systems, local incidents are known instantly and decisions are made at the highest levels. One consequence is that swift military "solutions" come to seem more appropriate than old-fashioned diplomacy. But in the future more refined systems will evolve, until not only are events known instantly but they can be anticipated by deduction from masses of computer-processed intelligence data. The logical consequence will be pre-emptive strikes to forestall action by the adversary. The men who have to implement a decision to strike will, at such a stage, be simply worse informed than the computer system, so that they may be obliged to follow its proposals. It is in that sense that computers may come to govern human affairs, and lead us into war.

Besides the computer, another radical development in human affairs during the remaining years of this century will be the exploitation, for civilian purposes, of the resources of the deep ocean. At the same time, developments in naval submersibles, including already existing nuclear weapons systems such as Polaris, are creating a new three-dimensional battleground of the greatest strategic importance. As Professor Nierenberg describes the trends, we must expect three concurrent hazards to peace: (1) attempts by nations to appropriate large volumes of the oceans for commercial or strategic purposes, (2) intensive development of undersea and anti-submarine weapons favouring or compromising the submarine-borne strategic missile systems, and (3) an intermingling of civilian and military activities, in the same stretches of ocean, which can only tend to generate friction and suspicion.

The naval technology [foreseen] includes both the development of operational craft capable of reaching the greatest ocean depths and the deployment throughout the oceans of automatic sensors providing continuous surveillance of activities at all depths. Although the submarine and the surface-to-surface missile will be so effective in the future that the sea lanes will be denied to all conventional shipping, the balance will be restored by the advent of big surface-effect vessels related to the hovercraft. These will be capable of speeds approaching 200 kilometres per hour, both for carrying cargoes and for naval purposes, including anti-submarine operations. The future of the aircraft carrier is put in doubt, even in a surface-effect version, by vertical take-off aircraft and an "oceanographic" aircraft of extremely long endurance, which Nierenberg [pictures]. We must also expect the creation of bases, in fixed positions on the sea: floating air bases anchored at strategic points around the world and submarine bases sited far from land at the edge of the continental shelf.

An indirect contribution of the oceans to future arsenals is suggested by Professors Fetizon and Magat, who note that certain fishes, notably the Tora Fugu, produce deadly poison. The potency of chemical weapons is probably greatly underestimated in current thinking about future warfare. Even if all research had stopped – which it certainly has not – military forces would still have the extremely effective "nerve gases" developed by the Germans during the Second World War. Against these gases, which can be absorbed through the skin and which kill by the interruption of the natural nerve control muscle, protection is very difficult for armies and virtually impossible for civilians.

Although lethal gases have not been used very widely since the First World War, other forms of chemical warfare have been perfected. For incendiary purposes, napalm is likely to continue in service in the decades ahead. The Vietnam war has brought wide-spread use of anti-vegetation poisons developed from weed-killers. For very large-scale destruction of vegetation or crops, heat from H-bombs is likely to be more effective; alternatively, chemical warfare in the future may include agents released by rocket in the ozone layer of the atmosphere which create a temporary "hole" in this layer. As the layer serves to protect [earth-bound] life from the intense ultra-violet radiation of the sun, its local obliteration, by chemical means, could result in fatal "sunburn" for all vegetation and exposed animals in the underlying region.

The chief current development in chemical weapons which Fetizon and Magat discuss concerns the "psychic poisons". Agents are already known which can have profound effects on the human mind, and new ones are being sought for medical purposes. LSD is the best known of the existing agents, but other types are also available for study. Typically, LSD given in controlled doses induces a state of temporary madness such as could make soldiers throw away their arms or sit down and weep like babies. Fetizon and Magat strongly challenge, however, the suggestion from enthusiasts for psychic weapons that here is a humane, non-lethal means of waging war. They point out that if most people in the target population are to receive effective doses, many will receive large over-doses, which will cause permanent insanity or death. Moreover, the military administration of such drugs to armies or civilian populations in the midst of their normal business will create horrific chaos in which many people will die.

Microbiological weapons have even more fearful consequences for human targets, possibly exceeding the killing power of all-out thermo-nuclear warfare. Professor Hedén describes how a cloud of infective micro-organisms could strike down by disease the human inhabitants of a whole province, or ruin their crops. Such weapons can be released swiftly from spraying vehicles over large areas or [secretly] by saboteurs against selected targets such as military staffs, crews of ships, or big public assemblies.

Biological weapons are easy to make and they may be especially tempting for nations unable to develop nuclear striking forces. Small groups of individuals may be able to upset the strategic balance. On the other hand, advanced microbiology may evolve novel forms of disease for military purposes. Defence against biological attack will be peculiarly difficult – most of all in the developing countries which lack good public health facilities.

Biological attack may, in practice, be indistinguishable from epidemics – and vice versa – so that [charges] of biological attack may become frequent and it will be hard to tell whether they are well founded. Reprisals can lead to an escalation of the intensity and virulence of the attacks. It will scarcely be possible to confine the diseases so evoked to the target areas. The very young, the very old, and the sick will be especially vulnerable to biological warfare.

The impact on weapons systems of electronics, and of compact computers in particular, may manifest itself in bizarre robots like the "walking bomb". Professor Thring forecasts the development of unmanned, expendable, and practically unstoppable tanks on legs, capable of finding their own way slowly but surely to their targets. Such a delivery system would introduce a novel psychological factor into the use of thermo-nuclear weapons, by allowing a rather long period for second thoughts between the launching of an attack and the first explosions.

More generally, robot foot-soldiers, aircraft, and submersibles may displace men from the conduct of the battle once and for all, as such computer-controlled systems come to surpass men in tactical skill and reliability. Once a decision to exclude men had been taken, the traditional role of infantry units in controlling ground might reassert itself even in situations where men simply could not survive. Important limitations on the design and performance of aircraft and submersibles disappear when the crews' requirements for comfort and survival no longer figure in the calculations. By such developments some purposeless loss of life among servicemen may be avoided, but human populations will still be the targets of the robot strategic weapons.

The possibilities of geophysical warfare, aimed at producing subtle or catastrophic modifications in the condition of the earth or its atmosphere, are largely [guess-work]. Economic [collapse] by drought might be brought about by systematic seeding of clouds in a prevailing airstream, to remove moisture. Hurricanes might be guided towards an opponent's coastline. Remote triggering of a major earthquake is not entirely incredible, nor is the creation of an artificial tsunami (tidal wave) by tipping loose material off the edge of the continental shelf. As an extreme form of geophysical warfare, one can imagine deliberate inauguration of a

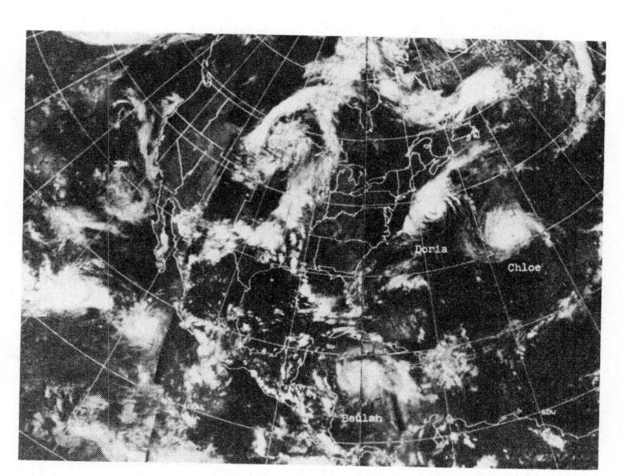

NASA

Three hurricanes shown in a photo taken from a weather satellite. Already, weather satellites are able to track the courses of hurricanes. Does this mean that weather control, and the harnessing of storms for war purposes, is possible some time in the future?

new Ice Age, by interference with the Antarctic ice cap.

[Professor] MacDonald also points out that human mental performance may be subject to geophysical influences. Although he admits that his scheme for timing lightning flashes to disturb people on the other side of the world is far-fetched, he thinks it very probable that environmental means of controlling behaviour will emerge within the next few decades.

The trends in weapons development already carry psychological implications. Professor Klineberg expresses a personal revulsion for the "psychic poisons" but he notes that this may be professional bias of one who has been concerned with mental illness; no really objective definition of "human" or "inhuman" weapons seems possible. On the other hand, the automation of warfare and the possibilities for attack from great distances must tend to dehumanize military operations and whittle away any remaining sympathy for the sufferings of one's enemies.

Knowing of the range of human mental reactions, and of the world's past quota of pathological leaders, Klineberg would require that candidates for public office be subject to psychological examination, but he has no hope that this will soon be done. He fears that new Hitlers may come to control nuclear weapons or other new systems.

Klineberg also points to the association between personal feelings of insecurity and nationalism – the finding of security in national identity and its irrational corollaries of racism and chauvinism. But new, frightening weapons may add to personal insecurity, thus heightening nationalist feelings and encouraging the further development and manufacture of weapons. The circle is complete and promises a grim future for mankind, unless irrational fears and apathy can be replaced by constructive, reasoning action in response to fears that are all too well-grounded in the facts.

Mr. Noel-Baker testifies to the possibility of remaining hopeful that the nations will agree on general disarmament and thus come to restrain the application of science to destructive purposes. . . . [He] is less concerned with the scientific and technological aspects of possible new weapons than with the phenomena of the arms race and rapid military innovation, which have a continuous history from 1870 to the present. . . . As long as men want ingenious ways of killing or dominating one another, the natural world, through the medium of science, will provide them. The same ingenuity and knowledge of nature can be applied quite otherwise, to creating a healthy, pleasant, and exciting environment for all mankind. But the worst forebodings will surely be fulfilled, and even the most modest visions of a better world will be smashed, if present military tendencies continue. Our loss will be a double one – both of what we have and of what we might have made – unless peace comes.

Discussion guidelines

1. From your own reading, supplement the weapons picture of the future as presented by the fifteen experts.
2. Resolved that: "In a major war, the use of biological and chemical weapons is more probable than thermo-nuclear devices." Debate.
3. To what extent do you think the predictions justify Calder's conclusion that "the worst forebodings will surely be fulfilled, and even the most modest visions of a better world will be smashed, if present military tendencies continue"?

Cross references

The First Atomic Bombing, page 256
Alliances Don't Work, page 269
The Munich Agreement, page 269
The Necessities of War, page 273

A HUMORIST'S VIEWPOINT

I Like Now
from *Man's Future and Who Needs It?*
by Eric Nicol

Whenever I get a little depressed with the way the world's going – which everybody seems to agree is downhill on a bobsled – I like to read the prediction by some scientists of what the world will be like in the future. The latest of these predictions, made by Dr. Wilton Krogman, anthropologist at the University of Pennsylvania, has been a real consolation to me. I think Dr. Krogman deserves a rousing vote of thanks.

According to the news story before me, Dr. Krogman predicts that the man of the future will transmit "thought waves" from a super-power brain, eat pre-digested food, and have roughly the shape of a parking meter.

Dr. Krogman is looking ahead to what man will be like five million years from now. This alone is enough to reassure me. Sometimes I wonder if anybody will be able to identify man after next Friday. Yet here is Dr. Krogman looking ahead five million years and seeing us still running around, on flat feet, he says, and living for an average of 140 years. Now, that's what I call comforting. On flat feet. For 140 years. Yes, it's good to be alive – now.

Let's take the first thing that Dr. Krogman sees in the world of the future – people who communicate by mind-reading instead of words. He explains this thus:

"A better way to put it is 'thought waves' which can be projected through space much as radio impulses are today. The electrical discharges in brain tissue – today called 'brain-waves' – will be so powerful that the brain will be both a sending and receiving mechanism."

I don't want to sound like a prototype or anything, but I've had some experience with this mind-reading business. As have most men, with members of the opposite sex. Right in our time we have women walking around who can pick up a brain-wave and make it the basis for a hit on the head. There are a lot of bugs in this type of communication that will have to be worked out before it can be safely made available to the general public.

Transmitting thought waves like radio impulses, instead of using words, may make for a quiet type of conversation, but static remains a problem, and there will always be those who object to having their *tête-à-tête* made subject to C.B.C. regulations. All in all, though words can get you into a peck of trouble, I think they may be less dangerous in the long run than trying to pick up a pretty blonde with a weak signal.

Dr. Krogman also raises some doubt as to how pretty the blonde of five million years hence will be. While the brain is growing in kilowatts, he says, the stomach will be shrinking, owing to the trend towards food concentrates instead of bulk, with all the necessary calories, minerals, proteins, and fats being packed into small tablets.

"Body build will be linear and slender," says Dr. Krogman, "and the front-to-back dimension will be especially reduced."

In other words, which Dr. Krogman has avoided using, probably for fear of causing a panic, the figure of the future will have fewer curves. The shrunken stomach will give people more or less the profile of a hornet, and probably much the same kind of temper. People that have to make a meal of small tablets are likely to carry a sting in their tail.

"The need for a digestive tract will lessen," says Dr. Krogman. "The stomach may atrophy to the size of today's appendix."

English people who underwent the austerity period will be familiar with this development. Many English folk had their stomachs shrunk to exactly the size necessary to hold a small sausage made of sawdust. This kind of atrophy never really caught on in England, however, and stomachs are now ballooning again over there, I believe, though not as aboriginally as on this continent.

Besides having a peanut gut, we shall terminate differently. "Feet will become flat," says Dr. Krogman, "more or less circular bases for legs." Well, I guess we've been headed for the lamp-stand base ever since we gave up swinging from trees by our toes. This is a shame, in a way, I have always admired a high arch in a foot, and a neat heel. In fact they have caused my own toes to curl at times. Now we are to lose all of these – arch, heel, toes, and curling, in favour of flat discs, sort of dishpan feet.

I don't suppose this will bother anybody five million years from now, any more than the absence of a tail dampens our estimate of beauty today. The plate-footed girl will knock a man off his circular bases just as easily as ever. But five million years doesn't seem like too long to get used to the idea.

Naturally one man's atrophy is another man's progress. Five million years from now they will be digging us up and saying we lived fifty million years ago and slid around in slime. "Look at the funny old atomic man," they'll say, dragging their kids around the museum. "He used to have to wear a belt a yard long to keep his pants up, instead of a paper-clip the way you do."

If it's *my* restored skeleton they're pointing at, chances are I'll be in no shape to answer the wisecracks they're thought-waving about my bay window and oblong feet, so that now seems as good a time as any to take a dislike to them. It's probably not a nice thing to say about your children's children, to the tenth power, but I think Dr. Krogman's man of the future is a bit of a goon. I wouldn't be surprised if all this business about having a brain discharging thought impulses, instead of using words, is just an act. The poor boob probably just hasn't got anything to say. These deep, silent types half the time are clods with just enough sense to clam up.

If this is the man, and woman, of the future – this flat-footed pill-gulper – I'd say that evolution will have taken a wrong turning someplace. Evolution was doing fine, up to me. I'd hate to see man go off at a tangent and finish up in some dead-end like the dodo bird and the rest of the flat-footed crowd.

But Dr. Krogman remains optimistic. While the mind is waving its thoughts and the body is shrinking, he says, there will be "a great change in the tempo of life . . . more thinking and less moving. . . . We will live slower as we live longer."

"More thinking and less moving" fits in with my own notion of the good life, but Dr. Krogman doesn't say what a man can think about for 140 years. Right now we spend a good deal of time thinking about food, or at least I do – looking forward to it, eating it, and digesting it – but you can't ponder a pill for long. With no words uttered, and everybody sitting around trying to think of something to think about, the world is going to look like the main lounge of a summer resort on a wet day.

Little wonder that we shall live slower as we live longer. With 140 years to go we'll be doing everything in slow motion to make it last longer. I can see a man spending a whole evening crossing his legs. This is progress?

I asked this question in another article recently, and a reader wrote a letter in reply, saying, "You have nothing to worry about, regarding life thousands of years from now. Man has a glorious future. That is, these are his last days. The end of the world is here."

It's nice of people to write you an encouraging letter like that. It gives you a certain confidence. You feel that even if man can't win, at least he has more than one way of losing.

One of these alternatives is space travel, which Dr. Krogman also touches upon. Careful selection, he tells us, may produce a breed of men with low oxygen needs, so they'll be well adapted for space travel.

The stomach was already shot – now here go the lungs. We'll produce a strain of men who are only comfortable on the moon. Presumably, careful selection will also provide men with padded shoulders and no teeth, for football players; champion swimmers with two sets of flippers; and bat-faced girls adapted to the perpetual gloom of the movie usherette.

What happens when a space-man with low oxygen needs falls in love with a lady glass-blower who is practically all oxygen needs? Dr. Krogman doesn't say, but I, for one, can see careful selection coming to a sticky end if it doesn't watch out.

All the more reason, then, to be pleased with the man of today, funny old crude us. The past always looks better than it was, whether of a people or a person. The future always sounds more exciting than it will be. Yet we make a career of running down the present.

Despite such terrors as the H-bomb and television, how many of us would accept an invitation to be shunted into the past, even back to a hundred years ago? Very few, I'll wager. And how many would care to be transported – lock, stock, and belly – into Dr. Krogman's world of the future? Even fewer, I'm sure.

The fact is, we're best adapted to right now. The person who is ahead of his time, the genius, is likely to have a miserable innings. I know several people with flat feet who live on pills and think they belong to tomorrow. They aren't at all happy. And the person who is behind his time is as badly off, since life has a way of putting the boot to stragglers.

Once again, therefore, I'd like to thank Dr. Krogman and all those other eminent men of science whose knowledge and vision provide us with these horrifying glimpses of the future. I believe they are performing a great service to mankind.

© *The Toronto Star*, with permission of Duncan Macpherson

Who's Who

ALLEN, William Sheridan (*historian*). Born in Evanston, Illinois; educated at universities in the United States and Germany; currently Associate Professor of History at Wayne State University; published *The Nazi Seizure of Power* (1965); has studied underground resistance to the Third Reich.

ARDREY, Robert (*playwright and novelist*) (1908-). Born in Chicago, Illinois; studied at University of Chicago (Natural Sciences); during World War II worked for the Office of War Information in New York; has travelled extensively in Africa and, partly as a result of his experiences and observations there, published *African Genesis* (1961) and *Territorial Imperative* (1966).

ATTLEE, Clement Richard, 1st Earl (*politician*) (1883-1964). Born in England; educated at Oxford University; called to the Bar (1906); Tutor and Lecturer in Social Science, London School of Economics (1913-23); M.P. (Labour) for Limehouse Division of Stepney (1922-50); Under-Secretary of State for War (1924); Leader of the Opposition (1935-40); Lord Privy Seal (1940-2); Deputy Prime Minister (1942-5); Prime Minister and First Lord of the Treasury (1945-51).

AUDEN, Wystan Hugh (*poet*) (1907-). Born in England; educated at Oxford University, where he was leader of a left-wing literary group; now Associate Professor of English Literature, Ann Arbor University, Michigan; won Pulitzer Prize (1948), Feltrinelli Prize (1957), National Medal for Literature of U.S.A. (1967); his published works total more than thirty-five volumes; one of the major British poets of the twentieth century.

AWOLOWO, Chief Obafemi (*politician*) (1909-). Educated at University of London; member, Supreme Court of Nigeria; Premier of the Western Region of Nigeria (1954-9); Leader of the Opposition in the Federal Parliament (1962); sentenced in 1963 to ten years' imprisonment on charges of treasonable felony and conspiracy; pardoned and released in 1966; Chancellor of University of Ife, Nigeria (1967); Vice-Chairman, Federal Executive Council (1967); publications include *AWO* (1960), *Path to Nigerian Freedom* (1965), *Thoughts on the Nigerian Constitution* (1966).

BAILEY, Thomas (*historian*) (1902-). Educated at Stanford University; member of Institute for Advanced Study, Princeton; Professor of History, Stanford University (1940-); publications include *Woodrow Wilson and the Lost Peace* (1944), *Times of Trial* (1958), *Maxims for American Diplomacy* (1969).

BALDWIN, James (*author*) (1924-). Born in Harlem, New York City; educated at DeWitt Clinton High School, New York; moved to Paris in 1948 and lived in Europe until 1956; on his return he became active in American Civil Rights Movement; made many visits to American South during early stages of racial integration; noted American black novelist, essayist, and playwright; publications include *Go Tell It on the Mountain* (1953), *Notes of a Native Son* (1955), *Nobody Knows My Name* (1961), *The Fire Next Time* (1963), *Tell Me How Long the Train's Been Gone* (1968).

BECK, J. Murray (*political scientist*) (1914-). Born in Lunenburg, Nova Scotia; educated at Acadia University and University of Toronto; Professor of Political Science, Dalhousie University (1963-).

BEHRENDT, Richard F. (*sociologist*) (1908-). Naturalized American citizen; born in Germany; educated at universities of Cologne, Basel, Bern, and London; adviser, International Bank for Reconstruction and Development, Washington and Guatemala (1950-1); Professor of Sociology and Director, Institute of Sociology, Free University of Berlin (1965-); has published works in eight languages in fifteen countries.

BERTON, Pierre (*author and broadcaster*) (1920-). Born in Whitehorse, Yukon Territory; educated at University of British Columbia; Associate Editor and daily columnist, *Toronto Daily Star* (1958-62); Contributing Editor, *Maclean's* Magazine (1962-3); screen writer, television commentator, and regular television panelist; host of *The Pierre Berton Show*; publications include *The Big Sell* (1963), *The Comfortable Pew* (1965), *The Smug Minority* (1968).

BISMARCK, Prince Otto von (*statesman*) (1815-98). Born in Schönhausen, Prussia; studied law at Göttingen and Berlin; ambassador to Russia (1859) and France (1862); President of Prussian Cabinet and foreign minister (1862); Premier of Prussia (1862-90); created German Empire after victorious wars against Denmark, Austria, and France (1864-71); became first Chancellor of the German Empire (1871-90); concluded Triple Alliance of Germany, Italy, and Austro-Hungary (1882); dismissed by Kaiser Wilhelm II (1890).

BOLT, Robert (*playwright*) (1924-). Born in England; educated at universities of Manchester and Exeter; wrote screen plays for *Lawrence of Arabia* (1962) and *Dr. Zhivago* (1966); has written many plays, including *A Man for All Seasons*, produced in 1960.

BURNS, John (*journalist*) (1944-). Born in England; educated at McGill University (Economics and Political Science); staff member, *Ottawa Journal* and *Ottawa Citizen*, before joining *The Globe and Mail*, Toronto (1967-).

CALDER, Nigel (*physicist*) (1931-). Born in England; educated at Cambridge University; physicist, Mullard Research Laboratories (1954-6); editor, *New Scientist* (1962-6); chairman, Association of British Science Writers (1962-4); publications include *The World in 1984* (1965), *Unless Peace Comes* (1967).

CARELESS, J. M. S. (*historian*) (1919-). Born in Toronto, Ontario; educated at University of Toronto and Harvard University. Chairman, Department of History, University of Toronto (1959-68); history consultant on C.B.C. radio and television programs; Governor General's Medal (1954, 1962); publications include *Brown of The Globe* (2 volumes), a major biography of George Brown.

CARY, Joyce (*author*) (1888-1957). Born in Ireland; educated at Oxford University; joined Nigerian political service (1913); retired after World War I and began writing. His novels include *Herself Surprised* (1941), *To Be a Pilgrim* (1942), *The Horse's Mouth* (1944).

CHAPUT, Marcel (*politician*) (1918-). Born in Hull, Quebec; educated at McGill University (Science). Worked as a Research Officer, Defence Research Board, Ottawa (1952-61); helped found R.I.N. (Rassemblement pour l'Indépendance Nationale) (1960); currently member of Parti Québécois; publications include *Pourquoi Je Suis Séparatiste* (1961).

CHASE, Stuart (*social scientist and author*) (1888-). Born in Sommersworth, New Hampshire; educated at Massachusetts Institute of Technology and Harvard University; investigated meat-packing industry (1917-22); publications include *Rich Land, Poor Land* (1936), *The Proper Study of Mankind* (1948), *Guides to Straight Thinking* (1956), *Roads to Agreement*.

CH'EN, Jerome (*economist*) (1921-). Born in China; educated at Nankai Institute and University of London. Reader in Asian History, University of Leeds; publications include *Poems of Solitude* (1960), *Mao and the Chinese Revolution* (1965).

CHERRY, Zena (*columnist*). Free-lance journalist; social columnist for *The Globe and Mail*, Toronto.

CHURCHILL, Sir Winston (*politician, soldier, author*) (1874-1965). Born in England; educated at Harrow and Sandhurst; fought in India (1897), the Sudan (1898), and South Africa (1899); elected to Parliament (1900); First Lord of the Admiralty (1911-15, 1917-21); Conservative Chancellor of the Exchequer (1924-9); Prime Minister, coalition government (1940-5); Prime Minister, Conservative government (1951-5). Awarded Nobel Prize in Literature (1953). Publications include a six-volume history, *The Second World War*, based on his personal experience as Prime Minister.

CLAUSEWITZ, General Carl von (*military theorist*) (1780-1831). Born in Germany; educated at Berlin War School; military instructor to the Crown Prince of Prussia; fought in Russian Campaign (1812-13); Director, Berlin War School (1818). Author of *On War* (3 volumes) (1833).

COLOMBO, John Robert (*poet*) (1936-). Born in Kitchener, Ontario; educated at University of Toronto; currently an editor-at-large for *The Tamarack Review*; publications include *The Mackenzie Poems* (1966), *Abracadabra* (1967).

CONOT, Robert (*author*). Educated at Stanford University; newspaper reporter; editor; television writer; chosen to supervise the writing of the reports on the U.S. riots of 1967 for the National Advisory Commission on Civil Disorders.

DAWSON, Robert MacGregor (*political scientist*) (1895-1958). Educated at Dalhousie, Harvard, and London universities. Professor of Political Science, University of Toronto (1938-51); received Governor General's Award (1947).

DE GAULLE, Charles (*soldier, politician*) (1890-

). Born in France; educated at St. Cyr Military Academy and l'Ecole Supérieure de Guerre; served in World War I; General of Brigade and then General of Division (1939); opposed France's capitulation (1940) and organized the Free French forces; returned to France after liberation of Paris (1944); interim President of France (1945-6); President of the Fifth Republic and most influential statesman of Western Europe (1959-69).

DEUTSCHER, Isaac (*author*) (1907-68). Educated in Poland; Polish journalist (1924-32); member of Communist Party in Poland and editor of Communist periodicals (1926-32); expelled for anti-Stalinist activities (1932). Polish correspondent in London (1939); on editorial staff of *The Economist* (1942-9), *The Observer* (1942-7); roving correspondent in Europe (1946-7). Author of a number of books on communism, including major biographies of Stalin and Trotsky.

DOOLEY, Tom (*physician*) (1925-61). Medical doctor, Muong Sing Hospital, Laos; co-founder of Medico; encouraged large numbers of American doctors to serve in underdeveloped areas.

EAYRS, James (*political scientist*) (1926-). Born in England; moved to Canada as a child; educated at University of Toronto, Columbia University, and London School of Economics; Professor of International Politics, University of Toronto (1952-); co-editor of the *International Journal* (1959-); Governor General's Award for Non-fiction (1965). Author of *In Defence of Canada* (2 vols.) (1964, 1965), *Minutes of the Sixties* (1968).

ENGELS, Friedrich (*political theorist*) (1820-95). Born in Germany; co-authored *Communist Manifesto* (1848); involved in revolutionary activity in Germany, and fled to England (1850); aided Karl Marx in the production of *Das Kapital* (1885-94), the book that sets forth in full the theories on which modern international communism is based.

FEHRENBACH, T. R. (*author*) (1925-). Born in Texas; educated at Princeton University; farmer; insurance agent; free-lance writer.

FINCH, Robert (*poet*) (1900-). Born in Long Island, New York; educated at the University of Toronto and the Sorbonne, Paris; currently Professor of French, University of Toronto; Governor General's Award (1946, 1961).

FISCHER, Louis (*author*) (1896-). Born in Philadelphia, Pennsylvania; American correspondent in Europe, particularly Russia and Spain, since 1922; member of the Institute for Advanced Study, Princeton University; recent publications are *Russia, America and the World* (1961), *The Life of Lenin* (1964).

FOULKES, General Charles (*soldier*) (1903-1969). Born in England; educated at University of Western Ontario; Brigadier on General Staff in 1st Canadian Army (1943); promoted to Major-General and took command of the 2nd Canadian Infantry Division (1944); led Canadian troops in the invasion of France (1944); Chief of General Staff (1945-51); Chairman of Chiefs of General Staff (Canada) (1951-60).

FRANKEL, Max (*columnist*) (1930-). Born in Germany; educated at Columbia University (Political Science); reporter for *The New York Times* (1952-68), Washington correspondent (1968-).

GALBRAITH, John Kenneth (*economist*) (1908-). Born in Iona Station, Ontario; Professor of Economics at Harvard University (1949-); served as United States Ambassador to India (1961-3); author of *The Affluent Society* (1958), *The New Industrial State* (1967).

GELLNER, John (*author and lecturer*) (1907-). Born in Trieste; educated at universities of Masaryk, Paris, Würzburg, and Vienna (Law); attorney in Brno, Czechoslovakia, until 1939; editor of *Commentator* (1964-).

GIMBY, Bobby (*composer and bandleader*) (1921-). Born in Cabri, Saskatchewan; composer of songs including "Malaysia Forever", a popular Malayan anthem, and "Canada", a centennial song; owner of four orchestras.

GINZBURG, Evgenia S. (*educator*). Russian Communist arrested in the 1937 purges, released 1955.

GOLDING, William G. (*novelist*) (1911-). Born in England; educated at Oxford University; teacher; writer; author of *Lord of the Flies* (1954).

GORDON, Donald R. (*political scientist*) (1929-). Born in Toronto, Ontario; educated at Queen's University, Kingston, University of Toronto, and London School of Economics; C.B.C. European correspondent (1957-63); Associate Professor of Political Science at Waterloo University, Ontario (1967-).

GUNTHER, John (*author*) (1901-1970). Born in Chicago, Illinois; *Chicago Daily News* correspondent in London, Paris, Berlin, Rome, Scandinavia, Geneva, Spain, Moscow, Vienna, the Balkans, and the Near East (1922-36); later turned to writing and travelling;

books include *Inside U.S.A.* (1947), *Inside Russia Today* (1958).

HAGEDORN, Hermann (*author*) (1882-). Born in New York City; poet; novelist; biographer; author of *Roosevelt Family of Sagamore Hill.*

HAGEN, Louis (*author*) (1916-). Born in Berlin, Germany; interned in concentration camp at age of seventeen; went to England in 1938 and was a glider pilot, then war correspondent in Far East; after the war, was correspondent in Germany for the London *Sunday Express* and then for Odhams Press; author of several books; now managing director of Primrose Film Productions.

HAINES, Gerald (*student*). Was a graduate student, Human Relations Department, University of Kansas, at the time of his death in a car accident.

HALL, Clarence W. (*editor and author*) (1902-). Born in Anna Maria, Florida; reporter; feature writer; senior editor of *Reader's Digest* (1956-).

HAMILTON, Edith (*educator*) (1867-1963). Educated at Bryn Mawr School, Baltimore; first woman student admitted to the Graduate School of Munich University; headmistress of Bryn Mawr School, Baltimore; author of *The Greek Way* (1930), *The Roman Way* (1932).

HEILBRONER, Robert L. (*economist and lecturer*) (1919-). Born in New York; educated at Harvard University; economist in government and business; lecturer to college, business, and labour groups; author of *The Future as History* (1960).

HERTZBERG, Hazel W. (*social studies consultant*). Educated at University of Chicago and Columbia University; teacher and curriculum consultant for New York State Education Department; student of the culture of the Iroquois.

HIBBERT, Christopher (*author*) (1924-). Educated at Oxford University; received the Heinemann Award for Literature (1962); author of *The Battle of Arnhem* (1962) and other books.

HITLER, Adolf (*politician*) (1889-1945). Born in Austria; became corporal in World War I; was a founder and leader of the Nazi party after the war; wrote *Mein Kampf* (1925) during imprisonment for attempted overthrow of Bavarian government; became Chancellor of Germany in 1933, then dictator in 1934; committed suicide in 1945 when faced with defeat in World War II.

HOBBES, Thomas (*philosopher*) (1588-1679). Born in England; educated at Oxford University; an acquaintance of Francis Bacon and Ben Jonson; first great English political theorist; author of *Leviathan* (1651).

HOFFER, Eric (*philosopher*) (1902-). Born in New York; self-educated after grammar school; factory worker; migratory field labourer; gold miner; dishwasher; longshoreman; author of *The True Believer* (1951), *The Passionate State of Mind* (1955), *The Ordeal of Change* (1963).

HOGARTH, Paul (*artist*) (1918-). His sketches have appeared in *Sunday Times*, *Observer*, *News Chronicle*; acclaimed as "Britain's best descriptive artist".

HUXLEY, Aldous (*novelist*) (1894-1963). Born in England; poet; essayist; satirist; winner of the American Academy of Arts and Letters' Award of Merit for the Novel (1959); author of *Brave New World* (1932), *Brave New World Revisited* (1958), and other books.

ISAIAH (*prophet*) (some time between 700 and 600 B.C.). Most influential of the Old Testament prophets.

JARMAN, Thomas L. (*historian*) (1907-). Born in England; educated at Oxford and Harvard universities; lecturer in Education (1934-62); reader at Bristol University (1962-); author of *The Rise and Fall of Nazi Germany* (1955), *Great Britain* (1960), *Democracy and World Conflict* (1963).

KAHN, Herman (*physicist*) (1902-). Director of the Hudson Institute; one of the founders of the "new science" of strategy games and policy prediction for decision-makers; author of *On Thermonuclear War* (1960), *Thinking About the Unthinkable* (1962).

KENNAN, George F. (*diplomat*) (1904-). Born in Milwaukee, Wisconsin; employed in American foreign service (1926-52); United States Ambassador to U.S.S.R. (1952-3) and to Yugoslavia (1961-3); professor at Princeton University (1963-); author of *Realities of American Foreign Policy* (1954), *On Dealing with the Communist World* (1964), and other books.

KENNEDY, John F. (*politician*) (1917-63). Born in Brookline, Massachusetts; served as Democratic Senator for Massachusetts (1953-60); became thirty-fifth President of the United States (1960); assassinated in Dallas, Texas (1963); author of *Profiles of Courage* (1956), which won the Pulitzer Prize.

KENNEDY, Robert F. (*politician*) (1925-68). Born in Massachusetts; attorney in United States Department of Justice (1951-2); Attorney General (1961-64); Democratic Senator for New York (1965-8); assassinated in Los Angeles (1968), while campaigning for the United States presidency.

KING, Martin Luther (*religious leader*) (1929-68). American black; religious and civil-rights leader; organized large-scale demonstrations that were partly responsible for the passage of the Civil Rights Bills through the American Congress in 1964 and 1965; winner of Nobel Peace Prize (1964); assassinated in Memphis, Tennessee (1968); author of *Where Do We Go From Here?* (1967).

LANGSAM, Walter (*historian*) (1906-). American historian and university administrator; radio news commentator; President of University of Cincinnati (1955-); author of *World History Since 1870* (1963).

LEIGHTON, Alexander H. (*sociologist*). Professor of Sociology, Anthropology, and Psychology at Cornell University; member of United States Strategic Bombing Survey of Japan (1945) – his article "That Day at Hiroshima" was based on his findings as a member of this group.

LEVINE, Irving R. (*news correspondent*) (1922-). Foreign correspondent for United States in Vienna and Paris (1948-50); N.B.C. war correspondent in Korea (1950-2); first United States television correspondent in Moscow; author of *Main Street, U.S.S.R.* (1956), *Main Street, Italy* (1963).

LOCKE, John (*philosopher*) (1632-1704). Born in England; educated at Oxford University; physician to the household of Anthony Ashley Cooper, later first Earl of Shaftesbury; an exile in France and Holland; author of *Essay Concerning Human Understanding* (1690), *Letters on Toleration* (1690), *Two Treatises on Government* (1690), *Thoughts on Education* (1693), and a number of other philosophical works.

LOWDERMILK, Walter C. (*soil conservationist*). Educated at Oxford University and University of California; conservation and land development adviser to Israel, Morocco, Tunisia, and the British colonies in Africa; member of the President's Water Resources Policy Commission; author of *Tracing Land Use Across Ancient Boundaries*.

MCCULLOUGH, Colin (*editor*) (1930-). Assistant editor of *The Globe and Mail*, Toronto; formerly Peking correspondent of *The Globe and Mail*.

MACDONALD, Bruce (*economics consultant*) (1926-). Educated at University of Toronto; correspondent and chief of the Ottawa Bureau of *The Globe and Mail*, Toronto; consultant in Economics Communications; author of *The Issue That Will Not Die*.

MCDOUGALL, Colin M. (*novelist and registrar*) (1917-). Born in Montreal, Quebec; educated at McGill University, where he has held the positions of Student Counsellor (1946-7), Director of Placement Service (1947-57), and Registrar (1957-); received Governor General's Award for Fiction (1959) for his novel *Execution*.

MACEACHERN, Ian W. (*photographer*) (1942-). Born in the Maritimes; free-lance photographer, with experience in television work; moved to Ontario in 1966.

MCGINLEY, Phyllis (*poet*) (1905-). Born in Ontario, Oregon; educated at University of Utah, where she began to write poetry; teacher; author of many volumes of poetry and prose.

MARX, Karl (*political theorist*) (1818-83). Born in Germany; studied at universities of Bonn and Berlin; theoretical founder of modern international communism; co-author of *Communist Manifesto* (1848); moved to London in 1849, where he wrote *Das Kapital* (1867).

MAYER, Milton (*author*) (1908-). Born in Chicago, Illinois; analyst, writing on social, educational, and religious issues; consultant and visiting lecturer; author of *What Can a Man Do?* (1964), *They Thought They Were Free* (1966).

MILL, John Stuart (*philosopher*) (1806-73). Born in England; educated by father; knew the works of Plato and Socrates and had begun the study of Latin and algebra when he was eight; wide experience in government of India; Lord Rector of St. Andrew's University; elected to Parliament 1865; publications include *Principles of Political Economy* (1848), *On Liberty* (1859), and a number of philosophic works.

MORE, Sir Thomas (*politician and author*) (1478-1535). Born in England; educated at Oxford University; acquainted with Erasmus and leading humanists of the age; Member of Parliament; Lord Chancellor (1529-32); retired because of religious differences with Henry VIII, was later imprisoned and finally beheaded on charge of treason; canonized by Roman Catholic Church (1935); wrote *Utopia* (1516).

MUHAMMAD, Elijah (*religious leader*) (1919-). Field boy; railroad labourer; automotive worker; Baptist minister; imprisoned (1941-6); founder, leader, and self-proclaimed prophet of Nation of Islam.

MYRDAL, Jan (*author*) (1927-). Born in Sweden; journalist; free-lance writer; translator; has travelled and lived in many European and Asian countries, including China; author of *Chinese Journey* (1965) and other books.

NEHRU, Jawaharlal (*politician*) (1889-1964). Born in India; educated at Cambridge University (Law); disciple of Mahatma Gandhi; imprisoned for a total of eighteen years because of nationalist activities; first Prime Minister and Minister of External Affairs of independent India; wrote *Glimpses of World History* (1936) and autobiography, *Toward Freedom*.

NEWMAN, Peter C. (*author and editor*) (1929-). Born in Austria; educated at University of Toronto; Assistant Editor, *The Financial Post*, Toronto; Assistant Editor, Ottawa Editor, and National Affairs Editor of *Maclean's* Magazine; Editor-in-Chief, *Toronto Daily Star* (1969); has written noteworthy books on Canadian politics, including *Renegade in Power* (1964).

NICOL, Eric (*author and humorist*) (1919-). Born in Kingston, Ontario; educated at University of British Columbia (French) and the Sorbonne, Paris; wrote radio and TV comedy series for the B.B.C.; columnist for *The Province*, Vancouver; free-lance writer for Canadian radio and TV (1951-); has won Leacock Medal for Humour three times; books include *An Uninhibited History of Canada, Say Uncle*, and *Space Age, Go Home!*.

PARKINSON, Cyril Northcote (*historian*) (1909-). Born in England; creator of "Parkinson's Laws"; lecturer in history at Harvard University and the universities of Liverpool, Malaya, Illinois, and California; author and journalist; wrote *Parkinson's Law: The Pursuit of Progress* (1958).

PEARSON, Lester B. (*politician and diplomat*) (1897-). Born in Toronto, Ontario; educated at University of Toronto; Assistant Professor of History, University of Toronto; member of Department of External Affairs (1928-57); President of the General Assembly of the United Nations (1952-3); Nobel Peace Prize winner (1957) for his work during the Suez Crisis; Prime Minister of Canada (1963-8); Chairman, Commission on International Development, sponsored by World Bank (1968-); publications include *Democracy in World Politics* (1955), *Diplomacy in the Nuclear Age* (1959).

REFORD, Robert (*news correspondent*). Educated at Oxford University; worked for British United Press bureaus in Ottawa, Winnipeg, and New York; Ottawa Liaison Officer for the International Service of the C.B.C.; editorial writer, *Ottawa Citizen*; United Nations correspondent for the *Montreal Star*.

ROBERTSON, Terence (*author*). Born and educated in England; served in the Royal Navy, including convoy patrol in the North Atlantic (1939-45); reporter in South Africa; news editor in England; magazine writer; author of several books, including *Dieppe: The Shame and the Glory* (1962).

SABOURIN, Louis (*political scientist*) (1935-). Born in Quebec City; educated at University of Ottawa, the Sorbonne, Institut d'Etudes Politiques de Paris, and Columbia University; radio and TV commentator on public and international affairs; writer of articles on Canadian foreign policy and international law; Director of Institute for International Co-operation at University of Ottawa; author of *Le système politique du Canada: Institutions fédérales et québécoises* (1968).

SEALE, Lewis (*news correspondent*) (1942-). City editor of the Quebec *Chronicle Telegraph*; chief of the Montreal *Gazette*, Quebec City bureau; correspondent for *The Globe and Mail* (Toronto) Ottawa bureau (1967-).

SEARS, Val (*news correspondent*) (1927-). Educated at University of British Columbia; journalist, editorial staff, *Toronto Daily Star*; London Bureau Chief, *Toronto Daily Star* (1968-).

SHAFER, Boyd C. (*historian*) (1907-). Educated at Miami University and University of Iowa; Chairman of the History Department, University of Arkansas (1952-3); Professor of History, Macalester College, St. Paul, Minnesota (1965-); author of articles, pamphlets, and *Nationalism: Myth and Reality* (1955).

SHIRER, William L. (*journalist and novelist*) (1904-). Born in Chicago, Illinois; educated at Coe College, Iowa; free-lance writer; newspaper correspondent in Europe, the Near East, and India; foreign radio correspondent in Europe; radio commentator; author of *Berlin Diary* (1942), *The Rise and Fall of the Third Reich* (1960).

SITHOLE, Ndabanigi (*politician*) (1920-). Born in Southern Rhodesia; educated at University of South Africa and Newton Philological School, Massachusetts; ordained Congregationalist minister; elected president of African Teachers Association (1960); Treasurer of the National Democratic Party; imprisoned for opposition to the government of Southern Rhodesia; author of *African Nationalism* (1959, revised 1968).

SMITH, Robert M. (*news editor and reporter*) (1940-). Born in Boston, Massachusetts; educated at Harvard University, University of Tübingen, and Columbia University; correspondent for Time-Life News Service; Assistant Editor, *Boston Herald Traveller*; reporter, *The New York Times*.

SNYDER, Louis L. (*historian*). Educated at St. John's College (Maryland), University of Frankfurt, and Columbia University; German-American Exchange fellow (1928-39); consultant in psychological warfare for U.S. War Department (1943-4); General Editor of Van Nostrand Anvil Books; Professor of History, City College, New York; author of a number of scholarly books on nationalism.

SORENSEN, Theodore C. (*former presidential assistant*) (1928-). Born in Lincoln, Nebraska; top policy aide and speech writer to John F. Kennedy (1953-63); lawyer, New York; author of *Decision-making in the White House* (1963) and *Kennedy* (1965).

TAYLOR, Charles (*news correspondent*) (1935-). Free-lance writer and broadcaster; public relations officer; correspondent for *The Globe and Mail*, Toronto, in the Far East, Africa, and Europe.

VOGT, Hannah (*civil servant*). Born in Germany; specialist in problems of civil education in Germany; author of *The Burden of Guilt* (1964).

WARD, Barbara (Lady Jackson) (*economist*) (1914-). Born in England; educated at Oxford University (Politics, Philosophy, and Economics); foreign editor of *The Economist* (1940-); member of the Pontifical Commission for Justice and Peace (1967); speaker of international repute; author of numerous books on politics and economics.

WEST, Bruce (*columnist*). Born in Huntsville, Ontario; correspondent and columnist for *The Globe and Mail*, Toronto; served on Wartime Information Board during World War II; has travelled extensively in Canada, Britain, Europe, and South America on special assignments; author.

WIENER, Anthony J. (*social scientist*) (1930-). Born in United States; educated at Harvard University (Law); Instructor in Political Science, Massachusetts Institute of Technology; Chairman of the Research Management Council at the Hudson Institute.

WINSOR, Frederick (*poet*). Author of *The Space Child's Mother Goose* (1963).

Supplementary Books and Aids

See "Key to Suppliers of Audio-Visual Materials" on page 349 for full names and addresses of suppliers.

GENERAL

Books

AYLING: *Portraits of Power* (Barnes and Noble)
BOYD: *An Atlas of World Affairs* (Praeger)
DAHL: *Modern Political Analysis* (Prentice-Hall)
DOYLE: *A History of Political Thought* (Humanities Press)
DUVERGER: *The Idea of Politics* (Henry Regnery)
EBENSTEIN: *Today's Isms* (Prentice-Hall)
ELLIOTT and SUMMERSKILL: *A Dictionary of Politics* (Penguin)
PARKINSON: *The Evolution of Political Thought: 1750 to the Present* (Viking)
SABINE: *A History of Political Theory* (Holt, Rinehart and Winston)
SCHULTZ: *Comparative Political Systems: An Inquiry Approach* (Holt, Rinehart and Winston)
STEINBERG (ed.): *The Statesman's Yearbook*, revised annually (Macmillan of Canada)
WATKINS: *The Age of Ideology – Political Thought, 1750 to the Present* (Prentice-Hall)

PART ONE
MEN AND THEIR GOVERNMENT

Organizing a Society

(*a*) *Books*

SOLZHENITSYN: *One Day in the Life of Ivan Denisovich* (Signet: New American Library)

(*b*) *Film*

King Rat, b & w, 134 minutes (Visual Consultants)

(*c*) *Filmstrip*

Governments of the World, colour, script (CG-CEA)

Nazi Totalitarianism

(*a*) *Books*

BULLOCK: *Hitler: A Study in Tyranny* (Harper and Row)
ELLIOTT: *Hitler and Germany* (McGraw-Hill)
OLIVER and NEWMAN: *Nazi Germany* (xerox, A.E.P. Unit Book)
SHIRER: *The Rise and Fall of the Third Reich* (Simon and Schuster)
WAITE (ed.): *Hitler and Nazi Germany* (Peter Smith)

(*b*) *Films*

Mein Kampf, b & w, 115 minutes (Columbia)
Minister of Hate: Dr. Goebbels, b & w, 30 minutes (Prudential)

(*c*) *Filmstrips*

Fascist and Nazi Dictatorships, 2 strips, 1-12", 33⅓ rpm record (EAV)
The Rise of Hitler, b & w, script (CG-CEA)

(*d*) *Film Loop*

The Rise of the Nazi Party, 8 mm, b & w, 4 minutes (SSSS)

(*e*) *Slides*

The Weimar Republic and the Hitler Regime, 30 slides (Medex)

(*f*) *Transparencies*

FENTON-WALLBANK: *What Caused the Rise of Hitler?*, colour, 8 overlays (Gage)

The Many Faces of Communism

(*a*) *Books*

BARNETT: *Communist China and Asia* (Vintage: Random House)
CARTER: *The Government of the Soviet Union* (Harcourt, Brace and World)
CHRISTIAN SCIENCE MONITOR: *The China Giant:*

Perspective on Communist China (Perry Peng Chang)
EBENSTEIN: *Communism in Theory and Practice* (Holt, Rinehart and Winston)
HOOK: *Marx and the Marxists* (Anvil: Van Nostrand)
HOUN: *A Short History of Chinese Communism* (Spectrum: Prentice-Hall)
MOOREHEAD: *The Russian Revolution* (Harper and Row)
OLIVER and NEWMAN: *Communist China* (xerox, A.E.P. Unit Book)
—— *Twentieth Century Russia* (XEROX, A.E.P. Unit Book)
RIEBER and NELSON: *The U.S.S.R. and Communism: Source Readings and Interpretations* (Scott, Foresman)
RIGBY (ed.): *Stalin* (Prentice-Hall)
SALISBURY: *Russia* (Atheneum)
SKILLING: *Communism, National and International* (University of Toronto Press)

(*b*) *Filmstrips*

Communist China, (New York Times: SSSS)
The Rise of Communism, 2 strips, colour; 2-12″, 33⅓ rpm records (Longmans)

(*c*) *Film Loop*

Czechoslovakia, 1968, 1-8 mm, b & w (EAV)

(*d*) *Projectuals*

FENTON-WALLBANK: *Russian Economic Growth* (EB: Gage)

(*e*) *Record*

Soundtrack: Dr. Zhivago, 1-12″, 33⅓ rpm record (Quality)

Democracy

(*a*) *Books*

CLASTER (ed.): *Athenian Democracy* (Holt, Rinehart and Winston)
COOK: *Canada and the French-Canadian Question* (Macmillan of Canada)
FOX: *Politics: Canada* (McGraw-Hill)
HALE (ed.): *The Iroquois Book of Rites* (University of Toronto Press)
MACLENNAN: *Two Solitudes* (Macmillan of Canada)
SMILEY: *The Canadian Political Nationality* (Methuen)
THORBURN: *Party Politics in Canada* (Prentice-Hall)

(*b*) *Films*

Advise and Consent, b & w, 138 minutes (Columbia)
All the King's Men (Visual Consultants)
Mr. Prime Minister (Manufacturer's Life Insurance Company)
The Sceptre and the Mace, colour, 30 minutes (Ontario Department of Education)

(*c*) *Filmstrip*

Parties and Elections – Canada, colour (NFB)

(*d*) *Play*

KING: *A Man at Westminster* (CBC)

(*e*) *Record*

PARKINSON: *Democracy*, 1-12″, 33⅓ rpm (EAV)

The Individual

(*a*) *Books*

LEWIS: *Babbitt* (Signet: New American Library)
LORENZ: *King Solomon's Ring* (Methuen)
MILL: *On Liberty* (Appleton-Century-Crofts)
MONTAGU (ed.): *Man and Aggression* (Oxford)
PACKARD: *The Hidden Persuaders* (Pocket Books)
RAND: *The Fountainhead* (Signet: New American Library)
SALINGER: *Catcher in the Rye* (Bantam)

(*b*) *Film*

Brainwashing, b & w, 30 minutes (Prudential)

(*c*) *Pamphlet*

Struggle For Individualism (L.E.R.)

(*d*) *Play*

IBSEN: *Enemy of the People* (Macmillan)

(*e*) *Record*

No Man Is An Island, narrated by ORSON WELLES, 1-12″, 33⅓ rpm (SSSS)

Protest!

(*a*) *Books*

BAEZ: *Daybreak* (Dial)
CARMICHAEL and HAMILTON: *Black Power* (Vintage: Random House)
FISCHER: *Gandhi* (Mentor: New American Library)

MASON: *Socrates: The Man Who Dared to Ask* (Beacon)
SIBLEY (ed.): *The Quiet Battle* (Quadrangle)
WOODCOCK: *Civil Disobedience* (CBC)

(*b*) *Films*

A Man For All Seasons, colour (Visual Consultants)
The Plots Against Hitler, b & w, 60 minutes (Prudential)

(*c*) *Pamphlet*

Gandhi and Non-violence (L.E.R.)

(*d*) *Records*

Bob Dylan, 1-12", 33⅓ rpm (ERS)
Songs of Struggle and Protest 1930-1950, 1-12", 33⅓ rpm (Folkways)
Vietnam – Voices of Policy and Protest, 1-12", 33⅓ rpm (ERS)
We Shall Overcome: PETE SEEGER, 1-12", 33⅓ rpm (ERS)

PART TWO
INTERNATIONAL AFFAIRS

Issues In Canadian Foreign Policy

(*a*) *Books*

BERTIN: *Target 2067* (Macmillan of Canada)
CLARK: *Canada: Uneasy Neighbour* (McClelland and Stewart)
CLARKSON: *An Independent Foreign Policy For Canada?* (McClelland and Stewart)
COX: *Canadian Defence Policy: The Dilemmas of a Middle Power* (Canadian Institute of International Affairs)
EAYRS: *Northern Approaches* (Macmillan of Canada)
MACDONALD: *Canada in Two Hemispheres* (Canadian Institute of International Affairs)
MINIFIE: *Open at the Top* (McClelland and Stewart)
—— *Peacemaker or Powder-Monkey?* (McClelland and Stewart)
PEARSON: *The Four Faces of Peace* (McClelland and Stewart)
SAFARIAN: *Foreign Ownership of Canadian Industry* (McGraw-Hill)
TUPPER and BAILEY: *One Continent – Two Voices* (Clarke, Irwin)

The Challenge of Underdeveloped Nations

(*a*) *Books*

ARNOLD: *Aid for Development* (Dufour)
BORGSTROM: *The Hungry Planet* (Collier-Macmillan)
WARD: *The Rich Nations and the Poor Nations* (Norton)

(*b*) *Film Loops*

Progress in Developing Nations – India, 8 mm (SSSS)
Use of Labour in Developing Nations – India, 8 mm (SSSS)
Village Life in Developing Nations – India, 8 mm (SSSS)

(*c*) *Play*

WIBBERLEY: *The Mouse That Roared* (Morrow)

The Meaning of War

(*a*) *Books*

BOUTHOUL: *War* (Walker)
FALL and RASKIN (eds.): *The Viet-Nam Reader* (Vintage: Random House)
FALLS: *The Art of War* (Oxford)
GRAVES: *Good-bye To All That* (Anchor: Doubleday)
HERSEY: *Hiroshima* (Bantam)
LEONARD: *A Short Guide to Clausewitz On War* (Ryerson)
LORD: *Incredible Victory* (Pocket Books)
MCLUHAN: *War and Peace in the Global Village* (Bantam)
REMARQUE: *All Quiet on the Western Front* (Premier: Fawcett World Library)
TUCHMAN: *The Guns of August* (Dell)

(*b*) *Films*

The War Game, b & w, 47 minutes (Film Canada Presentations)
Toys, colour, 7 Minutes (NFB)
Verdun: End of a Nightmare, b & w, 30 minutes (Prudential)

(*c*) *Filmstrips*

The First World War, colour, script (CG-CEA)
The Second World War, Parts I and II, colour, script (CG-CEA)

(*d*) *Film Loops*

Hiroshima and Nagasaki, 8 mm, b & w, 4 minutes (SSSS)

The Blitzkrieg, 8 mm, b & w, 4 minutes (SSSS)
The Normandy Invasion – D-Day, 8 mm, b & w, 4 minutes (SSSS)
World War I: Trench Warfare, 8 mm, b & w, 4 minutes (SSSS)

(*e*) *Plays*

MILLER: *All My Sons* (Dell)
SHAW: *Arms and the Man* (Penguin)

(*f*) *Records*

B.B.C. Scrapbook – 1914, 1-12", 33⅓ rpm (SSSS)
Bob Dylan, 1-12", 33⅓ rpm (SSSS)
Literature of World Wars I and II, 2-12", 33⅓ rpm (ERS)
The Causes of Aggression, narrated by ASHLEY MONTAGU, 1-12", 33⅓ rpm (ERS)

Nationalism In World Affairs

(*a*) *Books*

CARR: *International Relations Between the Two World Wars 1919-1939* (Torchbooks: Harper and Row)
CROWLEY: *The Background to Current Affairs* (Macmillan, London)
FULBRIGHT: *The Arrogance of Power* (Vintage: Random House)
GRAEBNER (ed.): *The Cold War* (Heath: Raytheon Education Company)
KENNAN: *American Diplomacy* (Mentor: New American Library)
—— *Russia and the West Under Lenin and Stalin* (Mentor: New American Library)
KOHN: *Nationalism* (Anvil: Van Nostrand)
NICOLSON: *Peacemaking, 1919* (Grosset)
SCHLESINGER: *A Thousand Days* (Crest: Fawcett World)
SNYDER (ed.): *The Dynamics of Nationalism* (Van Nostrand)
TREFOUSSE (ed.): *The Cold War* (Capricorn: Putnam)

(*b*) *Film*

Munich, b & w, 30 minutes (Prudential)

(*c*) *Filmstrips*

America's Global Commitment (New York Times; SSSS)
Nationalism: 1800-1920, 2 strips; 1-12", 33⅓ rpm (EAV)
Twenty Years of Cold War (New York Times; SSSS)

(*d*) *Film Loops*

The Munich Conference, b & w, 4 minutes (SSSS)
The Yalta Conference, b & w, 4 minutes (SSSS)

(*e*) *Game Simulations*

Crisis, class participation (Western Behavioral Sciences Institutes)
Decision-Making in International Affairs (SSSS)

(*f*) *Transparencies*

European Territorial Changes 1914-1939 (SSSS)
Western and Communist Blocs, 2 colours, 2 overlays (SSSS)

(*g*) *Record*

I Can Hear It Now – Volume I, 1-12", 33⅓ rpm (ERS)

Internationalism

(*a*) *Books*

Everyman's United Nations (United Nations)
FEDER (ed.): *United Nations: Man's Best Hope for Peace?* (Gage)
KELEN: *Hammarskjold* (Putnam)
LUARD (ed.): *The Evolution of International Organizations* (Praeger)
MCGUIRE: *The Peace Corps* (Collier-Macmillan)
MCWHINNEY and GODFREY: *Man Deserves Man* (Ryerson)
REFORD: *Canada and Three Crises* (Canadian Institute of International Affairs)
WATERS: *The United Nations* (Collier-Macmillan)
WAUGH: *Put Out More Flags* (Penguin)

(*b*) *Film*

Workshop for Peace: The United Nations, b & w, 30 minutes (Ontario Department of Education)

(*c*) *Filmstrips*

History of the United Nations, colour, script (MH)
Organization of the United Nations, colour, script (MH)

(*d*) *Record*

Voice Toward Peace, 1-12", 33⅓ rpm (ERS)

(*e*) *Tape Kit*

UNITED PRESS INTERNATIONAL: *The United Nations*, 30 programmed texts; 1 tape, 30 minutes; 1 manual (SSSS)

Future Prospects!

(a) Books

BURDICK and WHEELER: *Fail-Safe* (Dell)
CHASE: *The Most Probable World* (Harper and Row)
CLARKE: *2001: A Space Odyssey* (Signet: New American Library)
HUXLEY: *Brave New World* (Penguin)
KNEBEL and BAILEY: *Seven Days In May* (Bantam)
ORWELL: *1984* (Signet: New American Library)
SHUTE: *On the Beach* (Bantam)
WYNDHAM: *The Chrysalids* (House of Grant)

(b) Films

Dr. Strangelove, b & w, 93 minutes (Columbia)
Fail-Safe (Visual Consultants)
Seven Days In May, b & w, 120 minutes (Paramount)

(c) Filmstrips

Frontiers in Space and Undersea, 1 colour strip; 1-12", 33⅓ rpm (Longmans)
The Next Twenty Years (New York Times; SSSS)

Key to Suppliers of Audio-Visual Materials

Films

Columbia Pictures of Canada Limited, 72 Carlton St., Toronto, Ontario
Film Canada Presentations Limited, 1 Charles St. E., Toronto, Ontario
Ontario Department of Education, Learning Materials Service Unit, 559 Jarvis St., Toronto 5, Ontario
Paramount Film Service Ltd., 111 Bond St., Toronto 2, Ontario
Association-Industrial Films, 135 Peter St., Toronto 2B, Ontario
Visual Consultants, 23 Kellythorne Drive, Toronto, Ontario

Filmstrips

CG-CEA: Carmen Education Associates Ltd., Pine Grove, Ontario
EAV: Educational Audio Visual Inc., 29 Marble Ave., Pleasantville, New York 10570
MH: McGraw-Hill Text Films, 330 Progress Ave., Scarborough, Ontario
NFB: National Film Board of Canada, Decarie Building, P.O. Box 6100, Montreal 101, Quebec
SSSS: Social Studies School Service, 4455 Lennox Blvd., Inglewood, California 90304

Pamphlets

A.E.P. Unit Books: American Educational Publications, Education Center, Columbus, Ohio 43216
L.E.R.: Life Education Reprint Program, Box 834, Radio-City Post Office, New York, N.Y. 10009

Records

ERS: Educational Record Sales, 157 Chambers St., New York, N.Y. 10007
SSSS: Social Studies School Service, 4455 Lennox Blvd., Inglewood, California 90304

Simulation Games

Science Research Associates (Canada) Limited, 44 Prince Andrew Place, Don Mills, Ontario
Western Behavioral Science Institute, 1121 Torrey Pines Rd., La Jolla, California 92037

Slides

Medex: Medex Laboratory Supplies, P.O. Box 32, Station B, Toronto 2B, Ontario

Transparencies

EB: Fenton-Wallbank Series, Encyclopaedia Britannica, Britannica House, 151 Bloor St. W., Toronto 5, Ontario
SSSS: Social Studies School Service, 4455 Lennox Blvd., Inglewood, California 90304

Acknowledgements

For permission to reprint copyright material the publisher offers grateful thanks to the following publishers, authors, and agents:

American Historical Association and Boyd C. Shafer for "The Never-Ending Circle of Nationalism" from *Nationalism: Interpretations and Interpreters* by Boyd C. Shafer, pp. 10-12 abridged, published in Pamphlet (3/e) by the Service Center for Teachers of History of the American Historical Association, Washington, D.C. (1959).

Atheneum Publishers for "Juvenile Delinquency" and "Man Is a Killer" from *African Genesis* by Robert Ardrey, copyright © 1961 by Literat S.A.

Atlantic–Little, Brown and Company for "Student Rebellion", "Leaders Are More Important", and "A Dialogue on Protest" from *Democracy and the Student Left* by George F. Kennan, copyright 1968 by George F. Kennan.

Bantam Books, Inc., for "The Watts Riot: An Incident" from *Rivers of Blood, Years of Darkness* by Robert Conot, copyright © 1967 by Bantam Books, Inc.

Richard F. Behrendt for "Revolution?" from his article "The Uprooted" in *New Mexico Quarterly*, Spring 1949 edition, published by The University of New Mexico Press.

Burns and MacEachern Limited for "The Military Facts of the Case" from "Complications of Defence" by General Charles Foulkes in *Neighbours Taken for Granted: Canada and the U.S.* edited by Livingston T. Merchant.

Cambridge University Press for "Alignment?" and "The Dilemma" from *AWO: The Autobiography of Chief Obafemi Awolowo.*

Canadian Broadcasting Corporation for "Civil Disobedience: National and International" from *Conscience for Change* by Martin Luther King, Jr., CBC Massey Lectures 1967, copyright © 1967 by Martin Luther King, Jr.; "A Meaningful Voice" from *Fate and Will in Foreign Policy* by James Eayrs, CBC Publications, copyright © 1967 by James Eayrs; and "The Psychology of Poverty" from *The Underdeveloped Country* by J. K. Galbraith, CBC Massey Lectures 1965, copyright © 1965 by J. K. Galbraith.

Canadian Institute of International Affairs for "Canada's Sale of Weapons" from *Merchant of Death?* by Robert W. Reford from *Behind the Headlines*, October 1968 edition, published by CIIA, and "Canada as a Peace-keeper" from *Canada's Role as a Middle Power* by Donald Gordon.

J. M. S. Careless for "We Need America" from "Hooray for the Scars and Gripes!", his contribution to *The New Romans* edited by Al Purdy.

Chatto & Windus, Ltd., for "Controlling the Mind" from *Brave New World* by Aldous Huxley.

Zena Cherry for her article "Russians Descended Like Vultures, Czechoslovaks Say" from *The Globe and Mail*, Toronto, November 25, 1968, edition.

William Collins Sons & Co. Ltd. for "The Limits of Human Endurance?" from *Into the Whirlwind* by Evgenia S. Ginzburg, translated by Paul Stevenson and Manya Harari.

John Robert Colombo for his poem "O Canada", copyright 1968 by John Robert Colombo from *The New Romans* edited by Al Purdy.

The Cresset Press, Ltd., for "What Hitler Did for Germany" adapted from *The Rise and Fall of Nazi Germany* by T. L. Jarman.

Curtis Brown, Ltd., for "The Individual in Society" from "The Mass Mind" by Joyce Cary.

The Curtis Publishing Company for "Democracy in the Modern World" from "Can Democracy Survive?" by C. N. Parkinson, copyright © 1960 by *The Saturday Evening Post.*

The John Day Company, Inc., for "Neutrality?" adapted from *Independence and After* by Jawaharlal Nehru.

The Dial Press, Inc., for "My Dungeon Shook" from *The Fire Next Time* by James Baldwin, copyright © 1962, 1963 by James Baldwin.

Doubleday & Company, Inc., for "The Food Crisis" from "The Promise of Agriculture in the Less Developed Lands" by Walter C. Lowdermilk, from the book *Our Crowded Planet* edited by Fairfield Osborn, copyright © 1962 by Fairfield Osborn. Also "Russian Government in Action" adapted from *Main Street, U.S.S.R.* by Irving R. Levine, copyright © 1959 by Irving R. Levine.

Faber and Faber Limited for "Government without Adults" from *Lord of the Flies* by William Golding, and "The Unknown Citizen" from *Collected Shorter Poems 1927-1957 by W. H. Auden.*

Farrar, Strauss & Giroux, Inc., for "The Challenge" from *Promises to Keep* by Agnes Dooley, copyright © 1962 by Agnes W. Dooley and Malcolm W. Dooley. Copyright © 1961 by the Estate of Thomas A. Dooley.

Louis Fischer for "Does Dictatorship Create Order?" adapted from his book *50 Years of Soviet Communism* published by Popular Library, Inc.

John Gellner for his article "The Fears That Spurred the Russians into Action" from *The Globe and Mail*, Toronto, August 23, 1968, edition.

The Globe and Mail, Toronto, for articles appearing on pages 58, 92, 122, 168, 200, 227, 278.

The Hamlyn Publishing Group Ltd. for "The Compensations of War" from *My Early Life* by Sir Winston Churchill.

Harper & Row, Publishers, Incorporated, for "Lenin: Portrait of a Revolutionary" from pp. 172-4, 176-8 *Inside Russia Today*, New Revised Edition, by John Gunther, copyright © 1957, 1958, 1962 by John Gunther; "Leaders and Followers" from pp. 103-10 *The True Believer* by Eric Hoffer, copyright 1951 by Eric Hoffer; and "The Culture Concept" from pp. 74-80 *The Proper Study of Mankind*, Second Revised Edition, by Stuart Chase, copyright 1948, 1956 by Stuart Chase. Also "The Confrontation in Cuba" abridgement and adaptation of pp. 778-83 (Bantam edition) *Kennedy* by Theodore C. Sorenson, copyright © 1965 by Theodore C. Sorensen; and "The Facts Are –" from pp. 33-7 *The Great Ascent* by Robert L. Heilbroner, copyright © 1963 by Robert L. Heilbroner.

Robert L. Heilbroner for "Operation Humanity" from *Mankind's Children, The Story of UNICEF*, Public Affairs Pamphlet No. 279, published in 1959.

Heinemann Educational Books Ltd. for "The Duty to Conscience" from *A Man For All Seasons* by Robert Bolt.

Houghton Mifflin Company for "The Necessities of War" from *The Grand Alliance* by Sir Winston Churchill.

Hutchinson Publishing Group Limited for "The Use of Symbols" and "Propaganda and the Mass Meeting" from *Mein Kampf* by Adolf Hitler, translated by Ralph Manheim.

Alfred A. Knopf, Inc., for "Nazi Rituals" from *Berlin Diary* by William L. Shirer, copyright 1941 and renewed 1969 by William L. Shirer.

Longmans Green & Co. Ltd. for "A Soldier's First Experience" from *The Wheatley Diary* edited by Christopher Hibbert.

McClelland and Stewart Limited for "Negotiators at Work" from *Crisis* by Terence Robertson; "Our Free Society" from *The Smug Minority* by Pierre Berton; "The Pearson Image" from *The Distemper of Our Times* by Peter Newman; and "The Case for Quebec" from "Special International Status for Quebec" by Louis Sabourin in *An Independent Foreign Policy for Canada*, edited by Stephen Clarkson for the University League for Social Reform, 1968.

McIntosh and Otis, Inc., for "A Troublemaker" from *The Book of Courage* by Hermann Hagedorn, copyright 1933, 1938 by Hermann Hagedorn.

David McKay Company, Inc., for "A Powerless U.N.?" from *This Kind of Peace* by T. R. Fehrenbach, New York, 1966.

The Macmillan Company of Canada Limited for "Is Man Really a Killer?" from *Execution* by Colin McDougall, and "North American Defence: Its Background" from *Canada: A Story of Challenge* by J. M. S. Careless.

The New York Times Company for "Soviet-Czech Relations – See-Saw Between Pressure and Reconciliation" by Robert M. Smith, "Spheres of influence and Soviet aggression" by Max Frankel, and "1962 Cuba Crisis 'Was no other choice' ", all © 1968 by *The New York Times.*

W. W. Norton & Company, Inc., for "The Greek Example" from *The Ever-Present Past* by Edith Hamilton, copyright © 1964 by W. W. Norton & Company, Inc. The essay also appeared under the title "The Lessons of the Past" in the *Saturday Review* and was copyrighted in 1958 by The Curtis Publishing Company. And "The Case for Internationalism" from *Five Ideas That Change the World* by Barbara Ward, copyright © 1959 by W. W. Norton & Company, Inc.

Harold Ober Associates Incorporated for "A Stormtrooper's Reaction" and "A Businessman's Answer" from *The Mark of the Swastika* by Louis Hagen, copyright © 1965 by Bantam Books, Inc.

Oxford University Press, Canadian Branch, for "Select Samaritan" from *Select Samaritan* by Robert Finch. Also for "Stalin: Creator or Monster?" from *Stalin: A Political Biography* by Isaac Deutscher; "Adapting Communism to China" from *Mao – and the Chinese Revolution* by Jerome Ch'en; and "The New Nationalism" from *African Nationalism* by Ndabanigi Sithole.

Oxford University Press, Inc., for "The Right to Resist – Did It Exist?" from *The Burden of Guilt* by Hannah Vogt.

Pantheon Books, a division of Random House, Inc., for "Working with the Masses: A Case Study" condensed from *Report from a Chinese Village* by Jan Myrdal, © copyright 1965 by William Heinemann Ltd.

Prentice-Hall of Canada Ltd. for "Trudeau: His Image Has Everything" from *Pendulum of Power* by J. M. Beck.

Princeton University Press for "A World Symbol?" from *Democracy in World Politics* by Lester B. Pearson (for The Stafford Little Lectures), copyright 1955 by Princeton University Press. Text simplified by special permission.

Quadrangle Books, Inc., for "The Breakdown of Society" from *The Nazi Seizure of Power: The Experience of a Single German Town, 1930-1935* by William Sheridan Allen, copyright © 1965 by William Sheridan Allen.

The Reader's Digest Assn., Inc., and Clarence W. Hall for his article "Operation Crossroads Gets to the Heart of Africa" from July 1968 *Reader's Digest*, copyright 1968 by The Reader's Digest Assn., Inc.

Rutgers University Press for "The Historical View" from *The Meaning of Nationalism* by Louis L. Snyder, 1954.

The Ryerson Press, Toronto, for "I Like Now" from "Man's Future and Who Needs It?" in *Shall We Join the Ladies* by Eric Nicol.

Charles Scribner's Sons for a chart of "Weimar [German] Parliamentary Elections 1919-1933" from *Statistisches Jahrbuch, Statistik des deutschen Reiches, Vierteljahrshafte für Statistik des deutschen Reiches* (Berlin, 1920-34), English translation by Ludwig F. Schaefer. Reprinted from Volume II of *Problems in Western Civilization*, page 431, edited by Ludwig F. Schaefer, David H. Fowler, and Jacob E. Cooke, copyright © 1968 Charles Scribner's Sons.

Simon & Schuster, Inc., for "The Hydrogen Dog and the Cobalt Cat" from *The Space Child's Mother Goose* by Frederick Winsor, copyright © 1956, 1957, 1958 by Frederick Winsor and Marian Parry.

Gordon V. Thompson Limited, Toronto, for the words only of "Canada" (A Centennial Song) by Bobby Gimby, copyright by Gordon V. Thompson Limited.

The University of Chicago Press for "What Would You Have Done?" from *They Thought They Were Free* by Milton Mayer, copyright © 1955 by University of Chicago Press in Phoenix Edition.

The University of Kansas for "Government in Captivity" from "Stoerpenberg Camp" by Gerald Haines, unpublished case study of the Human Relations Department of The University of Kansas.

University of Toronto Press for "Knowing Americans" from *A Change of Pace* by Bruce West and "Democracy and Minority Rights" from *Democratic Government in Canada* by R. MacGregor Dawson.

The Viking Press, Inc., for "The Conquerors" from *Times Three* by Phyllis McGinley, copyright © 1958 by Phyllis McGinley.

Barbara Ward (Lady Robert Jackson) for introductory quotation, "Peaceful Stalemate!", and "The Case for Internationalism" from *The Village Planet*, text of lecture by Barbara Ward on November 4, 1967, published by the University of Alberta, Public Relations Office.

Photographs, charts, maps, cartoons, and diagrams are credited throughout the text.

Every reasonable effort has been made to trace ownership of copyright material. Information will be welcomed which will enable the publisher to rectify any reference or credit in future printings.

07 17 27 37 47 57 67 77 THB 9 8 7 6 5 4 3 2